Shanghai Pierce: A FAIR LIKENESS

SHANGHAI

PIERCE
A fair likeness

BY *Chris Emmett*
WITH DRAWINGS BY NICK EGGENHOFER

Norman: UNIVERSITY OF OKLAHOMA PRESS

By Chris Emmett

    Fort Union and the Winning of the Southwest (Norman, 1965)
    Shanghai Pierce: A Fair Likeness (Norman, 1953)
    Give 'Way to the Right (San Antonio, 1931)
    The General and the Poet (San Antonio, 1930)
    Texas As It Was Then (San Antonio, 1930)
    Texas Camel Tales (San Antonio, 1929)

Copyright 1953 by the University of Oklahoma Press
Publishing Division of the University
Manufactured in the U.S.A.
First edition, 1953
Second printing, 1955
Third printing, 1974

*Dedicated to that great band of old-timers
who mixed integrity and cussedness, opportunity
and natural resources, with hard work to form
the base of a sound southwestern United States*

"And it grew from that to this"

One of my first recollections is that of hearing the bellowing of a herd of bulls just as a spring day drew to a close. Those bulls, so I was told, belonged to Shanghai Pierce.

I was reared in Hamilton, Texas, on one of the spur cattle trails leading across Texas to merge with an extension of the main Chisholm Trail near Fort Worth. There was seldom a setting sun in the spring during the early eighteen nineties that did not shine upon a drover watering his stalking, bawling longhorn cattle in the little stream which flowed through that frontier town. That water, like the stream of hooves and horns that flowed northward with the rise of April grass, has long since ceased to flow; but the low of thirsty cattle and the bellow of menacing bulls are as fresh in my mind today as when I left my castle-building and pinfishing in a child's fright to scud to the protection of my mother so that Shanghai Pierce's "sealions" could not harm me.

Soon after those bulls brought me to a consciousness of the world around me, I began to inquire about ownership. I wanted to know who would want such ferocious things. And it seemed to me, according to the talk I heard, that all ownership of cattle centered around Shanghai Pierce. There was an aura of mystery about the man, for cattlemen referred to him in respectful terms. I absorbed it and thought of him as a colossus of irresistible strength, king of an empire, a man whom cattlemen sought to emulate. That I may have gained such impressions by having seen him I can not say after the passing of more than half a century. I may have seen him; I do not know whether I did or not. Perhaps my impressions arose from the then common cattleman's gossip about the man. I

Shanghai Pierce

was too young to formulate for myself the impressions of character I retained of him. I pictured him in my mind as loyal to his friends, ruthless to his enemies, faithful to his commitments, a "czar in my community."

Loyalty and reliability were valued qualities in men of the day of my youth. Fathers with an interest in the development of their sons impressed them with the importance of both. And Shanghai Pierce—that phantom who moved northward with large herds of cattle—symbolized those qualities in my consciousness, and, without intervening color of facts, the picture of the big man remained as I grew to manhood.

Many years later these early impressions came to life again when a change of residence brought me by chance one evening to Blessing, Texas. On the porch of an unpretentious hotel sat a longmoustached, gruff, talkative old man. He squared himself in his rocker upon my arrival and overawed me with local thrillers of the days gone by. Until I learned that he was Jonathan Edward Pierce, brother of the famous Shanghai, I had been inclined to cast him off as an inconsequential, talkative old man eager for a listener; but when I came to know he was both brother and partner of the colossus of my youthful imaginings, my interest soared.

Later through the kindness of Jack Hutchins, then in the employ of The Pierce Estate—subsequently president of A. H. Pierce Ranch, Limited—I sat one day in the shade of the A. P. Borden Company mercantile store, at Pierce's Station, Texas. There a withered old chocolate-colored Negro, Neptune Holmes, pensioner of the Pierce Ranch, was whiling away his extra allotment of days upon this earth, and I had from that inimitable character, who had been Shanghai's faithful servant, some of his oft-told tales. An acquaintance with Mr. Abel Pierce Borden, most beloved of the nephews, and with banker George C. Gifford, another nephew, added much color (but few facts) to my growing interest in the life of Shanghai Pierce. Those reticent gentlemen frowned upon inquisitiveness into private lives, whether theirs or that of their better-known uncle. Mrs. Edith Borden Greer added immeasurably to the facts as well as to the glamour of her great-uncle; and Ranch Boss Clay McSparren, as well as W. B. Grimes, son of the man Shanghai despised, 'Bing' Grimes, furnished intimate details of the acts of old Shang, as he was known by his close associates.

"And it grew from that to this"

J. Evetts Haley, onetime archivist of the University of Texas, and Jack Hutchins saved the Pierce Papers, which had survived storms and time. Thus hundreds of documents and letters became a part of the library of the University of Texas. Through the genial sufferance of Miss Winnie Allen, custodian, every paper—the first bearing the date, April 7, 1870, the last telling of Mr. Pierce's death, Christmas night, 1900—has passed under my scrutiny. This day-by-day record of Abel Head Pierce's life was supplemented by Judge J. C. Hutcheson, Jr., of the United States Court of Appeals, James V. Allred, onetime Texas governor, and United States Senator Tom Connally, who made valuable court records accessible to me.

Ranking with the most helpful in my quest have been members of the San Antonio library staff, Miss Grace Philippi being ever untiring in her search for a connecting link to a fugitive fact in this story. Russell E. Ward and his mother, relict of "Mr. Benn," read the manuscript to give me the benefit of their recollections. A host of Mr. Pierce's old hands, both black and white—including Old Idar (Ida) and Vi—were most helpful. Mrs. Arda Talbot Allen, Matagordian by birth, rummaged ceaselessly through the memories of her kin and friends (and whoever had more of both?) to lay another Shanghai story at my door. Fred and Janette Lowrey were indispensible critics of the manuscript. All these and many more contributed to the resurrection of Shanghai Pierce, Webster on Cattle.

Chris Emmett

San Antonio, Texas

Contents

	"And it grew from that to this"	vii
1.	"Mr. Pierce died this evening"	3
2.	"I was not born under the golden star"	10
3.	"My uncle fed me too many doses of sanctimony"	15
4.	"I was all the same as a major general..."	33
5.	"I owned nearly all the cattle in Christendom"	39
6.	"Once I went to hunt for society"	60
7.	"I thought a great deal of the man..."	78
8.	"A reckless and cruel disregard of my wrights"	87
9.	"A pretty big dog in the puddle"	94
10.	"There shall be no town naming to the exclusion of my perpetuity"	110
11.	"I'm scienced in ranchin'"	119
12.	"Now, sirs, I am a mystic knight of Bovina"	135
13.	"I am introducing religion into the community"	156
14.	"I recognize no obligation under the contract"	177
15.	"That damn Dutchman Bosky"	192
16.	"We will rob them Yankees"	203
17.	"My shotgun went off in the Pullman Palace Car..."	216

18. *"Every potentate in Europe except the Pope was gone from home when I called"*   239
19. *"Pluck my locks for souvenirs and charms"*   243
20. *"Trust in Providence if the breaching breaks"*   274
     Appendix: Bos Indicus   301
     Bibliography   313
     Index   321

List of Illustrations & Maps

ILLUSTRATIONS

Shanghai Pierce	facing page 46
William Bradford Grimes	47
Charlie Siringo	47
Thomas Jefferson Hamilton	104
Ben Thompson	104
Walnut Street, Ellsworth, Kansas, 1873	104
John Wesley Hardin	105
Captain H. L. McNelly	105
Lee Hall	146
Will Bill Hickock	147
George Washington Miller	218
Joseph G. McCoy	219
Fred C. Proctor	258
J. Clay McSparren	258
"There stands old Pierce"	259
Shanghai Pierce	306
Abel Pierce Borden	307
A "Brahmin" bought by A. P. Borden in India	307

MAPS

South Texas	page 120
The Pierce Neighborhood	121
Tacquard Squeeze Out	213

Shanghai Pierce: A FAIR LIKENESS

1. "Mr. Pierce died this evening"

Judge Proctor sat a long time looking at the copy of the telegram he had just dispatched. Finally he slid down from the tall bookkeeper's stool to stand before the frosty window. He took his handkerchief and wiped away the water accumulated on the panes, but the outdoor cold fuzzed over his view almost immediately. A mizzle of rain driven before a chilling wind whining out of the north came in gusts. Nature was providing a shroud, ash-grey and watery, in which to lay to rest America's most turbulent century,

Shanghai Pierce

to end the career of a man who was as resourceful as the era had produced. During the past one hundred years the vast southwestern part of the United States had changed from a little explored country, teeming with wild, rangy longhorn cattle and uncultivated acres, to a state with established order, extensive cultivated farms, and gentle graded cattle. Abel Head Pierce, the tall, lank, uneducated nineteen-year-old from Rhode Island, who had stowed away to Texas, had changed from an awkward youth of 208 pounds and six feet three inches of height to a pudgy, sixty-seven-year-old of great dignity and a profusion of beard, weighing 250 pounds and measuring six feet five inches. He had come with six bits in his pocket as capital with which to found a fortune, and his financial status, also, had kept pace with the progress of the century. In fact a most substantial part of the transition in the Southwest resulted from his foresight and industry. His own acres were to be counted in multiplied thousands. Railroads, banks, rice farms, cotton plantations, even a tea farm, were tangible evidences of his progressiveness, to say nothing of the all-absorbing theme of his life—cattle.

Thinking back over Shanghai's life, Judge Proctor moved slowly from the window. Few people called him "Judge," as his usual good humor and sprightly wit encouraged his friends to address him as "Fred." Today, however, he was more nearly the "Judge" than he had ever been. His friend, his most lucrative client, the man who had taken him as a boy lawyer, placed implicit confidence in him, and dubbed him "My Counsellor," the King-of-Cattle-Kings, banker, railroad builder, the last stalwart of the "Big Pasture Men," lay dead in his room above the ranch office. From there Judge Proctor had just telegraphed the news which would affect the lives of thousands.

As he turned back to the high-rung stool, Clay McSparren, ranch boss, slicker-clad against the weather, came riding slowly into the yard. The moaning of the ranch Negroes could be heard inside the house. The voice of "Old Nep," grief stricken and uncertain, carried above the whine of the wind. "Mr. Clay! O! Mr. Clay O! I is ruint. All us is ruint. D' whol' worl' am done ruint. Mr. Shang is dead."

Mr. Proctor ignored the increasing excitement, for he had unpleasant duties to perform. How he wished he had not failed Mr.

"Mr. Pierce died this evening"

Pierce's urgent message: "Wish you to come here tomorrow, saturday without fail." Perhaps the "Colonel" had had premonitions of fate! He may have wished to say something which would be directive now. Anyway, Mr. Williams would be apprehensive after receiving the telegram, and it positively would not do to let a New York bank president, who held a dead man's unsecured two-hundred-thousand-dollar note, get excited. He had promised to write. The letter must go forward today.

Sitting again before the slightly tilted ledger desk, he examined the pens in the wire holder. He discarded Mr. Borden's sharp-pointed Spencerian, then tested Mr. Pierce's ball-pointed Esterbrook. It was clogged with drying ink, showing much use. Then in even, concise strokes he wrote:

December 26th 1900

Mr. G. G. Williams
President Chemical National Bank
Broadway, New York City

Dear Sir:
    Mr. A. P. Borden asks me to advise you by wire of the death of Mr. A. H. Pierce and to confirm the same by this letter. To this end I first wired you
    "Mr. Pierce died this evening. letter follows"
which wire I now try to confirm by this letter.
    Mr. Pierce was only sick a short time and died from hemmorraghe of the brains.
    Of course your bank is his principal creditor and the balance of this letter is therefore opportune.
    I know that Mr. Pierce has a will drafted by me, and that he has conferred upon his executors free power to properly handle this estate and pay his debts. I also know that Mr. Borden is one of the executors and is Mr. Pierces nephew and fully conversant with his business affairs. I also take pleasure in stating that Mr. Borden is a good business man and will perform his Duties in a manner satisfactory to all concerned.
    Mr. Borden also asks me to say that he will write you when the will is read and as soon as possible give you a statement of his affairs. In addition I beg to say that Either Mr. Borden or I will take pleasure in giving you any and all explanations you may request.

Shanghai Pierce

Personally I add that I am sufficiently conversant with Mr. Pierces affairs to satisfy me that no creditor need feel the slightest uneasiness.

Very truly yours
F. C. PROCTOR

Well, that was out of the way; and most certainly no creditor need feel the slightest uneasiness. However, the situation held other possibilities far more dangerous to the integrity of the estate than one alarmed creditor. He had been the trusted familiar of Mr. Pierce ever since he had been licensed to practice law. First, he had given Mr. Pierce's business attention while a member of the law firm, The Proctors, father and two sons. Later Mr. Pierce had relied upon him almost exclusively. No man had been closer to the growth of the estate, unless it were the Colonel's nephew, Abel Pierce Borden. Most certainly he knew more about the estate affairs than did either Mrs. Pierce or his daughter, Mrs. Mamie Withers. How badly he needed Mr. Borden's counsel at this moment, but Abel Borden lay desperately ill upstairs with pneumonia.

The judge moved toward the big iron safe which stood wide open, showing neat packages of papers that filled it almost to capacity. It was probable that Hattie would try to discuss her husband's will before her stepdaughter, Mamie Withers, now en route from Kansas City, could arrive. Fred recounted to himself some of the difficulties he had had with Mr. Pierce while drafting the will. The Colonel had maintained that Hattie must "acquiesce in my better business judgment," but there was nothing in their marriage relationship which would give assurance that there would be such acquiescence; particularly might this be true if Hattie were to conclude that "Miss Mamie" and her lawyer husband would profit by accepting the will as written. He must find the will now at all hazards.

He fingered over the stack of papers. It would be a large package—some twenty legal-size typed pages, single spaced. He recalled the Colonel's fury when he delivered the completed document with a fee statement for one thousand dollars. With beard all aquiver, Shanghai had shouted so that people passing in the street stopped to hear: "Counsellor! My God, Counsellor! Just because you have got a good cow there's no excuse to milk her dry."

"Mr. Pierce died this evening"

Then the old man's anger had changed to mirth when "My Counsellor" replied: "Yes, Mr. Pierce; but a good milk cow doesn't kick."

Mr. Pierce had directed Fred: "Put the will in one of your envelopes that has Rubber snappes & I will put them all in my Safe & be loaded."

Yes; there it was; but it had four codicils instead of one. And bound to it by the "Rubber snappes" was another document written in Mr. Pierce's bold script. Fred read:

List of Assetts of A. H. Pierce & Indebtedness		
Due First Nat'l Bank Payable March 1st/1900		75,000
Due Chemical Nat'l Bank Pttg about		200,000
Due Adoes & Lobit Gal. Texas		20,000
		$295,000
Stock of Cattle Low Valuation		200,000
Pilkinton Bonus Pasture 22000 acres	2½	55,000
Mad Island Pasture 13000 acres	$5	45,000
Klopper Pasture 5000 acres	$5	25,000
Wire Pasture 15000 acres sold at $5 soon as Papers can be fixed up	½ cash	75,000
B U House Ranch Pasture 40000 acres S.P.R.R. soon runing through it & of $7		280,000
Convict Plantation 2300 acres well Improved & 85 Ricks 7 year old Bill B Mules Bills Receivable 95 Per cent fine.		160,494.93
Warrens Plantation on Caney Loaned 16 000 on it		8,000
86000 acres Land on Caney & Colorado East Side of River fine big of Land in Tex.		360,000
Cash in Banks between 6 & $10,000		6,000
Amts due on open accounts good		10,000
½ Int. in Avance Hotel in Hot Springs		15,000
		$1,319,494.93

This includes nothing of the W. Mc & Co
    Wrecked Assett or Gulf Interstate R.R.

Shanghai Pierce

Fred replaced the papers as he heard Hattie descending the stairs, musing half-aloud to himself: "Yes, a sizable fortune—$1,319,494.93 —despite the Colonel's errors in calculation—accumulated in just forty-seven years." He felt relieved over his prying now, for on the reverse side of the "list of Assetts" he saw in the unmistakable script: "if you desire you can submit this to Mr. Proctor. He knows all about my Property, but Remember this is Property not Cash but I can Handle it & get one & half Million Dollars out of It."

Early on the morning of the fourth day a hearse drew up before the ranch house. Ranch boss J. Clay McSparren directed the Negroes while six yoke of oxen were substituted for the span of horses. Then Clay, in his yellow slicker and gum boots, headed his horse across the prairie, and the funeral procession was on its way.

"My Counsellor" rode in one of the family carriages. Mrs. Pierce had avoided sitting in the same conveyance with "Miss Mamie." Mamie Withers was genuinely grieved over her father's death. The trip, consequently, was a silent one. This gave Mr. Proctor an opportunity to think over his years of association with this interesting family, as they moved slowly over the long muddy road toward the cemetery near Blessing. He recalled how Jonathan, the Colonel's brother, seeking a name for the new railroad town, had announced it should be called "Thank God." "But, perhaps Blessing is better," he added "It's God's blessing to us." So "Blessing" it became.

The cortege crawled slowly through an interminable downpour of rain. The hearse wallowed and bounced over axle-deep ruts. A church came out of the gloom, the same church the Colonel was so proud of having built.

As they drew nearer, Mr. Proctor understood what Mr. Pierce had meant when he wrote his banker a few days before his death in explanation of his losses in the recent storm: "I am badly torn up. I had built a nice church for my people all at my own Expence & the Good lord saw fit to give it a H—— of a lick & nearly wreck it."

From the service in the storm-battered church the body was moved to the burial plot where he had long since erected a tomb for himself. "I have," said the Colonel, "put up a statute, an exact likeness of myself which has been standing there for five years waiting for me to come. You will recognize it when you see it and say: 'There stands Old Pierce.'" In front of the "statute" a grave

"Mr. Pierce died this evening"

had been dug. The rain continued to fall. Improvised dikes overflowed, and the hole filled with water faster than it could be bailed out. Fred looked up at the marble statue. Yes, it was an exact likeness of his old friend, but a swarm of black wasps had taken refuge under the marble coattail. Mr. Clay, seeing the grave filling, gave the signal, and his friends lowered "Old Shanghai" into a watery grave.

2. "*I was not born under the golden star*"

Could one have looked back some twenty years before the Colonel's burial in the rainstorm, back to June 17, 1879, he might have seen a freight train crawl into the Kansas City stockyard as the shades of evening stretched to lay a gloom over the cattleman's Midwestern marketplace. A tall man—some six feet four inches—stepped from the caboose. A long full beard, flecked with gray but not white, and a definite stiffness in the movement of his back made him appear much older than his years, as he stooped along the sides of the cars, peering between the slats to see if his cattle were on their feet. He finally moved away from the freight terminal toward the St. James Hotel "on the hill." A grinning Negro followed close behind, carrying a small handbag. When they neared the hotel, the bag was passed to the large man, who sent the Negro away with the stern admonition: "All right, Nep. Be on time in the morning."

A peep inside that satchel, had one been so privileged, would have revealed several expensive white shirts, upon the left bosoms

10

"Not born under the golden star"

of which were embroidered the large letters A H P. On the shirts lay "a good deerfoot Bowie Knife," besides several miscellaneous papers. Obviously this man was traveling light and was ready for emergencies.

The stockman's speed continued unchecked by the ascent. His "wind" was good. The long, even, certain strides set him apart as one who knew exactly upon what mission he was bound. He took the steps to the porch of the St. James—eight of them—without falter. Then, swinging the door full back, he stood framed in the passageway. His large white hat, pointed upward at the crown as if to accentuate his height, dented as it touched the upper doorframe. His rough, soiled Levi trousers (he called them "britches"), weather-stained jacket, and the acrid smell of cattle lingering on his clothing catalogued him as a proper habitué of the old St. James of the seventies.

He looked at none except the newly employed clerk at the register, although all the available chairs and settees in the cramped lobby were occupied by men of dress not dissimilar to his own. There was even an overflow of guests. Some of them squatted on their haunches, the rowels of their spurs making a change of position precarious.

In a loud booming voice the new arrival demanded: "Is there any mail for me?"

The clerk, yet a stranger to the arriving guest, countered with the cynical query: "And who are you?"

The shoulders of the large man squared. He seemed a full two inches taller. The first sound was nasal, as if some wild animal in fright had snorted. Then in a full, even penetrating tone, a voice of high dignity and authority, he said: "I am Shanghai Pierce, Webster on Cattle, by God, Sir."

During the preceding quarter-century a great change had come over this man who had proclaimed himself the final authority on cattle and was now getting the attention of all in the lobby. From a lean gangrel, newly from Rhode Island, he had developed into a man of affluence, dignity, and poise. He was greeted by men many years his senior with a deferential: "Howdy, Mr. Pierce" or a more friendly: "Good day, Colonel. How are things down in Texas?" The life he had lived had been a rough one, not unmixed with hardships. To this his hands attested. His had been a life of nearness to both work and weather. Distended blood vessels tinged pink through wind-browned cheeks. There was a "Yankee twang" to his voice, a pompousness in his manner contrasting him with the calmness of Colonel Pryor and the genial indifference of Major Mabry, both of whom arose from their chairs to greet him as a friend.

That anyone—just anyone whosoever—would not recognize him instantly surpassed his understanding. His very bearing proclaimed self-sufficiency. His aloofness denoted importance; but the background from which he had come, no doubt, was of little concern to him. It was true his reminiscences, at times, lapsed back to a hard life on a Rhode Island farm, and he was prone to launch into bitter descriptions of memories of rising at four in the morning, of "biting cold winds" interspersed with "winter schooling in a small district school." He found nothing inspiring about the recollection of the "rough 20 x 30 structure known as the Judea schoolhouse" where he learned to read and write. Regretfully he would admit: "I am not like you. I was not born under the golden star. I came away from home very young, never learned. I can read and write very well, practice has made that, but I have never run up a column of figures in my life." Yet, what was his heritage back of the little Judea schoolhouse he had neither the time nor inclination to inquire. He was content in his conviction: "I stand pat I am the best cowman in Texas today."

This man was the product of the blending of strong lines of blood. That which flowed down to him would have pleased the most ostentatious of the vainglorious social climbers. However, ferreting out kinships was not one of his tasks. He was engaged only with the problems of his immediate life. The self-styled "Shanghai Pierce, Webster on Cattle, by God, Sir," as he stood framed in the doorway of the old St. James, whose mother had named him Abel Head Pierce, could have, in fact, traced his ancestry direct to the Mayflower. Seven generations separated him from Ann Marbury, and nine generations stood between him and John Alden and Priscilla Mullen. Through this family chain he was related to Henry Wadsworth Longfellow as well as to a president of the United States, Franklin Pierce, and also to Thomas Wentworth Peirce, New England philanthropist and builder of the Southern Pacific Railroad in Texas.

"Not born under the golden star"

Jonathan Pierce, Abel Head's father, was both farmer and village blacksmith. He and his wife, Hannah Head, were "hard working, shrewd New England Yankees, well knowing the worth of a dollar, and made good use of it." Jonathan's farming activities were constricted by the bleakness of his New England environment as well as by a paucity of land, so he supplemented the family income with earnings in the blacksmith shop, shoeing community horses and sharpening dull plowpoints. Thus he accumulated a fair competence with the passing years.

Hannah Head Pierce (in the language of her niece) "had an only brother, Abel, who had journed down to Petersburg, Va. had opened a store and was prosperous." The sister ranked brother Abel high in her life. "The success of my brother" was a phrase too familiar in the Jonathan Pierce household, causing the Pierce children to contrast New England hard-scrabble with Virginia opulence. The child to react most positively against the family environment was Abel, namesake of the beloved merchant-brother, now vaunting his prosperity from Petersburg.

Abel was Jonathan's and Hannah's third son, their sixth child. He was, as were his brothers and sisters, born on a farm adjacent to the village, Little Compton, Rhode Island. Miranda was born on February 22, 1824, a year and a week after the marriage of Hanna, and was ten and one-half years old at Abel's birth, June 29, 1834. By the time Abel was old enough to begin to understand some of the underlying causes for his mother's devotion to her affluent brother, he had developed a rebellious attitude toward stern parental supervision and financial scrimpiness and was casting a wistful eye in his uncle's direction, down in the "Old Dominion." Miranda by then had become a "strict stern New England School teacher strongly Puritanical"; and since "Sister Mira" was fending for herself and earning money disproportionately large as compared to the farmer-blacksmith income, Abel anchored his affections in his eldest sister, despite her much-disliked "puritanical sternness."

One of Abel's brothers was Frederick Horatio, a permanent cripple, who was the subject of great paternal concern. This favoritism Abel also resented. Thus he concluded: "I did not see much advantage for myself on the farm, and little pocket money, my thoughts turned to my uncle in Virginia, so helped financially and morally supported by Mira, I started to Virginia to work as a clerk in Uncle's store." He did not leave, however, until after he had precipitated a "family scene" over money. The dispute with his father culminated in the headstrong youth's giving vent to nurtured animosities against his father. He arose to his full six feet three inches and vowed in a voice loud enough for all kith and kin to hear (as well as the neighbors): "I'm going to leave and will not honor this family again with my presence until I can bring back a million dollars."

There was more than temper and boyish resolution in this railing. Abel H. Pierce was actually giving early expression to two of the tenets which were to be his philosophy of life: "Help your friends but never forgive an enemy; [and] strive to acquire, not for the money itself but for the control of those who have it." That he never forgave his family—particularly his father—for the restrictions they had sought to put upon him is to be gathered from a later letter to him from his sister Mary:

Fall River
June 19,1882

Dear Brother Abel
   Your letter reached me in due time But I have been very neglectfull. But beg to be excused for my neglect. But you will know my thousand cares. In your first letter you said your troubles with Susan were geting no better that I am sorry to here. I wish it could be diferent and you three could live peaceable. But I do certainly Know I would let My *Dead Father* rest. let him be now he has been gone over 15 years.

And when Mira heard of Abel's persistence she was "very much shocked at the language" and wondered "whar in the world will this stop."

3. "My uncle fed me too many doses of sanctimony"

The change from Rhode Island to Virginia did not soften the mounting urge in Abel Head Pierce. Troubles, such as were paramount in Rhode Island, he also found "in multiplicity" in Petersburg. His basic discontent did not pass away merely by changing his residence to that of the much talked about uncle. It was true he did not have to arise with the first signs of eastern light to feed farm animals, but on the other hand, he found Uncle Abel adamant that he should open the general mercantile store at an early hour. The floors must be swept to make ready for a chance customer. Broom-wielding to the boy savored much of the tasks for female menials, and besides, the dust stung his nostrils. He resented his chore for both reasons, but despite his repugnance for these tasks, they became daily duties. His status, he concluded, was "little short of a disguised apprentice." Not only was his employment unpalatable, but Uncle Abel felt it his holy duty to impose a restriction upon practically every activity of the nephew. And what was worst of all, Uncle Abel affected a positive religious mania and was horrified when his nephew evidenced no inclination to follow his Puritanical soul-saving directives.

Unacceptable as was the uncle's religiosity, young Abel might have devised methods for circumvention and survival had not "Uncle Abel persisted in being very exacting and paid small wages." The boy, thereupon, cast a balance. From father to uncle his outlook had not improved. He was yet in the hands of oppressive seniors. He saw no chance to get rich, which "discouraged me very much." He had, as he later said when he had acquired the cowboy vernacular, "traded a sorrel for a roan."

Working conditions were less objectionable after he was given an opportunity to observe the financial transactions going on between his uncle and farmers with whom a profitable farm-machinery business was being conducted. His watchfulness enabled him to understand some of the methods employed to make profit; and profit-making had much charm for him. "I can endure much," he vowed, "if it will get me out on the main road, contribute to my future welfare." Day after day, nephew and uncle discussed methods of trade and speculated upon the importance of men of wealth. These confidences he shared with a newly acquired friend, Chester Hamlin Robbins. Chester had been a clerk in the Head store, then admitted to a limited partnership, although his general relationship with the storekeeper was of the same character of "apprentice supervision" held by young Abel. Chester's father, Samuel Robbins, had entrusted his son to Mr. Head while he went off to a newly annexed state called Texas. The young businessman and youth therefore compared their plights, and they dreamed together of money and power. Chester claimed a kinship already with power, for he had an interest in the farm-machinery trade, and he understood that his father was a man of means in faraway Texas.

Letters seldom came from Texas, but what little he heard from his father impressed him with that new land. The nature of Samuel Robbins' employment was not clear to the son. It had something to do, however, with sailboats and cattle. News from Texas came almost exclusively through shipping connections of Richard Grimes.

Richard Grimes, familiarly known as "Captain Dick," was born at Rocky Hill, Connecticut. Captain Dick had inherited so

"Too many doses of sanctimony"

much of the lore of the sea that, at ten years of age, he boarded a ship as a stowaway. He continued adventures until he had sailed seven times around the globe and "entered every port ever entered by a whiteman and some where no other boat had ever ventured." But when steam began to displace the sailboat, he established himself on the Tres Palacios River and confined his seagoing activities to the Texas coast and the Atlantic seaboard. To his Texas establishment, which soon became more ranch than marine headquarters, he attracted Samuel Robbins, a kinsman of his New England neighbor, Philamon Robbins, of Hartford mercantile renown. And Chester gloated over Abel Pierce when letters arrived from his father, Samuel. It was therefore of much importance to the young dreamer that he had such a friend, closely connected to wealth, as was Chester.

Then tragedy came. Chester received a letter from Matagorda, Texas, signed by Captain Richard Grimes. Chester stammered out the news: "Father has been killed by renegades."

"There will be no money," the Captain had tersely written, "unless someone looks after the little property your father left." Samuel Robbins' estate seemed to consist, for the most part, of some ungathered cattle ranging wild in Matagorda County and a sailboat. Grimes said that the sailboat was at anchor in a cove near Palacios Point where Robbins had gone aboard, after having sold most of his possessions to Captain Dick. The pay he had taken in gold. The boat was ready to sail the next morning northward along the Atlantic coast to far-off Virginia and a meeting with his son, Chester. Captain Grimes conveyed the morbid information that he, in conjunction with others, had gone in search of Robbins; that they had discovered his boat at anchor and his body near by in the water, murdered. "It was the work of renegades."

Chester left the employment of Abel Head immediately, bade his friend Abel Pierce good-by, promised his sweetheart he would go to Texas and wreak his vengeance upon the murderers, recoup his father's fortune, and in due time return to make her his wife. Now Abel was more lonely than ever. His friend no longer had even the prospects of riches, unless riches could be had in Texas. That was worth thinking about. Samuel Robbins had acquired wealth in Texas. Perhaps Chester would do likewise, and why not himself! "Yes, why not myself?" repeatedly he asked himself. But long months passed. Uncle Abel continued to be "exacting" and paid small wages; and there was no news from Chester.

The situation at the merchant's home changed somewhat after Chester's departure for Texas. Abel Head's wife died, and his daughter Mary married Carter Bishop. These younger people, especially Mary, came more and more to determine the ambitious clerk's course of conduct. Mary was kind and sought to soften the rebuffs given by her father. She took much of the place in Abel's life formerly held by Mira, even contributing a sympathetic encouragement to his dreams of riches, but she could not entirely mollify her father's religious impressment. She had little of Mira's stern Puritanism. Abel was fast becoming reconciled to his Virginia environment. Then, as he passed his eighteenth birthday, Chester returned. He was vibrant with enthusiasm. He was returning to Texas. He would take a wife with him. Texas was the land of opportunity!

Long talks took place between the young men. Chester had visited, so he claimed, the "Etheopian Eden of America." It lay close to the waters of the Gulf of Mexico, with the Brazos River on the north, the Guadalupe on the south, and a verdant territory in between, approximating the size of the state of Rhode Island, bisected by the Colorado River, on the banks of which (and for some thirty miles in each direction) grew luxuriant native canebrakes. Wild game—ducks, geese, pheasants, even deer and bear—abounded in the land. Wild cattle could be owned by the simple expedient of branding them. Few white men had settled in the region, it was true, but those who had used good judgment survived the adversities of the new country. Negroes seemingly were immune to the scourges of coastal mosquitoes and the miasma which arose from the ponds, and white men erected great estates from their labor. "Then, too," Chester confided, "one may own Negroes if he wishes." These things Chester told Abel, and he was going back with his Petersburg sweetheart to live with the ease of Thomas Decrow, John Duncan, Captain Richard Grimes, the Holts, Rugeleys, the Keerans, and the O'Connors. It was the same region over which Álvar Núñez Cabeza de Vaca, Spanish conquistador, with his black Estevanico, after his shipwreck on the Island of Galveston, had trafficked with the Indians. It was the same territory over which the Frenchman, René Robert de La

"Too many doses of sanctimony"

Salle, had planted the colors of *La Belle France*, north of the Guadalupe, near Indianola, now the chief port of entry.

While the glory of Texas was fresh in the telling, Uncle Abel, with characteristic lack of discretion, renewed with increased determination his efforts to instill into his protégé a "certain amount of spiritual education." Every Sunday full-day sessions became the rule. More fervor than grace went into the efforts. Then came the fateful day when "Abel annoyed his uncle over some trivial matter, and he proclaimed to young Abel he never would be good for anything and would never earn a dollar, which discouraged him very much." Forthwith the disconsolate boy went to his cousin Mary, telling her his troubles and adding, "You know Cousin Mary, I always wanted to be rich." And she replied, "That you will, Abel," which (so wrote his niece) "comforted him very much and helped his spirits." He thereupon shouted defiance in the face of his astonished uncle: "Too many doses of sanctimony! Too many doses of sanctimony!" and cramming his hat down hard on his head, he departed from his uncle forever.

On June 29, 1853, his nineteenth birthday, the six-foot-four boy prowled the docks at New York. He was in search of a Texas-bound boat. He found a schooner of "ninety five tons burthen" destined for Indianola. On it he stowed away until the ship reached the high seas. When he was brought before the captain, the old salt thought him a "likely lad." Certainly he was big enough to earn his passage, so he went to work mopping the deck and heaving boxes at ports of call. It was December before the vessel came alongside the narrow wharf which extended far out into the water at Indianola. A part of the cargo went ashore, and the boat moved on up the bay to Port Lavaca, now assuming a place of importance in the cattle business. Some of the roustabouts intended to "jump ship" and take to dry land, but news was brought that an epidemic of "Yellow Jack" was in town. There was no inclination, however, on the part of Pierce to permit anyone to take his place. He stayed and tugged and shouted with the stoutest until the last bale of cotton was aboard. Thus, with his passage paid in good honest labor, "the long, lean, gangling boy with too short pants walked down the gang plank." He was in Texas, through with the sea forever.

A great transformation took place in the boy during the more than five months at sea. Hard work, exposure to the weather, and association with men who ranted and swore, had made whipcords of his muscles, bronzed his boyish face, and taught him to swear with the lustiest, the boom in his voice carrying far and wide. It was no wonder that Texans stopped to look "at the loud mouthed Yankee with the nasal twang and too short pants."

Abel heard bad news thick and fast. German immigrants, who were following Prince Carl of Solms-Braunfels to their new colony around New Braunfels and Fredericksburg, were dying in great numbers at Victoria only twenty-odd miles away. Those who could get conveyances were coming back to the coast, hoping to sail away again, or were trekking into higher country farther west where they hoped to leave the scourge behind. "They died so rapidly," said one from Victoria, "that there was no time to construct coffins or give them a decent burial. The bodies were wrapped in whatever the unfortunate people died on—sheets or blankets—tied at both ends—and then taken in the dump-cart, to the cemetery." If this had any effect on the plans of Abel, nothing in his conduct indicated it. He expressed no desire to depart with his ship. He did not so much as inquire of the little-explored western part of the state where so many of the immigrants were hastening. He did, however, ask for Captain Richard Grimes, known to him through Chester Robbins, "the most important cattleman in the region."

Abel felt the pang of disappointment again after talking with Captain Dick: He had no place, so he said, on the ranch for him. There was something, however, about the big, loud, bluff stripling, who spoke with a jaunty merriment, which caused the hard old mariner to offer him a ride across the bay in his boat. "Perhaps my son, Brad, may find use for you." In explanation, he told how he was getting old, now; that he was entrusting the family enterprises chiefly to William Bradford, his only son, and that he did not, in fact, have the heart to reject the appeal of the Yankee boy who was starting on a career much like his own.

Making good his promise, Captain Dick set down his unwelcome protégé at the doorstep of his son, suggesting: "You might use him, Bing." Bing looked him over and laughed: "Wonder if I've got a horse he won't break down!" Immediately young Pierce reacted unfavorably to the less courteous Grimes.

"Too many doses of sanctimony"

Half in apology the captain interposed in the boy's behalf: "But he does not have that lean, patient, dyspeptic look of the New England farmer." This feeble recommendation failed to convince Bradford, in whom there was no sentiment.

Young Grimes was responsible for his father's interest now, and he saw keen competition developing in the activities of Thomas O'Connor, J. M. Foster, and the Collins brothers. They were laying claim to nearly as great a number of cattle as Grimes had branded. The inroads of these industrious men to the south of the Tres Palacios were serious. They were encroaching upon Grimes' pre-emptions, and Brad needed ranchmen, but he was more than dubious about a tenderfoot from a mercantile store. Nevertheless, "Bing" looked at the large muscles, the powerful hands, the long arms, and he suddenly remembered: "I do need a hand to split rails."

Pierce would take the job, so he said. Then he astounded his new employer with: "Will it be all right with you, Mr. Grimes, if I take my first year's pay in cows and calves? I want to be a cattleman like you some day."

An agreement was reached. Pierce was to "batch" with E. A. Deming and was to receive at the end of the first year two hundred dollars in cattle. Thereupon young "gangle shanks" went about his employment with a will. Hefting several axes at the woodpile, he selected a heavy one and set out to the timber fringing Río Tres Palacios. He was wearing his entire wardrobe, an old straw hat, jeans pants, steel-clasp fastener shoes, and no underclothing. In his pocket jingled every solitary possession he had in the world, seventy-five cents in coin. The double-blade ax held rigidly over his shoulder pointed unmistakably to the fact that the spirit in the boy was equal to the task before him.

He arose early in the mornings, many times to be ushered off to the timber by Bradford Grimes without his breakfast. Near the path of his going stood the home of the "Widow" Ward—a kind old soul. And surmising, if not actually knowing his hunger, the old lady would watch for the boy, call him into the kitchen to a piping hot plate of hotcakes. She piled them high and laved them with butter and molasses; then he would eat until distended, and off to the rails he would go again. For the third time the kindness of a woman had influenced his life. His heart welled large for her.

Shanghai Pierce

Throughout his life he would repeat the story to any willing listener, climaxing the description of the quantity of his breakfast by measuring with four fingers: "She'd stack 'em that high. The best cakes I ever tasted. God bless the memory of the Widow Ward."

Many years later, Pierce was to become a man of wealth, while the Widow Ward's son became enmeshed in financial difficulties. One day L. Ward applied to Pierce's attorney, Fred Proctor, for a loan of $90,000, offering security which the attorney estimated to be inadequate. He therefore, without apprising Pierce of the facts, declined to make the loan, whereupon Ward applied direct to Mr. Pierce. Almost immediately Mr. Proctor received a telegram reading: "Let Ward have all the money he wants. His mother cooked good pancakes. A. H. Pierce." Thinking that Mr. Pierce had violated his rule of sobriety, Mr. Proctor again declined to make the loan, whereupon a storm came swirling into Proctor's office in the form of an infuriated Pierce. "Counsellor, by God, Sir, why don't you let Ward have the money?" Proctor explained; then Pierce replied: "Yes, that's true, but the Widow Ward fed me when I was hungry." And extending the four fingers of his hand, he shouted: "She stacked 'em up that high—Good pancakes—And so long as a son of the Widow Ward needs money and Shanghai Pierce has it, he can get it. God bless the memory of the Widow Ward!"

The rail splitter soon became general handy man around the ranch. The calloused palms produced by the ax handle, his aversion to Bing, and the kindness of Mrs. Ward he did not forget. Years afterwards in the prime of his affluence he would ride with strangers far out of his way to point out the "stake and rider fence" he had laboriously made with his rails and exclaim: "The folly of my youth, gentlemen! The folly of my youth!" but Bing remained for many years as unfinished business on his agenda.

The winter of 1853–54 broke off to a warm spring. Grimes and his crew of yelling, yipping cowboys were holding a large herd of Spanish ponies in the corral made of Pierce's unseasoned rails. Bradford Grimes was the owner of a number of Negroes, as well as cows and horses, and as fast as the bronc-busting crew would lead out a snorting, frightened pony, Bing would shove a Negro forward as rider. These horses gave an unusual amount of trouble. Time after time the full crew was required to master one sufficiently for the Negro to get astride. When turned loose, off he would

"Too many doses of sanctimony"

go, running, jumping, bawling above the laughter of the fence-sitters. Then a particularly unruly stallion came under the rope. Abel moved into the pen. Reaching out his long arms, he took the ketch-rope, walked quietly toward the horse, and pinioned his head firmly against his left shoulder. He was as deft and certain in his movements as if he had been accustomed to bronc-busting all his life. The "experienced" men looked on in dismay and in silence, while blustering Brad, with his weather-browned full beard waving in the breeze, ordered up another black rider. Pierce patted the quivering horse gently on the shoulder before releasing him. The animal trotted away, humping up a little under its unaccustomed burden; but suddenly the Negro slashed him with his quirt and raked him with his spurs. The stallion jumped high in the air, landed stiff-legged, threw his head between his forelegs, and, spinning a few times, dumped the Negro in the dust at the feet of the fence-riders amid shouts of "Ride him, cowboy," which he had demonstrated he was unable to do.

Just then a woman's high-pitched voice called from the ranch house: "Bradford! Bradford! Put Abel on the bad 'uns. Those Negroes are worth a thousand dollars apiece. One might get killed." The bronc-busters laughed hilariously while Abel looked them over. Giving Bing a withering stare, he shouted so that his voice carried back to the house: "Bring on your bad 'uns," and he went directly to the stallion which had just unloaded its rider. Abel mounted him and let him pitch, sitting firmly until he came finally under his mastery. Bradford thereupon recognized that his tenderfoot had more than "height and voice," so he was promoted to "ranch bronc-buster," with a promise of increased wages at the end of the year.

There was a sort of feudal, baronial character interspersed with Southern aristocracy about the Bradford Grimes household. Mary Louise Robbins, the daughter of Philamon Robbins of Hartford, Connecticut, who stood at the head of an old family of merchants, gentle and city bred as she was, contributed greatly to Bradford's dignity and added grace and charm to her husband's pose of stability. It was the custom, if there were guests, that the family would take their meals with some ostentation in the large ranch house dining room. Employees upon such occasions were expected to assemble at the "outside" quarters, some distance removed from, and at the rear of, the residence. Their meals would be served to them "cook-shack" fashion.

By mishap one day (or was it by design?) Pierce became a transgressor. The interpretable facts do not go beyond the incident and what both Pierce and Bradford had to say about it. Those interpretations were diametrically opposed to each other, as one might expect. Anyway, Abel rode to the front of the house one day just as Bradford's sister, Frances Charlotte, ushered the guests into the dining room. Pierce dropped his bridle reins and walked as if to enter. Bradford met him at the front door. What passed between them was heard only by the two. Abel squared his shoulders and strode measuredly back to his horse. Swinging into the saddle he rode resolutely away. Never had his shoulders been so square; never had he ridden so high in his stirrups. He was deaf to the calls and jeers of the hands as he passed the cook-shack; and he did not stop until he had pulled up his horse before the home of the Widow Ward. In that ride, so he told her: "I crystallized the philosophy of my life: 'Punish your enemies; reward your friends.'"

As Mrs. Ward heard the story from Abel, Bing had told him to "go to the back door like all other Niggers and Yankee whitetrash." Grimes reserved his version until many years had passed; then he said there was nothing amiss about the incident: he had merely informed Abel that the "hands" would take their meal that day at the cook-shack. But the oftener Abel told the story the greater was the offense. Mrs. Ella Talbot, having heard it many times, said that Mr. Pierce spoke with eloquent contempt of Mr. Bradford Grimes so long as he lived.

Any act, just at that time, which might lessen the social importance of Abel in the eyes of a feminine member of the Grimes family was certain to cause resentment, for Pierce found himself no longer inclined to conceal his love for Frances Charlotte, called Fannie, which brother Bing obstructed with every artifice at his command. Although Brad had no desire to have Abel as a brother-in-law, still he rated him as a "fust-rate cowhand." He had no cause to criticize his industry, so he promoted him to "range brander."

Nothing could have been more to Abel's liking than this assignment. He remembered his vow to the Widow Ward, and forthwith began to put into practice his life's philosophy. Thereafter he was on the range before the light came in the east. He rode all

"Too many doses of sanctimony"

day, seldom stopping for dinner. With him he carried three branding irons, one the RG (Richard Grimes), another WBG (William Bradford Grimes), the other HO (Frances Charlotte Grimes). Every time a fat heifer jumped from the bushes, regardless of probable ownership, Abel swung his loop and the heifer was soon writhing in pain and fright, smelling of burnt hair and hide from the fresh HO on her side.

Some of the observing boys noticed that Captain Dick got the fair ones, WBG went on the poor ones, and "My gal Fannie" got the fine ones. They, consequently, ventured discreet inquiry. "I am marrying them heifers, you know," was Shanghai's pointed reply.

Abel looked forward to the completion of his first year of employment with Grimes. On January 10, 1854, with less than two months' work to his credit, he rode into the town of Matagorda. It was a pleasant forty miles he had come, for he was looking over the country which Chester Robbins had talked about in such glowing terms. The Indians had once thought of this land as ideal hunting grounds, and now he was interested in it as a possible cattle range. He therefore went direct to the recorder of brands and drew on the brand book two large capital connected letters, AP, and claimed the brand as his own. It took him two days to return, riding up the Colorado, then crossing at Elliott's Ferry, and down the Juanita to the batch-shack and his friend Deming. He speculated on his riches as he rode. "At $7 for a cow and calf, $200 will give me 28 cows, 28 calves come December. A sizeable herd for one year's work." In his enthusiasm he told Grimes about his brand and talked the blacksmith into fashioning him an AP iron.

Time went on, but Grimes did not have any intention of delivering any cattle to him before his year was out in December. "I'll wait for the fall round-up. Your year will not be up until then. No cause to pay you in advance." Settlement day came, however, and Bing cut four old cows and three scrawny calves from a run of range cattle, burned the AP on them, and "threw 'em down on the mud flats." "There's your wages in cows and calves," said Bing as they ran away. Pierce figured rapidly: Grimes had charged him fourteen dollars for each cow and each calf when he had expected to get them at the range rate of seven dollars for a cow plus her calf, and besides, "those old cows looked to be ten to twenty-five years old."

25

Bing bragged on his cunningness: "I have given him the first degree in the cattle business." Then winter closed in, and the poor "old shelly bellies and swaybacks, fit for nothing but to sell," as Pierce explained it, were unable to lift themselves from the bogs; and they died, moaning for help. Three motherless spindle-legged dogies was all he had left from his year of hard work, and a tide of vengeance swept into Pierce's heart for his tricky employer. "There is another degree, the Royal Arch Degree," said Pierce, "and I will give it to him before I die."

Despite the treatment received from Grimes, Abel did not seem willing to quit his employer. Termination of the first yearly contract brought a renewal with increased wages. During 1855 he was to receive $22.50 a month. He demanded cash this time to be paid monthly. He would handle his own cattle purchases, provided he found it necessary to pay out money for cattle. He understood Grimes' method of acquiring herds now; and besides, Grimes' method seemed to be the accepted practice throughout the region. Cattle were to be had from the range for the branding, if you got your brand on first and someone did not "grub their ears" and counterbrand before you could sell them. To increase your cattle holdings on the range, you had to be industrious. He overheard Valcour J. Labauve call it the "grab game," and, according to the talk, the Lunn boys were experts at the game. "They will do to watch." Pierce did not know about that. He did know they were industrious branders, and they did not seem to be very careful to see whether an animal already carried a brand. In fact, he liked Ed Lunn, and they worked together whenever possible. He saw no difference in the methods of Grimes and Lunn. Grimes had a reputation; the Lunns were acquiring one.

No one called him "Abel" any more; most addressed him politely as "Mr. Pierce." Those who knew him better used his nickname, "Shanghai." "One day," said Gilbert Labauve, "I was over on the Carancahua. I had not crossed the path of Pierce before, and when I rode out of the bushes I was rather surprised to see coming toward me a young man, probably younger than I was. He had light brown hair, whiskers all over his face. He was riding a small pony. His long legs let his feet almost drag the ground. They, too, were large. Looked like shovels on long handles. I was more surprised when he spoke.

"Too many doses of sanctimony"

'Good morning, young man,' he said in a booming voice. 'What is your name, young man?' emphasizing the 'young man.' I told him and asked his. He said, 'Pierce . . . Shanghai Pierce, by God, Sir. . . . Just call me 'Shanghai'."

Labauve was tremendously amused and told his cousin Willie that night about the big boy with the bigger voice and shovel feet who called himself "Shanghai." But Willie had already heard the story from Pierce, who had stopped at the cow camp to spin a few yarns with the boys and to let Willie know that he did not object to the nickname which gave him distinctiveness.

There is an elusiveness about the origin of his sobriquet. He did not state it to be definite fact but intimated the name had been applied to him during his Little Compton school days. If so, it was then a term of derision, for shortly after he announced his intention to accept the nickname as a "brand of distinction," he let it be known that when previously employed it was a "fightin' word." He shrugged off this aversion to the word by laughing: "But you know I do not have time to fight everybody who wants to fight me. If I take that much time off I will not have time to take their money away from them." Then putting spurs to his horse he called back over his shoulder: "There are a few dollars old Shang hasn't got yet. I've got to go on after 'em."

Abel Pierce Borden, the namesake nephew, said, "People thought he looked so much like the long-necked, long-legged rooster from Shanghai that they called him after his counterpart." An undercover version (usually whispered during his lifetime) is that it came because he had "shanghaied" so many people out of their property. Legend has it, though there is no truth in it, that he was shanghaied off the dock at New York and brought to Texas. This, of course, was an attempt to make a dramatic story. The nickname most likely had its inception in the incident when Pierce had his blacksmith make him a pair of spurs. The rowels were unusually large, and when Pierce jangled them on his boots for the first time, he stood looking down at them, and exclaimed: "O, by God, Mr. Heyer, I look like a shanghai rooster."

Developing rapidly into a showman and fully appreciating the value of being one set apart from the common run of men, he encouraged all stories bandied around about him, repeated them himself, and added to their color to be certain they had currency.

He even went so far as to speak derisively of his towering proportions: "I was born in Rhode Island, you know, and it got too little for me. When I lay down, my head, like as not, would be in the lap of somebody in Massachusetts and my feet bothering somebody in Connecticut. I just got too big for the state, and I thought Texas would be big enough for me, and I came here."

Despite their mutual dislike a simulated truce developed between Pierce and Grimes. Pierce called Grimes "Bing," and he in turn was addressed by Grimes as "Shang." Bing was a practical man and he needed the tireless energy of the young man. Shang, at least, wanted the wages the richest of all South Texas cattlemen would pay, and while he drew his wages he was awaiting the day of his strength.

In 1850, before Shanghai arrived on the Tres Palacios, Matagorda County had 35,000 cattle grazing on the range. One-tenth of these were owned by John Duncan. By 1855, Grimes had his WBG on 5,500 of the then 51,090 branded cattle, while Duncan had fallen to fourth place. Grimes understood the importance of maintaining his position. Thomas Decrow, old sea captain turned cattleman, and James Kuykendall were actively contesting Bing's supremacy on the coast, and there were others, too. "J Foster of Indianola," reported The Colorado *Tribune,* October 29, 1849, "has for the last several weeks past, been engaged in this country in *purchasing* cattle for the New Orleans market." Since Foster continued to compete by actual purchase, Grimes realized more and more the importance of retaining the services of Shanghai. Bing, therefore, did two things: He employed Liege Dennis, who could facetiously say, "We skinned the cattle first, then looked to see if they belonged to Mr. Duncan," and he raised Shanghai's wages. He was promoted from common wrangler and bronc-peeler to "top cow hand." Forthwith, he was put in charge "trimmin' up the herd." Fewer and fewer "lonesome motherless calves" were branded to the AP, while a greater number of Crescent V calves appeared outside the Widow Ward's range. "Mr. Benn" caught Shanghai branding such a calf one day and questioned his mother's ownership of it. Shanghai laughed it off with, "You know, Mr. Benn, that's just interest on them pancakes."

Pierce's life at this time was not unhappy. He had not forgotten Fannie Grimes, of course, but he had extended his range

"Too many doses of sanctimony"

over to the doorstep of another neighbor, Fannie Lacy. When he was not "workin' cattle," his attention was given over to these young ladies. "I will not have a man in my outfit," he declared one day, "who does not love the ladies. They just do not have enough fire for me." But despite the lure of the women, he was happiest after all around the campfire, indulging in a little "common gammon with the boys," or out with the herd at night "singin' to the ladies on the bobtail guard," holding old "mossy horns" in loose herd on the prairie. His real love was "that cow out there."

No one was more welcome around campfires than Shanghai had become. He was jovial; he was rough as a last year's cob, profane as the most profane, and he could convulse his listeners with a good story. Credibility in his stories, however, was something to which he gave little thought.

In order to compete with J. M. Foster who was loading Morgan liners out of Indianola and delivering by water to New Orleans, Grimes had Shanghai "shape up a drive" for New Orleans. He hoped that driving would prove more profitable than paying steamboat passage. The tenderfoot boss was put in charge. Shanghai cut back all the culls, shelly bellys, wrinkle horns, and swamp angels and started north and east with as fine a herd of coasters as the Grimes crew could get together. He was intent upon finding a feasible land route to New Orleans. When he returned he gave a glowing account of his charges, voicing an affection for the brutes and paying a wonderful tribute to the cattle range from which they had been driven:

> The mud and water of the Louisiana swamps compelled us to pick every step. Why the public roads—where there were any—would bog a saddleblanket. My steers were nice, fat slick critters that knew how to swim, but they were used to a carpet of prairie grass. They were mighty choosey as to where they put their feet. They had a bushel of sense; and purty soon over there in Louisiana they got to balancing theirselves on logs in order to keep out of the slimy mud. Yes, they got so expert that one of them would walk a cypress knee to the stump, jump over it, land on a root, and walk it out for another jump. If there was a bad bog-hole between cypresses you'd see a steer hang his horns into a mustang-grape-vine, or maybe a wistaria, and swing across like a monkey. The way they balanced and jumped and swung actually made my horse laugh.

Shanghai Pierce

After his successful trip to New Orleans, Shanghai always commanded the best horse in Grimes' remuda. His employer grew more and more prosperous under his foremanship. Pierce also was giving evidence of prosperity. Money was being earned at a rate of $100 a month. His Yankee heritage made him keep a firm grip on it. Back in Rhode Island things were going well; also, Mira was punctual with her monthly letter. "Brother Jonathan," she wrote, "has acquired the mechanical aptitude of your father but not his physique. Farming and smithing, those occupations against which you, Abel, rebelled while young, have found lodgment in Jonathan Edward. He is now an efficient workman with his father. The farm our father owns is poor, but every art known to the skillful and scientific agriculturist is practiced to add to its productiveness. Father Pierce has taught his children to do thoroughly and well anything and everything they undertake. He impresses upon us the virtue of patience and perseverance. And Jonathan knows how to farm, he knows carpentering, he knows blacksmithing and even knows plumbing."

In a spirit of swagger to which he was much given, after receiving one of Mira's "family letters," Shanghai boasted to Bing of the accomplishments of his twenty-two-year-old brother "back up in Little Rhody." Grimes' dream was centering around the enormous cattle business now focusing at the port of Indianola. One year 21,685 cattle and 42,599 hides had been shipped from there, and he was aware that the business was small in proportion to the available grass on the coastal range. He was ranching in the middle of it, but he needed more men with cow sense, like Shanghai, to hold his own against encroachments of other industrious cattlemen. He, therefore, suggested that Jonathan be persuaded to come to Texas. "He could be useful. I will give him a job."

When the *A. C. Leverette* docked at Powder Horn in early December, 1860, after encountering three hurricanes at sea, Shanghai met his brother Jonathan, whom he had last seen when he was only seven years old. Both men had changed. Shanghai was tall and nimble, and he wore a full beard. Jonathan was stout and thick, of medium height, and almost barrel-torsoed. He wore a black moustache. He had not needed, so he said, "passage money and besides that I have some to spare."

Very soon after Jonathan arrived at the Grimes ranch, he was

"Too many doses of sanctimony"

indoctrinated with the first principle of sound horsemanship. He was furnished a saddle horse. Even the gentlest of Texas plugs is humiliated if one attempts to mount from the right side, which of course is the wrong side. It is not probable that brother Abel, contemplating brother "Johnathan's" initial ride, furnished the children's gentle old mare. It is known, however, that Jonathan—ever so unwittingly—was about to bring shame upon a Spanish pony as he swung for the saddle from the right side. Just at that moment, however, the horse wheeled out from under him, and he went rolling in the dust. Then and there with characteristic Pierce temper, he forswore the use of a horse's back "forevermore."

Indianola and Port Lavaca, south on the bay, were the chief Texas shipping ports, and, as a consequence, ranchmen bought their supplies there. Shanghai frequently had to go to these ports, especially Indianola, in the performance of his duties. There a loud-swearing genial chubby, red-faced Irishman conducted a general mercantile store. Indianola was a one-street town paralleling the water front. Ships came in as close to the land as the water permitted, and their cargoes were unloaded on a long wharf extending out from land. Down toward the most easterly end of the natural shell street stood the Daniel Sullivan General Mercantile Store. The merchant, getting quite far advanced in years, with characteristic Hibernian geniality, enjoyed the acquaintance of the Rhode Islander, and he captured the confidence of Shanghai immediately. "Me and Sullivan was particular friends; he was a regular old fashioned plain man. I was like him. Mr. Sullivan said, 'By God' when talking with me."

The diminutive roly-poly cussin' Irishman did more than greet Shanghai with profanity; he haloed him by magnifying, good naturedly, his tremendous voice. Pierce was pleased when Mr. Sullivan spoke of him as "that big, loud, and exaggerated jocular talker." And to keep the description going, Pierce would add: "Nothing new for me to talk loud. In Indianola, when Sullivan was asked if I was there (and here Shanghai would mimic his Irish friend) he would go to the door of his store, with his hand cupped to his ear, would say: 'No, sir. He is not in town.'"

Then with a grimace Shanghai would continue: "The town is only a mile and a half long, and of course he could hear me when I struck it."

Shanghai Pierce

One day Shanghai came to town making less noise than usual. He had something on his mind. He was playing with the idea of borrowing some money and venturing into the cattle business, like Foster, by purchasing instead of mavericking.

While he was passing the Catholic Academy, two boys came alongside him. One was a small blonde youth, a very reticent boy, who gave no name. The other called himself Billie Marshall. The courtesy of the smaller boy left Pierce reflecting as their ways parted, the boy going toward the rear of the store while Shanghai bolted into the front door, his mind on borrowing money. Later in telling the story Pierce said, "Much to my astonishment, when I said: 'Mr. Sullivan, I want some money, but I have nothing to put up,' he called to the back of the store: 'Danny, any money in the safe?'"

"Yes, Uncle," came the reply from the flaxen-haired boy, as he peered over the counter.

"Let Shanghai have it," crisply ordered the uncle, and then it was "I learned the nephew was also named Daniel Sullivan."

To be able to borrow money without security on his own account upped Shanghai's importance, even in his own estimation. Then the old Irishman added his bit toward dramatizing Shanghai: he ordered him a distinctive, large hat from New York. It was high of crown and elliptic, giving the already tall young man the appearance of added stature. When it came, Pierce called it "my Shanghai hat." Forever afterwards the Shanghai hat was part of his standard personal equipment.

4. "*I was all the same as a major general . . .*"

Jonathan Pierce's tumble from the horse did not keep Grimes from making use of what skills he did have. Bing put him to work as bookkeeper at the hide and tallow factory now going in full blast. His pay was to be twenty dollars a month. Someone was needed to keep account of the slaughter of hundreds of old cows and bulls which were driven in each day from the outside camp. Their hides were saved; their carcasses rendered into tallow. The meat was thrown to a large drove of noisy hogs that smelled to high heaven, making a paradise for flies.

Screens for houses were unheard of in that country at the time, and try as hard as the cooks might, flies were always guests at the dinner table. One day, when Shanghai was being served, the flies became bothersome contenders with him for his food. He pushed back the dish and shouted: "Take it back. Dip 'em off. Blow 'em back, and let me see if I can see to eat it then."

33

Jonathan was not aware of the fact that all cattlemen thought that nothing should be raised except stock. He therefore soon violated their first principle by wanting to know why all the land was given over to the cattle business while no planting was being done as far as the eye could see. He wanted to plant vegetables, but was told that the soil of Texas was not good for anything but cattle. He had, however, come from a coastal region much less favored by nature than Matagorda. Even if the men who claimed to know the land were older, he was not satisfied. He got together what seeds he could find, and the result was that Grimes' table thereafter was laden with vegetables.

Jonathan was fitting neatly into Grimes' needs. In some ways he served better than Shanghai, and Grimes had no intention of letting them leave his employment. But the spring vegetables had barely appeared upon Bing's table before news came to the ranch that there had been a telegraphic dispatch received at Indianola signed by General Winfield Scott. Fort Sumter had been fired upon. "Chivalrous Southerners" were fighting "Damn Yankees." General Scott had issued an order to establish an entrenched camp at Green Lake, southwest of Port Lavaca. "The object of the entrenched camp near Indianola," so the order read "is to keep a foothold in that State, until the question of secession on her part may be definitely settled among her people."

Many of those living in Matagorda County were former residents of the North, and Texas was too far away from the guns to incite haste. Some eager sons, of course, rode away to join the Confederacy, but others lingered at home or rode the range for moss horns and thought of the war as one of those things which would not come this far south to disturb them. One day, however, Dr. E. A. Peareson received authority direct from the headquarters of the Confederacy to organize a company. Matagorda citizens took an interest in the growing need for armed men and empowered Robert H. Williams, Captain John Rugeley, and John W. McCamely to solicit funds from local citizens to equip Company D, Sixth Texas Regiment. Williams and Rugeley were well thought of in the community, and McCameley, who had been part owner of a ninepin alley at Matagorda since April 1, 1840, and subsequently had been licensed to retail liquors and operate a billiard table, knew all the young men who ever came to the county site with spare time on

"All the same as a major general"

their hands. With equipment funds in hand, many of the young men of spirit acted under the persuasion of these respected citizens and moved out on the peninsula across the bay, facing the raft which clogged up the mouth of the Colorado. Among the number was the orphan, Thos. C. Nye.

Here from August to October, within easy AWOL distance by sailboat from Matagorda, they sought military training during the daytime, but used paddles and sails to get back to the mainland at night to view the bay in the moonlight with their ladies. But the sand-dune training was soon over, and Dr. Peareson moved his troop by boat to Port Lavaca, thence by train toward Victoria. They were off to war—so they thought.

While D Company's recruiting and training was in progress, Jonathan and Shanghai were going quietly about Master Grimes' business. All three were originally, of course, from the North. Jonathan, who was freshest from Yankeedom, was thought to lean with favor toward the preservation of the Union. It was questionable what Shanghai might do, for he had had residence in both Rhode Island and Virginia. Grimes had substantial financial interests in both the North and the South. He was pleased when neither Pierce made a move toward going off with the marching boys. He was more pleased that there was to be an entrenched camp near at hand, for certainly there would be a stable market for beef.

Outwardly, it seemed that Jonathan was satisfied with his situation. "At $20 per month," he wrote home, "I have worked one year as clerk, blacksmith, carpenter and general bottlewasher." Grimes had no way of knowing that all was not well in the mind of the newcomer. He, too, was resenting Grimes' stinginess: "For the year," he recorded, "I was charged with all loss of time and interest on advances to me before settlement at the end of the year, and I only drew $16 in advances." He hastened to tell his sister Susan, however, that "the 16 in advances has been used for good purposes: $.50 of this amount I gave for the digging of a well at the Tres Palacios Church. The remainder of the $16 went for brandy-peaches, candy and knickknacks for the girls. I spent a little cash in this way to keep from being called a 'stingy Yankee.'" And too, when Grimes sent him out on the prairie, "he fed me on old bulls and stags and called it fine beef."

Shanghai Pierce

Repugnant as was horseback riding, still he liked the wide-open spaces. The country awoke the poetic in his soul. "The air was laden with fragrance," he confided to one of his visitors. "The sun was just low enough in the great dome to show the prairie in its most picturesque and hospitable garnishments. We came to a spot with a glorious background of noble oaks and lordly elms. The first time I saw it I drove some stakes in the ground and resolved if life was spared to me and my fortune prospered, I would make my home there some day. Then I rode away and followed the herd, but I never forgot the land where the oaks and elms grew so thick, and I dream of the day when I will live there and have my own herd of cattle."

When Jonathan left the Rhode Island homestead, the circumstances were quite different from the day Abel started off to Virginia. Money, however, was the last subject of discussion between father and son, but this time it had a different emphasis. "My father told me that if I turned out to be a good boy he would give me a thousand dollars. When he decided to give it to me the Civil War had begun, and he could not send it."

Now that Jonathan had "turned out to be a good boy" he was not going to let a little thing like a Civil War stand in the way of his getting his reward, even though the two governments proscribed fraternizing with the enemy. A Yankee father with a thousand dollars ready for delivery was not an enemy of his; he, therefore, sought a solution to his problem. Fannie Grimes, beloved of Shanghai, had gone north for a visit at the old Connecticut homestead. The war had caught her there and she was stranded upon the generosity of her Union kinfolk. Jonathan sensed the situation and persuaded Grimes to induce his father back in Rhode Island to deliver a thousand dollars to Fannie in Rocky Hill, Connecticut, Bing, in turn, paying over a thousand dollars to him. Jonathan now had eleven hundred dollars in gold, and as the Confederate rate of exchange broke, he converted his gold into Confederate currency, sometimes receiving at the rate of seventy-five to one, and with this money he bought cattle, branding on his "Ace of Clubs" as fast as he could get them.

Then one day the brothers met. Jonathan bragged about the way he had come into possession of his father's money. He told Shanghai that he had it straight from Bing that Frances would stay

"All the same as a major general"

in Connecticut until the war was over. Perhaps she would not return at all, for her interest now lay in a young man named Joseph W. Camp. He had this direct from Grimes. She was going to marry him. When Jonathan had finished talking, Shanghai turned his horse and slowly they rode toward the ranch house. Shanghai was unusually quiet. Bing was there. Shanghai went straight to him: "I am through, Bing."

"Now about that $500 you owe me," continued Pierce. "I wish you would keep it for me until I come back. This war can't last long, and I'll need it when I get home." Grimes seemed pleased to accommodate him and assured Shanghai he would pay upon demand, without interest of course. Then the brothers rode off to war. They took the Confederate oath of allegiance and became members of D Company, First Texas Cavalry, at Texana, Jackson County, Texas. Captain J. C. Borden, late of Richmond, Texas, was their commander. The company joined with a sister company, August Buchel commanding, and here they met up with their old friends, T. C. Nye and "Little Danny Sullivan, of Indianola, the cussing merchant's nephew."

The prowess of Shanghai as a cattle rustler was known to Captain Borden long before he joined the company, and the cowboy, turned soldier, was a welcome recruit. Immediately he had a special assignment of duty. It was a long distance to the Confederate capital. Communication and promotions were slow. Hence in good old Texas style, disregarding army punctilio, Private Abel Head Pierce was elevated to the rank of "Regimental Butcher," and he was given a "staff" of aids. The army "Bible" neither designated such an officer nor described similar duties, but Captain Borden knew his soldier. And too, the troop had to be fed. Of all the troopers, the commander knew there was none other so well qualified to inveigle cattle from their haunts, and from their rightful owners, in exchange for Confederate currency—if need be— and into the regimental meat-box.

For two years the regiment did garrison and picket duty in the vicinity of Matagorda and the adjacent islands, finally being transferred to Louisiana. But Pierce missed all the fighting except the Red River campaign when his troop was used as a reinforcement. Buchel was killed at Pleasant Hill, and the war came to an end with Shanghai all in a dither to get back to the cattle country.

Shanghai Pierce

On the road home his comrades bragged of their battles, their wounds, their accomplishments, and, most of all, their rank. Shanghai could lay no claim to having been, in any sense, a war hero. All he had been was "Regimental Butcher"; but when a friend sought to tease him about it, he defended his status gallantly:

> "By God, Sir; I was all the same as a major general: always in the rear on advance, always in the lead on retreat."

With the directness of the proverbial Indian, Pierce struck straight as an arrow for the Grimes ranch house. He drove all his earthly possessions before him—two old loose-jointed oxen. Grimes greeted him quite cordially. He even seemed to want to prolong the initial pleasantries, but Pierce went straight to the subject nearest his heart. He would like to have his money.

"By all means! Yes, by all means," said Bing. "It was a deposit of $500, was it not"?

"To the dollar," said Shanghai, "and I can use the money right now."

Grimes became very solemn. He hesitated as if thinking, then said: "Let me see now. As I recollect that was for pay due in the first year of the war—during the Confederacy—wasn't it?"

"What has that got to do with my $500?" bellowed Shanghai.

"Nothing," said Bing, "except that since the work was done under the Confederacy, I shall have to pay you in Confederate money. There's a whole barrel of it in the corner. Help yourself, Shang, and take a big handful for interest."

When the meaning of Grimes' words was understood, the tide of anger, which he had suppressed since the very first day he had met Bing, burst forth. Rising to his full six-feet-four and with voice aquiver, he shouted: "By God, Bing. By God, sir, I'll put you on the Black Hills for this. I'll make you wish, damn you, that you could eat your no 'count money, barrel and all." With that he stalked toward Bing's horse lot. They had come to the crossroads. Never again would they travel together. But the Black Hills of the Dakotas, the cattleman's financial graveyard, was a long way off.

5. "*I owned nearly all the cattle in Christendom*"

Shanghai saddled up at the Grimes horse lot and rode southwest. His long beard stuck out as he squared his shoulders and threw back his head. "By the Holy Latter Day Saints!" he shouted to himself. "By the Holy Latter Day Saints! Now he's got to fish or cut bait, by God."

That night he lay on his blanket in the open. He hobbled his horse and tied the stake rope to his wrist, then went to sleep. Near evening the next day he rode into Victoria. He took a light toddy at Musselman's before calling at the law offices of Stockdale and Proctor; then he mounted his horse again and rode steadily toward Indianola, more than thirty miles away. "I have to see Heyer," he mused. "I'm going to need quite a number of branding irons. I'm glad I talked with Stockdale and Proctor, counsellors. Proctor is a gentleman lawyer, and Governor Stockdale, well . . . you never can tell when your counsellor should have political influence."

Blacksmith Heyer had ideas of his own about how to make a branding iron, protesting when Shanghai wanted the face brand three-sevenths of an inch thick, and decided for Pierce: "You make a mistake as that is too heavy for a brand so I do 'em myself as I t'ink best."

As for Stockdale and Proctor, well, that was merely a courtesy call. His acquaintance with Uncle Daniel Sullivan furnished the excuse and made the call proper. But Shanghai was the subject of more than passing comment between the two lawyers after he rode away. He had announced his intention to pay his respects to Uncle Daniel, then go on to Saint Mary's, some seventy-five miles farther on, to see John Wood, who, he had heard, had some cattle for sale. By the time he had gone to St. Mary's, and stopped off for a little confidential chat with Uncle Daniel, having to do with financing a few cattle deals he had in his mind, and after taking time out to spin a war yarn or two with Little Dannie, who had now discarded his cavalry horse for a grocer's peck measure, Shanghai consumed some valuable time. His trip to Indianola had been worthwhile, however, for he learned that Foster was shipping again by boat. He consequently called on the shipper and shared with him his option to buy the John Wood cattle. With this trade concluded, he headed back toward Deming's Bridge. He had not intended to be away so long. His thoughts were divided between a growing interest in that Lacy girl and plans he was making to head Bing toward the Black Hills. And he hummed as he rode:

> *His hoss'll go dead, and his mule'll go lame;*
> *He'll lose his cows in a poker game:*
> *A hurrican 'll come along some summer day,*
> *And carry the house whar he lives away,*
> *And swallow the land the house stood on.*
> *And the tax collector he'll come 'round,*
> *And charge him for the hole in the ground.*

He was also thinking about Jonathan, wishing he would come back, for he needed him now since he had to drive that John Wood herd to New Orleans. The last time he had seen his brother was during the war when Jonathan was riding southward toward Matamoros on a mule. Jonathan was then in his full stride, expatiating volubly of his prowess as a soldier. He wrote a letter to

"Nearly all the cattle in Christendom"

his sister Susan to invite her to come to Texas "as soon as we've whipped them damn Yankees thorough," and explained: "I was with Buchel's regiment of cavalry when we whipped General Bank's Thirteenth Army Corps quicker than a stuttering man can say 'Jack Robinson.' The Confederates made a charge through the fields of *waiving* wheat and captured about 4000 *Yankies*, 84 wagons and the Boston and Chicago batteries almost in the twinkling of an eye." Jonathan was a war hero. He could prove it by his own words, but Shanghai knew something about that battle himself, being near by, although in the rear. Despite immunity from physical fear and his great love for eliminating great numbers of Yankees, with the Boston and Chicago batteries thrown in for good measure, the southbound mule-riding cavalryman tarried long enough with his brother, Shanghai, to confess to a homesickness so great that when he "happened to notice a keg of nails marked from Bridgeport, Massachusetts, he involuntarily stooped down and hugged it."

As Shanghai had hoped, his brother Jonathan had returned during his absence. Before the war Jonathan squandered his substance at the rate of sixteen dollars a year, part of which went for well-digging at the church and "knick-knacks for the girls," but now Shanghai found him bragging of another accomplishment: "I have come to the estate of man. I have learned to drink one and one-half quarts of whiskey daily." Shanghai learned from Fannie Lacy that Nannie, "that other Lacy girl," thought Jonathan's great goodness of soul in providing a well for the church was quite commendable, but by no means did Nannie agree with Jonathan that "he was Lable to get Snake bit any day."

Shanghai found that Jonathan also had plans. He had not forgotten the day Grimes sent him out to tail the herd across the Río Tres Palacios. That was the day he had driven stakes in the earth to mark the spot of a "glorious back-ground of noble oaks and lordly elms." His resolve of that day had not dissipated: life had been spared to him, his fortune was prospering, and, said he to Shanghai, "I am going to build my home there where the prairie is dotted with Indian pinks and primroses, buttercups and daisies, marigolds and verbenas. I look to the time when within the confines of the gardens near the house will grow chrysanthemums and majestic roses, and they will nod their heads in the gentle breezes."

His conscience must have been pricking him, for the grog-loving tippler avowed he found great satisfaction in being so near the little Deming's Bridge Church. Within that church he would lave his conscience because of his persistent bad temper. "I am not really so mean, after all," he plead. "I would rather pray four times instead of three times a day. I won't let the sun go down on my wrath."

Now that Shanghai was aware of Jonathan's plans, he made arrangements for his own future as well. He wrote Mira that he too was buying a place "on the Caronkaway." The establishment of a home, however, was not enough for him. His visions were tinted with gold as he recalled the liberality of Uncle Daniel Sullivan: "You may have unlimited credit. Draw on me for what you need." He was also looking with favor upon the encouragement James Foster had given him. Foster would make a good partner. Then the vision grew astronomical as he encompassed the possibilities of those unbranded cattle near Bing's pre-emptions and as far north as the Old Caney. What he needed right now was a branding crew.

Hot irons were running fast near the Grimes Tallow Factory. The very thought of this put Shang in high dudgeon, and he reverberated his contempt for Bing: "By God, Sir. He will have to fish or cut bait. There is no time for delay. I'll put off nothing until tomorrow that can be done today." He recalled that his father had told him the family motto was "To think is to do"; and he forthwith proposed to Jonathan that they form a partnership. He would, so he said, own three-fourths of the stock and do the outside work. Jonathan might own one-quarter of the stock. "It is understood, John, you are to stay at Rancho Grande all the time." Thus came into existence "El Rancho Grande." It took several weeks though for the letterheads to get back from the Galveston printers. In the printing they took in more territory:

A. H & J. E. PIERCE
Stock Raisers and Cattle Dealers,
Tres Palacios, Colorado and Caney,
Deming's Bridge, P. O.
Rancho Grande, Texas.

"Nearly all the cattle in Christendom"

Rancho Grande was now established, that is, by oral agreement between the brothers and upon newly printed and ornate letterheads, but the advertisement the brothers gave their enterprise soon made it known throughout the coastal country.

With that accomplished, Shanghai swung lightly upon Old Prince. He tapped his flanks with the rowels of his spurs and pointed a course down the Río Tres Palacios. His mind was dallying with another venture. He stopped before the home of the Widow Lacy. His affairs could not wait, so on September 27, 1865, he married Fannie Lacy. If the bride fondled visions of "a homestead in its most picturesque and hospitable garnishments," such as was being dangled before her sister's eyes by brother John, she was doomed to sudden disillusionment. Realism was completely in control of the new bridegroom. Grimes was fast ridding the prairie of all cattle. The bridegroom just did not have time now to stay around home. Years later he bragged reminiscently of his industry: "You can judge how busy I was. When I married I only stayed home four days the first year."

The marriage ceremony was little more than completed before Shanghai set out for Matagorda to inspect the records of beeves being killed and driven from the county. He found that Borden and Earle were moving fair-sized herds regularly. Of one such herd of 145, Grimes had laid claim to 112. During a period of three months the clerk's files showed that seven other herds, totaling 803 head, left the county with his old army captain, Borden, in charge, and again Grimes claimed every animal as his, with the exception of one BU. This BU was the new brand Shanghai and his friend, Deming, had adopted for partnership cattle. Perhaps Grimes thought it best to say nothing about that one steer. At the same time, Grimes made a record that his Tallow Factory slaughtered from 25 to 112 animals each day. In addition, however, Shanghai found ten interesting documents, all of the same import. W. W. Lunn had, according to the files, "authorized W. B. Grimes to Collect and dispose of all cattle in the brands of John Pybus, John Spoor, Ella Jamison, August Schultz, John Holcomb, A. Guyle, G. W. Baucker, I. N. Fleury, Mary E. and Alley Pinchback . . . whereever found from Indianola to Columbus." The records were silent, however, as to where W. W. Lunn got his authority. But the contract on file which really amazed Shanghai read:

> In consideration of the above, W. B. Grimes hereby agrees to pay Asa H. Dawdy Two dollars and fifty Cents Specie per head for all Cattle he can find old and young sound healthy and diseased that can be driven to said Grimes Slaughter House.
> (*Signed*) W. B. Grimes.
>
> The Cattle east of the Trespalacios & below Blue Creek not to be taken on this contract.
> (*Signed*) W. B. Grimes.

At the Grimes Tallow Factory he found a crowd of "hangers-on" riding the corral fence. Charlie Siringo was having his fun with Bradford Grimes. During the Civil War, cattle had drifted before the cold winds, and many of them could now be found around the coastal waters, many miles from their owners and from the county in which their brands were recorded. Grimes was making good use of such straying cattle, slaughtering them at will. Siringo, who had had differences with Grimes, decided to even the score, so, unknown to Grimes, he had registered as his own a brand which was carried by a large number of North Texas strays. When Shanghai appeared on the scene, Siringo was demanding ten dollars a head for all of the newly registered brand, while Bing was contending the cattle could not belong to Charlie. "The cows are older than you are."

"Yes," said Siringo, "that's true, but you killed them with my brand on them and you pay!" He did, much to Shanghai's pleasure.

The news went throughout the cattle country that A. H. and J. E. Pierce would buy cattle at the market price and pay in gold. The Pierce brothers soon had a crew of hands, as motley a gang as one could imagine. Some were Mexicans, more were Negroes. There was a sprinkling of white men. Of the latter, a few were recently from the war and were hardened to the rigors of the saddle. Others were mere boys cheating their teens, who were fastened to their horses by a grim determination to ride with their elders. For instance, there was Willie Wheeler who bragged: "I

"Nearly all the cattle in Christendom"

was runnin' cattle before I could get on my horse. They helped me on." Then, too, no one will ever forget Wiley M. Kuykendall, who, at the age of seven, had ridden away from his Fort Bend County home astride a mule behind a Negro named Lark. Wiley was shoeless and carried his entire wardrobe tucked under his arm in a paper sack. The Negro dumped him down in Matagorda, where the happy-go-lucky child so readily captured the hearts of all who saw him that he became "Mr. Wiley" before the fuzz on his face turned to whiskers.

Mr. Wiley was one of the first Pierce recruits. In truth, he was more than a recruit. He came cow-driving but wound up courting the Pierce brothers' sister Susan, who had cast her lot with them in Texas. When Shanghai saw what was going on, he stormed at his sister: "I'm not hunting a brother-in-law, just a cow hand. If you marry that man, you'll starve to death. You can't do anything with him. He has Kuykendall fits." But "Kuykendall fits" did not dampen Susan's ardor for her new found beau. "We will never starve," she countered as she held up her strong rough hands before Shanghai's face, "so long as I have either of these."

Now that Mr. Wiley had become a brother-in-law, he took over as roundup boss. His love for Susan, liquor, and longhorns was only exceeded by his energy. As a boss he was harder than Shanghai. Long before dawn each morning he crawled out from under his blanket, lighted his big, smelly black pipe with a coal out of the campfire, and called the cook. Together they boiled a big black pot of coffee, cup after cup of which he drank piping hot. Then, very softly, he called to the sleeping cowboys: "Come, boys. Come. Get up and hear the little birds singing their sweet praises to God [Then continuing loud and harsh] ALMIGHTY DAMN YOUR SOULS! GET UP!"

On May 2, 1866, Pierce rode in from the range to find a celebration going on. Brother Jonathan greeted him with the news. "I have just become your brother-in-law. Nannie and I got married." Jonathan and Nannie were soon ensconced snugly in the new home they had dreamed about. They had taken Bing's most prized kitchen servant with them, and Aunt Eliza was forever thereafter an indispensable fixture in the Pierce household.

The house was the handiwork of the bridegroom, who bragged he did carpentry with such precision that "my measurements would come up to a chigger's eye. I did a tip-top job of it, even though *My* classical education was limited to reading, ciphering and geography, for it is the best built dwelling in all Texas. You could roll it over and over and not break off enough wood to make a tooth pick. Why, there's 2,200 pounds of galvanized nails in it, and the walls would stand a siege."

Under Jonathan's planning, El Rancho Grande began taking on the appearance of a self-sufficient community. In time, buildings arose all around the place. First, he built an office for the transaction of the affairs of the cattle company. Then came two carriage houses, a barn, a saddle house, a crib, a hide house, a store, a gear-and-smoke-house, a white man's bunk, and a house for Negroes. To these he added a carpentry shop, a blacksmith shop, a hide press, a hay barn, a potato house, a hog house, a goat house, and then he erected a church and a Masonic temple, all of which he proudly referred to as "The Department of State." Activities were not confined to the vicinity of the dwelling, however. In 1867, Isaac Thompson had introduced the wild rose into the county from South America. Jonathan immediately studied its possibilities. "That plant," said he, "will prove a blessing to the cattlemen of Texas," and soon he had under way the planting of thirty-five miles of wild-rose-hedge fence enclosing, as it grew, all of El Rancho Grande. Years later, and reminiscently, Jonathan stated: "I planted it to keep out horse thieves and other depredators. The thief who will penetrate a rosebush hedge is hardly fit for business after the trip. It was solely as a defense measure against thieves that I planted it, but I found that they were of greater utility. The hedge outlines the various pastures, but it serves as a windbreak, and when the northers blow the cattle seek the shelter the hedge affords and are protected. If you want to see the earth in all its glory, come here in the spring. The whole thirty-seven miles of hedge is then one great blaze of rose blossoms and the perfume of the air hereabouts is so sweet that those who visit me say they are in paradise."

Jonathan's transition from brother to brother-in-law had done wonders for him. We have it from his own mouth that there had been a cleansing of more than his prayerful soul. "Yes, you see when I worked upon the prairies and did service as a ranger I used but little water except for drinking purposes. I could rub the dirt

Shanghai Pierce, the last and best picture ever made of him
(Courtesy of Ed Bartholomew, Rose Collection)

William Bradford Grimes,
before the Black Hills

Charlie Siringo,
who later wrote his
famous autobiography
A Texas Cowboy (1886)
(Courtesy of
The Cattleman)

"Nearly all the cattle in Christendom"

from my face and hands while perspiring, but now I have reached a higher estate in this life's eventful pilgrimage. I have a young wife who keeps me clean, making me take a bath every night, something I never did before." This habit of nocturnal ablutions by feminine edict came easier, however, than breaking away from his daily three pints of X X Log Cabin whiskey. But he decided "to quit this habit that was ruinous to my purse and not especially beneficial to my health and morals or temper." Therefore, he publicly proclaimed that he was a teetotaler, but later when he was inveigled "into sipping a cup with three of my fellow citizens who were candidates for office, I felt," he professed "like I had stolen a sheep."

With Jonathan in control at El Rancho Grande headquarters, and Wiley Kuykendall calling out the boys on the range, the A. H. and J. E. Pierce cattle company was a substantial reality. However, one more thing was needed by Shanghai to give him the proper dignity and this was Old Nep.

Just how Old Nep came into the El Rancho Grande picture no one took the trouble to record or recall. Perhaps it just happened, just one of those natural things. But being a necessary part of the ranch, he appeared at the proper time. The Neptune of mythology is accredited with having ridden over the surface of the sea in a chariot drawn by sea horses while the waves were stilled at his approach. Neptune Holmes—the Old Nep of-the-sea-of-waving-grass—who rode in the wake of his boisterous master, just happened along to help still the anxiety of many a Texas cattleman from that day on. Shanghai rode into cattle camps followed by Old Nep on the jogging mule, announcing their welcome approach through the jangle of gold and silver strapped in bulging saddlebags. And for some thirty-five years, as long as there was an "earthly marster," as long as saddlebags served in lieu of bills of exchange, this almost illiterate, grimacing black servant slept on the prairies of Texas, pillowing his kinky head on bags of gold, bowing in obeisance only to "Mr. Shang."

Neptune's life was one of idolatrous service, unspoiled with pretensions. He knew no arithmetic. He made no claim to being a writing man. Humbly he evaluated himself: "I ain't much, but I can scramble [scribble] my name so you will know what I am trying to make."

Shanghai Pierce

With faithful Neptune trailing, Shanghai cut south for Saint Mary's. He stopped at Indianola to replenish his saddlebags and recruit a short crew, bedding down on the Woods' range for the first roundup. Jim Foster had made good his promise to stake him for half the profits, and he received the Woods' cattle. His destination, now, was New Orleans. He crossed the Guadalupe River at Victoria. Here his wild cattle gave him trouble. He sent out a call for help. "They sent down a man with a tin cup and a long rope. He was on a pony and his legs were dragging on the ground. I said: 'Young man, what is your business?' He was a lawyer but he wanted to go cowdriving. I said: 'Young man, go right back. You can learn cheaper from someone else; when you run one of these steers off, you run off $20.' I discharged him before he got to the top of the hill. I told Mr. Peticola I did not need him, but the law did, and I saved him to become one of the best lawyers I ever knew."

The drive went on without the long rope and tin cup. Foster followed across the Gulf by ship. The cattle were sold, and "Foster got half we had and I got the other," he recorded. "We whacked up in New Orleans. Foster treated me badly; gave me a shotgun settlement." But with fourteen hundred dollars' profit in his pocket the bright lights of New Orleans were too much for Shanghai. "I spent mine," he lamented. "I don't know what Foster did with his."

The shotgun settlement turned Shanghai back to Daniel Sullivan, but in the change of bankers there lingered an unredressed grievance. Foster was making more money shipping cattle across the Gulf than could be made by driving them. The voyage was made more rapidly. The freighter cost was commensurate with the expense of trailing. Where Pierce's credit had been good with Uncle Daniel Sullivan, now it was unlimited with Little Dannie.

Foster was skimming off the cream of the cow business by holding a corner on vessels plying the Gulf. He was trying to force those in competition with him to market their cattle by the slower overland route through the Louisiana swamps. Foster, however, reckoned without computing the astuteness of young Dan Sullivan. Allen and Poole were extensive shippers operating chiefly out of Galveston. They owned the freighter *Alabama,* and as it was idle at the moment, Mr. Thompson, the agent for the shippers, was not averse to accepting one thousand dollars in hard money and making a contract to ship a load under Pierce's instructions for

"Nearly all the cattle in Christendom"

one-third of the profits. And too, Allen and Poole were not blind to the possibilities of enlarging their business. A connection with a merchant-banker who loaned funds with such a lavish hand could not fail to bring profits, they reasoned.

When the *Alabama* docked, there was a herd ready to dive down into the hold to escape the yipping cowboys. The Lunn boys, who had joined the Pierce forces, were on hand to see the *Alabama* steam out into the Gulf. She turned, not northeast toward New Orleans, but southeast toward Cuba. She docked at Matanzas and Shanghai took $5,000 in profits. This was an accomplishment of a magnitude most pleasing to him. When back in Texas he boasted of his success, his reliability, his virtues, and his stamina: "I will do just what I tell I will if it takes the hide and my *Panns* off at my Belly." To attain this reliability, he avowed: "I have been through Hell many times, crawled into the brush & slept with rattlesnakes many a night to keep the Commanche from scalping me, Live'd on aligator Eggs & Monkey stew, all this by no means a bed of roses." However he had five thousand dollars, and it was his own—all except the 25 per cent he was allowing his brother for El Rancho Grande management.

Fearing another competitor now, who owned a ship, more than he did Foster, who only leased his vessel, Pierce accepted the offer of the Galveston operators and a new partnership was formed. The firm was called Allen & Pierce. Steamers docked with such regularity thereafter that Pierce saw the wisdom of annexing other partners to add to the immense net which was being dragged across the coastal region, bringing more and more mavericks under the AP branding iron. Collins Brothers were invited into the scheme. They agreed that Pierce was "quite some man" when he boasted: "by this time I got to be a pretty big dog in the puddle. All Little Dannie had to do to get $50,000 or $60,000 for me was to send my note over to a man named Taylor at New Orleans. He'd cash it."

The Pierce sugar lump was now attracting a myriad of human flies. True to instinct, they were not content to sit upon the sweetmeats. Men of serious mien occasionally visited the camps of Pierce's new company. These newcomers talked little, but obviously they were not pleased with the efficiency of the Pierce layout. One day a neighbor cattleman stopped off to chat with Shanghai

Shanghai Pierce

and to remark sarcastically about the great number of cattle now roaming the range wearing the AP; at the same time he directed Pierce's mind to the fact that it was only yesterday, as time is measured, since he came back from the army, flat broke. "Yes," said Pierce, "and it all came from the yoke of old oxen I drove back from the war. You just never would have thought two old oxen could possibly have been that prolific."

Rumors came to Pierce that his camp visitors were outriders for the Taylors. The Taylors and Suttons had been feuding west of Shanghai's pre-emptions, and they held no enterprise in high esteem which had for its purpose the wholesale branding of mavericks unless the Taylors were doing the branding. Although the Lunns had been favored by the Pierce brothers, they were now known to be more and more in the company of the camp visitors. The Lunns were not disliked in the coastal region, but these new associations caused men like B. Q. Ward, Tom Nye, and the Pierces to hold long confidential talks. Then Shanghai spoke out one day —and of course, everybody heard him—"If these Lunn boys don't change their runningmates, some of these days somebody is going to say: 'There comes a bad man on a good horse, and that horse is apt to lose its owner.'"

The casual inspections of the El Rancho Grande camps were followed by rumors that came down from De Witt County that the Taylors and Suttons were on the warpath again. And, too, there was evidence that the Suttons were spreading their branding range as far as Matagorda County. The Taylors lost no opportunity to push into the same territory; and as the Taylors drove large numbers of cattle from the interior to the port of Indianola, there was a constant apprehension among all cowboys that these factions would clash within the Pierce ranks. Then, one day, a big-jowled ruffian, who gave his name as "Smith," rode into the territory. He was immediately dubbed "All Jaw Smith." In order that he might impress others with how tough he was, he laid claim to have ridden with Quantrill's gang during the recent war. He referred to a brief sojourn in Jacksonville, Texas, where his society, he let it be known, was not appreciated and where there was too much law and order for him to enjoy his surroundings. The Matagorda region was more to his liking, and true to suspicion, the El Rancho Grande boys soon knew he was conniving with the Taylor outriders. Old Jack

"Nearly all the cattle in Christendom"

Helms, long at enmity with the Taylors and particularly one of their new gunmen, John Wesley Hardin, shook his head and recalled the Taylor motto: "Who sheds a Taylor's blood, by a Taylor's hand must fall." Jack Helms smelled trouble, so he talked earnestly and privately with Shanghai. Some days after the conversation, Captain Joe Tumlinson, renowned Indian-fighter, came riding quietly through the country. He reported to "Old Jack" that he had enlisted two hundred "regulators," and this time Brad Grimes was not at loggerheads with his enterprising neighbor.

Before Captain Joe Tumlinson could complete his regulator recruitment and give mavericking a semblance of respectability, the Pierce brothers had formed other partnerships—one with the Widow Ward's son, B. Q. Ward; ("Mr. Benn," as Shanghai wrote it), and one with W. H. Kyle. These connections extended Pierce's interests from West Columbia to Victoria, on the Guadalupe River. This organization's success served to unleash in others an equal greed, which contaminated the acts of nearly all of the mossy-horn hunters throughout the region. The running iron took its place alongside the branding iron. Nearly every saddle skirt carried one of each. With Pierce's dozens of cowboys ranging from the Guadalupe River to Old Caney, all working for A. H. and J. E. Pierce or one of their partners (when they did not take a little time off to increase their own stock by a few head), the slicks and brush-splitters in Bing's territory were getting extremely hard to find.

The Allen and Pierce partnership was netting a substantial profit. A loading dock was built at Palacios, and the *Charley Morgan* and *Harlan* sailed with almost clocklike regularity every tenth day. On board, Allen and Pierce had cattle in nearly every brand registered in South Texas. The crews on the range were having to hustle to keep up with the sailings. One day, Shanghai rode into a cow camp where a few of the boys were patterning after the more enterprising barons, such as Grimes and himself. He found them scorching their monograms on wild mavericks, thus hoping to turn them for a few dollars to some ambitious purchaser. As Pierce neared the chuck wagon, he rose high on Old Prince, standing full height in his stirrups. With one raised hand he signaled back to the walnut-colored Negro who followed on a small horse, leading a trotting mule. "Dump it down, Nep," shouted Shanghai. The Negro dismounted and walked quietly to the mule. He released the cinch and two large saddlebags filled with Little Danny Sullivan's "hard money" clinked to the ground. Shanghai then turned to the approaching cattlemen and held up his arms. His voice carried to the farthermost: "Round 'em up, fellows. I'll take all you have. Pay you in gold." And George Saunders, hard pressed for money, at first not believing his ears but finally understanding the significance of Pierce's statement, called out: "Our Redeemer has come."

On July 17, 1867, Pierce took time off to celebrate the birth of a daughter, whom he christened Mary, but was "Mamie" to her father and "Miss Mamie" to all at the ranch to the very day of her death. From the moment of her birth, Mamie's welfare held top position with her father, even beyond "that cow out there." His first act was to start a cattle brand in her name; in fact, he bought the entire Bundick brand, and from that day the famous BU cattle were known from the Gulf to Canada. They belonged exclusively to Miss Mamie. Looking a little further into the future, her father bought 6,200 acres of land. "I put my daughter's cattle in there," he said. "I went to Missouri and bought 100 bulls, and a good many thorough-bred and graded bulls. I commenced grading her cattle up." Miss Mamie was surely on the road to riches!

Mary's birth merely added zest to Shanghai's passion for wealth. Had it not been for his implacable love for the little baby he would have spent less time at his Tres Palacios home. His expanding cattle business was absorbing all his time and energy. "After being out in the prairie," he complained, "I go home at night. I want to sleep. I had a heap to do."

Now that Shanghai had partners all around him, he was getting thousands of cattle under his brand. Great numbers of old bulls and stags had taken to the timber and canebrakes, and there they defied the cowboy and his rope. Some of these animals had lived in the timber so long that their horns were fuzzy, a few carried strands of moss dangling a foot long. If they could not escape by flight, then they tried it by fight, but neither was successful when pursued by such doughty cattlemen as Pierce's nephew Abel Pierce Borden, Tom Nye, and Asa Dawdy. Thus, Shanghai was ready every April with drove after drove of mossy-horns which he shaped up for the long northward walk to Kansas. Jesse Chisholm, the squaw-man who never actually drove a cow over the trail which bore his name, marked out a feasible route connecting North Texas

"Nearly all the cattle in Christendom"

with the westward-building railroads in Kansas and Nebraska; and Shanghai was one of the first to drive his fresh roadbranded AP and BU herd northward in search of a better market than New Orleans. If he did not have a good trail boss, he led the cattle himself, and his high carrying voice could always be heard above the crackle of hooves and knocking horns.

Trips up the trail began to take more time than was at his disposal, now that he had irons in so many fires. Consequently, it became his practice to ride with the herd until they became "trail broke." Then leaving them in the care of his boss, he would take the train in time to meet them at the northern market. Shanghai had a particular affection for Asa Dawdy as trail boss, even though he knew Dawdy to be "one of those happy-go-easy fellows who was always sticking his nose in everybody's business. He was as full of wind as myself, only a good deal more windier than I am. Yes, Sir; he was bigger bellied and had more wind than I have." Although he was willing to trust his cow-brutes on the trail to big-bellied Dawdy, still, "windy" Dawdy was no man to sell them. "Yes, sir," said Old Shang, "I never sent the boy to the mill. I always went myself."

On July 17, 1870, Shanghai returned to his home to find himself a father for the second time. This time he had a son, whom he proudly named "Abel." Five weeks later he buried his son at the Deming's Bridge Cemetery; and on December 18, Fannie followed in death.

Jonathan and Nannie took over the immediate care of Miss Mamie while Shanghai increased his frenzy to accumulate more and more cattle. Some of his better nature died with Fannie. Those days, he rode the range alone. He carried a Winchester rifle strapped to his saddle within easy reach of his hand. His lariat was held in place by a leather thong. He was not passing up a chance to brand a maverick. He was taking no chances with strangers. "Yes, sir," he said, "you see I got my start on the back of a pinto pony with an unbranded calf on the end of my rope!" If anyone attempted to approach him on the prairie, he would be halted by a sweep of the Shanghai hat. It was safer, those who knew him said, to stop for identification. He was a most determined man now that his wife was gone.

In the early days of April, 1871, sixteen-year-old Charles

Siringo, who for the past four years had been acting as a "full-fledged cowboy, wearing broad sombrero, high-heeled boots, Mexican spurs and the dignity of a grown man," showed up at Tom Nye's camp, at Palacios Point. He was leaving Grimes, he said, and wanted to become a Pierce boy. Just at that time twenty men were leaving for El Rancho Grande headquarters. Charles went along. In addition to Jonathan's dwelling and his church house, the company store had been erected. Old Hunky Dory Brown was in charge. Old Hunky Dory invited Charles to charge to his account at the store the things he thought he needed for his venture. Charlie, therefore, bought a full cowboy outfit, "including saddle, bridle, spurs, pistol, bowie knife, bedding, sombrero, silk handkerchiefs, slicker, and high-heel boots." Thus decked out he proclaimed he "looked like a thorobred cow Boy from Bitter Creek." Then he went out, so he wrote, to see Shanghai Pierce arrive "just from the Rio Grande with three hundred Mexican ponies for the spring work. Pierce had paid two dollars and fifty cents a head for them. They were what was termed 'wet' ponies on the Rio Grande. In other words, were stolen stock."

With a crew of fifteen men Charley went to work at the peep of day with "never a thought of eating a noon meal." When darkness came they returned to their campfire, where they were served "fat heifer calf, corn bread, molases, and black coffee." Their assignment was to round up eleven hundred mossy-horn steers, ranging from four to twenty years in age. They started on the Navidad where the timber was thick and the bulls thin and wild. A certain Mr. Black, who was a Kansas blacksmith turned cow trader, had paid down his cash to Shanghai for these particular cattle. The crew went over to the Snodgrass pens, where they established headquarters, as their cook said, "Usin' our backs for a mattress and our bellies for a covering." Black impatiently waited for the arrival of the herd he was to put on the trail. With him was a "short-horn" crew who were as green as the April grass on which they slept. Some of them had never seen a longhorn, to say nothing of a mossy-horn, which hides in the dense timber in the day time and ventures out in the open prairie only at night to nibble a paunch full of grass and is ready to dispute any man's attempt to control him at all times.

The Pierce boys, at least Tom Nye and the older men, were

"Nearly all the cattle in Christendom"

fully aware of the craftiness of these old brush-poppers, so long before there was light in the east Charley and the other fifteen riders were in their saddles cutting the herd off from the timber. Without the protection of the brush they soon fell prey to expert ropers, who immediately threw them to the ground and sewed their eyelids together to blind them temporarily and prevent them from traveling except by sound.

During the night half the crew held the cattle on the prairie while the others slept. When stormy weather came, Shanghai would appear on the scene and ride the night through, singing to the cattle in true cowboy fashion. Jonathan, however, remained at home and "was never so happy as while ploughing with a yoke of oxen."

In due time Black's cattle were ready for delivery. He and his Kansas softies headed them "toward the promised land" wholly unaware of the cause of their apparent docility. It was but a short time, however, until the threads holding together the eyelids rotted away. The blinders thus taken off, they looked upon a strange land. The old mossy-horns, finding that the range was new and that they were hedged about by leather-pounding cowpokes astride jughead horses, inaugurated an ever recurring series of stampedes and frantic dashes for liberty. Mr. Black and his crew pulled up to the Red River and "crossed into the Indian Territory with nothing left but the grub wagon and horses." "Lots of the cattle," wrote Siringo about the incident, "came back to the range and 'Mr. Shanghai' had the fun of selling them all over again to some other greeny." But this was not to be the end of the matter. Shortly thereafter Shanghai made a trip to Kansas. There he met his onetime customer, Mr. Black, who "cursed Texas shamefully, and swore he would never, even if he lived to be as old as Isaac, son of Jacob, dabble in longhorns again."

After the Black herd trickled back onto the home range at their leisure, Wiley Kuykendall enlisted the energies of Siringo for a little mavericking with him. It was Charley's rare good fortune that he was transferred to Mr. Wiley, for this Pierce brother-in-law "concluded it would look more businesslike if he would brand a few mavericks for himself, so he put his own brand on all the fine looking ones." Then, wrote Siringo, "to keep us boys from giving him away, he gave us a nice egg apiece—that is, a few head to draw to. Of course, after that I always carried a piece of iron tied to my saddle so in case I got off on the prairie to myself, I could brand a few mavericks for myself, without Mr. Wiley being the wiser." The scheme ran with greased wheels until "the big chief heard about the private racket." This caused both Charley and Wiley to conclude they were not going to work there any more and Siringo decided to move along before he evoked the wrath of Old Shang. He therefore headed into Old Hunky Dory's store and demanded a settlement.

Old Hunky Dory was ready and, looking over the books, said: "Charley, we owe you three hundred dollars. Then he deliberately counted out three hundred dollars in silver and stacked it neatly on the counter. Again he opened his book and peered at the record for a long time. "But Charley," he said, "you owe us two hundred ninety nine dollars and twenty-five cents." Then he raked all the coin into the till except seventy-five cents. Charley shoved back the coin and picked up a bottle of peaches and a stick of candy, and mounting his pony rode off to Grimes where he knew a job was always waiting for him.

Over at the Grimes Tallow Factory, cattle-branding was going on in much the same fashion as around El Rancho Grande, but the son of the old seafarer from Connecticut had not been able to keep pace with the sons of the Rhode Island blacksmith. The county records showed that Grimes was assessing only 7,000 branded cattle while A. H. and J. E. Pierce assessed 35,000 of the 70,000 branded cattle in the county. These 35,000 branded cattle were exclusive of the Allen and Poole, and other partnerships. Now the chief owner thought the time had come to boast of his accomplishments. "Yes, sir," he said, "I owned nearly all the cattle in Christendom once. I believe me and Allen, Poole and Company must have owned one time more than 100,000 cattle. I branded 18,000 calves, or thereabouts, and 1,154 yearlings this year."

Now that unbranded cattle were hard to find, rumors became more and more persistent that a long-loop gang was operating at night around Newell's Grove on the Carancahua. Cattle with plain brands on them drifted into the thickets and were never seen again. Owners of branded cattle were becoming restive. And Joe Tumlinson increased the frequency of his rides to the ranches and talked with the Wards, Tom Nye, and Grimes. Youngsters like

"Nearly all the cattle in Christendom"

Henry Bates and Clay McSparren understood from the way their elders talked that matters of importance were being discussed. Jack Helms, so the rumor went, had found a large kettle six feet in diameter down on the Carancahua, near the Lunn brothers' headquarters. It was such as was used for tallow-making. There was evidence that scraps of slaughtered animals had been cast into the Carancahua. The word went out that all "Regulators" should watch the Lunn brothers and "All Jaw" Smith. Then Shanghai rode into Bing's camp one day, where Charley Siringo and others of his punchers sat feasting upon a fresh killed calf. Shanghai alighted, walked deliberately to the hide, inspected it very carefully, then read out so all could hear—"AP." He then drew close to the men and said firmly: "Boys, the time has come when every man will have to learn to eat his own meat." With that, he mounted his horse and rode slowly away.

Charley Siringo did not work for Grimes very long this time until misfortune overtook him. Lolling on the soft velvety grass was quite as pleasing to Siringo as mavericking. He was thus enjoying himself one sunny day when Sam Grant, a well-known "nigger-killer" rode up. Siringo's pistol was out of his reach. Grant threw it aside and remarked: "Why don't you have a good pistol like mine?" At the same time he fired point-blank at the boy's heart. The bullet struck Charley's doubled-up leg at the knee joint and lodged there. Liege Dennis, renowned for skinning cattle first, then looking for Mr. Duncan's brand, came out of the brush at that moment, and Grant, avowing an accident had happened, rode away for a doctor. A doctor did not come, but Jonathan Pierce did; and Nannie carefully nursed Charley back to health at El Rancho Grande.

Siringo always believed "a certain wealthy cattleman hired Sam Grant to kill me account of my boldness in branding mavericks." It was thirty-five years, however, before Nolan Keller confirmed Charley's belief, but then the "wealthy cattleman was dead," and Siringo preferred to let those who were interested speculate on "which of two men did it."

With the word out that all mavericks were to be unceremoniously dealt with, and with Joe Tumlinson doggedly riding the range in search of suspicious characters, and Charley Siringo fighting for his life over at El Rancho Grande with an assassin's bullet in his body, there was a feeling of impending tragedy in the air. Tall, desperate John M. Smith was now living across the Carancahua. He had sent Shanghai word he would kill him on sight. Pierce now rode with his Winchester resting in the crook of his arm. Then late one evening a tire on a hide wagon, driven by a Negro, worked off. This delayed the three Lunn brothers and "All Jaw" Smith from loading out their kill and escaping down the Carancahua by boat. Inopportunely a Pierce boy came along, and in the effort to avoid detection the culprits took to the water in the slough. They carried cap-and-ball pistols. After getting them wet, they were unreliable. It took time to dry them out, and the rider disappeared.

At dusk that evening, as a fog lent somberness to approaching night, the Pierce boy bobbed up and down as he hastened toward El Rancho Grande. "The Lunns! The Lunns!" he said. "The Lunns and "All Jaw" Smith. Down at Well's Point. I caught 'em in the act near Newell's Grove." There was a scurry for bridles and saddles. Riders fanned out toward neighboring ranches. Before morning, some seventy-five or eighty men converged on Newell's Grove. There was a run for the bushes; but finding themselves surrounded, four men and a boy came out into the open with their hands up. Ropes swished over their heads and tightened around their necks. Ed Lunn tried to shoot, but his brother shouted: "No! No! My God, No! That's Mr. Ben." Wilborn was not with them. His horse had fallen with him, and his discharging pistol had wounded him in the knee. Realizing what was going on, he crawled away to safety.

Mounts were furnished and silently the concourse moved toward a convenient dead tree. None had seen Wilborn as he slithered into the fog and darkness. Four of the five men were quickly identified. All sat their horses in silence until a big voice said: "Men, let's let little Eddie go. He just got in bad company." For a moment there was an impressive silence; then the boy spoke: "Hang my brothers if you dare. Shanghai Pierce, you old son-of-a-bitch, you were the first man to teach me to steal a cow; and if I live, I swear before my dying brothers that I'll kill you if it takes my last breath." There was another moment of silence, then the five horses moved out from under their riders. The morning found three Lunns, All Jaw Smith, and a stranger dangling at the ends

"Nearly all the cattle in Christendom"

of ropes. Shanghai was wry when questioned about the incident: "Well, Sir: you never can tell just how much human fruit that old dead tree might have borne had it only been green."

The Matagorda County grand jury registered the feelings of the men of the region by forthwith indicting W. W. Lunn for stealing cattle hides. There was murder, too, but proof was lacking of the identity of the hangsmen. So, on June 16, 1871, the sheriff of Matagorda County, lacking evidence for filing a charge of murder, put Abel Head Pierce under bond of two hundred dollars "to appear as a witness for the State of Texas in the case of W. W. Lunn for stealing cattle hides." Someone, at least, hoped thus to hold him, pending developments. This was the danger signal to Shanghai. There was a quick cattle trade. Allen and Poole paid over to A. H. Pierce $110,000 in gold. Shanghai credited his brother Jonathan with his personal indebtedness and pocketed $100,000. To his more intimate friends he complained that "the athmosphere is getting rather heavy . . . . The pressure is heavy. It affects my lungs." Then too, "the society is not good"; and Shanghai Pierce mounted Old Prince and disappeared northward before a gathering storm.

6. "Once I went to hunt for society"

Men of the West of 1871 were prone to think of one who carried a walking stick as physically crippled or stricken with an incurable case of "down-East Dandyism." When, however, the bewhiskered A. H. Pierce came out of the St. James Hotel to stroll the streets of Kansas City, rhythmically tapping the sidewalks with his ornate cane, showing no sign of physical disability, and wearing apparel which, to the minutest detail, refuted any semblance of foppery, passers-by stepped aside to gaze after him in amazement. Surely here was a man quite different from the common run-of-the-mill swaggerers who could be seen throughout the Midwest as they clicked their boot-heels on the sidewalks or tipped a shiny boot-toe to the sun while they lounged before the accustomed cowmen's hotels and saloons.

"Once I went to hunt for society"

Regardless of what cattle port he hailed from, a cattleman was thought of as being "Texian." The greatest number who reached the Midwest in the early days of cattle driving, in fact, were from Texas. A few were born there. Others were Texans by adoption, having moved westward from the old South to avoid the clashes of Reconstruction. Still others came from north of Mason and Dixon's Line to vie with their recent Civil War foes in marketing the vast hordes of cattle which had covered the prairies while the men were busy fighting. But, now, since all had a common business—cattle—there was a kinship which showed itself in their everyday attire. Even their habits became much the same.

The attire of cowmen while on the trail grew out of the necessities of the business. There was such a similarity of clothing worn on the road up and such a uniformity of change of garb when the trail's end was reached that one familiar with the west could tell about how much time had elapsed since the cowman hit town.

On the road up, the boss was not distinguishable from the other men as far as clothing was concerned. All wore heavy woolen shirts cut to fasten high around the throat but flung wide to the third button except in the coldest weather. Their boots, form-fitting and of the finest leather, extended well up over the calf of the leg. The boot tops were either sewn ornately with variegated thread patterns or embellished with different colors of leather. If the boots were not custom made, which they usually were if the wearer could afford the price, and if the cowboy was "fresh up from Texas," then the make was almost certain to be Star Brand. The large Lone Star which showed at the top of each boot made other identification unnecessary.

Their pants were of durable woolen material. Frequently a pair of Levis would be drawn over them, but regardless of what material they were, every cowboy wore his pants stuck in his boots. Spurs, sometimes large and loose of rowel, tinkled rhythmically with each movement of the foot. A yellow slicker—a "Fish Brand Oil Skin," the boys called it— was tied securely behind the cantle of each saddle; and never, except when headed into a gale, was the rider out of the range of its spermaceti smell. So similar, in fact, was the clothing of the men of the trail that the common query for a stranger to make when he rode up to a herd was: "Who is the boss here?"

Shanghai Pierce

Upon arrival at any cattle delivery point north of Indian Territory, the "jerkin-and-slicker democracy" dissolved. The common cowhand tied his horse to the nearest hitchin' rack and headed—buckskins, chaps, woolen shirt, boots, spurs, dust, and all—straight toward "The First Chance" or "The Emporium for the Dispensation of Liquid Tarantula Juice." There he'd wet his whistle for the frivolities to come.

Pistols, of course—and two of them—were necessary parts of his accoutrement. He may not have shot at even a cottontail rabbit on the seven-hundred-mile drive, but once in cow town, he would have felt too light on his feet if not wearing two six-shooters, or out of balance at the hips were he wearing only one.

The owner of the herd varied his procedure sharply from that of his "boys." He left his hands and veered off to "The Big Brownstone Bunk House." If the journey's end happened to be Abilene, then the bunk house might, likely as not, be the old six-room log house, the Bratton Hotel. There grizzly John P. Simpson claimed to be the proprietor. If the year happened to be 1871, the Drover's Cottage was where he would go. The Cottage was built by Joseph McCoy himself, but it was now operated by Moses B. George. If the new arrival had trailed cattle to Abilene before, McCoy's old place was sure to be his preference. If the Drover's Cottage could not put him up, he would amble over to the Gulf, the American, or the Planter's House. Not so likely the Planter's House, for the name savored of squatters who were drifting south and west in increasing numbers and giving cattlemen "a heap o' trouble." But if Kansas City was the end of the trail, then the St. James Hotel, on the hill, was where the boss-man would bed down.

After sleepin' quarters were arranged for by the drover, there would be a brief refreshing stop at the Alamo Bar and a dodge in for a moment at the Bull's Head to shake hands with Phil Coe and Ben Thompson, owners of the "drink-dice-dump." After thus making it known that he was in town, the dirt-smeared boss took out for the tonsorial parlor where a favorite barber would be ordered to "give me the works."

During the interim of delay, tailors were called. They feverishly plied their needles to deck out their customers with what O. Henry called "Texas full dress—black frock coat, soft white hat and lay-down collar three-quarters of an inch high, and black

"Once I went to hunt for society"

wrought-iron necktie." When released by the barbers, tailors, and haberdashers as fit to appear on the streets of "cow town," Mr. Cattleman trod the boardwalks majestically. With boot tops concealed by black broadcloth trouserlegs, with long frock coats glinting velvet-faced lapels, with Texas hats both white and wide, and with six-guns swung from either hip, conveniently within reach to puncture an offender or punctuate the air—just to celebrate a growing satisfaction with new environs—he was quite a different person from the boss man who had successfully wangled a thousand steers through an Indian-infested land. It was understandable, therefore, that some would seek the gaming table, while others stood with one foot on the brass rail mixing whiskey-straights with a bit of sociability. And soon "the gorgeous Jesse Hazel" or "a girl named Lola" came in for attention.

The Texas tuxedo was a hybrid. It grew out of a simulation of the dignity of the Southern gentleman crossed with the necessary weapons for personal defense. The clothing represented the manorial dignity of the aristocracy of the South. The pistol display was thought to be necessary—and often was—for the assurance of that dignity. Then, too, the men who so attired themselves, in many instances, were also hybrid in character. Some stood with the law or made such pretense; others were deadly foes of constituted authority.

At the end of the drive some drovers banished the thought of cattle to engross themselves in the ever present poker game. Lady Luck beckoned. Few, in fact, were strong willed enough to pass her by, especially if there had been indulgence in his Satanic Majesty's liquid libations. A potent brand was Snakehead Johnson's Special Blend.

The gentleman with the ornate walking stick, however, who trod the streets of Kansas City early that July day in 1871 was one apart from the common run of men to be found in the West. There was firmness in his tread. If liquor had passed his lips—and it probably had—it truly had been of small quantity. No more than a light toddy. His appearance vouched for his assertion: "By God, Sir, I am not one of those low-down picayune fellows that goes in a back room and gets a five-cent drink and a nickel cigar." In fact, the use of tobacco in his presence was enough to incur his displeasure, but whiskey to him represented a means of mild stimulation

Shanghai Pierce

His thin brownish beard, which grew thicker on the chin than on the jaws and face, crinkled almost into waves. A thin moustache grew well up to his nose but left a distinct bare spot at the middle of the upper lip. His moustache always went untrimmed and blended smoothly into the other whiskers of his face. His hair was light brown and heavy. It lay one-third over his ears and showed a long absence from the barber, although it had been neatly parted on the side and combed. He did not wear the Texas tuxedo, but a dark brown suit, instead, through which was interwoven a lighter but barely noticable pattern. The lapels, pockets, and sleeves were trimmed with a narrow satin binding. His shirt was plain white. A large A H P monogram showed on the bosom. There was a soft white collar and a neat white tie. The attached cuffs were soft. His vest was faintly cream, of basket weave, in which interwoven threads of gold showed plainly. His hat was white, its brim broad. This day he had the crown of his hat mashed in to form a circle. In his right hand he carried the heavy walking cane. A friend met him and chided him upon his appearance. He replied: "I am out to hunt for society."

Picturesque Shanghai Pierce with pistols on his hips might have been too good a target for some rambling rowdy with an itchy finger, but gentleman Pierce, devoid of foppery, except for the ornate cudgel, was reasonably immune from bad-man molestation. In fact, Pierce knew that the code of the West, "Never shoot an unarmed man," was inviolable. So popular, in fact, did the tall Pierce make his gesture of inoffensiveness that he became known as "the man who introduced the walking stick into Kansas."

The arm of rowdyism was long at the time Pierce was preparing for defense through simulated inoffensiveness. Lack of respect for law reached from the coastal plains of Texas across the Indian-infested territories above the Red River. Lawlessness held sway in the new cow towns, Abilene, Ellsworth, Wichita, Dodge, and even Omaha. The elbow of this arm was Kansas City. Wyatt Earp, straight-shooting, law-and-order man, called it "the metropolitan playground for frontiersmen who hankered for the finest and fanciest in entertainment, food and drink, or the latest style in weapons and accoutrements for man and horse." This law man left out women, unless he intended "fanciest in entertainment" to include the ladies. "Market Square," according to Earp, "was where

"Once I went to hunt for society"

traders, teamsters, hunters and cowmen made headquarters in their holiday on the edge of the encroaching East."

In this metropolitan playground the inoffensive man with the loaded walking stick, out "to hunt for society," was certain to meet acquaintances, both desirable and undesirable, from the Matagorda country he had so recently fled to avoid appearing as a witness against W. W. Lunn for stealing cattle hides. To some of the bad men who came northward driving cows, drinking whiskey, and intermittently pumping cow towns full of hot lead, Pierce's facetious explanations of his absence from Texas were insufficient. They heard of his desire "to hunt for society," chuckled at his avowal that "my health is not good," and understood quite well that "the political conditions in Texas," with which he was not in accord, focused upon a certain dead tree, from which had dangled the lifeless bodies of the Lunns and "All Jaw" Smith. Pierce was also aware that he and his vigilantes had committed themselves to the opposition camp against the bad men and that he could expect reactions wherever he went.

Tom Speer was city marshal in Kansas City. He was a genial soul who tried to keep the peace and, at the same time, hold the friendship of potential law violators. Therefore, "Speer's bench," on Market Square, became the rallying point for most of the well-dressed cowmen. Some perched themselves before the doorway of the city marshal to enjoy his good company; others sought unvexed tranquility and felt themselves to be in a simulated custody. And, too, trouble-seekers reasoned that it would do them no harm to be thought of as minions of the law. Consequently Tom Speer's bench became the loadstone to which all Texans were drawn. Here they sunned themselves and digested every rumor that came their way.

Down on Market Square, Pierce heard a disturbing report. From over Abilene way came the story that the boy-thug, John Wesley Hardin, had "treed" Wild Bill Hickok, along with the entire Abilene constabulary. That a rowdy had treed a constable was not unusual; but when anyone flourishing shootin' irons had put Wild Bill Hickok between a rock and a hard place that was news enough to cause a thorough discussion. Shanghai was not opposed to the fun that the cowboys had at almost every trail's end; in fact, he was known to have indulged quite freely in the sport himself.

However, he was thoughtful over the rumor which was whispered to him that he, in conjunction with Tobe Driskill and Ben Thompson, had "squared" Hardin, the pistol-totin' killer, with Wild Bill; thus leaving Hardin free to shoot his way through Kansas, as had been his delight in Texas.

John Wesley Hardin was a few days older than eighteen when he rode into Abilene during early June, 1871. He had been on the road up since March. Pierce had not jumped his Matagorda County bond until after June 16, when it became evident the Lunn faction intended to force him to testify in the theft case, thus hoping to elicit testimony which might be used as a predicate to indict someone—probably Pierce himself—for murder. John Wesley Hardin had heard of the fate of the Lunns. In fact, the lynching had assumed great proportions in the repeated tellings and had engendered intense animosities. Hardin, who was as handy as any man with a branding iron, could not have felt kindly toward the Helm-Tumlinson-Pierce vigilantes, who sought to curb illicit branding. Pierce knew he could expect trouble from the Hardin gang since the tie-in with the Lunns was so close. He was especially concerned when the rumor came over to Kansas City that "They accuse you of being somewhere in the vicinity of the lynching."

Jack Helms was the renowned self-appointed captain of the vigilantes. At the time when mavericking could not be distinguished from thievery and illegal branding, he had been foreman for A. H. and J. E. Pierce. As wild cattle became scarce, Helms was more and more determined to assist on the side of order and uphold the feeble arm of the law.

Captain Jack had returned from the war to find the black belt of Texas anything but secure after emancipation. Negroes were numerically predominant in Matagorda County, in 1870, at the ratio of 2,120 to 1,254. Helms led in the thought that there must be no "Black insolence." But one day, when he was riding near Rancho Grande, a "free nigger" mounted a stake-and-rider fence and began whistling "Yankee Doodle" at the former Confederate. That was an error, not of marksmanship on the part of the Captain but of a musical selection on the part of the Negro. The first bullet struck the tune-maker "square between the eyes," and his bleached skeleton lay for years where the body fell, as a grim reminder to musically inclined Negroes.

"Once I went to hunt for society"

"Potting" an offending Negro occasionally, however, only made the situation more tense, and violence broke out more and more frequently. Governor Davis, "the Black Republican of Reconstruction," had but one choice when he found that former Confederates would not serve under him. He picked his police force from the ranks of the recently freed Negroes. Therefore, Jack Helms and men of his kind took it upon themselves to keep the peace after their own fashion and independent of the constabulary.

Helms and John Wesley Hardin might have been in the same camp except for the accident of kinship. When Wes was fourteen years old, he showed his callousness by stabbing a schoolmate. The next year, when a Negro tried to flail him with a club, Wesley shot the Negro dead. This double trouble put Governor Davis' troops after him. He thought he could not afford to stand trial in a Reconstruction, Negro-dominated court, so he went on the loose, seeking the protection of his kinsmen, the Clement brothers, who ruled and pillaged the range near Gonzales and west of the Staffords, Pierces, Grimes, and Wards.

The Clements were related to the Taylors, who had been feuding with the Suttons for so long that even the participants could not recall where the trouble began or what its origin was. It is reported to have "started back in the Carolinas, flourished in Georgia in the forties, and was brought to Texas with the household goods of the Taylors and Suttons, who oddly enough, elected to settle in De Witt as neighbors."

One of Jack Helm's most trusted vigilantes was Bill Sutton. Jim Taylor killed him, and Hardin gave the killer his support, which was the signal for Captain Jack to let it be known that he intended to shoot the young desperado on sight. This put Hardin immediately in the anti-Pierce camp, but before Captain Jack could get a bead on the boy, the Negro troops were so close on his trail that he accepted an invitation from the Clements brothers to trail a herd to Abilene and let things die down in Texas during his absence.

The trip up was a fairly uneventful one for rambunctious Wes. He killed only two Indians and five Mexicans en route. By the time he reached Kansas and put out the news that Shanghai was aiding him with Wild Bill, his two and one-half years on the loose had netted him the gory record of eighteen dead men, not counting, as he said, "Indians and Mexicans." It was, therefore, understandable that Pierce—fresh from the scene of the dead-tree gallows, where men had died who might have been of the Taylor faction—would avoid any appearance of being "heeled," and that he would remain perfectly quiet, neither giving credence to, nor denying, the story that he, with Tobe Driskill, the Texas cattle baron, and Ben Thompson, the notorious pistoleer and gambler, had "squared" the boy-bandit with Wild Bill over at Abilene. In truth, he visited Tom Speer's bench with discreet regularity, picked up what gossip he could, but pretended he had heard nothing disturbing.

Now that Shanghai was out of Texas, George Durham fabricated a story which had for its purpose directing more attention to himself than to Pierce. George was not averse to the limelight and was quite willing to be dubbed "the only survivor of the death squad of McNelly's Texas Rangers," thus linking himself with the rumors about Pierce and the vigilantes. Of course Ranger Durham was on the side of the law, while Pierce was in the potential bad-man class. According to Durham, Ranger Captain McNelly had been steeped in the Taylor-Sutton doin's before he left his home in Georgia to make his residence between the two fighting factions. "Captain McNelly," as Durham chronicled it, "knowed pretty well the background of the feud. He had knowed it back in Virginia before the war, and he was th'ow'd into it again in 1870 when he was called back into the harness as a peace officer, when he was asked by the Republican Governor Davis to form and organize and handle a force of state police." McNelly, however, had merits which Yankee-hating Texans could approve, for just as soon as he carried out the orders of the governor, he resigned "because he wouldn't work for no damn Republican longer than necessary."

But before McNelly had time to wash off the black of "damn Republicanism" he had to go into De Witt County and "try to take them Taylors and Suttons off each other's necks," and in the effort, recounted the redoubtable Durham, "A bunch of Sutton fighters —The Pierce boys—captured McNelly."

It appears that McNelly had left home upon call during the night to protect a prisoner whom the Pierce boys were in the act of hanging. McNelly went to the rescue so fast that he did not

"Once I went to hunt for society"

notice that his wife had slipped a little old two-shot derringer in his holster instead of his reliable six-guns. And when once on the scene he found it impossible to stand off the lynchers with his "little old two-shot," so he bargained with the Pierce boys: he would take the prisoner's place, if they would turn their intended victim loose. "The crowd agreed and began looking for a tree."

"Damit," the Captain swore, according to his narrator, "why do you have to look for a tree when you got a man to kill? You've all got guns. I'm not fightin' back. I'm your man. One of you take a gun and kill me."

"That mob fingered triggers and unholstered guns. But no one took the shot. Finally one of the Pierce boys—and there was six of them—came forward. This was old Shanghai Pierce. 'You know damn well, Captain,' he said, 'there ain't a man in this crowd that could hold a gun on you and pull the trigger. You take it too easy . . . you looking us in the eye.'

"He won old Shanghai then and there. He took him into camp; and Shanghai brung in his brothers, but he promised Shanghai he would never forget it; that he would never, in all his life yet coming to him, bother either Shanghai or his brothers."

This Texas Ranger brag, aiming to put Pierce in with the pistoleers and against the officers of the law, was ignored by Shanghai with the same silence he had employed against the effort of the Hardin gang around Abilene to get him to speak.

Instead of trying to bolster a sagging reputation as a bad man, Pierce turned his mind to other activities. He had one hundred thousand dollars in gold, and he proposed to make it earn something for him. First, he picked out a banker. Herman Kountze, who lived in Omaha, was one of four brothers living in New York, Indianapolis, Omaha, and Denver. They owned the banking institution known as Kountze Brothers. The branch banks at Omaha and Denver loaned much of their surplus capital to stockmen. As a consequence, Pierce made a trip to Omaha. Shanghai talked so enthusiastically and so loud that Herman was quite embarrassed for fear his customers would conclude bodily harm was about to be dealt him; thereupon he invited Shanghai up to his home for a light toddy, and there they held all subsequent conferences beyond earshot of curious people.

Back in Kansas City again, he employed L. C. Slavens, of

No. 18 Orr's Building, with whom he conferred as an attorney. He was not ready to forsake his hunt for society, but he was ready to mix business with pleasure, so he notified brother Johnathan (as he always spelled it) to get together what herds he could and put them on the trail, admonishing him to have them in Abilene before the winter season set in. Then he boarded a train and rode out of Kansas City.

He found Abilene to be all John Wesley Hardin had pronounced it: "I have seen many fast towns but I think Abilene beats them all. The town was filled with sporting men and women, gamblers, desperadoes and the like. It was well supplied with barrooms, hotels, barbershops, and gambling houses, and everything was open."

Abilene had been the center of cattle operations since its establishment in 1867, and remained such until 1871. At the height of its frothy growth it had a population of seven or eight thousand people. The census showed they had come from twenty-seven different states and thirteen foreign countries. There was no record that any of the people carried into Abilene with them "regrets of departure" or a "God go with you."

Shanghai arrived when the place was at the height of its activities. It had a new and much needed brick courthouse, a stone school, a railroad depot, a newspaper, a theater, two banks, four hotels, a calaboose, and two churches. Seven saloons, not counting the bars in the hotels, stood open at all hours. The Beer Garden or the Devil's Addition, as it was also called (depending upon one's predelictions toward the area), housed the Jezebels and Delilahs. No one thought to take the census there, or to hazard a guess as to anyone's destination upon departure.

Almost on the day John Wesley Hardin pointed his cattle toward Abilene, it started its existence as a city. Joseph McCoy, the avowed cattleman's friend, was sworn in as its first mayor. The office of city marshall took on color and assumed prestige under the six-shooters of Wild Bill Hickok; and when John Wesley Hardin hit town and strutted around for a short sixteen days, Wild Bill realized he had a job on his hands. And the situation did not improve as more and more Texans hitched their saddle horses before open saloons. Wild Bill sensed a crisis and called upon the city council for aid. Two policemen were forthwith put on the marshal's

"Once I went to hunt for society"

paid shooting staff. Several others volunteered for emergencies "just for the fun of the thing."

Between the time that Wes came to town and the unannounced arrival of Shanghai, Hardin had renewed his acquaintance with Ben Thompson. None—not even the youthful Wes—held as much pre-eminence as a killer as big moustachio Ben, whose reputation had been acquired around the capital of Texas. In Abilene, he and genial Phil Coe were the prosperous proprietors of the Bull's Head. Abilene had but one other saloon comparable in elegance. Phil Coe had been promoted from card-table cowboy, down in Washington County (within a hundred miles of Shanghai's El Rancho Grande), to the Bull's Head's best dealer. He had learned the art sitting on the corner of a spreading saddle blanket.

Ben Thompson was a man of sartorial elegance, who wore his top hat and similar fine clothing even upon the dusty streets. He had a fine good humor when sober but lusted after human blood when drinking, and he drank a great deal. The fact that he was credited with being the slayer of twenty-eight men refutes any claim to average sobriety.

When Hardin called to pay his respects to Ben and Phil, he found them on the verge of a clash with Wild Bill Hickok. The city had other saloon men and gamblers, claiming to be "original residenters" and entitled to a fair share of the loot, who could not hold the Texas trade against the Bull's Head. They were, consequently, responsible for the appointment of Wild Bill as marshal. He understood that it was a part of his duty to cause these worthies to move along, but he did not relish the undertaking and did nothing about it until Wes came to town. Ben and Wild Bill both saw Wes as a convenient tool, and each sought to set the six-shooter boy against the other through half-truth insinuations. Wes, however, stood aloof until Wild Bill indiscreetly declared Hardin to be "a dangerous man with pistols swung to his hips!" This Wes interpreted as a threat. He had come to Abilene armed, he said, and he proposed to stay that way. Then when Wild Bill decided to disarm him, he found, to his amazement that he was right, for the only things Wild Bill could see were the bores of Wes' two guns staring him in the face. Recognizing this as his closest view of death, Wild Bill Hickok stood quietly while Wes Hardin stripped him of his guns and set him adrift to face the contempt of Texas drovers.

Shanghai Pierce

Hardin left town, killing a Mexican as his last token of disrespect for Hickok, and then he turned back toward Texas. All of this took place with great speed while Shanghai was making arrangements to receive Jonathan's cattle which were on their way. Then he doubled back to Kansas City. Now that Wild Bill had more cause than before to see Ben Thompson on his way, Ben thought it a proper time "to take the cars" east and visit his wife at Kansas City.

Thompson was met at the "metropolitan playground" by his wife and son, but they were soon in an accident. Mrs. Thompson was severely injured and Ben had his leg fractured when a runaway team upset their buggy. This accident was the subject of much conversation on Tom Speer's bench, but Shanghai elected to ignore Ben's predicament, even though he knew Coe was having a hard time scraping together three thousand dollars to send to his injured partner. Then the news came to Market Square that Wild Bill had killed Coe, presumably over the gambler's attentions to Wild Bill's girl friend, Jesse. Again Shanghai side-stepped the turmoil and went west to order his trail herds marketed at Ellsworth instead of Abilene. It was now obvious that Shanghai was avoiding all connections with rowdies. His friends at Ellsworth, therefore, decided to play a prank on him, inasmuch as he had not altogether forsworn his hunt for society. There was a certain fair lady sojourning at an Ellsworth hotel who had commented favorably upon the appearance of the tall man, and his friends seized upon this opportunity to lure him in her direction, even though it was common knowledge that an interested bad man had served notice that his fair one was not to be molested by any cattleman.

The trap was baited for springing on the night Pierce intended to leave with a train of cattle. The engineer of the train was secretly informed of the scheme, and he agreed to refuse to stop on signal at the place where cattlemen were accustomed to board their outbound train. Shanghai was induced to walk alongside the lady's hotel window for a last look, perhaps more than a glance upon her countenance. He saw her within the dimly lighted room. Reaching over, he tapped gently upon the open window. She gave no heed to his signal. He repeated it. Then a man, resembling her six-shooter friend, appeared at the window with a cocked pistol in each hand. The picket fence which separated him from the rail-

"Once I went to hunt for society"

road tracks crashed flat with Shanghai's first charge. He ran rapidly to the accustomed place to board the train and hid in the weeds. He could hear men searching for him. The train approached with the engineer holding the throttle wide open. Shanghai could stand the pressure no longer, and, making a run for it, he tried to flag the engineer. When the caboose passed, laughing men fired their pistols in the air. Again he took cover and lay in the grass throughout the night, only to learn when morning came that he was the little goat his drover friends had left behind.

Shanghai was now definitely surfeited with society. Abilene was too tough for men of Pierce's inclinations. Besides that, the cattle business was shifting to Ellsworth, sixty-five miles away. Even Joseph McCoy, mayor, hotelkeeper, promoter, and the cattleman's friend, could not hold the cattle to his stockyards now that yardage prices were rising and desperate men were bullying the marshals. The situation at Ellsworth, however, soon vied with that at Abilene. The *State News* took notice of this in these words: "As we go to press, Hell is still in session at Ellsworth."

Seth Mabry, the little, five-foot-three, genial cattleman, had arrived from Austin just before Pierce reached Ellsworth. There was barely enough festivity at the new cattle town to satisfy the urge of the little cattle king. Therefore, lacking entertainment, he hunted up Pierce and they set about more dignified undertakings. They invited "One Arm" Jim Reed, just up from Goliad, to join them. He, like Pierce, had some cattle that were late reaching the market, so they decided to cast their lots together and hold over some three thousand steers on the Kansas prairies and have them ready for early 1872 sale. But cattle kings, whether little, one-armed, or towering, when once freed from the tedium of nursing a herd of cattle on the road, return to this labor reluctantly. To give themselves the freedom they wanted, hands to keep the cattle during the winter were needed. A godsend came to them in the person of Thomas Jefferson Hamilton, late from Kentucky.

Orphaned when young, Tom had been under the care of a grandmother and uncle. His grandmother was a devout Roman Catholic whose every wakeful hour was employed in furthering his education so that he could enter the priesthood. Long hours over books showed in the boy's sunken, piercing, grey eyes. His shoulders were stooped, putting him slightly at a disadvantage as he stood alongside Pierce, although both men stood more than six feet in height. His black hair and straight full beard made him appear much older than he was. A driving energy and firmness—perhaps, too, the similarity of youthful religious training—drew these two men together. He was hired to winter the Texans' cattle on the Kansas prairies.

These cattlemen were aware of the fact that there were pitfalls in the scheme to hold three thousand steers on the prairie in cold weather. Consequently, when an Indian agency, seeking cattle in lieu of the fast-disappearing buffalo to feed the Indians, approached Pierce with a bid for one thousand cattle, he knew that manna was about to fall to him as well as to the poor Indians. The price was agreed upon, and some "green horn army men" were to receive the steers on the prairie. Pierce (so he often told the story) "got the idea that those leather bumping horse soldiers were not up to snuff in their ability to receive cattle on the range." He, therefore, talked pompously of his skill at counting cattle on the run and hoped "them green horn army men" would take a "running count." This the cavalrymen agreed to after having heard him brag, for they were not willing to admit Pierce could count them faster than they could. "Me and my foreman," related Shanghai, "were to count the cattle as they came through between us, and the army men were to count for themselves. The steers were wild and ran past us like greased lightning. I lost the count several times myself and started over at a guess, and when I thought about *so many* had passed, I cut them off and sang out: 'Just an even thousand! What do you make it, boys?'

" 'Just an even thousand,' replied my foreman." Tom Hamilton was departing rapidly from his grandmother's training.

"The army greenhorns didn't like to admit that they couldn't count a thousand cattle as well as anybody else could, so they didn't ask for a recount, but accepted the cattle."

When the cattle were shipped, however, they found they were 118 short.

"They wanted," laughed Pierce, "to come back on me to make good, but shucks! I told them they were too late. How did I know but what their Jim Crow outfit had let some of the critters get away overnight!"

He left his cattle with Hamilton and moved out of "rowdy-

"Once I went to hunt for society"

land," intent upon visiting Herman Kountze again. As he rode across Nebraska, he observed conditions to be the same as in Kansas. Organized gambling was a leech, drawing the very lifeblood of the new country, at the same time that the Nebraska legislature was bemoaning its inability to raise sufficient money by taxation to relieve the state from financial embarrassment. Pierce thereupon called on the legislature and offered to come to the aid of "your busted institution." He proposed to post a ten-thousand-dollar deposit annually for the exclusive privilege of dealing monte bank on trains within the state. A ripple of laughter went across the state when his cynicism was understood. Then following up the attention the public had given him, he convulsed all Nebraska again. The legislature hesitated, it said, "to give such a lucrative franchise to an individual," but Pierce countered with the same offer "for the exclusive privilege of dealing the game against only such passengers as *profess* to be *clergymen* or *missionaries*."

After about eighteen months of trading in Kansas and Nebraska, making more money than he lost, the news came from brother Jonathan that "athmospheric conditions" down Texas way were clearing up. His venture with J. D. Reed had been successful, for they now owned seven thousand steers, which they were pasturing free in Kansas. But his mind kept reverting to the Matagorda prairies and to Galveston, where Hattie James was having difficulties managing her father's estate since he had been confined in the state hospital for the mentally deranged. And, too, he began to shudder over the realization, which for some time had been a surmise, that his investment of one hundred thousand dollars in bank stock was actually in jeopardy.

A Kansas banker, aided by cattleman-banker Andy Wilson, had painted the life of a financier in alluring colors, and his one hundred thousand dollars in gold went into bank stock. Dividend time came, but there were no dividends. He became inquisitive, but there were no assurances. "Then," said Pierce, "I began to realize that the gilt on the edges of the bank stock certificates which I had received from Andy Wilson and his banker-accomplices was not of the same fineness as the gold which I had given for the certificates, so I thought of a way out of my troubles."

The thought brought forth this action. One day Mr. Pierce entered the bank with the appearance of great excitement. He

Shanghai Pierce

went to the bank's books, checked his deposits, and chuckled loudly to himself until he brought forth the inquiry from his banker-associates: "What's in the air?" At first he refused to tell "even you." Under persuasion and a pledge of secrecy he told them: "A great herd of cattle is coming up the trail. I know them cattle. I know the owner. The cattle are fine. The owner is dumb enough to drink mean whiskey. The cattle can be bought on the trail. A fortune is waiting for me at Ellsworth. God has signalled at last that he will smile on me. I am going to buy them, and I am going to get rich."

The possibilities dethroned the caution of the bankers. They asked Pierce for an enlargement of their association: "We are partners, so why should we not also share in this good fortune?" Shanghai was reluctantly convinced. If they would cash his one hundred thousand dollars in bank certificates—he needed the money right now for the cattle purchase—he would take them into partnership with each man sharing his part of the cost of the cattle. The deal was made. Pierce put his one hundred thousand dollars in his little black satchel. On top of the money he placed a clean shirt and the ever present Bowie knife. Mr. Wilson elected to accompany Pierce down the trail to purchase the cattle. Shanghai invited Tom Hamilton to go along and drive the buggy and come back with the cattle. An early start was made. Hamilton drove according to instructions. Pierce kept a wary eye on his black satchel. Andy Wilson talked of good times to come.

Their route was such as to intersect the railroad running back to Kansas City. Pierce was almost fussy with Hamilton for "mistreating a good team," but with the same breath he urged him on: "Keep going, Tom." Hamilton's timing was good. Just before train time the fagged horses were brought to a stop at a wayside station. Suddenly Hamilton professed a great thirst and asked Mr. Pierce to hold the team while he and Andy Wilson walked around behind the depot to get a cool drink from a community well. The train came and departed during their absence. As the rear coach pulled from behind the depot, Andy Wilson was shocked to see Shanghai standing on the rear platform. He was laughing. In one hand he carried the little black satchel. In the other he held his big black Shanghai hat. He was bowing very low. "Fare thee well, brother Andy! Fare thee well," came the booming voice of the Texas-bound Shanghai. "Fare thee well, brother Andy . . . I am going to Texas

"Once I went to hunt for society"

... and out of the banking business ... Fare thee well, you Kansas sons of bitches ... I'm going to Texas ... You can go to hell."

"Fare thee well, brother Andy! Fare thee well." Back came the voice of the bowing Shanghai just as long as the train could be seen in the distance.

7. "*I thought a great deal of the man and took an interest in him— a 12% interest*"

Now that Shanghai had parted ways with his Kansas partners, forever, as he hoped, his roaming around brought him back into the jurisdiction of the Matagorda County courts. He had been away almost two years. Despite his uneasiness about the "political, atmospheric, and social conditions," he was now ready to admit, "Society in Texas is better than I am," and he had a genuine desire to be back at El Rancho Grande. Conditions in Matagorda County, however, made his personal security uncertain. The sheriff wanted him for jumping his bond, and, because of the rumors he heard, he was unwilling to trust himself in the presence of some Matagordians. He would, therefore, enter the county and leave again,

"I thought a great deal of the man"

testing the temper of the people much as a woman tests the heat of her flatiron with her spittled finger. He touched and jumped. "I was in and gone; off and on, until the atmosphere became pure and the society got good; then I returned to stay."

He went back again to his brother Jonathan at El Rancho Grande and arranged for the return of his daughter, who had been east with her Aunt Miranda while he was in Kansas. He learned that his appearance bond at Matagorda had been forfeited and that the sheriff had an execution order for two hundred dollars. He arranged for McCamley to pay the judgment and stay the execution.

Shanghai, of course, inquired about the outcome of the case of *The State of Texas* v. *W. W. Lunn,* and he was amazed to learn that Lunn, instead of fleeing the jurisdiction of the court (which he might have done without hindrance) had remained quietly within the county. He conducted himself in a manner to please all those who were not attached to the cattle clique. Not only had Lunn not run away, but on the day previous to his trial he voluntarily presented himself to the deputy sheriff and requested that he be remanded to jail to await the fortunes of tomorrow. Deputy Sheriff Perry was extravagantly polite to the young accused. Publicly ignoring his attempt to surrender, he invited Wilborn to dine at his home that evening, and he spoke so that passers-by would surely hear.

Lunn, fresh from an eastern college, sat that evening at dinner with his educated Irish host and nonchalantly discussed early English literature and many other subjects, but not once did they mention rustler hangings or brand-blotching. A little girl of the household listened in wonderment to the conversation, and she began to feel that the boy's reputation had been besmirched "by a greedy band of powerful men who had charged him with the abhorrent crime of stealing cow hides."

Time for retirement came. Officer Perry showed embarassment, now that he must perform his duty under the law and imprison his guest. Mrs. Perry sensed the situation. She called a servant; and clean sheets, pillowcases, towels, and even a bowl and pitcher with fresh water, were provided. When everything was reported in readiness, Officer Perry and his prisoner disappeared quietly into the darkness. When morning came, there was no delay in serving breakfast, for host Perry was again at his home with his guest, and all were too courteous to inquire even as to the soundness of their sleep. When court convened, with punctilious formality, W. W. Lunn was declared "not guilty."

Pierce regretted the loss of the two-hundred-dollar forfeit money. The loss of any money caused Shanghai to wince; but he reasoned that two hundred dollars was a small price to pay to avoid placing his testimony on record, especially after he learned how sympathetic the people had been with the boy who had been generally thought of as a cattle thief. This caused him to say that, though he had "more or less interest in things, it was considerably mixed up. I owe nobody to run away from them, still I had a feeling there was somebody after me."

Pierce then made a trip to Indianola which served to relieve the tension somewhat. He met Little Dannie, and they were happy to see each other again. Little Dannie tried to explain Pierce's absence as a small matter: "He just had a little difficulty with the Lunn family and left the place. When he returned I took him up again."

Sullivan had news, both good and bad. Uncle Daniel Sullivan was dead. "That is most regrettable," consoled Pierce. "Not so bad," demurred Little Dannie, "for I succeeded to the business." Then continued Sullivan: "Mr. Pierce, as a pure matter of friendship, because you are a working man, working up without security, you may have credit with me unlimited. Whatever you draw I will pay. I will take neither security nor note. You pay back when you please."

To the incredulous, who knew Sullivan, he sought to explain his liberality by professing: "I thought a great deal of the man and took an interest in him." He did not, however, at that time, make known his intentions to charge his friend "1 per cent per month compounded monthly, a generous reduction on my part, for I was getting 2½ per cent per month with good security from all others."

Shanghai exercised the dubious privilege of drawing unlimited on Sullivan every time "a traffic or trade" appeared which seemed to have any profit in it. Little Dannie continued to deduct his "1 per cent compounded monthly" until one day Shanghai looked over some statements little Dannie had furnished. "There" said he, "I saw: 'Interest, so much.' It was an enormous amount.

"I thought a great deal of the man"

It scared me. I do not see how I lived. Thereafter, I resolved: I'll keep my money biling all the time."

Consequently, he crossed over to Hamilton's Point to observe Bing's activities and see if he could persuade his contrary brother-in-law, Mr. Wiley, to cast his fortunes with him again. At the Tallow Factory he saw a young former Confederate bookkeeper at work. He called himself George Stidham Hamilton, but he was evasive when someone asked him why his brother signed himself "Stidham." He explained: "I have done nothing criminal. The cause is *feminine* in character," and all he was willing to tell about himself was that he was from "No'th Georgaw." Pierce understood that he was predisposed to Jonathan Pierce's "three pint befuddlement" and that he "played poker and took a little too much tea." These vices were pardonable in Shanghai's eyes since he was a good bookkeeper. Consequently, before riding off up the Carancahua, he hinted to Hamilton that he was again enlarging his business, that he was taking over the old Hunky Dory Brown store, and that there was money to be made if he would keep store in conjunction with his brother and serve as bookkeeper for A. H. and J. E. Pierce at the same time. To make his argument a little more forceful, he suggested the impropriety of a former Confederate soldier working for a damn Yankee who had not even fought for Yankeedom but had stayed in the South and made money by selling Texas cattle to the Army of the Republic. That was enough for George!

Then Pierce was given some information which alarmed him terribly. Wes Hardin was back in Texas, running amuck and filing notches in his six-shooter barrel. The news that traveled this time was true. Wes had literally loaded down with buckshot the body of his old friend, Sheriff Jack Helms. The feud had flared up so violently that old Joe Tumlison, who only grudgingly ever missed a fight, had thought it discreet to extend the olive branch. The two factions, as a result of old Joe's concession, had met in Old Clinton and signed a "treaty of peace." Evidencing their pacific intentions, they caused the clerk of the county to make the document a public record, so that friend and foe alike might feel safe within shooting range of any of them.

Hardin, however, was not safe from the state police, even though every Sutton, by terms of the contract, was under obligation to pass him by. Consequently, the boy bandit moved away from Old Clinton and sought protection from his Clements kinsmen the second time. They put him under cover in their cattle camps, which were spread from Gonzales down through Pierce's territory to the port of Indianola.

Charlie Siringo had gone over to the Pierce camp again and was fully aware of Pierce's alarm over marauding Wes Hardin. One night, said Charlie, "while I was employed by the great and only Shanghai (Abel) Pierce, who stood six-feet-four in his stocking feet and had a voice equal to a fog-horn on a river steamboat, [a young man who was] jovial and full of fun" came riding into camp. Wiley Kuykendall recognized Wes immediately, but kept his identity a secret until after he had ridden away the next morning. When Shanghai learned of his brother-in-law's finesse in steering Wes out of his path, he confessed: "Wiley is a hunney."

It was not comforting to Pierce to know that Wes was trailing through his territory, and he thought it might be profitable for him to get back into Kansas for a short time. At Victoria, Tom O'Connor told Shanghai that E. P. Byler intended to trail a thousand steers to Wichita for "One Arm" Jim Reed. Byler had worked for Pierce in Kansas, and Shanghai had good reason to believe that the cattle would go through in good shape. Also, he knew that seven hundred of the herd were good cattle from the O'Connor range. He therefore drew on Little Dannie again, bought the cattle en route, and set out for Wichita, where he intercepted Byler and ordered him to try to run the quarantine and deliver the herd to him in Missouri.

Texas cattle were not allowed to pass into Missouri without waiting through the quarantine period. Shanghai knew, of course, that if he could get the herd into Missouri ahead of other cattle, the market would be higher. The fact that Missourians believed that the influx of Texas longhorns into the Middle West had brought Texas fever to the native stock was of no concern to Shanghai at the moment. What he wanted was a market. He would risk the consequences of the law.

Byler, with Shanghai's promise of a bonus if he were successful, was so anxious to get down into Missouri that he neglected to burnish up his road equipment. He left the "old coonie" under the wagons which showed both recent and long use on the road. This belied any assertion Byler might make that the steers were win-

"I thought a great deal of the man"

tered above the quarantine line. When Byler got into Missouri by a circuitous, little-used road the old beef-hides were still swinging all bespattered with mud and grime. This looked suspicious to a sharp-eyed native who rode into camp one evening and asked Byler's name "and a few fool questions." He returned to camp within a short time bringing with him "several men riding long-tailed horses and carrying muskets." Without ceremony they served a writ and announced: "E. P. Byler and crew! Consider yourselves under arrest."

Byler persuaded the officers to escort him to a near-by town where he telegraphed to Shanghai at Wichita. Shanghai soon got there with a bunch of men. They counselled and a course of action was decided upon. Pierce got very intimate with the guard, and after adequate liquid social persuasion had tempered his resolution, Shanghai and the guard went off in the moonlight for a buggy ride. Then "E. P. Byler and crew rattled their hocks for an Indian reservation about ten miles away." When the buggy ride was over and the moon had gone down, there was neither Byler, crew, nor cattle to be seen. Pierce, of course, "got into a wrangle with the authorities about the cattle but it was compromised," reported Byler, and there was enough left over after the compromise from the cattle sale to net Shanghai a profit from his "wintered" steers.

When, in the year just passed, Shanghai stood on the rear of the train shouting "Fare thee well" to "Brother Andy," he was earnestly wishing it to be an everlasting adieu. Such, however, was not to be his good fortune, for Andy and the bankers were not willing to take it lying down. Now that they had him back in Kansas they ensnarled him in expensive lawsuits. One suit was for $23,000 damages, in which they alleged false representations. In another suit, judgment was rendered against Pierce for $4,900, and a deposit by Pierce of $3,500 went over to Brother Andy Wilson when Jim Reed assigned the money to him, claiming that one-half the money was his as a result of the Pierce-Reed partnership. Pierce howled to Attorney Slaven: "He had no right to do so as I always was all the Pierce & Reed Business & money matters & he had no Wright to Sign My Name two years after we quit business."

Slaven had lost Pierce's suits, but he counselled Shanghai to attempt recovery by suit against Reed. The threat of suit, however, did not scare "One Arm" Jim, who declared positively: "I don't propose to pay anything on that account." Reed, however, reckoned without Shanghai's ingenuity. Pierce knew that a cattleman's most vulnerable spot was his credit. He therefore laid the transaction before R. J. Brackenridge of the First National Bank of Austin, who was carrying Reed's paper. Brackenridge deposited $1,743.14 to the account of J. H. Pierce (in error) and charged Reed's account. Shanghai wrote critically of the error but forgot to thank Brackenridge for the kindness. Brackenridge admitted "it was done but by Mistake." Then he harked back to Shanghai's forgotten Sunday-school lesson and admonished him to "Do unto others as you wish others to do unto you. So I won't tell you to go to h——.R. J. B."

Just as soon as Shanghai finished fighting and paying his way out of Kansas litigation, Brother Andy turned tormentor again. Away up in Topeka another suit appeared on the docket of the federal court against J. D. Reed and Company, with the allegation that the "company" was none other than A. H. Pierce. This time the treasurer of James County sought to collect taxes on two herds of steers, one numbering 810, the other 6,500 head. The strange part of the matter was that some unknown party had actually rendered the cattle for taxation with the statement: "The cattle actually belong to Pierce and Reed," and "They are the same cattle once in the possession and under the control of Andy Wilson."

When Pierce promised Slavens he would pay fees for fighting the suit, Slavens encouraged him to go on with the litigation, for, said he, "take it all around we will beat them, but it will be the first time any Texas man ever got out of paying a tax on cattle." But when Pierce's cash fee was delayed, judgment suddenly was entered against Pierce and Reed for $2,200. Pierce understood what was happening, and wrote: "There is no use in squirming. It will have to be paid." Again he called on "One Arm" Jim to pay his half. Jim called Shanghai's attention to his previous letter—"I always was all the Pierce & Reed Business & money Matters"—and refused to pay. Pierce replied by threatening: "I will wait 20 Days for an Answer and if I here nothing I then will refer the matter to Mr. O'Connor & see what he has to say." Mr. O'Connor, like Mr. Brackenridge, said "pay," and Jim did.

Shanghai was more than happy to get out of Kansas this time and return to his Texas schemes. He found El Rancho Grande going along well under Jonathan's supervision. George Hamilton had

"I thought a great deal of the man"

taken over the old Hunky Dory Brown Store, which was being financed now by Pierce, Kyle, and Pierce, and a set of cattle-company books were being well posted. Grimes was not pleased over the loss of his bookkeeper, but the growing community reacted favorably to the genial former Confederate storekeeper, Shanghai's sister-in-law stating of him: "I would rather trade with George and *Know* I was being cheated than with others and expect to be."

With Kyle, Sullivan, O'Connor, Allen, Poole, and George Hamilton in the Pierce camp, Grimes saw that Pierce was spreading his loop wider and wider. But there was one more man in the region whom Shanghai wanted on his side. Benjamin Quinn Ward (Shanghai always wrote it "Mr. Benn"), although friendly with Grimes, had not been one of the thirty men of the region who had contracted to let Grimes have first bid on their cattle.

At the age of twenty-four, two years before Pierce came to Texas, B. Q. Ward joined his two brothers, LaFayette and Russell, on Carancahua Bay, about thirty-five miles from Grimes. There the Wards built a ranch upon industry and integrity. It was no inconsequential matter, then, when Ward decided to accept a partnership with A. H. Pierce. The partnership, however, was not consented to without long and thoughtful consideration on the part of Mr. Benn. Ward was a man of independence of thought and spirit. He had pride of possession and he was willing, only with reluctance, to merge his identity with others. Time after time, Pierce had sought to entice Ward into the Pierce-dominated alliances, but Mr. Benn was coy. Then one day, during the absence of Mr. Benn, Shanghai appeared at the home of his mother, Mrs. Eleanor Shannon Ward—the Widow Ward—and sought to effect his plan by an appeal direct to the mother. She asked Pierce pointedly: "Why do you want Ben to be your partner?" Shanghai squared himself, looked her straight in the eyes, and spoke truthfully: "Madam, I want the name." He had won his case.

Although Shanghai had spoken truthfully to the Widow Ward, whom he respected beyond any living person, still he had not told all the truth. Ward fitted into a scheme which he was slowly but surely bringing to completion.

Mr. Benn did not marry until he was thirty-seven years old. He had fought through two wars, crossed the continent on horseback to dig up a small fortune in California gold, and now he was ready to anchor himself to the soil by purchasing the land upon which his cattle fed. This meant, of course, that Ward's purchases would restrict Grimes' range. Pierce had remembered that Bing had spoken disparagingly of the coastal land: "I prefer to leave the country in preference to buying a chunk of it." A buyer of land, reasoned Pierce, will help put the encircling squeeze on him.

With his scheme in fair shape to put a little more pressure on Bing, Shanghai took time out, trekked down to Galveston, put on his topper and frock-tail coat, and married Hattie James. Hattie had the care not only of her insane father's property, but of some of her own, and a disposition to direct the course of her life after her own inclinations. This made it mandatory that the bridegroom adapt himself, for a time at least, to strange surroundings and displeasing customs. "We went to Galveston to hunt society," lamented Pierce. "Mrs. Pierce had to go to the hotel to board, at the Tremont, to be in society."

He appeared occasionally in the dining room of the Tremont and at social functions wearing topper and tails. His six-feet-four, thus bedecked, focused attention upon him. This he enjoyed, but he felt very uncomfortable without his boots. He declared: "I don't like them Congress shoes." He sensed, too, that his voice was too loud for "in-door use." It functioned better around the cattle pens at El Rancho Grande. Therefore he proposed that they return to the ranch. The bride was not amenable. Pulling on his boots, he rammed his Shanghai hat hard down on his sleek hair and announced, as he hied off alone to the ranch: "By God, Madam! Remember that old Vi has everything I need for my comfort and dignity down on the ranch."

8. "*A reckless and cruel disregard of my wrights*"

En route to the ranch the disconsolate Shang played with the idea of building a lavish ranch up near Wharton. There would be a fine house for Hattie, something to compete with the Tremont. He would have fine cattle, and he would not have to bother with Wiley and Susan and "that old grumbler, Johnathan." He selected a place, in his mind, across the river from Wharton. There was heavy timber to the north and east and level prairie as far as his eyes could see to the south and west. It was an ideal spot. But when he got to El Rancho Grande the old grumbler, as usual, had bad news for him. His scheme to "circle Grimes in and all others out" had slipped the noose during his absence. Bob Stafford, who ranged with his brother over west toward Columbus, was giving evidence that not only would he welcome trouble but he was out hunting for it. So house-building must wait, for Stafford would not.

The aggressive Stafford brothers of Columbus had been running large numbers of cattle on the open range east of Columbus for many years. They were on the periphery of Pierce's much desired domain, and some of their cattle were actually on the land where he now wished to build his ranch.

Bill Kyle, partnering with Pierce, had been grazing this land with the Staffords without friction, but to make matters worse, Kyle had made it known that he was dissolving their partnership. He would, so he said, "come off the prairie and th'ow my cattle up the Guadalupe above Victoria."

It was known that Stafford had been on the range checking the number of cattle in the Pierce-Kyle brands and that Shanghai was taking his partners for the purpose of using good men as buffers. Bob, therefore, construed this as a "trespass-by-design" and forthwith announced that not only had he no intention of receding from the expanding Shanghai Circle, but he proposed to convert the free-grass issue into a personal one and intended to bring it to a climax the very first time he crossed Shanghai's trail. And he went out looking for the trail!

One night Pierce blustered into a Victoria hotel to register. Lobby-sitters lounged in chairs as usual. It was common knowledge that the ill will between Bob and Shanghai was at the action point and that Bob was "cuttin' for sign" of Pierce's presence. Shanghai picked up the pen. Then he put on his glasses and peered carefully at the hotel register. The name he saw fresh-inked before him was "R. L. Stafford—Columbus." Without a moment's hesitation, Pierce replaced the pen, and pointing to the name stated: "Gentlemen, I know this is a comfortable hotel with ample accommodations for ordinary men, but, by God, Sirs! It is entirely too small for Bob Stafford and Shanghai Pierce at the same time." Quietly he left the hotel.

The Shanghai Circle was not the only worry Bing had. "Over on the Leona," according to his son Bradford, "there was a choice herd of Grimes cattle. Circumscribed as they were and separated from his other holdings, it was difficult for father to give them protective supervision. All the ranch bosses, except one, stole all the profits and the natives killed that boss." Under such circumstances, Bing decided to drive that herd of cattle north. The drive netted him such a good profit that he became "Kansas conscious." He therefore began emptying the Pierce Circle by transferring his

"A cruel disregard of my wrights"

cattle to Kansas as his Texas range conditions dictated. With a pasture in Kansas, there was less incentive for Bing to continue the fight; it was also much easier for Pierce to tighten the circle.

Grimes, however, was unwilling to desert the range before Pierce's onslaught without at least one resolute fight. He, therefore, backed down on his decision not to invest in land and bought 3,074 acres right in the "big middle of Shanghai's circle." This acreage he used as a nucleus to combine with the holdings of ten of his neighbors, and they formed "an association for mutual protection." The association held 10,303 acres, and their combined holdings encircled 50,309 acres which were either owned in whole or in part by Pierce or controlled by him. (A circle within a circle!) Across the only feasible outlet to the Pierce range and wholly upon the "association properties," the "mutual protectionists" erected a plank fence, at great labor and expense, from the Colorado River to Williams Creek. Into this enclosure they "pushed twenty thousand cattle and four hundred horses," enough to destroy Pierce's grass like a wind-fed fire.

This retaliation came as a surprise to Shanghai. He doubted their intentions and made overtures to the fence-builders. He asked to be permitted to participate in the cost with an agreement that the fenced area would not be overstocked, but construction went on. Thereupon he sought an attorney, selecting D. E. E. Braman, who, by the strangest of coincidences, happened to be the brother-in-law of the presiding judge of the district. And he complained to Braman: "Grimes is proceeding with a reckless and cruel disregard for my Wrights and is forcing Great numbers of cattle and other stock within the enclosure and against my urgent and continued protest."

A suit was filed. Pierce sought to enjoin the fence-builders from proceeding with their scheme. He asked for a receivership of the association and prayed for "the authority to eject all cattle from within the enclosure save and except one animal for every six acres owned by the fence-builders." Shanghai had confidence in the integrity and legal ability of Attorney Braman, but he summed up his opinion of the judge in these words: "Why I paid that man to render a decision in a suit for me once, but after he did it, he promptly granted a new trial to my opponent. When I jumped him about it he claimed he had lived up to his bargain: he did agree to give me a judgment, but he did not say he would not reconsider!"

Pierce viewed every movement in the suit with suspicion. Trusting Braman but fearing Burkhart, when all defendants except Grimes had filed answers in the case, he caused Braman to get the suit transferred to DeWitt County. There it would be heard before Judge Pleasants. Also, his regularly retained "counsellor," D. C. Proctor, would be near by to see that things went well, and no man spoke more softly to gain the ear of Judge Pleasants than did "the elder Proctor." So, true to expectation, before the case came up on its merits, Judge Pleasants entered an order that "T. C. Nye [shall] be the Commissioner or Receiver [and he is] authorized and empowered to take and exercise such control over the pasture described in Plaintiff's petition as will prevent the same from being overstocked by the parties to the said suit during the pendency of the same; that is to say, he will prevent the parties from putting into said pasture, or keeping in the same, more than one head of cattle to every six acres of land owned by them . . . and said receiver is authorized to turn such excess out of such pasture."

The ink was not dry on the order before Tom Nye, ever loyal to Shanghai, was in the saddle. He was accompanied by a complete Pierce cowboy contingency, and they began chasing every WBG they could find out from behind the plank fence. They were not careful, either, to keep from frightening Stafford cattle when they came upon them. When cow-chasing got in full swing, Pierce became apprehensive about the outcome of the affair. Judge Pleasants had granted a temporary injunction which was effective during "the pendency of the suit." It was therefore quite possible that Judge Burkhart could regain jurisdiction and "reconsider." "He is," lamented Pierce, "the same sort as our County Judge & Negro County Commissioner."

While the cow-chasing went gleefully on, Bing was away in Kansas City, out of the jurisdiction of the court. He knew of the injunction suit, although he had not taken Shang's counterthrust seriously, but now that eleven thousand cattle had been wangled out of the country by the never tiring Nye, he saw real shadows of "the Black Hills." They began to lay a pall over his property, under the guiding genius of his implacable enemy. He therefore disclaimed further residence in Texas and claimed his right under the

"*A cruel disregard of my wrights*"

Constitution of the United States as a nonresident to be sued in the Federal Court at Galveston.

The interval of time between Judge Pleasants' injunction and the removal of the cause of action to the Federal Court was all Shang and Tom Nye needed. They swept the pastures clean of Grimes' cattle. Pierce had accomplished his purpose, and Grimes' recourse lay in an action for damages. However, he was unwilling to meet the ingenious Pierce in such a battle.

Grimes' removal from Matagorda County practically nullified him as a power at his old home. Old Shang was, on the other hand, riding high, but he was not content with half-measures. He knew that Grimes, or any landowner within his range, could be troublesome. He therefore tried the sly method—indirection. He employed Nelson Clements, land agent in far-off New York, to undertake to buy the remnants of the Grimes holdings. Nelson was unsuccessful, and Pierce became impatient, as usual. Clements reported: "I am crowding Grimes all I can. As soon as I hear from him again I will let you know." He did hear, but the crafty old fellow had smelled the mouse. "I have a letter from Grimes," so wrote Clements again, "this morning from Victoria where he has gone to see a Sick Sister—He says he thinks I am trading with Shanghai Pierce and *if I am he will not sell.* You must have leaked, for I have not. I shall write him I am trying to Sell to an English Company." But no results came from the "English Company," and the New York agent threw up his commission, declaring: "I will not give him [Grimes] anymore of my time. I can do better at Something Else."

B. D. Crary was also interested in Grimes' departure from the state; consequently, he reported developments to Shanghai. "Grimes," wrote Crary, "is cleaning up over 3,000 at your Switch, Bulls, Cows, and Calves—everything. You won't feel very bad over this I think."

Bradford R. Grimes now began assuming his father's responsibilities. He rode the cattle train northward and assisted his father to relocate on the old Spade Ranch, in the Indian Territory, and at Kiowa, Kansas. The trip was not a very profitable one. He doubled back from Wichita Falls and again spent the night with Crary. Crary wrote a note to Shanghai, keeping him posted: "Young Brad Grimes stayed here last night on his way back from Wichita Falls

Shanghai Pierce

where he went with the cattle. They lost some 40 head including Calves on the cars."

Despite his father's feud with Pierce, young Bradford Grimes took little interest in the fuss. At Wichita Falls he learned that horse thieves had stolen three horses from one of Pierce's passing herds. He ransomed them for Shanghai for ten dollars each, but the following evening the thieves descended upon him again and stole them the second time. Brad stopped his herd and scoured the country for nearly a week, but he was forced to write to Shanghai: "I was unfortunate to lose all three of your D horses, and am out $30." A few days later he encountered thieves again. This time he picked up three of Pierce's steers. He took them away from the thieves, put them with his drive, and notified Shanghai that he had them. This made him bold enough to write Shanghai for a recommendation. From the Spade Ranche he wrote:

> Mr. Pierce   Dear Friend
> Will be glad to look after the cattle and horses you are out; wish I could have met you in town.
> I wrote you sometime ago, but don't think I ever sent the letter, it was in substance that I would like to have you recommend me to any layout with any outfit where I could get better wages than a $100. a mo. I am worth more.
>   Respy
>   B. R. Grimes, Kiowa, Ka.

Bradford, however, did not get his recommendation "to a layout with an outfit" which paid better wages, so he branched out into merchandising.

He advertised on ornately printed stationery:

OFFICE OF
B. R. GRIMES
DEALER IN GENL. MERCHANDISE

Spade Ranche, I. T.   Tres Palacios, Texas
Kiowa, Ka.

Using one of his letterheads, he wrote the second appeal to Pierce for assistance. He wanted to move some steers from Texas, and he needed money with which to buy corn to feed them. "Would like,"

"A cruel disregard of my wrights"

so read the letter, "to borrow one to five hundred dollars from you to buy corn with, say for a year. I wouldnt mind giving you a lien on it, or buying it in your name. Would like to get some capital to help work out my obligations on, but moving the steers is mainly what I need. Am doing better now and think in a year or two will pay out probably."

Shanghai, however, was not interested in buying corn for Grimes' hungry cattle, neither was he concerned about shipping money, but he was still interested in finishing the job of putting Bing "on the Black Hills." Therefore, when Clements failed him, he turned to the Liverpool and London and Globe Insurance Company. Its agent soon reported:

> I am offered all the property of Mr. W. B. Grimes—on Tres Palacios including everything—Except about ten acres—on which is the Family burial ground for $10 000.00 Cash—Land, fences—Houses, barns—Machinery tools—of course cattle are not included. Should you think well of it, I can probably be of service.

Shanghai read the letter, again and again, while his mind reviewed the long struggle between them. Then putting the letter down, he said:

> I have initiated my old employer into the Royal Arch degree. All accounts are squared. I can honestly say: "Peace to his ashes."

9. "*A pretty big dog in the puddle*"

"O, my God, I got to be a pretty big dog in the puddle. I was borrowing one hundred thousand dollars at Galveston at a time. I stand pat there is not a better cattleman in the state—in the land. There is not a man in the United States of America can beat me on a ranch. I have some stuff to show for it, too, Sir."

The Colonel—it pleased Shang these days to be called "the Colonel"—was speaking in more grandiloquent terms than was his custom. He was in an expansive mood. "By long effort," he said, "sleeping with the rattlesnakes, wearing my *panns* off even with my belly, I can begin to see my empire in the making. I am rid of Grimes."

For some years now his great herds of cattle had moved regularly each spring toward the Middle West. There they had fanned out, some to go to the packers in the East, some to follow the course of the North Star into Canada, others to move westward into Colo-

"A pretty big dog in the puddle"

rado and Wyoming. All had taken the name of Shanghai Pierce with them. "Sea Lions" and "Shanghai Pierce Coasters" were synonymous terms wherever cattle were bought and sold; and the Colonel was feeling his importance.

Not only could he lay claim of ownership to large numbers of "sea lions fresh from the waters of the Gulf of Mexico," but also to many acres of land in the name of A. H. and J. E. Pierce. His score was evened with the crafty Grimes. That bewhiskered old gentleman would find little profit feuding from faraway Kiowa and Kansas City, but Bob Stafford was still a sharp thorn in his flesh.

Bill Kyle had not proved to be an aggressive associate. His cordial entente with Stafford had endured despite the partnership with Pierce. Then Kyle had withdrawn from Pierce after two years' association, and he gave as his reason, "Just a little misunderstanding," upon which he would not elaborate. Thus the "buffer," which Pierce had so thoughtfully erected, had disintegrated, and Stafford cattle roamed eastward again without hindrance. They could now be found as far away as the Pierce-Ward pasture. Pierce was wholly unwilling that this "aggression" should go unchallenged.

Again Shanghai drew on Little Dannie, and, recalling Grimes' plank-fence scheme, he and Mr. Benn began building a fence from the Gulf of Mexico to the Navidad River. When the fence was up, Pierce boys were at the heels of every animal in the area which did not wear a Crescent V. The high-mettled Stafford learned that his cattle were being combed unceremoniously out of the country, and his anger rose to the breaking point. "I resolve," he said, "to shoot Mr. Pierce on sight." And there was nothing wrong with Bob's vision.

Soon after the warning went out, Bob Stafford met the gentleman with the walking-stick technique, face to face, in the vestibule of a train standing at a way-station. The Colonel recognized Stafford instantly, and wheeling, he turned his back and, at the same time, said plainly: "Bob Stafford is too much of a gentleman-of-the-code to shoot an unarmed man in the back." Then, without casting a backward glance, he walked deliberately off the train and disappeared up the street of the village. Even old Bob had to admit: "I admire the Colonel's quick thinking."

Now that money was easy to borrow—"By God, gentlemen, I was borrowing one hundred thousand dollars at Galveston at a time!"—Colonel Pierce checked over "the multiplicity of his business" and gave serious thought to Little Dannie's "1 per cent per month compounded monthly." He wondered what Little Dannie had meant when he said: "Mr. Pierce, I am not the best cow man nor 'boss-anything-else.' I make a living; that is about all." Consequently, Shanghai called in his bookkeeper, who did some "running up," and they concluded the little banker was too expensive.

The Colonel grew philosophical and speculated on why he had continued with Sullivan for such a long time and on such an extensive scale. He shrugged it off, however, concluding: "It is like everything else you get in the habit of doing; going to mill, you go to a certain place. Then you go there regularly. You go to a certain place to get your drinks, then you go there regularly; but there is one thing I am certain about: while Dannie was furnishing me money from 1 per cent up, I had to rustle. I now know why I could not be very religious about the trades I made. I had to get the interest for Dannie. He needed it in his business. I was contributing to his future welfare."

Good fortune came Pierce's way just as he decided "to go to another mill." "Along came Mr. Matthews," he wrote. "He was being financed by Sullivan also. I made a trade with Matthews. It was an immense amount of cattle, 9,480 head I sold him . . . and that gave me lots of money."

As soon as the big deal was closed, the Colonel headed straight to Indianola. "I went down there; got there one night. The next morning we fixed up our accounts." When Little Dannie came down to open the store that early morning, Shanghai greeted him with: "Mr. Sullivan, when in luck I worked for myself two days; when out of luck, I worked for you every other day. Fant works for you two days in good luck and out of luck, all the time. Poor Matthews works for you all the time. He never gets out of your debt. I am going to pay you up—*and with your own money!* I made a trade with Matthews. . . . Dannie, I have got to go where I can borrow money cheap. I have to have it for less!"

Mr. Sullivan did not appear to be surprised at the Colonel's rebellion, and tauntingly consoled himself over the loss of a good customer with: "Well, I have made one hundred thousand dollars out of you, Mr. Pierce. If we cannot make it out of you rich men, where can we make it?"

"*A pretty big dog in the puddle*"

And back came the retort: "But, Dannie, when you were robbing me, I was robbing someone else."

Mr. Pierce now needed a banker of his growing proportions. Again he turned up trumps. This time it was in the person of Herman Kountze, the "Omaha brother" of the four New York bankers, who was making a tour of the lumber belt of East Texas and the coastal cattle country.

Herman Kountze's visit to Texas was predicated upon important economic developments. Texas had launched into railroad-building. Its legislature had been generous in an effort to induce construction, but like all other sparsely populated states, it had a paucity of money and an amplitude of unused acres. The state owned much land. Therefore, it set aside many sections to railroad construction companies in lieu of cash bonuses.

Among the corporations acquiring acreage in Texas was the International and Great Northern Railroad Company. The landgrant company organized a holding company, The New York and Texas Land Company, Limited, which issued six million dollars in stock certificates. Four million dollars of these certificates were "reserved" from public purchase by large companies which had furnished railroad construction funds. Of course, there were some speculation holders, but with two-thirds of the certificates held off the market, railroad lands in Texas remained relatively high. The certificates which had gone to various owners were, from time to time, purchasable on the New York Stock Exchange. When the price on the board was low, Texas land, obtainable through certificates, sometimes fell to fifty-five cents per acre. These facts were well known to Mr. Pierce as well as to the Kountze brothers.

"My Omaha Brother," as Augustus referred to Herman, "was first attracted to Pierce during his 'Kansas walking-stick days.'" Herman Kountze had promised Mr. Pierce he would make a financial connection with his "New York brother," should Pierce ever need an eastern connection. At that time, with $110,000 available, Pierce had not needed a New York correspondent, but now that he was "a pretty big dog in the puddle" and no longer able to afford the luxury of Little Dannie, he was more than pleased when Herman Kountze sought an interview with him.

Mr. Sullivan's New York correspondent had been Donnell, Lawson, and Simpson. The little business Pierce transacted in New

York naturally gravitated to them, until the Colonel passed through New York to Rhode Island for a visit with the home folks. While in the big city he decided to go around to 120 Broadway and pay a social call on "My New York brother, Augustus." As he entered the bank, he found only busy clerks engaged in routine duties. Looking about a moment and seeing he had entered unnoticed, he boomed out: "My God, sirs! I want to see Augustus Kountze." Almost instantly a placid stern man appeared from an inner office. Bowing, he invited: "Come this way, Mr. Pierce."

Snorting his surprise, Shanghai exclaimed: "My God, Brother Kountze! How in the hell did you know it was me, Sir?"

"O," replied the courteous banker, "you carry your introduction with you."

When Shanghai departed, his importance was more puffed up than usual. The New York banker had not only tendered the facilities of the New York, Omaha, and Denver banks for his accommodation, but August had expressed a desire that Herman, who was more or less an authority on cattle, should visit Pierce's ranch in person and advise them on the feasibility of buying grasslands on the coast and timberlands in East Texas. "You know," said banker Kountze, "that railroad sections may be bought on the New York Stock Exchange to our mutual benefit, provided, of course, Mr. Pierce, that you will be so kind as to direct the location of the certificates upon valuable lands after we have bought them for our joint account."

Shanghai had known the route to cheap railroad lands long before Kountze suggested the joint account. In fact, at that very moment, he had an order with Donnell, Lawson, and Simpson to buy twenty thousand dollars' worth of such certificates. Now, with the lure of a joint account with a banker, he neglected to call on his brokers and close out his account. He wanted more time to think about the Kountze Brothers' offer.

The neglect was fateful. A rumor got to the board that Kountze Brothers and Pierce contemplated extensive investments. The market jumped from fifty-five to sixty cents. Donnell, Lawson, and Simpson heard that Pierce had been in New York and surmised that he was going over to new brokers. They railed at him in a letter: "We remember you well. Any such amount thrown on the market, or inquired for, would materially affect the price." Then

"A pretty big dog in the puddle"

they bought on a rising market, but before the certificates could be delivered, the brokers went bankrupt.

Shanghai now turned to Augustus Kountze, in a dither, and Augustus smilingly rescued him with a minimum of loss. Kountze Brothers were now the trusted representative of A. H. Pierce.

Herman Kountze acted upon his brother's suggestion and was in Texas sooner than Shanghai had expected. Together they inspected thousands of acres of purchasable grasslands. Pierce laid stress on the land where Bob Stafford's cattle roamed. He called attention to the fact this former Kyle-Pierce buffer country was either railroad-grant land or owned by nonresident Texas army veterans. "The railroad land can be bought," he told Kountze, "through your brother on the stock exchange." The veterans had received their grants from the Republic of Texas, and many of them had removed from Texas to live out their declining years in comfort "back in the States." "They will sell their land cheap if we pay cash."

A special inspection was made of the land lying between the Crescent V Ranch (Ward and Pierce) and Pierce's prized BU Ranch, which extended along the Colorado River and far up into Wharton County. "Here," he said, pointing out to the prairie, "is grass belly deep to any old coaster—two hundred thousand acres of it. It has recently been turned over to Ira Evans. He represents the I. and G. N. RR Grant down here."

As Herman looked across the miles of waving grass—so different from the short grass country of the Platte—he was enthused with its possibilities. Forthwith he proposed that Kountze Brothers should go into the cattle business on an extensive scale in this region. "Kountze Brothers will furnish the cash," said Herman, "for the purchase of 200,000 acres, if you, Colonel Pierce, will supervise the selection and purchase of the land and the cattle to stock it. Of course, we will cut you in for an undisclosed one-sixth interest in the profits on the cattle."

One part of Kountze's mission was now accomplished. His "New York brother," so he said, would write the contract for signatures. Now he must visit the pine-timber section of East Texas. "Will you go along, Mr. Pierce?" Pierce would not. "Hell, no," he scoffed. "That damn walrous country won't raise anything but straight swamp angels."

The purchase of two hundred thousand acres by friends, with Pierce holding an "undisclosed one-sixth interest" without cost to himself was the ideal arrangement he had visualized. "This beats peacible Bill Kyle all hollow," he wrote to Jonathan. What he now had to do was buy the land.

He could not wait for the contract to come from New York to put land agents into action. I. N. Dennis operated out of Wharton. H. H. Kirkpatrick, clerk of the United States District Court, worked cautiously through H. M. Trueheart and Company, realtors; but lawyers, J. L. Croom and Son, aided and abetted by Attorney Masterson, arose in the path of the agents to confuse titles and demand extra legal fees and agent's commissions.

Spanish land-grant titles were complex enough at their best. Continuity of titles was not simplified by those San Jacinto veterans who had accepted land bonuses from the Republic of Texas, filed their deeds for record, and departed "to the States," leaving the fruits of their Mexican fighting to the "ravages of the Kings of the Ranch." Often as not these war veterans died without their heirs knowing of their Texas holdings. These complexities pleased Croom and Masterson, and they made the most of their opportunity.

Daniel Erasmus E. Braman, veteran and resident of Matagorda County since 1836, was not of the Masterson stripe. His information and recollection were amazing, and he was most helpful to Pierce in his efforts to untangle the chains of title for Texas veterans. More and more, the Colonel leaned on "Don Erasmus," as Pierce facetiously dubbed him. Croom, on the other hand, tried to win him over and put him against Pierce; then, when he failed, he lost his temper and stormed at Pierce: "I see you are just from Victoria, and I suppose you got information from our ancient and honored friend, Don Erasmus, the Up duke of Matagorda; and, of course, since Croom is interested, he has 'stuffed' you full. But be sure he has not 'rammed' the stuffing in the wrong end."

Colonel Pierce became aware of the fact that, at times, Croom could also be helpful. He could serve, if he would, as well as obstruct. Therefore, he sought to lure him away from the influence of Masterson. Finding Croom in need of money, he furnished it and defended his liberality in a letter to his attorney. "You see," he wrote, "I was Wright about letting him have the $35 it got him

"A pretty big dog in the puddle"

Coming my way & by todays Mail I will write him & give him Lotts of Taffy."

Masterson was more ingenious than penny-pinching Croom; and furthermore, he played for higher stakes. He was remarkably adept at finding "clouds" on titles to land which Kountze Brothers needed to establish their ranch. Consequently, Pierce came to hold the busybody lawyer in high contempt. On one occasion, Tom Nye made a land purchase for which, of course, Pierce furnished the money. Masterson suspected the subterfuge and forthwith brought suit for a Mr. Curry to try title. Repeatedly Nye caused the case to be set for trial, but Masterson, lacking merit in his suit, importuned the court to continue the cause of action. He was hoping that by this means he would force Nye to seek settlement on Masterson's terms. One day, after another continuance had been granted on the plea that "Plaintiff Curry has been away from the county on an extended tour and has had no opportunity to prepare his case for trial," Masterson approached Nye to ask who, in fact, was backing him in the litigation. When informed, Masterson replied: "Well, Tom, old Shang will see you through."

Late that evening Clay McSparren met Pierce at the ranch house. The weather was cold and damp, and the Colonel was in a fret to go out into the pasture and see how "that cow out there" was getting along. He ordered his buggy and team. He instructed Clay to have a big fire burning in the hearth. He would be late in returning.

Rain began to fall just as a stranger came up the walkway. He inquired: "Is this the Pierce Ranch?" He declined to enter the house, preferring to seek the Colonel in the pasture. Clay told him such would be useless, for even though by chance he might find him, still Mr. Pierce would talk to no one on the range. "He is still carrying that 30-30 rifle with him." The stranger, thereafter, was content to pace up and down the porch with his overcoat collar high around his ears. Finally night came, and with it the Colonel.

Old Nep met his master, took away the horses, and Pierce hastened to the house, where he was accosted on the porch by the stranger. Shang looked at him carefully, then said: "Mr. Curry, you have been hard to find these days."

"Yes, Colonel," replied Curry, "I have been traveling rather extensively of late."

Shanghai Pierce

"And I rather think," countered Pierce, "you will go places yet before you and Masterson get any of my money."

Then resuming a courteous demeanor, he opened the door to a pleasant fire, and bowing the unbidden guest into the room ahead of him, he made a hooking motion with his head toward McSparren as if to force him in to hear the conversation. He seated himself only after the others had been made comfortable. Then turning steady eyes on Curry, he waited.

With some sly hesitancy, Curry entered into an off-color proposal about the Nye lawsuit. The Colonel waited until the statement was complete, then said: "Mr. Curry, Colonel Peareson of Richmond, Texas, is my lawyer."

Again Curry made an approach. Again, Colonel Pierce stated: "Mr. Curry, Colonel Peareson of Richmond, Texas, is my lawyer."

A third and a fourth proposal were made. Each brought forth the identical reply. Then simulating anger, Mr. Curry arose to his feet, making the statement as he moved toward the door: "Colonel Pierce, I do not believe you are going to commit yourself on anything." With a smile, Pierce let fly his last shaft: "By God, Sir. When a man owns a dog, there is no use for him to do the barking himself."

As the sound of the retreating footsteps died away, Pierce turned to McSparren. "Clay," he said, "By God, Sir, never again will I try to buy a piece of land that Masterson has ever walked over until I get a quit-claim deed from him, whether he claims an interest in it or not."

Augustus Kountze was slow in preparing the agreement for Pierce's signature, consequently, he decided to visit his home folks in Rhode Island and sign the Kountze papers while he was in New York. He went by train to Fall River. There he hired a horse and carriage and drove down to West Port Harbor where he spent a month at a hotel kept by Captain Sowle. The Captain had married one of Abel's cousins. Each day he drove about the countryside heralding his approach by his stentorian voice. He never failed to drop in at the old farm house for a visit with Miranda and his cousin Flora. Long before he reached the house, he would call out what he wanted for dinner: "Cobb pie, sweetened with spiced apples, cooked in a kettle with beaten biscuits dropped on top . . . a good cup of black coffee." Then when he had eaten, he would inquire

"A pretty big dog in the puddle"

individually after all the neighbors, with his voice at the highest pitch: "How is Isaac Snell? Sam Jennings? John Luce . . . and all the crowd?"

Herman Kountze delayed him in New York much longer than he wanted to stay while the ranch agreement was being prepared. When the paper was presented to him, Pierce protested signing it "without my counsellor's advice," because, he said, "It is one of those long-winded documents full of 'whereases' and other stuff that is all foolishness and other bosh." It was neatly printed by a new machine which Augustus called a "typewriter," and the Colonel became so interested in the machine that he forgot the "whereases and other bosh," signed the agreement, and ordered a typewriter sent to the ranch, giving no thought to the fact that no one there would know how to operate it.

Pierce found that his troubles had only begun when he arrived at the ranch with a copy of the signed contract. One of his old Kansas associates had observed him growing from a whelp to "a pretty big dog in the puddle," so a mystical Thomas C. Martin, who was "just passing through the country," stopped long enough at El Rancho Grande to inquire of Shang's whereabouts. He scribbled a note and left it with the Widow Ward:

> I come down to see you on Busness that we Spoke of Seveal Years ago in Kansas. I could not make up my mind at that time to give you the information or evidence that you So Much Wanted against Sertain parties that had Ronged you. if you are Still in the Same Notion you was in Kansas we can work together. I can place you in a position that you can approach them allmost unsuspected of your intentions. Now Shang Write me Soon as you return home & if you want to Work at this it is a Sure Winning. I will come and give you dats that will open your Eyes, if you decline Write any How & *Keep This letter from Public Eyes.* I cannot work alone & have picked on you for the Most Sootable partie in my Knolage.

Shang kept the note in his pocket more than thirty days before he gave the conspirator his answer:

> It has been so [much] time Since I Saw you in Kansas I have almost forgotten to what business you refer—but never the less—I am getting old & health bad & while I know I have been treated badly by parties I think best to let by gones be forgotten. Should you

be in this Section at any time Call & See me & I will treat you as well as I know how.

After this link with the past was disposed of by an adroit side step, Pierce gave his attention to an irate neighbor who wrote his positive conviction that A. H. and J. E. Pierce were "trying to possess five beeves to which they had no title": "Shangs statements are all faults. I don't mean any violence—would not harm a man for the world—but if a man was to take my old hat and I told him to Stop he best do it. I will call and See you if necessary." It was not necessary.

Next to register a complaint was the Widow Robb, who would like to have the long overdue money Shanghai owed her on some hides. She would, she said, "be much obliged if you can Settle that little account without delay. Be sure and don't let anything keep you from a Settlement *this time* but Send me the Money and oblige a Friend in need. I want to take my little blind girl to the Dr."

Troubles had been left in the wake of the real estate agents, also. In the effort to buy 200,000 acres for Kountze Brothers, Pierce's agents had bought in such a fashion, in many instances, as to place owners of small tracts within the Pierce Circle. Alexander Morris was one of these. This man had moved off to Gonzales County and left his cattle, but "each year I found fewer and fewer of my cattle than I expected." He also found that Pierce had "fenced him around" and was refusing to pay him a rental on the land he had enclosed. Morris forthwith demanded that the land be cut out of the Pierce Circle or that rentals be paid. "You certainly do not Expect me to by land for you to Enclose & Graze without Cost and pay the taxes on it in the bargain. I have stood for it [a] long time & Wont Stand it any longer. Your excuse that you do not need the land does not release you from Compensate me for the use of it as long as you graze your cattle on it."

Fred Sparks was another "inside owner" who could neither be swept aside nor fenced around without trouble. Before the trouble developed fully, however, good news was relayed by Shanghai to his bookkeeper: "I understand our Illustrious Friend Fred Sparks has taken his departure from Edna for Hell no doubt if there is Such place."

Left: Thomas Jefferson Hamilton, who studied to be a priest
Right: Ben Thompson at the age of twenty-nine, as he appeared in Wichita, Kansas, in 1872 (Courtesy of Ed Bartholomew, Rose Collection)

Walnut Street, Ellsworth, Kansas, 1873 (Courtesy of the Kansas State Historical Society)

John Wesley Hardin,
after his trip to Kansas
(Courtesy of Ed Bartholomew,
Rose Collection)

Captain H. L. McNelly,
who worked long enough for the "black Republicans"

"A pretty big dog in the puddle"

Over on the Colorado River, a Mr. Charlton was hanging on tenaciously "to My place where I have lived so long and worked so hard." Before he would go, he wrote Pierce, "I have one thing to ask of you and I hope you will be kind enough to grant it. I want something for what I have here. You know my improvements are common but comfortable and convenient. I am in debt. I have a wife and three children to support; to vacate the house I built, the fields I opned for nothing is hard indeed; and you must remember I have enemies in this country and the lies they tell about me are not true. I have never done a hair's bredth of injury in no way. I appreciate your energy in accumulating so fine a fortune, and I think you will enjoy it still better after you have given me something for what I have."

The Colonel read Charlton's appeal and remarked: "Yes, not much more than half them damn lies they tell about me, either are true." The letter was passed over to J. Y. Phillips, who soon reported: "I have digested all matters with Charlton. I find him to be a hard *Case* to put it Mildly. I bought his cane to get possession."

Mrs. Maggie E. Minnich, who with her sister, Mrs. Golden, owned an interest in a tract of land within the Pierce Circle, was not as easy to dispose of as the "Pierce-fearing" Charlton nor the "Hellbound" Sparks. Kountze Brothers' agent learned that Mrs. Minnich had no intention of disposing of her property. As a consequence, the Colonel bought a tax title to the acreage, then turned his cattle on to the land to graze it clean. Of course, Mrs. Minnich complained, and Pierce replied with an inadequate offer of purchase. Shanghai had little hope that Mrs. Minnich would weaken, but he thought the land might be bought through her sister whose "husband is a S. B. Labor leader and will soon need money." In this he was right, but not before Mrs. Minnich had demonstrated she was not subject to bluff. "I receaved your letter," she wrote Shanghai, "but I would mutch rather Sean you personaly. I am not willing to sell my interest in that land. what I wanted to See you for was to See if you was in earnest when you Sead you would take your money back and give me a quit clame to my interest & Mrs. Goldens interest. Now give me a business answer. I am tired of foolishness. I mean to buy the rest of that land or inter Suit for the rest of it. Anyway I could not Sign the deed you brought me & besides I would be Selling more land than was in the place there.

and you had misrepresented things to me. and If I sold to you for that cignifigent Price I would Spite myself & I know if I Sell to you that you will never pay Mrs. Golden anything and she is my Sister & I am duty Bound to do my duty by her. as you Seamed to regrett as you call it to not have the pleasure to quarell with me any more, I will alow you that pleasure. You Seamed very Mutch offended at Something I wrote if I wrote anything out of the way, I am Sorry. I would not insult any one *by letter*."

Shanghai Pierce was not the only "Big Pasture Man" who was encroaching upon small ranchers and "nesters" and fencing them in. This caused the Big Pasture Men to get a thorough airing before the Texas legislature. So much pressure had been brought upon a legislature which was normally a cattleman's legislature that this honorable body was considering the enactment of both a "herd law" and an "anti-enclosure law." When the news came to El Rancho Grande, Pierce stormed: "That will cook my bacon crisp before I am ready to eat it." This was an inopportune time for legislative interference. He had not completed purchasing the 200,000 acres for Kountze Brothers, and he had many other acres he wanted to buy, also, for himself. Therefore, he wrote to his lawyer, already a member of the legislature: "McCamley, it is time to set out some wolf bait," and Fred McCamley became not only the legislative representative from Fort Bend County, but the trap-setter for the Big Pasture Men.

McCamley's first report was encouraging:

> I ret'd from Austin last night and will return again this week. Anything like a herd law will not pass and the only thing now to do is to oppose and fight the fool legislation on the subject of opening roads and making it punishable for one man to build a fence enclosing another's land and a great many other measures having for their object the destruction of the large pastures and the only consolation is that if such measures are passed that they are either unconstitutional *or can never be enforced in this section.*

To this information on the status of the cattlemen's affairs at Austin, McCamley appended the query: "Would it be asking too much to request you to advance me at this time the $500 which will be due for services at Austin?"

"A pretty big dog in the puddle"

In spite of the services of the five-hundred-dollar inside lobbyist, the "nonenclosure law" passed. This gave courage to some who had not previously known how to contend with the Big Pasture Man. W. S. Sartwell, who identified himself as "Grand High Priest of the Grand Royal Arch Chapter H.T.W.S.S.T.K.S.," now called upon Pierce in terms both firm and gentlemanly to give him justice:

Col. A. H. Pierce,
Dear Sir:
When we feel aggrieved, I believe it always best to state candidly the matter to the party offending, consequently in my long life I have had no vexatious lawsuits and unpleasant relations with my fellow man. Years ago you and your brother got up your first large pasture and I helped you all I could by leasing to you (my voluntary offer) for Ten Years all our lands some 2,800 acres at a nominal Rent. You left these lands in such a Shape that I had great difficulty in getting justice from Mr. Ward, but I am happy to state that Mr. Ward has paid Satisfactory rent for our lands in his Pasture Since Your Ten year lease expired. Since that time you have without my consent, or without even consulting me, 354 acres of my land enclosed in another Pasture of yours.
I presume Col Pierce then in your numerous engagements, and great press of business, you have overlooked this small matter, when presented to you; whether there is much or little grass on my land is not the question. You know the law relative to enclosing or fencing in another man's land without permission, and I must believe that you will be willing to do what is right, fair, honorable and gentlemanly. I therefore ask you to pay me five cents an acre per annum for the land since you had it enclosed.

Herrin and Wren were other "inside owners" who availed themselves of the new law. Again Pierce resorted to the expedient of a tax title, but the owners sued him, recovering judgment, and charged him with the cost, but not until Pierce had blocked their ingress and egress by building a fence, wholly on his own land and using the impassable river as one fence line. He then grazed it to the grassroots, and advised the owners: "If you don't like what I've done, I know of no law prohibiting you from moving your land from my pasture!"

Mr. Wren did not like it, and he said so, in convincing terms:

> When I alluded to the fact that I will take steps to have my interest placed, or fenced, outside of your pasture, I was not dealing in mythical ideas or physical impossibilities; and when you say you know of no law prohibiting me from moving my land from your pasture, you show signs of want to *Squeeze* me. I do not desire to squeeze you nor to be squeezed by you.
>
> But as you invite me to take my land bodily from your pasture— a physical impossibility—you, in effect, say to me that it is in my pasture, no one else will buy it, and I have you at my mercy.
>
> Now let me say to you in all candor that I have rights and know them fully, in support of which assertion I refer you to the general laws . . . an act to prohibit the unlawful fencing and enclosing, or keeping enclosed, of the lands of another. and upon conviction fined in the sum of *not less* than 50 cents nor more than one dollar per acre each month so enclosed, or fined and imprisoned in the county jail for any period not over two years. . . . I could give you a lot of Trouble. . . . I must in justice to myself proceed against you.

Not being willing to test his strength against one who wrote so convincingly, Shanghai called upon his "counsellor," who made the best trade he could.

Through buying, trading, bluffing, and enclosing without consent Pierce had cut the very heart out of the free range which was so highly prized by Bob Stafford. B. D. Crary and F. C. McReynolds took over as superintendents of the K and KO ranches, but Shanghai's job was yet incomplete. He had to find twelve thousand steers with which to stock the ranches.

A. H. and J. E. Pierce already had the greater portion of the purchasable better grades of their neighbor's cattle under contract. Consequently, Kountze's cattle would have to come from distant ranges. Augustus Kountze began to push him. "Time is passing rapidly," he wrote, "and I do not see that the 12 000 head of yearlings proposed to be driven into the enclosure of Ranch No. 1 are ready to be branded & occupy the field. I earnestly hope that you will not fail of success. I can assure you I greatly appreciate your kind offer in this matter and I am quite sure Col. Crary will feel glad all over. Keep me fully advised by letter or telegram of the situation as to yearlings & progress made day by day in stocking Ranch No. 1."

"A pretty big dog in the puddle"

Buying twelve thousand steer yearlings and turning them loose on a new range was far from Pierce's idea of being the most profitable way to run a ranch; consequently, he telegraphed Kountze: "We are better off to buy heifers than to buy one year old steers." This sagacious advice fell on deaf New York ears, and protesting volubly that all he could expect to buy would be "Little Hard Eastern Texas Devills, swamp angels, and saddlepocket dogies," he and a crew fanned out deep in the piney-wood region of Texas, two hundred miles from Ranch No. 1. With the closing days of August (1885), bookkeeper G. S. Hamilton sent a memorandum to New York: "The last one and Twos received were from Dayton. They were very good ones. Have contracted enough to fill out the 12 000." Pierce's job was finished, but it would be two years before he could collect his "undisclosed one-sixth interest."

10. "*There shall be no town naming to the exclusion of my perpetuity*"

While the K and KO ranches were being formed, Pierce's agents also took title to a vast area from the Tres Palacios to a point north and west of Wharton on the Colorado. This was his dream ranch. Headquarters was established on the fringe of the timber, facing out toward the Kountze prairie. Carpenters built a comfortable dwelling. George Stidham Hamilton moved up from El Rancho Grande with the A. H. and J. E. Pierce books. Brother Jonathan, Susan, and her husband, Mr. Wiley, were left to their own resources.

One day the Colonel was reading the San Antonio *Light* when he saw the headline:

"There shall be no town naming"

>Mrs. Mackay
>Revised Details of Her
>Interesting History
>from the Working
>Woman.

These "revised details" gave color to a rumor which had been making the rounds that a railroad was to be built from a connection with the Southern Pacific, near Richmond, west of Houston, straight through Wharton, Victoria, and into Mexico. Such a railroad, of course, would bisect both his and Kountze's pasture. He pored over the paper, absorbing every detail. Colonel D. E. Hungerford was to be the new vice president of the railroad. Hungerford's promotion to a colonelcy had been like Pierce's—assumed. Mackay's story had its day in print in California. Now the *Light* copied it, since Hungerford was transferring his operations to Texas.

Hungerford had been a journeyman barber in New York, but when the Mexican War broke out he joined General Winfield Scott to carry a musket toward Mexico City. On the march across Texas, the coastal grasslands impressed him immensely. After many close shaves in the land of the Montezumas, Hungerford stacked arms and started wielding his razor again, this time in fabulous San Francisco. In that faraway city his employer was George W. Ciprico, or "Dago George," as he was better known.

George's shop was really the *ne plus ultra* of all the West. He named it "The Montgomery Baths" to suggest westerners' Saturday-night needs. It was to this place that gold panners and gentleman-rats flocked to measure the yellow metal by the pinch in exchange for the inevitable Saturday-night spree. Hungerford became known as "Jack-the-barber." He was little more than settled in his employment before he began trumpeting the beauty of his daughters, Edna and Louise, whom he had been forced to leave in New York because of a lack of funds. Ciprico was so captivated by the descriptions of their beauty that he advanced five hundred dollars for boat passage to Frisco. The girls arrived in due time, took up a seven-year residence in the home of Ciprico, and became bosom friends of the Ciprico daughters, each family teaching the other its native tongue.

Shanghai Pierce

Just as Louise reached her nineteenth birthday, Jack left his benefactor to set up a shop for himself at Mokehunne Hill. Louise acted as her father's housekeeper in a one-room lean-to at the rear of the barbershop. There a Dr. Bryant who lived at Nevada City about a hundred miles away discovered her, and they soon married. The doctor's propensity for "potent potions" (according to a news account) labeled him as "a man of dissolute habits." After three years of marriage and unrestrained indulgence, he developed an advanced case of the "wobbles" and died of delirium tremens.

From this union Louise had a child she called Eva. The doctor had left no property with which they might keep bodies and souls together, so Louise deferred soul-saving for the time being and turned camp-follower. In the language of a news reporter, "she tried a hand at keeping a boarding house for miners." At the boardinghouse she met J. W. Mackay, superintendent of a bullion mine. Mackay was comfortable, owning a cabin of two rooms, and these he shared with Louise and Eva. The new Mrs. Mackay fitted into the life of the miner until he struck it rich, becoming fabulously wealthy overnight. Now with more money at her disposal than she had previously thought existed, she felt the need for globe-trotting, so, taking her rich husband back with her to San Francisco, she recruited for a cruise. "Pappa" dropped his "Jack-the-barber" nickname and appropriated a "colonelcy." Both he and his daughter, Edna, were quite willing to travel with Louise and Eva at the miner's expense. The party, therefore, put to sea, and, as the girls had acquired fluent use of the Italian language, the Mackay-Hungerford party made port in Italy.

The Bonanza Queen became the talk of European society at the Riviera. She even attracted a count, Joseph Telferner, to Edna for a husband. When interest in his American wife lagged, the Count was forced to hear fabulous stories from voluble Colonel Hungerford. But when he told of the trek across the grasslands of Texas, Count Telferner's interest was aroused. Telferner had previously ventured in railroad-building, and he yet dreamed of finding a new land where he might colonize his overcrowded people. This dream now took form. With Mackay's money he would build a Texas railroad. His own people would furnish the labor. "Italians will colonize the region and reap the harvest. My family will live in perpetuity."

"There shall be no town naming"

A. H. Pierce saw newspaper rumors turn into surveying parties. Colonel Hungerford escorted Count Telferner and Mr. Mackay through Texas. They planned the general route of the railroad. In its ethereal stage it stretched from New York to Mexico. They applied for a charter and christened it the New York, Texas and Mexican Railway Company. Joseph Telferner was elected president; Colonel Hungerford graced the vice-presidency; and Victoria was corporate headquarters. The finances were assured to be secure in the hands of Treasurer G. A. Levi. Legal advice was to be had from the Proctors. Then six hundred Italian laborers swarmed in with picks, shovels, and spike mauls. Rail-laying began at both Victoria and Rosenburg, building toward the middle. A connection was made at Rosenburg with the Galveston, Harrisburg and San Antonio Railway Company, which had already been constructed toward the west by Thomas Wentworth Peirce,[1] Shanghai's kinsman. Local Texans found the corporate name clumsy upon their tongues, so, observing the chief diet of the Italian construction workers, they dubbed the railroad "The Macaroni."

Town-naming soon came up on Count Telferner's agenda. "Yes, my family must live in perpetuity," he said, and stations were given these names: Telferner, Mackay, Hungerford, Louise, Edna, and Inez. Town-naming, Pierce conceded, was the prerogative of the owners. In this case, though, it would have to be different. "The road runs over my land, and town naming must not be done to the exclusion of *my* perpetuity." Therefore, he reserved for himself two stations, "Pierce" and "Shanghai." Then, in an afterthought for his nephew, he added "Borden."

Now that the railroad had established shipping points along its line, Pierce was ready to load cattle instead of driving them. The general manager, Allen McCoy, made arrangements to handle the business that Pierce offered. "I will," he wrote, "have a man go over to the Site for Pens Friday or Saturday so as to be there when your Nephew is to Stake off the ground." He would not, however, build the pens at the expense of the railroad, but he said: "We will charge on the Lumber less than car load the same as for a load, which is very little you know, as our Lumber rates are nominal &

---

[1] Thomas Wentworth Peirce later changed the spelling of his name to *Pierce*, as his kinslady, Flora Bodington, said, "to show he belonged to the aristocrats."

Shanghai Pierce

non-paying." The shipping pens were erected, and on March 25, 1884, Shanghai placed an order for "one hundred cars Stock April 15 proximo." Allen McCoy was prompt with his reply:

> We will be ready to begin this movement of your 100 cars Stock April 15 proximo. But it must be borne in mind that barring accidents to prevent, this does not mean on or *about* that time.

There was nothing Pierce could do about this railroad attitude. He conformed to McCoy's demand and the cattle went on their way. He did not, however, forget the tone of the letter. Later, while in Galveston, he called at the freight office of the G. C. and S. F. Ry. Co., which had ample shipping facilities at near-by Rosenburg and which was a real competitor of the N. Y. T. and M. R.R. Co. He then took more than a common delight in informing the N. Y. T. and M. freight agent:

> I was in Galveston yesterday & saw Mr. Resique of Santafee in regards to Stock Cars & he informed me if the Cars was to be had he would get them for me. I know, or feel fully Satisfied he will have them. Will there be any trouble about your moving them. My Cattle go to Cuba, therefore I Cannot name the exact date, as the Ships arrival depends on the Good Lord Wind & Weather.

Until N. Y. T. and M. engines began running through the BU pasture, Pierce's cow ponies were the fastest things on foot around the ranch. Some of the boys were not willing to concede that even a "Macaroni" engine could outdistance them, so one day Pierce's men set out to run a race with an engine, and a horse fell, killing itself. Pierce, who was on the train, presented a claim for damages to General Manager McCoy. After referring the bill for damages to Mr. Whalen, "who," according to McCoy, "makes adjustments (after investigation) of Stock Claims," the general manager wrote:

> As to the Horse which you claim as having been killed, you will find that the facts in the case will not warrant or justify our entertainment of any claim for this animal. The accident was caused by your men *running a race* with our train & the horse in question having become unmanageable ran across the tracks with rider & fell as he crossed but was not touched by our Engine. And it may be

"There shall be no town naming"

you will call to mind the circumstances *as you were on the train at the time.*

As time went on, Allen McCoy was succeeded by Mr. M. D. Monserrat, who held the title of General Superintendent of both the N. Y. T. and M. and the Gulf, Western Texas and Pacific Railway Company, which had consolidated. These roads, in turn, went to the Southern Pacific. General Freight Agent W. J. Craig held Pierce to a strict compliance with the company regulations. Pierce lost his temper and fired a blast at the freight department, but Monserrat tried to placate him in his reply:

> I have your favor 14th., enclosing letter from Mr. W. J. Craig, G.F.A., and your reply thereto.
> You call my attention to your letter and say: I was uncommonly mild, being religiously inclined and tomorrow being Sunday.
> I congratulate Mr. Craig on the fact that you were so inclined; had the contrary been the case, and the next day not been Sunday, he would have fared very hard if the enclosure is one of your religious addresses. I trust that we shall never have occasion to listen to or read any of the other kind. I shall write to Mr. Craig and enclose your letter.
> In concluding I beg that you will exercise your well known patience and I have no doubt that in the end you will be satisfied with Mr. Craig's action in the premises.

At this juncture, the newly appointed trainmaster, L. S. Daniels, took notice of the Colonel's ruffled feelings by passing along a few bubbles of soft soap when he wrote:

> I Know you *Can* appreciate the situation, while there are some who *cannot* or Will *not*. We have been in great stress for Stock cars for 3 Weeks, during which time orders have poured in. I have had to battle hard to "Keep the Peace," and, so far, no broken bones, though 2 or 3 parties have wanted to "punch" me while others have wanted to "Wine" me, but I didn't want either. Much prefer BU *Milk*. I have ordered cars for you for tomorrow, and hope you will load them on arrival, as is characteristic of You.

Several of Pierce's cattle got in the path of engines, and one steer went under a locomotive, causing a passenger-train wreck. These incidents did not add up to increased good relations. Then another animal was killed near the stock pens at a point where the general superintendent had wanted to fence the tracks, but the Colonel had objected because the narrow crossing over the tracks did not provide enough space for easy handling of his cattle. As soon as the animal was killed, Colonel Pierce filed a claim for damages, and Shanghai forthwith was the recipient of the following letter:

> Mr. C. S. Wells, our stock claim agent, has handed me your favor 26th, inst, in which you inform him that one of your steers had been killed at the end of the switch for which you put the price down to $10.00, which you say is little over half the price and leave it to me to say whether it shall be paid. I am sorry you placed me in that position. I have given the matter much consideration and have decided against you for the following reason. The company desires to fence in all its track, except at crossings where cattle guards would be placed on both sides, thereby reducing the killing of cattle to a minimum, and of course, except in cases of gross neglect, would not be responsible for any killed on the crossing. The openings which the company proposed to put in, and which are required by law, were considered by you insufficient for your business, and in compliance with your request no fence was put up between the bridge east and the end of the switch west of Pierce Station. You will remember the conversation we had on the subject at the time, and although you did not actually agree not to put in any claim for any animal we might kill, yet it was tacitly understood by both of us, certainly by me, that you would make no claim for cattle killed within that space as long as proper care was taken to avoid killing same. Under these circumstances, and by reason of the authority given me by you to decide whether the steer should be paid for, I am constrained to decide against you; and as you have so liberally struck off one half the value of the animal, I shall be no less liberal and strike off the other half, hoping that there will be no more killing in the neutral ground.

The Southern Pacific traffic department got another one of Shanghai's "religious addresses" soon thereafter. Mr. C. C. Gibbs parried that by writing: "There is so much human nature in your letter that I am overpowered, and have given the Agent the notice to give you the rate." Then Mr. Gibbs was succeeded by Mr. Gerken,

"There shall be no town naming"

who tried to hold the Colonel in line by promising: "I hope my actions will prove to you that I am as willing as my predecessor to accommodate you, having bought a supply of elasticity."

The "supply of elasticity," however, was insufficient when Pierce brought up the subject of construction of a new depot for his accommodation. He wrote his complaint in positive terms and couched in it a threat of reprisal:

> Mr. T. D. Forbes
> Victoria Texas
> Dr Sir
>
> You have been promising to build a depot Here for Last Two years & Make a ditch to carry the water of that corner down for 3 miles West of me through your R.R. ditches & turn it loose on me Now Forbes the two New Rice farms believe me are shipping Lotts of frt to this point & no place to put it & forbearance has ceased to be a Virtue & my Entire stock of Patience exhausted & I want to know wheather or not you Intend to build a good respectable Depot at this Place or not & not some old depot moved from some other Point.
>
> Let me hear from you & oblige.

The Colonel did hear from Forbes, but he was not "obliged" with a new depot; whereupon Pierce proposed that he would buy the lumber, provided the railroad company would ship the material and erect the depot without further cost to him. This proposal was given the usual railroad "in-channels" handling, but ultimately Mr. Gibbs gave him an answer:

> Your favor of the 21st inst. was duly rec'd and would have had earlier attention but for the fact that I wished to get Mr. Monserrate's views on the subject, he being the Superintendent. The matter of construction of depots, warehouses, etc., is entirely under his supervision I am happy to say that I have just heard from him, and he looks favorably upon your proposition. I will therefore take pleasure in deadheading the car of lumber from Lake Charles, whenever you are ready to ship Please advise me when you wish to ship, so that I may give the necessary instructions beforehand.

Finally Pierce's depot was erected. Clay McSparren and Shanghai sat on a pile of lumber watching the painter put on the finishing touches. On the end of the depot he was painting:

PIERCE STATION

Suddenly, Shanghai jumped up and pointed his finger toward the new sign, shouting at the same time: "Hold on there, by God, Sir. Put the apostrophe S on it. I own it, don't I? I paid for it." Accommodatingly, the painter stenciled:

PIERCE'S STATION

and it so remained for many years afterwards.

11. *"I'm scienced in ranchin'"*

Mr. Pierce sat in his "counsellor's" office. He was by no means pleased that anyone would undertake to suggest how he should run his business. "No, Sir," he snapped. "It is the custom of the country, Sir, not just the custom that prevails among cattlemen. That is one thing I think I'm scienced in—running a ranch. I never make bad breaks. But I am eternally lawing; up to my eyes now. I will never get out until I'm dead, or all the lawyers and surveyors are dead. Then I would have it all my own way."

Despite the handicaps of lawyers and surveyors, the new BU Ranch was taking on an appearance which even pleased Hattie. The residence stood one mile east of the "Macaroni" station. A front room on the lower floor had been set apart for Mr. Hamilton and his big books. The upper story was furnished comfortably for Mrs. Pierce and Miss Mamie, during such times as she would stay at the ranch while Hattie was there. Mr. Hamilton ("G. S. H," as he signed himself, or "HL" connected, his brand, if he happened to be taking a little too much "tea" and thinking in terms of his own

South Texas, showing the area of Shanghai Pierce's interests

"I'm scienced in ranchin'"

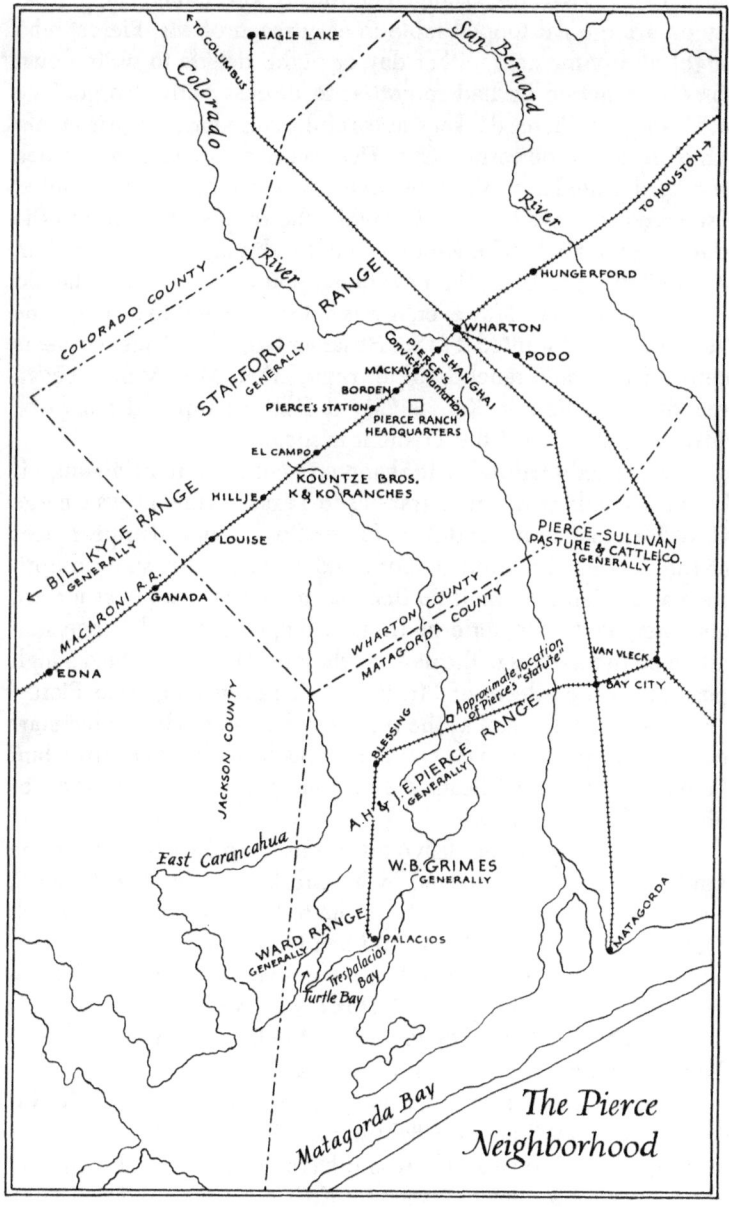

The Pierce Neighborhood

cattle) supervised the arrangement of his workroom. The journal lay on a large flat-topped table in easy reach of Mr. Pierce, who might at any moment, either day or night, decide to write down some transaction he had forgotten to discuss with George. The A. H. and J. E. Pierce docket was carefully stored in a large iron safe which stood in the corner. G. S. H.'s fine, sharp-pointed pen stuck in a spring holder on the table. Near it was a blunt, ball-pointed Esterbrook reserved for the Colonel, who dipped it deep into the black copy ink when he wrote his multitudinous letters. Hamilton was delighted to be at the new ranch house, "away from the old crank, the grunter." However, it was not turning out to be the home the Colonel had wanted it to be. He lamented, "It took me two years before I got me a ranch built all right," then Miss Mamie began spending her time in Kansas City if Hattie happened not to be down at Galveston at the Tremont in society.

It was only natural that Shanghai's cobb-pie tours among his kinsmen would result in migrations to Texas. His nephews George C. Gifford and Frank and Abel Pierce Borden put in appearances at the new headquarters. Gifford and A. P. Borden showed aptitude as cattlemen. Frank Borden was more than handy as a clerk and merchant. A coterie of friends, employees, and hangers-on attached themselves to the new ranch. John McCroskey held a high position in the esteem of Mr. Pierce. "I raised him," said Pierce. "He is as honest a man as the sun ever shown on. He did not start out to beat anybody. You can tell by his looks. I would trust him behind a mountain!" Besides that, John was a distant relative of Shanghai's deceased wife.

Isaac Flagg did not leave his former employer with the same kind of a reputation enjoyed by McCroskey. At least that was T. W. Babcok's opinion, which he wrote to the Colonel: "Mr. Pearch Dear Sir   after Respects to you i Send you isac flags Bill for groceries to Wich if you can collect for me you will greatly oblige a friend the sum of $58.38½ cts i Think isac had Better Pay Me as i hav acomotated him with Provishon Medacens & Clothen when he could not get the favors anywhere Elce."

Casper Bell was another one who bore a reputation. He was known as "something of a fightin' man," and loyalty and fightin' were qualities Pierce surely would have need of. Loyalty was not to be confined wholly to Casper, for Ed Taylor professed his friend-

"I'm scienced in ranchin' "

ship to Shanghai while at the same time calling for money: "Mr. Pierce   Dear Sir Will pleas Send to me ten dollars 10.00 By My Brother Reuben   I want to pay My Taxes, and Fixs My Business up, before I leave for work. I Ever remain Your devoted friend untill death. I am ready to move at your Call."

Ed was to get that call much sooner than he thought!

Then, too, there was William Chin, who "had to have $20 Sent to Anner My wife by first opportunity," and Jack Beans, who "has no money to grub himself," and "the nigger dude from Gainesville," whom Pierce did not want around anyway. Other Negro cowmen, not to forget the indispensable Neptune Holmes, were Robert and John Norman, Charlie Ellis, Ed Roberts, Jasper Singleton, and the genial, poker-playing Gabriel Sims, who didn't think "Mr. Pierce was ever a fightin' man, just a citizen-man." The most colorful man on the ranch, not excluding Shanghai himself, was Podo, the tall Kaffir from Zululand, Union of South Africa. He moved about the ranch with a dignity in keeping with his pastoral people. Taller than Mr. Pierce, carrying a staff even taller than himself, and wearing abbreviated pants in lieu of a breechcloth, Podo would wend his way unhurried over the ranch in contrast to the general bustle found there. He was, however, a source of constant annoyance to John McCroskey, for upon him fell the responsibility of keeping Podo supplied with liquor. Mr. Johnnie would write to Shanghai: "Send half bariel two Dollar whiskey per gal. for Podo. He wants it"; or "Ship thing for Podo, ½ barriel Whiskey, 1 barriel flour, 50 pounds Coffee, down to Podo Bridge."

Those serving at the ranch house were Elvira Miller—"old Vi," as the Colonel called her—"Violet," as her son Jesse called her —and Mr. A. P. Borden's faithful Ida Malone, known as "Idar" to Colonel Pierce. To these, Colonel Pierce added G. W. Carson, Willie Labauve, Ed Partain, and last, but not least, Clay McSparran; and he was ready to market his cattle.

"Big Belly" Asa Dawdy gathered a herd from the southern part of the range and started them northwest. They stampeded at Gonzales during the night. Without pants or shoes, he mounted his horse, and lost his little toe as the horse collided with a tree. Nephew Gifford got off to a better start, but from Hackberry, Indian Territory, this trail boss wrote the Colonel some of his troubles.

> Cattle are doing well, not So with the horses thay look worse than Thay did when you wer her three of them are dead and thair is two or three moore that I think will die Soon unless thay improve very fast. we are washing them with sheep dip but have seen no great improvement. Hamilton & I have been to the Eagle Chief country and we like it better than eny place we have seen yet. We will hold thair if we can do no better. July 14–2 Head of cattle killed by lightning one bull and two steers have died. no one has paid eny taxes yet and I shall hold off paying as long as posible. Regards to Willie and love to all the young ladies rite soon.

Bernard Miller nursed his fever-ridden horses as far up as Ogallala before he registered his troubles. "I write you this afternoon," he told Pierce, "to tell you I am Still taking care of all your Horses except that poorest one in the bunch it has died." After posting this, he thought he had not been sufficiently explicit; therefore, he mailed another letter:

> Mr. Pierce, your horses have all had the pinkeye and they all got well but two and they have gone to rest, but they have the worms very bad and if you will furnish me with Salt and Copers I think I can cure them.

While the trail drivers were having their woes, Shanghai decided to follow along after them. The season was unusually warm and the country along the route was extremely short of water. Local cattlemen were pre-empting near-by watering places and preventing transient cattle from drinking up the limited supply. One Pierce herd had suffered intensely because of the water shortage, and Shanghai was greatly pleased when he finally came upon a water hole. He was disappointed, however, when a local cattleman, fortified with a sufficient number of Winchesters, positively forbade Shanghai to let a single cow stick her muzzle into the precious water. The Colonel talked loudly about his right. Then he tried "taffy." He even offered cash, but to no avail. He was wasting his breath.

That evening Pierce moved his cattle along the trail and bedded them down dry. When the cattle got quiet, he held a "star council." He and some of his trusties then disappeared in the darkness and headed back toward the water hole. Some hours later a

"I'm scienced in ranchin'"

small bunch of the water-hole owner's beeves, with Shanghai and his boys whanging them hurriedly along, overtook and passed around the Pierce herd. Shanghai was particular that they should be driven along the regular trail. "Drive 'em hard toward Kansas till their tongues drag the ground," shouted Shanghai as he dropped back with his own herd. When daylight came, he looked earnestly over the horizon, but no cattle were to be seen, except his own thirsty brutes. The morning was well spent when the gentlemen with the Winchesters appeared. Not too politely they informed Pierce: "We have lost a herd of beeves. We would like to cut yours."

"Sure, boys. Help yourselves. Take it easy. Look carefully. We are in no hurry."

The Winchester men made their ride through the cattle. Nothing except the BU brand was found. They apologized and headed south again. On the second day, and again on the third, the same men came back with the same request. On the fourth day, old Shanghai met them with his full force armed with his own Winchesters. "No damn grease sack outfit," he said in understandable terms, "can trail cut my herd four successive days. Get goin'."

As Shanghai afterwards told it: "When I did finally catch up with them advance cattle I just didn't take any time to show 'em the way back home. And come to think of it, considering the natural increase of cattle on the road, that was a rather profitable drive, although pretty dry."

Somewhere along the trail, Shanghai heard that one of his bosses was having trouble over on Dodge prairie. Good cowboys were at a premium and he had to hire a nester to help out in an emergency. The chief accomplishment of this new hired man had been the growing of a long black moustache. The granger knew none of the arts of handling cattle. His awkwardness instantly incurred the displeasure of old Shanghai, who stopped long enough to help shape up the herd. The new hired man went about his work in plodding, plow-handle fashion.

"Get some action on yourself, Moustache," shouted Shanghai. "You ought to have hold of them plow handles right now."

Of course this brought a laugh from nester-detesting cowmen. It also goaded Old Handlebars into action. After a few moments, Pierce's high-pitched voice could be heard over the noise of the lowing cattle.

Shanghai Pierce

"Cool down a little, Moustache. You have already run over a cow, knocked down a yearling, and killed a calf."

When the work on Dodge prairie was finished, Pierce rode into the city to "shoot the bull" with some of his Texas cronies. They met in the Wright Hotel. It was a colorful aggregation—Dun Houston, Uncle Henry Stephens, John Blocker, Lum Slaughter, Ike T. Pryor—representing Texas' best cattle ranchers. They were his competitors and friends. Even Ike Pryor, who had lost his wife and was now heavy on the social side of the Bob Stafford fold because of Bob's attractive sister, welcomed old Shang to the party. They were such "big bore" men that the hotel had reserved a table for them separate and apart from the common herd. At the head of the table Shanghai took command.

It was into this scene that Andy Adams realistically stumbled. Andy was making his first trip up. He had drunk nothing invigorating since he left Texas, so, when he pulled into Dodge City, he began bar-hopping until his barrel-fever status caused his boss to suggest a cigar for a "top off." With unlighted cigar in his mouth, Adams marched off to the Wright Hotel dining room. "There," said Andy, "I saw, last but not least, Shanghai Pierce, the most widely known cattleman between the Río Grande and the British possessions. He stood six-feet-four in his stockings, was gaunt and rawboned, and the possessor of a voice, which in ordinary conversation could be distinctly heard across the street." Shanghai was chiding a cattle solicitor who wanted him to stop his herd at Dodge instead of moving them farther northward. "No, I'll not ship any more cattle to your town," boomed Shanghai's voice, vibrating with indignation, "until you adjust your yardage charges. Listen! I can go right into the heart of your city and get a room for myself, with a nice clean bed in it, plenty of soap, water, and towels, and I can occupy that room for twenty four hours for *two bits*. And your stockyards, 'way in the suburbs, want to charge me *twenty cents a head and let my steers stand out in the weather.* No! I'll not ship any more cattle to your town."

He was not going to let Dodge mistreat his sea lions, and the cattle moved on toward Ogallala. As a matter of fact, those identical cattle had been under contract to be delivered to Seth Mabry, at Ogallala, since the previous March. Seth had lured Shanghai to drive and ship two thousand steers, promising to pay twenty

"I'm scienced in ranchin' "

dollars a head "at Ogallala, if they are full age Cattle this spring and the shipping don't injure them to Much this Shipping is a new thing and I cant Say how cattle will look I must winter the Cattle and can't afford to buy poor ones but if they are in fair condition will take them."

Seth Mabry's March 17 letter reached Shanghai at Fort Worth just after he had delivered some of the best cattle he owned, and he did not have two thousand cattle that would meet Mabry's requirements. Such a little obstacle, however, did not deter him. He put out orders to brother Johnathan at El Rancho Grande to supplement their own cattle with purchases from neighbors, putting a $15.50 ceiling on what he could pay. He also added, significantly, that "We pay Herd 12 & 15 for any Stray Cattle that he puts in." If Jonathan could get other neighbors to put in a large number of strays, for which he would allow twelve to fifteen dollars after they were shipped, then Mabry's twenty-dollar offer would give him a substantial margin of profit.

Jonathan was so successful in his buying that Pierce rode down the Gulf, Colorado and Santa Fé and established shipping headquarters at Milheim Station. He selected H. C. Coates, G. C. Gifford, A. P. Borden, T. C. Nye, Casper Bell, and Mr. Johnnie, the man he "would trust behind the mountain," as trail bosses. Ed Taylor, Pierce's "devoted friend untill death," reported "ready to move at your Call" from down on "Cancue Creek." William Chinn asked to be placed with Coates' crew. Gabe Sims joined Mr. Johnnie. Old Nep chose Mr. Borden. Cattle by the thousands were soon converging on Milheim Station. At the end of the first day of shipping, after Shanghai had soundly cursed the locomotive engineers for frightening his cattle, he wrote G. S. H.: "Just got of 659 Cattle today having a great deal of Trouble Cattle running a great deal." On the eleventh of May both Coates and Gifford received their herds off the cars at Wichita Falls. They wrote of their progress as they left Texas, via Doan's Crossing, into Indian Territory. Each man was apprehensive, especially over the shortage of water. Using the border merchant's elaborate stationery, Coates' message read:

Shanghai Pierce

          OFFICE OF C. F. DOAN & CO.
     Wholesale and Retail Dealers in Dry Goods,
            Hardware and Groceries
       Trail and Ranche Outfits a Specialty
              Established 1875
                Doans: Texas,
           May 11, 1883, Vernon.
A. H. Pierce,
    Dr. Sir, we arrived at Doans Store this morning all well. The Cattle are suffering for water, but I hear at this place, that there is water three miles ahead on north fork of red river. We cut out fifteen cattle at the fall for Collins, he told me that he could not find any of the cripples we left except dead ones. We will be in Dodge in about 20 or 25 days if we have no trouble.
              Yours very Truly,
                         H. C. Coates.

Gifford also reported that he had "crossed red river today am getting along very well I left five head of Steers with Done that wer crippled on the cars and I thought they would not make it through   I have got in my herd 3,260 head Coates 3,282   water has been Scarse for the last two days but think will find plenty from this on."

It took Tom Nye more than a month to get his cattle out of Wichita Falls. He was not in a hurry, though, he said, for he was "just fooling along with the horns."

    A. H. Pierce Esq.
    Dear Friend
        You see we are here and in good fix only one dead on the cars a very old cow, but two calves have since died—I only put in 25 cows and 30 twos 40 ones & 62 calves to the car & they rode it out finely. We are now only a few miles north of Wichita just fooling along with the horns letting them rest & fill up on the way to Doanes Store   Grass pretty good & water plenty with plenty of rain & two such nice little storms but a beautiful country neverless & such cattle twice as large & fat as ours & very few on the range at least we have seen very few. I inquired for your two horses at Spanish Camp but could hear nothing at all of Them. I suppose I

"I'm scienced in ranchin' "

will hear from you about time of delivery of Horns. I hope you will have a nice time on your Trip north as I am having a nice time up here. Our cattle are recovering from the effects of their trip fast & are no trouble to hold Two men at a time on watch hold them very easily as they lay down all night. So with Kind wishes to Mrs. Pierce Mamie & Mrs. Gifford, I remain as ever your
   Your
      Friend
         Tom Nye.

John McCroskey's crew had taken the lead and ran into real troubles. He was pleased when the other drives closed up near him. The McCroskey herd had little more than penetrated Indian Territory before hungry Indians "began dogging my tail demanding Wo haw." This Indian-coined word was the most accurate the red man could employ to designate a cow. They had heard the bullwhackers call to their oxen, "Gee, Whoa, Haw," as they cracked their whips to urge on slow moving wagon trains. And "Wo-haw" came to mean cattle or beef to the hungry Indian.

The migration of the buffalo had been checked by hunters before Pierce herds came into Indian Territory. Buffaloes had crossed the Strip on their last run. The United States government with the use of "buffalo soldiers" had hedged the Indians about in an attempt to confine them, first to the Indian Territory, then to the Strip. The buffalo, of course, was not there to feed them. A generous Great White Father had sent the news that he would send cows in lieu of buffaloes, and the Indians felt that any cow which ate their grass should in turn be eaten by them. The Strip, consequently, became a stalking-ground for hungry Indians, and Mr. Johnnie was trailed into each camp site.

The more intelligent Indians acted under the encouragement of white men and demanded Wo-Haw from each drover as an Indian's right in payment for the privilege of passing over Indian lands. More practical Indians prowled around the herds at night until they stampeded. Then they ate the strays left behind. One night Mr. Johnnie's outfit was stampeded. When the melee was over, he checked short seven horses, two beeves, and a fine jack that Shanghai had hoped to sell in Kansas for a good profit.

Gabriel Sims, the genial Negro member of Mr. Johnnie's crew, was always apprehensive over the intentions of the camp-followers. He bowed to no man, black or white, as a horse wrangler or bone wangler while he used a saddle blanket for green felt, but those glum Indians made him uneasy while he was plying his arts. After a saddle-blanket session under the chuck wagon one hot day, Gabriel was left in full possession of all the hard money in camp. He leaned leisurely upon the blanket, ladling up the silver with one hand and pouring it back again to hear the clinking. His defeated bone-shaking companions had sought rest in other wagons. Suddenly a big brown hand flashed through the spokes of the wagonwheel and scooped up Gabe's winnings. Gabe turned. A big, greasy buck, all decked out in war paint and feathers, confronted him. Without ceremony Gabe retired into the presence of Mr. Johnnie. Mr. McCroskey side-stepped the honor of dealing with this interloper and passed him along to Mr. Borden, who greeted the Indian with a tremendous "How!" The red man replied by holding up two fingers, adding, "Wo-haw." Borden was all for ending this long-winded conversation by cutting out two fat beeves, but Mr. Johnnie, from within the comparative safety of the wagon, kept shouting orders: "Cut out one stray, and tell him to get the hell out of camp."

Gabe was then put to the ushering out of an old crate of bones which wore the unmistakable brand of a widely known Indian Territory cowman. The Indian stood stoically aside until the old buzzard bait wobbled forth. Then, raising his arms in a gesture of imprecation and looking Borden square in the eyes, he sneered: "No! Fat white man heap thief bastard." Then he pointed to a fine beef: "Indian take big D damn quick." He did.

That night Neptune discovered a turkey roost. With rising glee, old Nep lay awake until the moon rose high enough for him to undertake the killing of several of them before they could fly away. Just about the time he was ready to shoot, dim figures began closing in on him. An Indian spoke from the darkness: "No kill turkey. Belong to Indian." But Nep crawled back just before daylight. He tapped one turkey on the head with a stick and ate Indian turkey that day anyway.

Before Pierce's boys left Indian country, they had become more or less accustomed to begging, bluffing Indians. One day when an old buck demanded his Wo-haw, a McCroskey boy, in a spirit of reckless fun, twirled his rope and caught the old fellow

"I'm scienced in ranchin' "

around the neck and upset him in the dust. The Indian sprang nimbly to his feet. There was dignity in his bearing, determination in his eyes. His movements were catlike. Grasping the rope around his neck to relieve the pressure, he ran swiftly around the mount of the laughing cowboy, entangling the horse. Then he began climbing the rope to the rider. McCroskey was some distance away, but he saw the flash of the tomahawk. He shouted: "Shoot him! Shoot him in the guts." But the warning came too late. The Indian brought down the hatchet with a dreadful thud.

That afternoon the Pierce boys held the funeral. They lost little time, however, in kicking clods back into a second grave before they shoved off toward Kansas.

While Pierce was making his way northward, visiting one herd after another, he received a distressing letter from Hamilton. It bore the news that the collector of internal revenue had summarily assessed a fine against Shanghai for selling tobacco without an excise tax; and worse yet, the collector was threatening to have a federal indictment returned against Pierce for selling tobacco to his cowboys without a license. Hamilton had paid the fine and attempted to explain away the danger of the indictment on the grounds of Pierce's lack of familiarity with the law; but Hamilton warned: "Get your story straight if you are required to make a statement."

The slowness of the movement of the cattle gave the Colonel an opportunity to make a side trip to Kansas City before he intercepted his herds again at Dodge. His wife and daughter met him at Kansas City. He left them at the hotel and rode south to Caldwell where he found some mail awaiting him at the Leland Hotel. A Texas cattleman named Burchfield got aboard the stage at the Leland Hotel and was in the act of departure when suddenly Pierce left off reading his letter and bolted out to the stage, holding a letter in his hand and calling to the stage driver to stop. The horses were reined in. Shanghai came alongside and addressed himself to Burchfield in his usual tones. He told the sad news he had just read. Mrs. Ward,—the Widow Ward—known to both of them, was dead.

"You know what a fine woman she was," he continued to call aloud. "She was the mother of us all." Then he began reading the letter so that all could hear. The manager of the stage line, seeing

131

the cause of the delay, called out: "Drive on." Pierce shouted back: "Hold on just a minute," and continued with his letter. The manager insisted that it was time the stage should be on its way, and it pulled out with Pierce running alongside the coach reading the letter above the crunch of wheels and clatter of hooves. Finally, he was outdistanced. Then Shang turned to the crowd he had attracted. He took off his hat and, without lowering his voice, solemnly read the obituary, adding a parting praise for his friend: "The Widow Ward is gone."

The stage went west to Kiowa, with Colonel Pierce as passenger. There he hired a double team and buggy and cut out into the prairie to intercept a lagging herd. Eddleman, a cattleman with headquarters at Doan's Crossing, had been following herds northward and buying cattle from disheartened drovers when he could drive good bargains. A tall, vivacious boy, just breaking out of his teens, had maneuvered a bunch of two hundred cows between two Pierce herds, and he was having trouble keeping his cows from joining up with Pierce. This boy, John P. Lowery, saw a double-team buggy coming across the prairie. It was driven by a large whiskered man. John began to fear that his violation of the rule of the trail was going to terminate in unpleasantness.

The driver reined up his team before the young man. They looked each other over carefully. Then in a loud but pleasant voice the big man called out: "Whose steer is that out there?" pointing to a poor old beef seeking shelter under a mesquite tree. In a flash John replied: "Sir! That is the poorest, mangiest D that Shanghai Pierce ever tried to fatten free off Indian lands; and he has some poor ones here, too, sir."

"Git up," laughed the double-team driver as he wheeled rapidly to the rear. Late that evening the same man stopped alongside John again. "Have you sold your cows, yet, son?" he inquired solicitously. "You know that Eddleman is giving a pretty good price on the trail, don't you, son?" Then he moved almost out of hearing before he reined up again and called back: "Son! Better take it from old Shanghai Pierce, now is a good time to sell."

John Lowery bedded down his cows that evening, and rode back to find Eddleman. "Surely," he reasoned, "old Shanghai has some motive in suggesting that I sell." Early the next morning Pierce was back at the Lowery camp. "Son! Did you sell them cows

"I'm scienced in ranchin'" last night like I told you?" When told that Eddleman now owned them, the Colonel showed he was pleased: "Well, son, I'm mighty glad. I couldn't tell you yesterday because I was afraid you'd think I wanted your cows. I have more cows now than I can get rid of. They're strung out from Texas to Cheyenne. Even have a herd turning back right now from Colorado to Ogallala that nobody will take. I'll flood the Ogallala market. I can stand it, son, but you and your two hundred cows might have a hard time wintering up here." He lifted the reins and started moving, shouting: "I sorter liked the way you answered me about that old D the other day, son."

The cattle progressed too slowly for Pierce's pent-up energy. He, therefore, pushed ahead to Ogallala where he quietly made arrangements to hold the cattle, in the event Seth Mabry decided they were not "in fair condition" after the new experiment of shipping. Having some time on his hands he rode westward to inspect some Wyoming-bound steers. Shanghai overtook the herd at Horse Creek just before entering Wyoming. Here Andy Adams saw him in action again. A lad dropped back from the Pierce herd to tell Andy the news. The luck of one of Pierce's best peelers—a Matagorda County boy (no one seemed to know his name)—had run out. A man-killer had fallen back on him. Pierce was greatly perturbed over the accident. He had caused the outfit to lay over a day. The earth was hard, and there were no tools for grave-digging. Old Shanghai, therefore, selected a site near a clump of cottonwood trees. The earth was softer there, and they dug as deep as they could. Then they built a pen with cottonwood logs and heaped the hollow square with cobblestones to "keep the coyotes from gnawing his bones." Then Pierce took off his hat and bowed his head before the cattle moved on.

With the funeral over, Shanghai rode back to meet Seth Mabry. Seth was even better than his word. Before Pierce could retrace his steps into Ogallala, Mabry had inspected the cattle and greeted Shang upon his arrival with the good news that he would accept them, and, in addition, he would buy his herd of horses. Then he selected G. C. Gifford, Casper Bell, Sam Evans, Neptune, John Allen, and William Chinn, raised their wages, and started them toward Denver with the herd.

Pierce celebrated the day by writing from the office of the county clerk of Keith County, Nebraska:

Shanghai Pierce

Ogallala, Neb, July 4th 1883.

Merchants National Bank   St. Paul Minn
   Gent
      Enclosed plese find drafts
on your Bank as Follows
   one Drft at Sight $ 61,178.76)
    " " " "   50,000.00) 111,178.76
   one Draft at 30 Dys   20,000.00
  all Payable to your order which Please dispose of as follos   Send to Bank of New York   New York City to Credit of Island City Saving Bank of Galveston Texas $100,000 & Forward to Me at Kans City M. o. Care St. James Hotell 11,178.76 in Sight N. Y. Exchange & also plese Send me Draft on N. York for the 20,000 Payable Augt. 3rd Please forward Exchange Kans City as I will have to Wait there until it arriaves
Res Yours
A. H. Pierce
Please Send the 111,178.76 in five Drafts

After posting his instructions to St. Paul, Shanghai moved on to Kansas City, where, three days later, he reported to his bookkeeper:

> Your favors boath rec'd on my return from Ogallala the boys got through all Wright in good shap—delivered Cattle to Mabry—all o k & he was well Pleased   Sold him & another man all the Horses—Gifford & a Lott of the boys took the Cattle on for Mabry he paid them good wages here   take Neptune one side & tell him I will fix up with him the balance when I Come home but for him to tell the other boys he only got $25 per Mo.
> When Willie La Bauve gets back, collect 25¢ a pair of sox I forgot.

12. "*Now, sirs, I am a mystic knight of Bovina*"

"Something unusual is taking place within the bailiwick of San Antonio's Alamo Plaza Chili Queens," said the San Antonio *Daily Express*. Earlier that day a traveling man had called at the office of the mayor. He had asked permission to erect a barbed-wire fence within the corporate limits. Armed with permission, John Warne Gates, a salesman for I. L. Elwood's barbed-wire company, chose Alamo Plaza, a place familiar to every cattleman who visited the historic city. With a gang of laborers, heavy cedar fence posts, and coils of wire, Gates set to work. News went down to the Manchke, to the Southern, and across the street to the Menger Hotel, where kings of the ranches were accustomed to sit in the shade of the

135

Mission City's downtown trees. Skeptical cowboys and curious cattlemen gathered, dividing their attention between the brunettes and bustling Gates, who strung wire with sharp barbs on it from post to post. "The crowd," reported the evening edition of the *Express*, "does not know whether it will be a free circus, a group of traveling acrobats or a medicine man's show. But whatever it is, it is different."

Drummer Gates was ready! (He was yet to acquire his sobriquet, "Bet-a Million Gates," in a slightly higher than penny-ante poker game.) He stepped right up and made a speech in typical style. "Gentlemen, bring on your steers. Bring on the cattle from a thousand hills. This is the finest fence in the world. Light as air. Stronger than whiskey. Cheaper than dirt. All steel, and miles long. The cattle ain't born that can get through it. Bring on your steers, gentlemen!"

This time, at least, Gates was betting on a sure thing. He had made certain that the show would go off according to form. Before exhibition time he had hired cattle for the test. They were the tamest but the most ferocious looking to be found. Not even Shanghai could have produced from his old-time Matagorda mossy-horns any to look the part more fittingly. Once within the enclosure, after being prodded a few times, they bucked and snorted and tore around to the entire satisfaction of the man who, so realistically, was trying to introduce barbed-wire fences into Texas; but not a steer tested his shoulder against a strand of wire.

Shanghai was not convinced. "It may keep 'em in, by God!" he commented. "But my cattle would cut themselves and die from screwworms, and I'll be damned if I treat my critters that way."

The fence fight with Grimes, however, had convinced Shanghai of the merits of fencing, so, when Mr. Benn told him that he was fencing a pasture with "flat wire with barbs," Shanghai rode over to the Ward ranch to discuss the innovation with his partner. While the cronies were talking, a herd made a run toward the fence. "Here comes the test," shouted Shanghai. Not a cow got through. Forthwith an order went off to Lambert and Bishop, Joliet, Illinois, for a full carload of wire. And, too, he convinced Augustus Kountze that his ranches also should be enclosed. Consequently, fence-building occupied much of Pierce's attention, until his Buena Vista Ranch became known as the "Wire Pasture," and

"A mystic knight of Bovina"

Kountze's two-hundred-thousand-acre enclosure stood between his new BU Ranch and Bob Stafford. Shang was no longer a free-range man. He recognized the effectiveness of "bob wire." He had become a Big Pasture Man.

After the K and KO ranches were put under fence, Pierce checked up on his land interests. He found that he owned, either in partnership or entirely by himself, approximately two hundred thousand acres. This did not take into consideration his holdings with Mr. Benn. "We have there," he said, "10,000 or 12,000—a big stock of cattle—Mr. Ward and I." He, therefore, decided to "consolidate."

Shanghai's relations with Mr. Benn had been, without exception, cordial and pleasant. There was no personal reason why the association should not continue. However, he told Hamilton: "The cattle are running all up the west side of the Colorado to Columbus. Now Kountze's pasture will hold the range on the west. I must dissolve with Mr. Benn."

Shanghai waited patiently for the opportune time to break the news to Ward. Then Mr. Benn announced the arrival of another baby at his home. "This is it," said Pierce, and he rode straight to the Crescent V Ranch. He would not even get down from his horse but called Mr. Benn out of the house, and, in simulated seriousness, announced: "Mr. Benn, I am going to have to go out of the cattle business with you." Ward was quite surprised, and asked the reason why.

"You are giving too much of your time and strength to other interests, Mr. Benn," answered Shanghai. "I am only interested in the cattle business."

Ward was agreeable to the dissolution of the partnership. He accepted from the ninety-thousand-acre partnership holdings the Crescent V Ranch. Shanghai took the greater portion of his division in cattle, and insisted that Mr. Benn should round up and deliver them. "You have your own hands [sons]." J. E. Pierce, at this point, came to Ward's rescue: "You damn old fool," he said to Shanghai. "Don't you know it's cheaper to *hire* hands than *raise* them?"

The time came when the cattle were to be counted and delivered. Shanghai called the tally while Ward kept the record. On the chute fence sat his seven-year-old son. The lad watched the cattle as they passed. When the tally was complete, Mr. Benn casually remarked: "I sure thought we had more cattle than that."

"You did, pappa," spoke up little Dean.

Ward caught the significance of the child's statement and demanded a recount. This time both men made the count, and it agreed with Dean's figures; whereupon Shanghai guffawed: "My God, Mr. Benn, why don't you leave them babies at home?"

What was plain to "them babies" could be seen, also, by another Crescent V rancher. Sam Evans rode over to Indianola and penned Shanghai a note which expressed without equivocation his intentions regarding wrong he'd suffered.

> I reckon this will surprise you and I Serously regret that it has occured, you told me positively that you would leave that cow in pilkington bend. I have information from the one that moved her out that you told him to take that cow. Mr. Pierce We have got to Settle that Some other way. I think I have as good a claim to her as you have. I would'ent of treated you in that way without a cause you have acted Just like you thought that I had been trying to increase my Stock and decrease yours. If you think So please say So! I have tried to meet you but have failed to so far. I would like for you to answer this if you dont I will hunt you up! I have saved Several Cows for you in this pasture by pulling them out of bogs; that is the thanks I get from you.

Ike Pryor had been one of those who shouted with George Saunders, "Our Redeemer cometh," when Shanghai and old Nep appeared on the scene with Little Dannie's money bags, but now that Colonel Pierce had become "scienced in ranchin," Ike dealt with him with misgivings. He, therefore, thought it to his interest, after he had bought some cattle from the "scienced" man, to warn him regarding his too thrifty inclinations. He did so with a note borne by his brother:

> Mr. A. H. Pierce
> Dr. Sir
> The Bearer of this Mr. D. C. Pryor (My Bro) will receive and settle for the cattle I have bought from you Dont try to put off any more little yearlings on him than you can help. Hoping you will both agree I am yours truly
> I. T. Pryor.

"A mystic knight of Bovina"

If sister Susan's version was correct, then, brother Abel was not confining his thrift to dealings with experienced cattlemen like Ike Pryor. Consequently, she, joined by her husband, Wiley Kuykendall, filed a suit in the justice court at Matagorda for possession of "one cow now in the possession of one A. H. Pierce." Court-day came. There was a big crowd in town that morning. The news had been relayed from neighbor to neighbor that Susan was "lawing" her brother. The first case on call was *Wiley M. Kuykendall, et ux* v. *Abel Head Pierce.* The spectators had filed into the crowded courtroom. The presiding justice tapped for order and called the case. Suddenly there was a disturbance in the courtyard. Old Shanghai was seen to be tying a cow to a hitching post. His booming voice carried into the courtroom: "I think the best evidence in the world is the witness, so I've brought the old cow up to let her tell her tale. I'll let the court pass on her."

"Judgment in favor of the defendant," solemnly pronounced the judge.

Then Shanghai unhitched his cow and started leading her down the street.

"I'll give you ten dollars for her, Colonel," someone jokingly shouted as he passed.

"Sold," answered Pierce, pocketing the money just in time to get it out of the reaching hand of sister Susan. For the moment, at least, Susan forgot her sisterly love, and she ground the knuckles of her fist on the end of her tall brother's nose. "If I were as big as you are," she shouted, "I'd twist your nose completely off."

Smiling blandly, Shanghai answered: "Well, just for that, sister Kuykendall, I'll keep the ten." Then, in an aside to the onlookers, he stated very slowly: "Wiley's my brother-in-law, you know. Just as apt as not to indict me. He takes a Kuykendall fit once in a while. I can't do anything with him when he takes a Kuykendall fit. The lion and the lamb have been lying down together now for a long time, but he has to have his outbreaks occasionally."

Shanghai was right about it: there was an indictment. In fact, the grand jurors of Matagorda County presented two indictments against him. What astonished him was that Joseph Pybus, his brother-in-law, was the foreman of the jury which charged him with counterbranding a yearling in Case No. 704; and in Case No. 727, Tom Nye, his ever faithful Tom, had been the witness in the indictment for the offense of selling hides without having them inspected.

Pierce had need for his political lawyer, again, so Fred McCamley took over, and Pierce was held to be "Not Guilty" in the counterbranding charge. A year and a half later, a docket entry was made by the judge in the remaining indictment: "December 4th, 1884, Dismissed by State with permission of the Court, for want of merit in the case."

Fred had earned his fifty-dollar fee, and Shanghai thought that perhaps McCamley could serve him profitably in another matter. While purchasing land on a wholesale basis, Pierce had acquired a three-fifths interest in a five-hundred-acre tract. A two-fifths undivided interest was held by the Dawdy estate. The heirs agreed to a partition and named County Surveyor Robbins to provide the field notes, which he did, forwarding them to Pierce, who sent them along to McCamley with his suggestion. "I think," answered McCamley, "all the heirs signing—and the Old Lady, Mrs. Dawdy—makes the partition and deed legal. They can never dispute it. You suggest that I reduce the distance on the line going west from the river 100 vs & say nothing about [it]. I cannot do this as I have Robbin's field notes before me and to put them in only partially correct would be a deliberate changing of the field notes which would not be exactly right, and then again the Dawdys w'd sign under the impression that they were acting and conveying under his survey, and they would, perhaps, be mislead in this way.

"According to Robbin's Survey this West line is 1460 vs & taking off the 100 vs w'd leave 1360 vs. I leave this distance blank in the deed to be filled in as you think best."[1]

Now that the Colonel had made the change from a Free-Range to a Big Pasture Man, troubles developed in new forms. Not only were his cattle being stolen from the enclosures, but the fences were being ruthlessly cut so they could escape. "As to the scientific manipulators of the branding irons," said old Shang, "we can't help that: that is a natural consequence. Why, I knew a man up north to sell a wagonload of branding irons. They were for 500 cattle. But this stealing by 'skally wags' has become Epidemick."

J. W. Heard rode over to discuss the epidemic with the Colonel. He had intercepted, so he related, a full carload of cattle al-

---

[1] It was many years before the Robbin's "error" was discovered and a correction deed secured.

"A mystic knight of Bovina"

ready under bill of lading at Louise. "They were all stolen cattle, Mr. Pierce. One two-year-old steer has a BU on it." This made the Colonel recall that a prized young horse had been missing for some days. He, therefore, sent Clay off in a hurry to search for him. "I think you can find him over at Watkins," he shouted. "Send down and get him. Take a gentle horse and tail him to him. I am afraid that Watkins layout have killed him." But McSparren came back to report: "The Watkins would not say anything about him."

After Mr. Heard left the ranch, Pierce wrote, instructing Borden:

> It is a good Idear now that so many of our stock are missing to take a little round in Reeves Pasture Sometime & Proably you will find the red bull yearling makes no difference where you find him bring him home & put him in the Pasture in front of the house.

While the bull hunt was going on, the Colonel had to make a business trip to Arkansas City, Kansas. To that point Borden directed a report, showing his discomfort:

> I went to Wharton today. I saw Reeves in Town and he was to[o] mad to talk. He said you and I insinuated that he took the steer out of you[r] pasture and then he said he would sure see you about it.
> Fleas about to eat me up so I will close.

Pierce was little concerned with what John Reeves thought, that is, at least, what he said in his reply to his nephew:

> I dont care for John Reeves being mad let him stay So & I will Notify him when I get home so if desirous to See me that he will have No trouble in finding me If you never get hurt, Bordon, untill John Reeves does it you will live a long time. Let him Cool—he has a Lotta time to do it.

Borden also kept his eyes on others besides John Reeves. He wrote to Pierce, who was spending more and more of his time up in Kansas, that he had heard:

> Ed Roberts is going to Slaughter a beef on this side of the river, and I went to see about it. I will try to keep him in check if I can.

While over ther I saw Dick Lee and Prichard come over hunting and Gus told me that they come three or four times a week and kill deer, so I waited for them to return. They had no meat with them but had done some killing of some kind as both had bloody hands and boots and clothing. I said nothing but watched the bridge until 2 A. M. this morning. No one showed up on the bridge but after moon went down two men passed up the river in a boat and returned later. Will try and catch onto them if I can. Will have Clay moove all the cattle from the sandbars, and, as the mosquitoes are bad in the bottom, I think they will stay out.

When Borden found a party of eleven make-believe hunters in the BU pasture who refused to leave, he called on his uncle for instructions. "Is there not a way to break them up?" he asked. "I am thinking about putting out poison." Shanghai was prompt with his reply: "You best take some beef & a bone to Drug [store] & say nothing to no one & go down & Put out Wolf Baits Enough to Kill Every dog they Have. I will see Proctor & I think I can give them some trouble as Trespassers."

Pierce, however, went out of his way to differentiate between "that gang of thieves," "skally wags," and "damn rascals," who preyed on the Big Pasture Men and the deals "Big Men" had with each other. "What they do," he explained, "is legitimate. It is putting up a job on a man." Then, he illustrated his point:

> For instance, Dillard Fant once inspected a herd belonging to "Old Man" Fleming. I heard that Dillard was going to offer the "Old Man" twelve thousand dollars for all the cows he had in a certain brand. I slipped down there before Dillard could make the offer, and hurried up and bought every critter in that brand, except one poor one. Then Fleming, who buys his own drinks when he should of been buying me one, too, wrote a bill of sale specifying "every cow I own," and he took Fant's money.... Yes, sir: that was a square deal ... and besides that, Fleming "set-em-up" so often to keep me from telling it, that I almost drank myself to death.

The Colonel was not the only Big Pasture Man having enclosure troubles. The Kountze managers, McReynolds and Crary, were having their troubles, too. Crary, therefore, appealed to Pierce:

> Grimes has moved all the cattle he could get hold of into the Territory. We have worked the cattle, and there was a great many

"A mystic knight of Bovina"

of them outside our fence, and on your tank, two or three times. Stafford worked through our Ranches 1 & 2 about the time Grimes was gathering—took out some Beeves, cought and branded some calves, and left.

With this information, Shanghai went into action. Ed Taylor (who had avowed to Shanghai: "I ever remain Your devoted friend untill death. . . . I am ready to Move at your Call"), got that call and went over with McReynold's Winchester, which he was "taking home for a *visit*." The effect of this action registered in faraway New York. Augustus Kountze wrote his appreciation: "I note that Taylor is now busy turning out of Ranches Nos. I & 2 the Stafford Cattle."

Shanghai was familiar with the fact that the *Western Stock Journal*, in its first issue, in 1875, had set itself up as the defender of the rights of the stock raisers of Texas. That journal started its existence by quoting with approval a resolution which had been passed by the Stock Raisers Association of Western Texas:

> The custom or practice of selling cattle without the authority of the owner, which has existed for a long time, opens the door to abuses which have caused incalculable injuries to the interests of the cattle-raisers, ought to stop. The cattle thieves and hide purloiners should disappear, if to do this, it is necessary to call in the gallows to enforce the right of property, even though this be only cattle. It is also essential that the *grab game* cease.

When the *Western Stock Journal* echoed the sentiments of the Stock Raisers Association of Western Texas, Pierce was not far away from that old dead tree which had borne so much "human fruit," and the *grab game* was equally familiar to him. And, too, the time soon came when he was not eligible to membership in the association, for Fred McCamley had yet to quash a couple of vexatious indictments. The situation, now, was different. George Littlefield and George West had reversed their shields and were now seeking protection from cattle thieves and fence-cutters through union with the Cattlemen's Association. The Colonel also heard that prominent members of the association had ventured to discuss the propriety of accepting his membership now that his "record had been officially expunged." "Well, I never was tried," he said, "if I was indicted. McIntire did it. He indicted every man he could strike. He indicted me, but the fact that a man was indicted for cowstealing does not, itself, prove that he is a cowthief. If he is convicted of cowstealing . . . if he is a notorious cowthief . . . that goes a great deal further."

While Pierce was toying with the idea of lining up with the Big Pasture Men, he received information that his membership was acceptable. The association also drew on him for $558—"your yearly assessment." He roared his protest, but when the other big fellows paid up, he did likewise, observing that "they only jump on the fellows who *could* pay."

Now that he was a full-fledged member of the Cattleman's Association, he thought a little visit with "the boys," many of whom he had not seen since Dodge City days, would do him good. Therefore he notified the secretary to reserve him a room at the old Capitol Hotel, in Austin, where the cattleman's convention was to be held. As he walked off the train with his little satchel, he met some roaming cattlemen who were already lubricated to the talking point, and they told him that Ben Thompson was back in town.

Since he last saw Ben, that pistol artist had been both in and out of trouble. The citizens of Austin had entrusted him with the office of city marshal, but San Antonio's jail had detained him so long on a murder charge that he had resigned his office and was now dividing his time between running a gambling dive and engorging raw red whiskey. It was a much-talked-of fact that Ben had a positive dislike for several men who were in attendance at the convention. Shanghai and Texas Ranger Lee Hall were two who would not be cordially greeted by the former marshal. Despite this, Colonel Pierce registered quietly at the old Capitol Hotel and prepared for a week of entertainment.

The convention built up momentum in true cattleman's style, but not all of the speeches were made in the assembly hall. There was much talk in the saloons and on the streets. The San Antonio *Express* sent over a reporter to listen to what was being said. The *Express* set the "boys" up in capital boldface: THE CATTLE BARONS. The paper circulated on Austin streets in prophetic warning. It told how the cattleman thought he owned Texas, "who counted his horns on an hundred hills." Then it referred to a similar convention, previously held at Dallas, where "500 sat down to a

"*A mystic knight of Bovina*"

$5,000 banquet. They drank champagne from big goblets. Diamonds as big as the pecans which grow in the Concho country sparkled on the bosoms of the barons' wives and daughters." It told how, when he wanted legislation, the baron sent down to Austin and got it; how he ceaselessly shouted "free grass" and sneered "nester" at the farmer who settled on the water courses of the range. "His cowboys are his feudal following and know no law but his decree." Then the reporter told of another such assemblage in Austin:

> One night near the end of the session of the legislature, the barons and their friends entertained behind closed doors. It had been a period of satisfactory lawmaking for the cattle interests. Everybody present was feeling good. A governor, who once had said that Texas didn't need immigration, sat at the head of the table. Speech after speech was made. The cattlemen were eulogized. The "nester" was ridiculed. Such newspapers as had begun to rebel against the arrogance of the barons came in for hard raps; and finally, the governor, in a spirit of fair play, called for the only newspaperman present to defend his craft. Nettled by the sarcastic flings to which he had been listening, the speaker replied half angrily:
>
> "Gentlemen, you may have your sport tonight at the expense of the despised nester. You may think you are strong enough to defy the press and public sentiment, but let me tell you one thing: A man with a hoe has poked his nose over your wirefence and is looking at you today. You will kill him, of course, but tomorrow two men with hoes will be looking over the same fence. It isn't in the nature of things, gentlemen, for an acre of land, which will raise twenty bushels of wheat, to be given up for all time to the possession of a five dollar cow."

The few barons who took time off from "sillybrating" to read the *Express* gave little thought to this prognostic omen. They were having a good time, while giving their serious thoughts to the interests of the Big Pasture Men and the "depredating nesters." Consequently, under "Plans as Devised by the Mystic Knights of Bovina," the convention went on record "for larger rewards for the conviction of cowthieves—$200 for the conviction of a whiteman and $100 for the conviction of a Negro." With such resolutions off their minds they came to the grand finale of the convention.

Shanghai Pierce

The more dignified ones sauntered up Congress Avenue and into Simon's Café, carefully selecting their seats at the banquet table. The crowd gathered slowly. The blubber-bellied, white-apron fraternity was extra busy in an adjacent saloon shaking up a bit of tanglefoot and pouring "conversation water" to calls of "nominate yer pizen." While the preprandial turmoil was engaging the attention of the men of the range, the Honorable L. E. Edwards, attorney and staunch friend of Mr. Benjamin Thompson, one-time marshal of the capital city, more recently from the environs of San Antonio's clink, sauntered none too steadily into Simon's and seated himself at the long table which was already piled high with savories. Someone sufficiently sober and officious enough to differentiate between baron and lawyer, but too tippled to recognize the intruder as one who walked with marshalcy, ushered Ben's pal unceremoniously out to the sidewalk. The dinner went on—for a time at least—undisturbed by the absence of the uninvited guest.

Shanghai came in late. Since he could not grace the head of the table, he chose the foot. As they ate, the diners grew noisy— so noisy, in fact, that even Shanghai was unable to engage the attention of the custodian of the turkey at the farthermost end of the board. It was a double insult to be deprived of the turkey and not to be able to make himself heard. So, shouting, "Well, sir, I will get that bird," he slipped off his boots and mounted the table. Picking his way step by step, his head almost to the ceiling, gingerly dodging the gravy here, the cake there, and then the salad, he put his foot flat in the custard pie and came to an abrupt halt when the street door opened. There stood Ben Thompson, pistol in hand, demanding: "Who in the hell says my friend Edwards can't stay in here?"

Lee Hall, who had been standing on a chair, caricaturing for the amusement of the banqueters, sensed the situation, and, dropping his hands, stood motionless, looking the killer straight in the eye. Congressman William Henry Crain (Congressmen were even then special guests at such functions!) stepped between Thompson and Hall, and spoke calmly: "Give me your gun, Ben."

Then there was a terrific crash. Shanghai was stepping through the window, taking sash, screen, and all with him. Ben handed over the gun, but the merrymakers—all except Lee Hall and Con-

Lee Hall, ranger, manager of the D.H. &D. Ranch, and Indian agent

Wild Bill Hickock, 1876 (Courtesy Western History Collections, University of Oklahoma Library)

"A mystic knight of Bovina"

gressman Crain, according to the old Negro waiter's version—"had done already adjourned wid out de benediction."

Shanghai hurried back to the ranch. The season was far advanced, but he had not been able, so far, to make ranch-gate delivery of cattle, so he opened Peyton Montgomery's telegram with misgivings.

"So Shoot you Mouth off and Say—'I go you,'" concluded the message which made him an offer on seven thousand threes and fours if Pierce would "guarantee that they are cattle raised west of the Brazos River, or in other words, no *Swamp Angels.*"

His friend, Seth Mabry, had peddled the news to Quinlan, Montgomery and Company that he had made money on Pierce's cattle the previous year, and now both Montgomery and Mabry wanted herds of seven thousand each. He was not certain that he could deliver fourteen thousand cattle which would meet the classification of "no swamp angels." At least, he could not depend on Kountze Brothers to help, for theirs were all swamp angels. To add to his perplexity, a message came from Denver offering "nineteen-fifty for two thousand straight twos." He solved his dilemma by wiring Montgomery, "I go you," and set off to find Jim Heard. Jim admitted that he had been "trading partly for other parties. I will not have over three hundred head, but you can have them at your offer." "Three hundred," Shanghai said, "is a mighty little fish in such a big pan," but he took them and moved on over to see "that damn Dutchman Bosky." Bosky had come over from Italy with Count Telferner and was now holding 8,402 acres in Shanghai's Circle. Not only did he control the land, but he was advising his Italian friends not to market their cattle through Pierce. Undaunted, however, Shanghai instructed brother Johnathan to comb the coastal section and start driving everything that would class toward the BU Ranch. Then he took the train to Galveston and, from the Island City Saving Bank, drew two sight drafts, each for $10,000, on Montgomery and Seth Mabry, as earnest money on their contracts. The livestock agent for the G. C. and S. F. Ry. Co. called at the Tremont during Shanghai's absence and left him a significant note, which read:

> You need have no apprehension about cars for Millheim. You know, of course, that we will take care of Shippers from points on our line in preference to those coming from other roads.

Shanghai Pierce

To the note were pinned two annual passes on the G. C. and S. F.: "One for you—one for your brother."

This little thoughtfulness on the part of the G. C. and S. F. Ry. Co. caught the N. Y. T. and M. napping. The pens, being built over at Pierce's Station out of Shanghai's lumber, were not yet ready for use, so the Colonel placed Jonathan in charge of 1,903 beeves and 25 horses, billed for Mabry, and the Santa Fe pulled them out of Millheim on the first leg of their journey toward Wichita Falls. When the cattle were unloaded, Jonathan wired his report: "Collected $33,692.50. The cattle stood the trip tolerable well. Tell Pryor the grass is tolerable."

This suited Pierce perfectly. Consequently, he started the first shipment to Montgomery. To a sixty-day sight draft on Montgomery and Osburne, he attached a carefully itemized bill of particulars:

```
being for
    1037 Beeves at $22.50          $23,332.50
      13 Horses at  35.00             445.00
                                   ----------
                                   $23,787.50
    Int. 63 days at 10%               416.28
                                   ----------
                                    24,203.78
```

Receipt attached to the draft & will be surrendered upon acceptance.

With the beeves drawing 10 per cent interest as they rode, plus three days of grace, the Colonel now turned his attention to another order which had come from Montgomery. He wanted five hundred dry cows and "all the 4 to 6 year old Steers you will ship at $25." This order gave Pierce the opportunity he had wished for. He put every animal he could round up on the trail, spacing the herds along under his best trail bosses. He struck out ahead of the cattle, selling along the route to local men, promising delivery from the advancing drives. "Now," thought he, "I can get rid of my swamp angels. I will follow and make collections."

Things went bad from the start. Bordon and Gifford got as far as Pond Creek, Indian Territory, where they quarrelled. Bor-

"*A mystic knight of Bovina*"

den wrote in his notebook: "We have lost nearly half the cattle. We have got a *fine* boss, I am sorry to say. We do not get along well together. I do not know how long I will be here."

Squabbles between nephews were not to be the worst news Shanghai would receive. The Island City Saving Bank reported his sight draft on Montgomery had been returned, protested for nonacceptance, and, too, the Davis Cattle Company notified him that they were unable to deliver all the cattle they had contracted to furnish. Thus, with thousands of cattle en route and his contracts defaulting, Pierce headed his big bay up the trail, collecting swamp-angel sales as he went.

He met a tide of dissatisfaction over the grade of cattle wherever he stopped. The indignation reached its crest one day as he reined in his mount to the greeting: "Shanghai Pierce! Get down, damn you! I'm going to beat hell out of you as soon as your feet hit the ground."

Shanghai sat bolt upright in his saddle and calmly replied: "Hold your horses, young man! Jesus Christ, son! I could have got whipped a hundred miles closer to home any day this week."

The Colonel finished his collections and retraced his route to the ranch. Frank Bates had come down from the Spade Ranch, where he and Bradford Grimes had been talking about the sea lions, and he wanted some "she stuff which would warm up quick" on a new range. Shanghai immediately offered to sell him one thousand heifers. "The finest bunch of two-year-olds in the State of Texas," he avowed. Not only were they the finest bunch of heifers in existence, he added, but they have other qualities: "I am grazing them on an island out in the bay, and I've got 'em well trained. I swim 'em across the lagoon to the island every morning to graze and swim 'em back to the corral on the mainland at night. They can outrun a deer and swim like a duck. Not one of 'em will drown as they cross the Red into the Territory. Better take 'em! They're a bargain."

This was the first time Bates had been in conversation with the Colonel, and he did not know what to make of the bombast. Therefore, he backpeddled to his horse, jumped astride, and headed off to buy his "she stuff" from someone else.

McCroskey, who seemed never to be out of trouble as he trailed northward, wrote Pierce with unceasing regularity. One

Shanghai Pierce

day he had "Sold to Haul² and Fisher 174 two year old and 1 cripple Steer for the Some of $15 dollars per head." Also he reported: "I have c[r]ossed Red River. they say I cant go near Ft. Cil [Sill] so I will after [have to] drift down Red River until I can see further grass and warter."

A few days later he encountered more trouble:

> We are holding on the Little Washita and are getting along very well, but I am satisfied that Forsythe's man beat me out of 11 head. He gathered them right where I had a stampede and was not willing to give them up. Addington has offered $16.25 for the herd. I told him I did not know what you would ask for them. The cattle seem to have some disease among them. We have had 20 die. Our horses are very poor and sick. We had ten stolen a week ago. Everybody is down on a Texas herd and are strictly on the steal. If our horses dont die or some rascal dont steal them we can hold the cattle until about the middle of July, but I will ceep cuming up the trail untill I am Stop.

Tribulations, however, were not confined to McCroskey. For a long time the Indians in the Territory had been content to accept Wo-haw, but, when drifting cattlemen turned resolutely against tribute, the Cherokees sought results through a more substantial union of their tribes. As a consequence the Honorable D. W. Bushyhead was made principal chief of the Cherokee Nation. One R. Bunch became acting principal chief, and J. W. Jordan secured the appointment of United States marshal through the Commissioner of Indian Affairs. With such a showing of authority, Jordan, as Shanghai put it, began "molesting us cattlemen."

The marshal's report to Bushyhead, at least, gave evidence of zeal. It said in part:

> In haste I here with submit a limited report of our affairs . . . and ask you use your influence to secure Agent Owens presents [presence] here to give force to cleaning up of the Strip of intruders by his authority and direct orders. Also your presents is of great importance to our interest in Rid[d]ing this Country of a great Curse and Seting up full and Complete controle under our Nationality. My U.S. Court papers are expected every day and our Troops will return . . . on the 28th. we have ex[p]elled a colony

² Hall and Fisher, cattle dealers.

150

"A mystic knight of Bovina"

of Boomers. . . . I have no force at present and while hunting alone yesterday in Among Boomers was rounded up by them but no attack was made aside from Cursing and threats . . . they were well armed and mounted—I made a stand and they left without opening a Ball. . . . After my life is Sacrificed in a Common Cause it will be too late to aid me. . . . One at home at pease Can have no idea of the works of Kansas Robers in the open Country. it is clear to my mind that we must Settle this part of the Strip with Cherokee districts or loose it. Many licensed Stock men are Boomers Simply holding for this land to come in for white Settlers . . . and covering our land with men who come to stay.

Jordan's final report was replete with assertions of his determination to rid the Cherokee Nation of intruders. The report was voluminous. "A full account of my Services," he wrote, "would make a volume."

I have the honor herein of submitting My final report embracing my last years Service and state of affairs, giving the different lines of duty I have found necessary to perform in behalf of the Cherokee Nations rights and property.
Acting U. S. Scout after receiveing orders of ejectment from the U. S. Authority—and submitting them to the Military officer in Command—I then had to lead the Cavalry—to find Said intruders —identify—Capture—expell—and destroy all improvements.
To August 12 '87 was constantly traveling preparing and reporting intruders for removal—also applying U. S. law by prosecution in the Courts.
On August 13th I began service with T Troop of the 15th U. S. Cavalry—and kept busy with them. . . . Cleared a large scope of country on the Arkansas and Cimmarron Rivers—burned out a Settlement of Boomers on each river—destroyed all improvements, farm implements, two hundred tons of hay—and nearly fifty acres of corn and potatoes—put several men in jail—turned the majority over the Kansas Line—and opened fire on several that run to escape arrest. At the time the Troops on the Strip were ordered to Sill, our entire country was clear of all intruders except a few Boomer Ranchmen. . . . I sign Myself obedient Servant of the Cherokee Nation, J. W. Jordan, Assistant Ex-Secretary of the C. N. west of 96 M.

Gifford, McCroskey, Partain, and Borden were keeping as close to each other with their herds as the country permitted, and they were drifting slowly as possible, fattening as they moved. As a consequence, Bushyhead's troops were soon after them. Gifford reported his progress, or rather, the lack of it, and his troubles with the United States soldiers to the Colonel as they moved along.

On May 24, 1887, from "Oklama," he wrote to the Colonel: "Your letter in regard to route to hand. I will have no trouble as I am pretty well acquainted with the Country. I croosed the river yestardy don't expect to be able to stay here very long but shall stay as long as possible. I think after staying on this side of Cimaron as long as we can, we will be able to stay on the other side of Cimaron on Turkey Creek. It is in the Oklama Country but we will not be disturbed thair as it is off the rode and now [no] Shoulders [soldiers] to bother we could have stayed a few days longer in the Chicksaw Country but some of them were making sow much fus that I thought it would be better for us to leave for we might get in truble and have to pay something to get out."

Just a week later, Gifford again recorded the happenings, writing on the envelope: "Will give this letter to the first one passing to mail":

Sandies Creek 5/30–87

Mr. A. H. Pierce
  BU Ranche
    Texas

Dear Sir
  Having a few minutes leasure this morning thought I would drop you a few lines as we are now Camped on Sandies it is one prong of walnut Creek wich emptes in to the Cadian River at the R. Road at Persil [Purcell]) which is the name of the town we are about 12 miles from thair it is my entain [intention] now to grase up walnut and stay as long as possible in a place. . . . I dont know yet but I think probely that after I have stayed in this country as long as I can I will come back down the Cadian and Cross and try to give Soulders the slip.

Gifford did not have the good fortune to "slip the soulders," as he had hoped, for Major Sumners anticipated his intentions, and kept him moving. Back on Turkey Creek, one week later, he wrote again to Mr. Pierce:

"*A mystic knight of Bovina*"

I am now on the north side of the simeron because Major Sumners orders were to keep all herds mooving 8 Miles per day, and *special orders in regard to the Pierce herds*, the Old fellow has not forgot your telling about the 15 days we stayed in thair last year. I had no trouble with any of them and stayed 11 days between the Cadian and simeroon we are still in Oklahoma and are going to stay as long as possible I have been to Reno while in Oklahoma to see Agent to get pass to go through Chyine Country dont think will have eny trouble in getting it   shall stay out of Chyine Country as long as possible and stay in as long as I can after geting thair   I will be at Drum & Snyders Pasture July 1st redy to diliver if sumner dont get me which I dont think thair is much danger of as the Liut that has Comand of Indian Scouts is a first rate fellow. We have to put in a few days on the Trail to Kill time but we have been able to beat it so far.

While the herds were drifting toward the north, Shanghai was struck with a wanderlust and made his perennial trip to Rhode Island, but he doubled back to Kansas City, not even waiting for the arrival of his daughter, who was attending Virginia Female Institute. In fact, Shanghai left Rhode Island in something of a huff over the report which came to him about his brother Jonathan.

Jonathan had heard of Shanghai's ride about the countryside, shouting his "cobb pie and black coffee" dinner orders to impress his kin and friends; therefore, knowing that brother Abel was about to tour again, he took his dogs and went down into the canebrakes on Old Caney to trail down a bear. Having early success, he returned to El Rancho Grande with a cub, which he dubbed "ettar, the bear." The Pierce children soon brought it under their charm, and the little fellow became quite gentle, although inquisitive and nosey. Then Jonathan set out for Rhode Island taking not only his entire family, but also "ettar the bear," which wobbled along with the travelers on the end of a chain. Upon arrival in Little Compton, Jonathan took great pains to inform Hamilton: "Lots of people came to see me, too, this time. I got through all right with ettar the bear, and there has been hundred of people here to see us. Tomorrow John and Abel enter her at the fair—she is docile and very playful."

Jonathan had captured the people's attention, this time, and

Shanghai did not wish to compete. Therefore, he left for Kansas City sooner than he had planned, and waited there for Miss Mamie, who brought along her nephew, Johnnie. She also brought her quarterly report card from Virginia Female Institute, signed by Mrs. General J. E. B. Stuart, principal. The report rated her accomplishments:

Bible Lessons	9.3
Reading	9.5
English Composition	7.
Evidences of Christianity	9.69

and there was a special bill for equestrianism and a note showing: "Balance Due—$206.61—Send Northern Exchange if equally convenient, if you please: Southern checks are always discounted."

Shanghai put Mrs. General J. E. B. Stuart's statement of account and note in his pocket and waited until he saw his banker, Levi, some weeks later. "See that," said Shanghai, pointing to the word "equestrianism." "My God! Levi what has she done now?"

When told that it was a charge for horsemanship, he waved his hands and cried out: "O, my God! Here I am paying out money to teach her to ride a sidesaddle in Central Park and she was *raised* riding straddle on a bareback Texas pony."

The "equestrienne," who rated so high in "Evidences of Christianity," made it quite plain to "my dear pappa" that she preferred to be left in Kansas City while he made the trip to sell and deliver his cattle. Hattie observed that Miss Mamie seemed to be enjoying the attentions of Henry Withers, a Kansas City lawyer, and Mrs. Pierce told Shanghai: "If given a little time, something may come of it."

"Withers," countered Pierce, "is getting grey around the temples, Madam, and nothing to show for it! And by God, if it's money he's after, he'll never get a dollar of it."

Pierce was out of Kansas City three days before the last of the reports from his herd bosses reached him. He was unable to sell his heifers, so he made arrangements to winter them. He was willing, so he wrote his bookkeeper, to make Turner Revis a loan of one hundred dollars, "but the papers must be fixed up Iron Clad." After that, he began worrying about an unsettled account Kountze Brothers had with him for rental on horses. "I cannot See

"A mystic knight of Bovina"

why the K Horse Account is not Correct," he wrote. "I have not charged him the actual Cost & only charged up what there actually was, this Spring, & if any has died Since, that is his own Loss & they are all acclimated & worth fully $5 per head more than horses Just brought in—I do and will do my full Show of Work on K Cattle & it is nothing Wright nor do I perpose to Stand any Loss of the K Horses, & I want to Settle up with K Bros & Want the Money— If I owe them $10 [for] 10 Minutes they Charge me Int on it & why Should they owe me for Months & No Int. Push Crary to Settle up all his accounts as it will Stop that Much Int. with K. Bros."

Seth Mabry paid Shanghai fifty thousand dollars at St. Paul, and the Colonel put two thousand dollars in his pocket. He announced to Hattie, who had found it convenient to take to her bed, claiming illness, at Kansas City, that he was en route to Omaha, where Mamie had gone to visit the Herman Kountze family. From there they were to make a tour of Canada. And would finally go to Saratoga, New York, for a week.

13. *"I am introducing religion into the community"*

The Canadian tour started on schedule, but he "left the cars" at Chicago, and Mrs. Pierce had more than a little trouble getting him out of the Chicago stockyards where he put in his appearance day after day. With a sagging stock market, he had no heart for the journey. Nevertheless, he set down his itinerary, in the event someone at the ranch wished to communicate with him: "Thursday for Quebeck from there to Portland & then Boston & Fall river. Will be at Fall river about Augt 3rd." At Montreal, instead of seeing the sights, he remained in his hotel room and shunted off instructions to the ranch: "I suppose Dawdy will be in with our Horses pretty soon—Tell Nye best Rope every one of them & take

"*I am introducing religion*"

his time in Picking them—the Cattle Market is drooping . . . bound to Effect the young Cattle Market & Stock Cattle will go to $15 all over our Country before Frost."

The Colonel had wished to see his brother Jonathan before he returned to Texas, but Augustus Kountze detained Shanghai ten days in New York while the others in the touring party went on to Saratoga and Vineland, New Jersey. Kountze Brothers delivered his mail upon arrival, including a letter from J. E. Pierce advising that his plans had been spoiled by the women. "I have had a pleasant trip, but they're fixing up the old home here—the furniture is all in the house—and they are putting down the carpets, so you see the jig is up about the folks returning with me. The children dont like it any better than I do. the weather is very cool her. Abel cried this morning for Warm Water to wash his face in."

Shanghai kept in constant communication with Hamilton by letters. In one, he admitted. "I made a serious Mistake in delivery of my Cattle . . . it will be expensive Mistake." In another, he inquired again about the Kountze horse account:

> You did not write me anything about Col Crarys Making any Settlement of our old account and horse account. If he wont settle I dont want the Horses used, and whatever is lost will have to come out of his part, and we will divide them as soon as I return home, as I propose to Stand No Loss but my own and no foolishness is the matter.

Then turning to other collections, he directed:

> Write Mr. Benn about his Note & get the Int & Int on Int. . . . The Int Must Come   I need the money & Must have it. Money Matters is very tight in N.Y. & Mr. Kountze says no prospects of any better for 4 Mos   It has been almost a panick for Last Month in Wall Street, but if you can get the corn, *good* corn, but it *Must be good corn*   No Free Nigger Stuff—and Dry when weighed & well slip-shucked—at 30 cents you best get a big car load. It wont cost anymore frt for 400 Bus than 300.

Hamilton sent the Colonel a letter which had been received at the ranch. This was the first information Pierce had that marauders were making trouble again about fences. The letter read:

Shanghai Pierce

Mr. A. H. Perce   Wharton Co. Texas
    Dear Sur
    I wood like to git Per mishen from you to Jorne my Fele Fence on to youse Pasture Fence   I will Kepe the Parte I Jorne on up and will olso Put youre Cattle that is on the outside in the Pastur
                              From Yours as ever
                                            B. J. Jarvis.

After the cattlemen concluded their convention at Austin, other newspapers, made bold by the San Antonio *Express* reporter's attack on the cattle barons, shouted the merits of barbed-wire fences. "Barbed wire," said one Texas daily, "makes it possible for the citizens of Texas to own and control the land of Texas in common with the Lords, Dukes, and Mighty Sirs of Europe." Word of this attack, along with the other bad news, came to Shanghai before his eastern visit was complete, and Shanghai relayed his anxiety back to Hamilton: "I am Just in rect of letter from John McCrosky in which he Says Somebody Cut about 3 miles of Duncan Ranch Fence & he Expects they will cut the BU fence I hope they wont but if they should do the best you can about getting it Fixed up as soon as possible if it should be done   I would take one Strand of new Wire & Stretch at once wherever it is cut   not Stretch it too high & that will keep Cattle in untill the others can be mended & I would like if you think necessary to take your Horses and Skirmish around some where you think most needed. I leve here tomorrow. If you think any Extra Winchesters needed on the ranch, I will bring them."

After getting ready to leave, the Colonel walked out of the Metropolitan Hotel to roam the city, asking questions and talking with whomever he met. People stopped to listen to his booming voice, to laugh at his witticisms, and they crowded around to hear him pipe up a lively Texas tale. Among those lured to the vocal loadstone was a teen-age lad with a roll under his arm. When Shanghai stopped again in the lobby of the Metropolitan Hotel to spin his last yarn, he was surprised to see the same youth crowding up close into the circle of listeners. Suddenly, Shanghai stooped low over the boy and asked: "Now, son! Just what do you want?" Back came the reply: "Please, sir! I just want to hear you talk!"

"I am introducing religion"

"That you shall, son. That you shall," boomed the Colonel, as he patted him on the shoulder and asked about the little bundle of clothing tucked under his arm. Before the boy quite understood what was happening, the Colonel was saying: "Just the boy I've been looking for. I'll take you down to the ranch in Texas. You should be there right now . . . making something out of yourself. Come on, son. Let's go. I'll sell you a horse. I've got a nice little bay, bottomed just right for a boy your size. I could give him to you, son; but that won't do. You should work for what you get. You'll keep it after you work for it. I'll charge you interest, too. No hurry about the pay. The thing is: Buy what you get in this world, son. It may come hard but it won't go easy. It's better to cry over what you've got before letting go of it than to cry after it after it's gone."

The next morning Shanghai and his new protégé left by train. Their first stop was Louisville. He would, so he told the boy, show him the fair then in session. They took a cab direct to the Galt House, where Shanghai registered, and, suddenly remembering the waiting boy, asked: "By the way, son. What is your name? In my multiplicity of business my old head doesn't seem to hold all these things."

Some thirty-five years after Shanghai registered for himself and the boy who just wanted to hear Pierce talk, two prominent Texans were hunkered down in a duckblind near Indianola, Texas. A cold, raw, early morning had suddenly changed to a murky mist as the sun rose to add its heat. The duck flights stopped. Geese called to their mates, out in the marshlands. Both men, one ranking as the dean of the medical profession, the other a substantial Texas merchant, knew that the day's shoot was over.

The doctor reached into his pill bag and, passing a small flask to his crony, said: "They won't fly any more today. Let's take a drink."

"A bit of it, Doctor."

Again, there was silence until the doctor spoke: "I've known you a long time, but I've never known whether you are "an original G. T. T."[1]

For some moments there was no reply; then he answered: "I suppose you could call me such." And he told the story. "I was born

[1] G.T.T.—Gone to Texas. An expression commonly used when a person left the "States" hastily for "cause."

in Liverpool. My father was as crusty an old salt as ever skippered a ship. For long periods of time he would be at sea, while I took advantage of mother's leniency to roam the waterfronts in search of whatever deviltry I could find. I had just turned thirteen when the Skipper came home one trip to hear that I had been more disobedient than usual. The old man grabbed me by the scruff of the neck and marched me down to the docks. There he talked long and positively with a master. A bargain was struck. The captain of the ship took a belt of coin, five hundred dollars of which was to be given me at my journey's end.

"Now go learn the ways of the world. I hope I never hear of you again," shouted my father as the vessel pulled away from the shore.

"The boat docked at New York, and the captain, true to his promise to my father, strapped my money around my waist, and cut me loose to fend for myself.

I wandered a long time; then I heard a commotion. Many people surrounded a tall man with a big beard and a bigger voice. I joined the crowd. He was telling of the wonders of Texas, his cowboys, his ranches, his cattle. I followed him into the hotel. Then he demanded: 'Just what is it that you want, son?'

And, Doctor, when Shanghai Pierce asked me my name there in the Galt House that morning, I gave him the first name I could think up. I did not want my father's name. I have never spoken it since. I shall never let my family know my real name. . . . You can say I am a 'real G.T.T.,' and you can say also that Shanghai Pierce was a great man. Everything I am and have dates back to the advice he gave me."

When Shanghai arrived at the ranch with the boy he found distressing news. Tom Nye, instead of "taking the cars" back to Texas after delivering Pierce's cattle, had ridden back through the northern part of Texas and bought some land—some for Pierce's cattle which he could not market, and six thousand acres for himself. Also, he had drawn on the Colonel for $5,000. In explanation, Nye said:

> We stopped our cattle in Wichita County, just north of the river the men up there had built there pastures and left about 17,000 acres outside, surrounded by fence except 2 miles Nobody

"I am introducing religion"

in there, so we bought 6,000 acres next to the gap & we then built the 2 miles of fence & have got the cattle we took up there in a pasture. up in that County Every Rancher up there, Whether he owns the land or not, Claims all the land 25 Miles of him & if you go in anyhow, they with there Scalawag hands could make it too hot for a Small man with a few cattle. Some men have got 3 and 4 hundred thousand acre pastures fenced & only own 50 or 60 thousand acres. I see thair is a great deal of fence cutting up in that section of country & I do not blame the cutters Much under the circumstances.

Nye's troubles piled up fast and furiously on Pierce. The Colonel sent Tom some checks which Nye neglected to cash. The shaky condition of the Island City Savings Bank was known to Pierce, and he had been careful to get all his money out, but Nye's failure to cash the checks caught him short for a substantial sum. "I had just come to the Conclusion," explained Nye, "to return the Checks when I See in the Morning paper the failure of the Island City Savings Bank. Bad Luck to them!! I do hope that they have not hurt you badly. I was holding the checks never dreaming for an instant that the Island City would bust; rascality & DisHonor is the Cause. Dont Cuss me to Much as I thought I had the Rock of Gibralter behind me. I am going to do in the Matter what is right, if it loses me the whole amount & I only hope that they have not hurt you Severely."

In order "to do in the matter what is right," Nye sold some of his Wichita County lands to Jonathan Pierce, and then he and Pierce sold to a Mr. Lombardi and John G. James, the latter being president of the Panhandle National Bank. Shanghai was greatly displeased to learn that Jonathan had been given the opportunity to purchase the land, and he made his displeasure known. To this Nye, replied: "I have studied over the letter you wrote me on February 14th, in which you gave me such a talk & it has worried me no little. I am afraid that you think that I did you some dirt in our deed of trust business. I am not aware of having done you any wrong in the matter at all, unless it was wrong for me to sell John Pierce the Wichita land that he proposed to buy himself. Now I am willing to do what is right about paying what I owe. I now propose to sell out my land & cattle to you so that all I owe you will be paid. I would thus be enabled to pay my debt to you included in the deed of trust. All my cattle & all my land, about 15,500 acres more or less, you can have & pay at your own convenience & whatever rate of interest you think right, for the balance comeing back to me. Make your own terms! You have always been my friend & I am not complaining Now at all: but after reading your letter I have come to the conclusion that you would rather have the money that I owe you back again."

However, if Shanghai was displeased over the sale to James and Lombardi, he got a real shock when James wrote him:

> Mr. A. H. Pierce:
> I write to say that I have just found out that the title to the Dembreski Survey, in the so-called Nye Pasture, near here—nearly 2,000 acres—rests upon a Forged title. I have written Mr. Nye. I have acquired an interest in this land with Mr. Lombardi, who purchased from Nye & Pierce. I have written Mr. Lombardi, also, and neither he nor I expect to pay any more on the notes. If you can, go back on your warrantors & let the land go. I feel it my duty to notify you & I trust you will duly inform your brother, J. E. Pierce.

Now that both his friend and brother were in financial troubles, caused by "forgers and Skalawags," the Colonel went into action. First, he made certain that Lombardi and the Panhandle National Bank would undertake to carry out the trade, as Mr. James had said he would, if the title could be cleared. Finding their intentions good and both men financially responsible, Pierce next turned to the real heirs. Nye furnished the information that three young women actually owned the property, one was married, and the other two were properly represented by a guardian. Shanghai, thereupon, sent J. E. Pierce off to New Jersey to "see that this evidence is jenuine & Not false." Finding it "jenuine," Shanghai came across with $1,500 on behalf of his friend, Nye, at the same time, letting brother Jonathan do his own trading. Now, with good record title, at a cost of $1,500, Nye could relax and write his friend: "First, I will tell you all the news. It is not quite so hot here this summer. Maybe it is my imagination, because Lombardi has paid me up in full."

When Pierce arrived from New York with the extra supply of Winchesters and the British lad in tow, he found the fence-cutting situation not as serious as he had feared. The K and KO

"I am introducing religion"

Ranches had suffered some damage, but Pierce was able to wire Augustus Kountze that the raid had been of a minor nature. To this Kountze joyfully replied: "I note that you feel quite sure that few, if any, cattle escaped out of Ranches 1 and 2 in consequence of fence-cutting. Evidently you are lying awake at night in consequence of losses which Mr. Stafford may sustain."

It was a different story, however, when the boys with the snips struck again in the night, laying down both Pierce's and Kountze's pastures. Again Augustus Kountze thanked Pierce for relaying the information so promptly and hoped "that the damage done by fence-cutting will be restored soon and the loss will not be very large." A third report went on to New York, and Mr. Kountze thought: "Its contents are certainly of a very reassuring character. I thank you for the courageous resolves, and I doubt but that they will be faithfully carried out, viz: That you are ready to meet any and all emergencies which may arise to protect your and our property. I most heartily approve of the punishment of all crime whereever detected. I earnestly hope you (you and Crary) may discover the miscreants and bring them speedily to punishment."

What Kountze did not know was that the Winchester men were already riding to protect the Kountze ranch. This information came in a note delivered by horseback to Pierce and Crary. It read:

A. H. Pierce and Colonel Crary:
My man has arrived. He has sent for another man who will be here in a few days. Treadwell will likely be over at your place tonight.
J. M. Mathis.

Since the men with the snips had found the answer to the impositions placed on them by the Big Pasture Men, fence-cutting, Pierce said, became "Epidemick." Governor Ireland, consequently, was importuned so persistently to give relief that he called a special session of the Texas legislature. A large number of cattle barons, some of whom had laughed at the nester when he poked his nose over the barbed-wire fence, now converged upon the capitol. They buttonholed every available legislator. They demanded a law penalizing anyone convicted of "the wanton destruction of a fence."

Shanghai Pierce

Pierce joined the conflux. T. M. Mathis was there, insisting that a "representative influential group" should call upon the governor in his office and lay their views before him. Shanghai went into action. He assembled the group and led the way, Mathis following along. The governor was friendly, and the conversation drifted from fence-cutting and pasture-firing to the merits and demerits of the sundry breeds of cattle. Mathis seized the opportunity to garnish the qualities of a herd of Jerseys he was developing down on his Rockport property. Pierce tried to say a word in behalf of his experiment with Brahmans, but, for the second time in his life, he was unable to make himself heard above Mathis' enthusiasm. Suddenly as if to cinch his advocacy, Mathis stopped talking on a high note, shouting: "Why, Governor, I have a cow down there that will give five gallons of milk every day!"

Pierce leaned forward and spoke into the face of the Jersey exponent: "If I had a cow like that I'd never touch a tit."

Mathis wanted to know why? The Colonel repeated: "Mathis, if I had a cow that would give five gallon of milk, I tell you, I'd never touch a tit. I'd make her stick out her tongue, and I'd dip out the milk with a long-handled gourd."

The legislature gave the barons the law they wanted, making fence-cutting an offense punishable by imprisonment from one to five years. It added grass-firing into the statute, as if for good measure, but offset the friendly gesture by circumscribing the cattle barons with another provision which permitted anyone to cause a fence-owner to install a gate every three lineal miles.

Pierce's legislative success caused him to turn his attention to the notice he had received from "my Denver Brother" that some prominent cattlemen of the West were to assemble in Denver to discuss quarantine laws. This was an opportune time, so the Colonel thought, to take his daughter on a western tour and divert her mind from that grey-templed Kansas City lawyer. Therefore, Miss Mamie and her father set out to the West. They stopped at Saint Paul, toured Yellowstone Park, and registered at the Palace Hotel in San Francisco. From there, the Colonel wrote Hamilton:

> Write all the neuse to Kansas City care St. James Hotell. The Weather is fine here fire Everyday overcoats in demand a fast City went last night with a crowd of policeman through the Hells

"I am introducing religion"

of Chinatown it is a Hell beyond description   will leave for Salt Lake in about 3 days.

En route Denver the "neuse" caught up with him that Willie Labauve, his most efficient ranch boss, "has resigned his position unconditionally and is going off to school." Hamilton proposed the appointment of Clay McSparren as Labauve's successor, saying of Labauve: "I don't think you will be much hurt by him leaving your Employ. After he goes to school he will be too much of a dude to be any use to you."

To this observation, the Colonel made prompt reply: "I don't think I will take the bankrupt act on account of his resignation, but try & Collect What he owes us before he leaves for Colledge—as it is Customary for all officials to be prepared to Settle up when they hand in their resignation."

Upon arrival at Denver, the father and daughter registered at the Windsor Hotel. Miss Mamie toured the region, while Pierce closeted himself with the western cattlemen. Their chief complaints were hinged on the vexatious question of the cause of so-called Texas fever and the quarantine laws which had been passed in several states in an effort to prevent the spread of the disease.

Texas fever was not a new subject among cattlemen. In 1868, a Chicago firm had driven two herds into Illinois. One of these herds had originated in a Texas coastal county. At Red River the cattle had been put aboard a river steamer and unloaded at Cairo, Illinois. The other herd had gone by ship all the way from Port Lavaca. Both herds suffered a large number of deaths. It was contended by some that overcrowding and heating on the boats were responsible for the losses. Others contended that Texas coastal cattle were disease-carriers, that the disease became active after there was a change of climate. The fact that indigenous northern cattle contracted a disease and died soon after coming into contact with the Texas cattle gave weight to the latter contention. The disease first became known as Spanish fever. Later it was known as Texas fever.

Other herds brought the disease along with them. In some instances, a trail of devastation lay through the states passed through. Incensed local cattlemen and farmers held protest meetings in many places. Northern and western cattle raisers who had cattle for sale saw their markets being crowded with longhorns. Fever or no fever, they resented the invasion and joined in protest with the farmers, and ill feeling was soon fanned into a high rage against the Texas cattlemen.

The citizens of Champaign, Illinois, made it clear by mass-meeting resolution that: "We will be justified in making personal efforts by forcible means, if necessary, to prevent any further admission of such cattle into our country."

A newspaper waved the red flag of violence when it stated: "The citizens are fully aroused, and I don't think it would be safe for a Texas steer to be seen in these parts, nor would I vouch for a man having them in his possession."

With these blasts at Texas cattlemen, Champaign citizens indicated their willingness to put an end to the driving of Texas steers through their country by purchasing a plot of ground without the corporate limits, and—that all might take notice of its intended use—a large sign was erected, reading:

COWMEN'S CEMETERY

Other towns followed the pattern of the Illinois city. This gave Old Shanghai an idea. One day he brought his herd up to the city limits of a Missouri town which was unco-operative with cattlemen, and there Pierce saw a sign which read: "Speed Limit 10 Miles per Hour. Violations Prosecuted." Obviously, the restriction was designed to limit the show-off activities of local "bloods" who prided themselves in ownership of fast sulky horses.

Shanghai called a parley of all hands. Finally he announced: "Boys! I don't know whether they can make it or not, but we'll sure try."

Later, Shanghai told the story: "Well, sir, we held up at the edge of town, and us in back of them old longhorns, at a prearranged signal, charged 'em waiving our slickers and chaps, yelling and shootin' off our guns. Then them old critters had an idear of their own. They went down onto that village rather sudden, and they waked them people from their tranquility. The rumble was like thunder. A dense cloud of dust and all hell broke loose on 'em at once. Citizens took shelter where they could get the quickest. Some climbed gate posts, some went up trees. Others looked at

"I am introducing religion"
my passing herd from roof tops. Fences went down. Clothes lines disappeared. Flying destruction went through there on the horns of my cattle, and you know, Sirs, all of us were out of Missouri and into Kansas before them long horns quit runnin'."

After the vituperation meetings in Champaign, the people of Illinois took up the cry against Texas fever. This caused the governor to call a convention of experts. Joseph McCoy, friend of the Texas longhorn, attended. He branded the participants as "a collection of quandam quacks and impractical theorists and imbicile ignoramuses without equal."

He found, so he wrote:

> Delegates in attendance from most of the northern states; also two or more from the Canadas. A portion of the delegates were esculapianse of the most deadly type (Others mere political bummers) sent to that convention by their respective governors to relieve the community, for a short time at least, of a pestilential crew. Others were so prejudiced as to be utterly unfit to deliberate on, or investigate, anything. A portion were of that class who will enjoy special immunity on the Final Day, if it be true that "unto whom little is given, little will be required." There were a few earnest seekers after truth and information on the subject of Spanish fever and the importation of Texas cattle and "what to do about it." The convention, as a body, was a prejudiced, impractical one, filled with a burning hatred of longhorn kine.

After thorough discussions by the Denver assembly on Texas fever, the "grab" of the Cherokee Strip by a thrifty group of cattlemen who undertook to lease the entire Strip from the Indians, and means to be employed to pass Texas cattle through the Colorado quarantine, Pierce and his daughter headed eastward, making a stop at Kansas City, where the Colonel met his prospective son-in-law.

Henry Withers was an easy-going, jovial young man, whose friends habitually greeted him with nicknames or abbreviations of his real name. This familiarity Pierce interpreted as a lack of manly dignity on Withers' part. One morning, when the Colonel and the young lawyer were walking down the street, a chance acquaintance passed and called out, "Hello, Hen." The Colonel shook his head and went on. Then another passer-by called out, "Hi! With." Pierce stopped squarely in the walkway, and, addressing himself to his prospective son-in-law, he said, in disgust: "My God, Sir: Doesn't anybody in all this big city know you as *Mister* Withers?"

Before Miss Mamie left to continue her studies in the East, she made a request that her father prepare a definite statement of the condition of her deceased mother's estate. She wanted her property rights acknowledged, now that her father was married the second time and she was contemplating marriage. This put the Colonel in quite a huff, but he promised he would comply with the request just as soon as he could see Mr. Proctor. Immediately upon arriving in Texas, the Colonel called on Proctor and Stockdale and put the responsibility of drafting a property statement and a prenuptial agreement upon D. C. Proctor.

Hattie Pierce owned some property in Galveston, in which other members of her family were also interested. Now that Mamie had given evidence that she might want her mother's interest in the family estate set aside to her, Pierce was anxious to separate the two estates. He, therefore, called on Captain Nick Weekes, one of his old Confederate compatriots. Weekes, until the failure of the Island City Savings Bank, had been associated with that institution. He had been very popular in Galveston, being something of a politician, and had drawn to his bank a large following of city politicians and political hangers-on. He, quite naturally, in view of such acquaintances, held the deposits of the City of Galveston.

"Political control in Galveston," according to a current newspaper, "is vested primarily in saloons on the prominent corners in the business district and grocery stores with a room attached where beer and whiskey is sold in the residence portion of the city, enabling those in political power to come pretty close to saying who shall be mayor and who shall represent the twelve wards on down to the lesser offices."

With tentacles reaching out into every phase of life in the city, with Nick Weekes and his political connections always available, Pierce soon found an avenue of approach to his problem of selling his Galveston property. Therefore, he called on Hattie's kinsmen J. H. Blagge and confided to him Captain Weekes' suggestion of "the mode of easy sale." Before the trap could be snapped on the unsuspecting purchaser, however, a terrifically cold wave swept down across Texas.

On January 8, 1886, Pierce waked up at the Tremont Hotel,

"I am introducing religion"

to learn that, for the first time in the recollection of men then living, Galveston Bay was completely frozen over. He turned his mind to the affairs of his ranches, and, boarding an early-morning train, he started toward the BU Ranch. From Rosenburg he wired Augustus Kountze: "Severest cold weather ever experienced in Texas. I fear losses of cattle from blizzard will be large."

The blizzard brought the mercury down to fifteen degrees. This alarmed Pierce, and again he telegraphed Kountze at New York: "Still snowing very hard and cattle are bound to freeze to death tonight in large numbers."

Three days later, the weather moderated, and Pierce wrote Kountze that "in all my thirty-five years experience in Texas, I have never encountered any weather in Texas of such severity, still, relatively speaking, your loss in cattle is very much greater than I have experienced."

J. E. Pierce took a skinning crew for Shanghai and went out into the snow. On January 26, he sent a note up to Shanghai, which said:

> I Came out of Bend Last evening have Skined all the grown cattle that froze to Death have between 225 & 250 grown cow hides. think 350 will cover the total Loss. [Hensley] over on the K & KO Ranches, did not have such good luck. . . . Skinned about 1,600 . . . All hides on fence and heads stretched.

Augustus Kountze, who was not taking the report of disproportionate losses too philosophically, pressed Pierce to make a disposition of the cattle, but he was not agreeable to Pierce's suggestion that he (Pierce) be permitted to take out his one-sixth of the cattle and let the management go over to Colonel Crary and Mr. McReynolds. "In regard to your suggestion," Kountze wrote, "of making a division, we can hardly respond favorably, as we have never contemplated any disposition of the cattle except under your direction and management." Then the banker dangled a counterproposal before the Colonel. "We prefer," he said, "disposing of the herd to you at a lump sum on about the same terms of payment as those proposed by Smith & Forsythe—terms of payment liberal, so as to meet your convenience as nearly as may be."

The Colonel passed up the suggestion that he purchase the

entire herd and, forthwith, caused his nephew Gifford to turn his own cattle within the K and KO enclosures. Of course, this information was relayed to New York, and Kountze registered his protest, although mildly: "I consider Mr. Gifford anything but a reasonable man, and we in turn intend to be the same, and I am not finding fault with the number of cattle he has in these enclosures, which I understand to be about three thousand head. I only express the wish he shall add no more to the number, and that no one else should do so, and accordingly I ask you the favor that you would kindly render me your good offices in accomplishing this end."

Kountze said he would also like to know why there was such a large loss in the K and KO brands. In a sarcastic telegram, Pierce replied:

Too many cooks and hence the broth was spoiled.

After the weather warmed up, Blagge got Nick Weekes' scheme functioning. It seems that "Old Man John" owned a most respectable residence adjacent to the residence which Pierce wished to sell, and, of course, he did not wish any riffraff for a neighbor. As a consequence, Blagge gleefully gave his report:

Dear Uncle:

Acting on the advice given by you at our last meeting I am glad to say has brought good results. H. M. Trueheart & Company, real estate agents, have had an offer of $2,700.00 from a Lady of rather doubtful reputation, and Old Man John has been made aware of this fact.

I saw him today, and he seems to be very much alarmed at the idea of having such a neighbor, and said "he would have some money in a few days, and would make Adriance an offer at once," *although Adriance had told him he would not sell to the Lady.*

It seems to me it would be just as well to inform Mr. A. that you intend to sell to the highest bidder, Reputation to the contrary notwithstanding!

I can assure you they will have more offers in a day or two, and I suggest that you do not sell to John for less than $3,000. *Please destroy this after perusal.*

When the Colonel went back to Galveston to close his deal with "Old Man John," he found a letter awaiting him at the Tremont from George W. Littlefield. Littlefield was chairman of the execu-

"I am introducing religion"

tive committee of the Texas Live Stock Association, and he wanted to know:

> Are you going to Denver to that meeting? If so, write me at once, so we may get up Blank Certificates that you may fill out with the name of any member of our Association who you may meet there and is not a delegate. You being a member of the Executive Committee You Must give your influence to build up our State Association. Let me hear from you at once and where I can forward you the Blank Certificates.

Forthwith, Pierce dispatched a letter to Augustus Kountze suggesting that the K and KO ranches be charged with his expenses incident to a trip which he would be willing to make to Denver to meet a convention of cattlemen. "I would state," answered Augustus Kountze, "that should you deem it advantageous to attend that convention, that the K brand would be willing to contribute say— $150—toward defraying your expenses which may be incurred in making said trip: and if during your stay there you should have a favorable opportunity to dispose, at good prices, of a portion or all of the K brand, that you may do so, *provided* that you can do so on terms that would leave a favorable margin of profit over the cost of cattle, including interest and all expenses of whatever name and character."

In the meantime Colonel Pierce had received a letter over which he pondered for a considerable time. Mrs. J. Clay McSparren had written him:

> Mr. Pierce
> It is not often I ask a favor of anyone but I am going to call on you.
> The Ladies are going to have a barbecue dinner for the church to make money to pay a note due first of June. We bought a house and lot for a parsonage and paid one note down, and must not lose what is paid.
> Now Mr. Pierce, what we want you to do is: give us some beef for the dinner   they charge so high for meat we cannot buy it here
> You send over half of a calf on Tuesday's train. I will be at the train to receive it and we will be under lasting obligations to you. If you are in town next Wednesday you must take dinner with us. We will have it in Mrs. Ford's store building

If you send the meat be sure send it Tuesday.
Don't tell clay I wrote this
He does not like me to beg for churches but God does, and we are told to obey "God rather than man."

A few days passed and there was no answer from the Colonel. Then one morning Mrs. McSparren looked northward from the high porch of her home, and she saw the Colonel mounting his horse at Neptune Holmes' little shanty. Pierce rode as if to go across the prairie to the railroad station. Suddenly, he changed his course and spurred his horse straight to the McSparren home. He was almost to the high porch before he wheeled his horse and stepped to the ground, letting his bridle reins fall loosely at the horse's feet. Then the Colonel sat down on the porch. His long legs reached the ground; his shoulders were even with the saddle. Mrs. McSparren's little daughters stared out of the open door at the bewhiskered man. Without a word, he smiled and crooked a beckoning finger toward the girls, who went to him without hesitation. Grasping them gently but firmly, he seated one in the saddle, the other one behind the saddle, while they tugged playfully at his beard. He then addressed himself for the first time to Mrs. McSparren who had stood silently, looking on: "Good morning, Mrs. McSparren. I'm hungry. Got any of that good corn bread you make?"

Mrs. McSparren invited the Colonel into the house. He shook his head, demurring: "Just corn bread, Mrs. McSparren. Just corn bread. Nobody makes good corn bread like you."

Mrs. McSparren returned to the porch with a large pone of bread which she had cooked in a circular pan. She also held a pitcher of milk. Looking at the milk, again, he shook his head. However, he picked up the bread from the plate, and, holding the children on the horse with one arm, he offered the bread to them. After they nibbled, he bit generously into the pone until it was gone. Then, carefully, he lifted the girls to the porch, and, mounting his horse, he turned to Mrs. McSparren with his thanks: "Mighty good corn bread, Mrs. McSparren. Nobody cooks good corn bread like you."

He moved away a few yards before he called back: "That's all

"I am introducing religion"

right about Clay and God and the Church; and old Nep will take care of the calf."

Several days later the Southern Pacific Railroad Company received a letter from the Colonel. He was sorry, he wrote:

> But I tryed to get to See you & Inspection Crowd and failed. I am pioneering in another matter. I am trying to introduce religion in the community and the least your corporation can do is to haul in the tools. The People of this Community want a school, Road & Church but owing to the failure in Crops this year & all being Poor and unable to build. Now will your Company Dead Head 2 Big Cars Lumber from Mills to Pierce if I pay for it & Build and Paint the House. it will Cost me at Least one thousand dollars & your Great Corporation can certainly afford to D. H. 2 Cars Lumber toward the enterprise.

In the same mail, an order went to Jacoby Spears Manufacturing Company for church fixtures. "I enclose," so he wrote, "a diagram of my building Showing the spaces I want filled with seats and the length of the seats. Trust same will be plain to you and that you will be able to make prompt shipment together with pulpit and chairs as ordered."

Under the driving energy of the Colonel and the careful supervision of his nephew Borden, the tools for the introduction of religion into the community soon were being used by "my people." The Colonel was quite well pleased with his pioneering, and, when visitors came to the ranch, he pointed to the church with evident satisfaction. One visitor, not knowing what else to say when the church was shown to him, asked: "Colonel Pierce, do you belong to that church?"

"Hell, no!" sounded off the Colonel. "The church belongs to me."

Before Pierce was ready to leave for Denver, Jot Gunter wrote that he intended to be at the Denver convention and that he had *"honest Texas Salad* enough to feed some steers." This, of course, Pierce interpreted as an overture to purchase some cattle. Since Jot Gunter was a partner of the cattle firm of Smith and Forsythe, the Colonel thought the prospect warranted further investigation. Consequently, he wrote Gunter: "I leave for Denver in about an hour."

Shanghai Pierce

The Denver convention was a typical cattleman's get-together. They discussed the best means of delivering Texas cattle into Colorado. It was Mr. C. B. Kountze's opinion that no effort should be made to change the quarantine laws, for the quarantine board was composed of "fair and honorable men." If the cattlemen from Texas would merely drive their cattle "leisurely so as to arrive at the south Colorado line about the 15th of June, the cattle would be admitted without remaining the 90 days." This discussion gave Shanghai an opportunity to read aloud an excerpt from a letter he had just received from John McCroskey:

> As to cattle & horses, are doing fine and the little bulls are clear of ticks that greasing that I gave them when you was over there worked like a charm it cleaned the ticks of and they look fine.

He also put in a word for his Brahmans, which were interesting him immensely these days. This time he quoted Ike Pryor, who had some of Pierce's steers over in Kansas:

> Every one that has Brahma in him is hog fat. Be careful how you price them. You won't know the cattle this fall. They will make a "darling" bunch to winter.

Then he tried to explain that northern cattle died in Texas as fast as Texas cattle died north of the quarantine lines. "My brahmas get hog fat in the North," he shouted. "and any new bull that I bring to my ranch from the North, that has no Brahma in him, or that has not been greased, will die, even though I pour a double dose of Epson salts down him every morning before breakfast."

The subject, however, which engaged the most serious consideration of the assembled cattlemen was whether Congress would permit the continuation of leasing from the Indians, authorize a tax on trailing through the Territory, or open the lands for white settlement. Every cattleman was admonished to confer with his congressmen.

When Shanghai arrived at Kansas City, he found two letters awaiting him. One was from Federal Clerk Kirkpatrick, who undertook to bring him up to date on the prohibition election campaign being carried on in Texas. A newspaper reporter sought an interview with him. He brushed off the questioner by stating that

"I am introducing religion"

he knew little about the issues down in Texas, other than what Kirkpatrick had written. Then he read from the letter:

> There is considerable interest taken in local option elections in Northern Texas. It is of sufficient interest that Senator Coke and Congressman Mills together with a hundred lesser lights have taken the stump in opposition claiming that it is undemocratic to prohibit the sale of intoxicating liquors, while Lieutenant Governor Martin and a great many others, including all the preachers, are on the other side, and the result is that the excitement is much higher than during an ordinary campaign.

As Shanghai prepared to leave his hotel, the reporter observed that he carried an XXX Log Cabin silver whiskey flask. It was molded in the shape of a log cabin. The spigot was a replica of a closed door. Through the glass windows, the quantity, if not the quality, of the refreshment it held could be determined. It was a present from N. M. Uri and Company, wholesale distributors of XXX Log Cabin whiskey. In explanation of his prized present, Shanghai chuckled: "I carry it all the time, but I seldom take a dram. My friends, you know, rob my house every day."

The other letter which came with his mail was from the then renowned Pennsylvania politician Congressman Thomas Ryan. This politician had taken advantage of the public discussion of the leasing of Indian lands in the Territory, and addressed the Colonel on the subject. What concerned the politician most, of course, was how to get the most profit out of a cattle company which he proposed to organize. The letter said:

> It is important to know what Congress will do, if anything, in regard to Indian leases. My impression is that Congress will confirm the System of leasing. I think an arrangement can be made by which you can stock the range on terms very advantageous to you and profitable to the Company.
>
> Why can't you come to Washington. You want to see the Capitol anyway, and could kill two birds with one stone: have a good Enjoyable visit and put money in your purse at the same time.
>
> I am satisfied it will pay you from every standpoint to come on.
>
> The proposition would be to convey to you an interest in the Company taking payment in cattle on such terms as might be agreed upon.

> The proposition is to[o] large and involves too much of detail to make much progress by mail.
>
> I mentioned a proposition that might be considered. I do not mean that any *one* of a dozen propositions would not be acceptable.

As Shanghai rode toward Texas, he turned over and over in his mind this invitation to a new adventure: Free lands in the Indian Territory; partnership with a successful politician; protection through a Congressman; "any one of a dozen propositions." This was what the Colonel had seen in his dream for power.

When once back on the ranch, he jogged across the prairie in his buggy with Neptune and took out the letter and read it again. Neptune was not enthusiastic over Pierce's disclosure that he was heading for Washington and "my great future with the Indian Territory cattle company." Finally old Nep found his tongue long enough to ask: "Mr. Shang, hadn't we better stay out of that p'litical bizness you don't know nothing about, and stay with our cows we do know somethin' about?"

Shanghai's reply was slow in coming, but at last he said: "Well, Nep, I guess you are right. I don't part my hair in the middle, and sons of bitches and damn rascals, like Galveston citizens, are fine collectors, but damn poor paymasters."

14. *"I recognize no obligation under the contract"*

The effect of the prohibition elections in Texas had been to arouse a polyglot political situation in Wharton and adjoining counties. The impending trouble in Wharton County had been long in the making. When carpetbagger Republicans swept down into Texas after the return of Confederate Texans to their homes, Republicanism, in a form, stayed to fashion the destinies of the so-called "black counties." Few real carpetbaggers, in truth, played important roles in Texas politics, but the preachment of the "forty acres and a mule" office-grabbers had taken the Negroes away from the Wharton, Matagorda, and Fort Bend County plantations. Negroes had become conscious of their numerical superiority. They became clay in the hands of the unscrupulous. Those who gave the Judas kiss were not wholly subscribers to the Republican hegemony. Some native Texans, even some Confederates, eschewing principle, took into their hands the certain means of controlling local elections, and they voted the Negroes en masse. When unscrupulous men ascended to political power, they used the Negroes to the fullest.

It was of this situation that Jonathan Pierce had written his brother after a Matagorda County election: "I hear we have two niggers and Alic Burkheart for commissioners ... a very able sett endowed with great executive abilities."

The political situation was even worse in Fort Bend County. As early as 1869, the Negroes, under the guidance of a few white men who called themselves Republicans, took over the political affairs in the county. Each year they held their convention, nominated a ticket, and regularly elected it. The Galveston *News* gave a picture of one such convention:

> The presiding officer was J. C. Williams, white and heavy: William Reynolds, half white and short, was secretary. J. C. Smith, white and long, was doorkeeper.

Out of this convention came nominee Walter Moses Burton, Negro, who was elected to the Texas senate, representing Fort Bend and Wharton counties. Seven years later, Fort Bend County again elected Negroes for sheriff, treasurer, county attorney, and justice of the peace. In 1880, Walter Moses Burton again went to the Texas senate, and he had, as colegislator from Wharton County, Doc Lewis, also a Negro. It was in this latter contest that W. H. Burkhart was elected district judge. In 1882, Tom Taylor, a notorious cattle thief, became commissioner; and so it went for many years.

A cry of "graft" went up from the "outs" as the officeholders engaged in the construction of public buildings. The old courthouse was torn down, and a new, two-story brick structure, with clock and steeple aloft, took its place, but it did not reach higher than the cries of "graft" from Fort Bend citizens.

The second year after the Civil War, two young men left Matagorda in search of a new home. They stopped their horses in Richmond for a rest. Peareson decided to stay while Wells Thompson rode on to Columbus. There he came to dislike Bob Stafford.

At Richmond, Colonel Phillip E. Peareson associated with such men as Sid Winston, J. H. P. Davis, W. I. McFarlane, the Gib-

"I recognize no obligation"

son boys, and the Frost brothers. Henry Frost was already letting it be known that the political situation was most irksome to him. Frost ran the "gentleman's bar," and, almost by common consent, his place became headquarters for the opposition to Negro control in the county.

Colonel Peareson counseled organization and patience, so, on July 7, 1888, the first mass meeting of white citizens of Fort Bend County, marched into Richmond. Their banners showed: YOUNG MENS DEMOCRATIC CLUB OF FORT BEND COUNTY.

Colonel Peareson made a speech. "We will," he said, "dig the 'ins' out of their holes."

Then a half-witted Negro chanted the mystic Negro spiritual:

*The jaybird flew to the woodpecker's hole,
and said:
"Damn your soul."
Walk, jaybird, walk.*

The "ins" repeated the lines of the Negro spiritual in derision, but the "outs" realized they had a slogan. Thus came into existence the political nicknames Jaybirds and Woodpeckers.

Some unwanted Woodpeckers were visited by the Jaybirds with invitations "to walk" and leave no addresses behind; but J. M. Shamblin gave public notice that he would not permit any political agitator of whatever affiliation to visit his plantation. That night he was shot as he sat reading by lamplight in his home. On his gate post was found a rambling note which started: "i am Just From town and Full of Hell in the neck for all dam misleaders, Mr. Shamblin."

A few nights later, two shotgun blasts were directed at Henry Frost; one tore away the brim of his hat, the other struck him in the right arm and neck. Then, to the surprise of the Jaybirds, a "defection" ticket was named. On that ticket was Kyle Terry, who had been in the forefront of the July-day marchers. Obviously, he had chosen to desert his friends for political preferment. The Republican convention endorsed the "defection" ticket, and the nominees were publicly proclaimed by the Jaybirds to be "apologists for assassination"; but when the election returns were counted, the Woodpeckers had again gone back into their well-feathered holes.

No person, after the election, was so thoroughly despised by Jaybirds as was Kyle Terry. Volney Gibson shared that opinion with his Jaybird associates. Kyle Terry, who was a large man, met Gibson and knocked him down on the street in Richmond. Some time later, Tod Fitzgerald, a close friend of Kyle Terry, was arrested at Wharton, accused of rebranding another man's cow. Ned Gibson, brother of Volney, was a witness in the case against Fitzgerald. Ned Gibson and Little, the owner of the rebranded cow, appeared on the streets of Wharton on the day of the trial. Unknown to either Gibson or Little, Kyle and Fitzgerald hid themselves in Malitz and Barbee's Saloon. As Gibson and Little came within range of the saloon, Little, by mere chance, turned away. Kyle, however, stepped out and killed Gibson with a blast from his shotgun.

Shanghai was away from the ranch when the Fort Bend County feud exploded on the streets of Wharton. Hamilton, however, supplied the news:

> All quiet in Richmond, but if you get the Gal News you know as much as I do about it. Of course, most of Wharton's officials are on the "Woodpecker" side, but a large majority of the best Citizens are on the other side. I have only been to Wharton once for an hour since you left so know but little of what they think of the Richmond affair. No one seems to know where Kyle Terry is. I look for him to turn up as a night assasin in & around Richmond. It is thought by many that he will never come to trial, but will forfeit his bond. If I was one of the "Jaybirds" I would hunt him down as I would a mad dog.

It was not necessary for him to stand his trial. On the day his case, which had been transferred to Galveston, was called, someone from the rotunda of the Galveston courthouse shot him dead. The presumption was that Volney Gibson fired the shots, since he was in the city that day.

When the Colonel returned to the ranch, he learned that the Wharton County officials had taken a page out of the Fort Bend County book, and they, also, were going to build a new courthouse, despite the fact that the county was unable to pay its current debts, except through the issuance of script. Pierce was the largest individual property holder in the county. Only two corporations, the

"I recognize no obligation"

Southern Pacific Railway Company and Kountze Brothers, of New York, exceeded his taxable possessions. Tom Nye had abandoned his Matagorda residence and gone to Cotulla as ranch boss for Dull and Dull. He preferred one hundred dollars a month he received there to some of the irksome conditions in Matagorda County. Captain James K. White had moved out to West Texas. From there, he tried to get Pierce to join him, writing: "What a contrast between a Whiteman's country and a Negro country—that Walrous and Negro country with a Burkhart for a judge!" But Pierce had stayed. Now he must submit to increased taxation or fight the politicians. He chose to fight.

Shanghai saw that there was a direct connection, in Wharton, between the anti-prohibition leadership, the saloons, and the control of the Negro vote by the "ins," who held the political offices. Tom Nye summed the situation up in one of his letters to Pierce.

> Wharton County went Nearly solid Anti Prohibition under the leadership of A Dawdy, Tol Taylor, W. J. Croom. They voted the Negro solid. I am strictly with the Pros for the Saloons are beginning to run the Country & it is time to Choke them to death. Every Scalawag & nearly all of the Negroes & foreigners voted Anti.

W. J. Croom, in his official capacity of county judge, announced that the courthouse and the jail were to be dismantled and that forty thousand dollars of interest-bearing bonds would be issued to defray the expense. The Colonel's first move against this plan was to secure the co-operation of the Southern Pacific. C. C. Gibbs, land commissioner for the railroad, expressed "full sympathy" but remonstrated against the cost of the contest, thinking Pierce's estimate of "the cost to accomplish your object too high." He was willing, however, to contribute $300, provided Pierce and Kountze would contribute $300, with Pierce "getting as much help as I know you can from other sources."

Kountze replied that Pierce should try "vigorous remonstrances," and, should that not succeed, then the Colonel "should take counsel with some of your best lawyers and see if Croom cannot be restrained from doing so by injunction." Shanghai followed Kountze's plan of action, and he was soon able to write:

Last Monday we had a very long meeting of the citizens of the Co. at Court House and Petitions with 560 Tax Payers against incurring the expense of building new Court House & Jail the present one being good enough and went before Commissioners Court and they paid no attention to our request although all the prominent citizens of the County were present, they went ahead and received plans for Court House & Jail which will cost the Co. over $40,000.00 before completed all useless.

I had injunction papers prepared at once and went to our District Judge and he would not grant the injunction he being the same sort of man as our Co. Judge & negro Comr. court.

I then went to Houston to see Judge Masterson. he declined to grant it as it was out of his district, but said it was just and should be granted.

From there I went to Cuero to Judge Pleasants, but found him very sick, left papers with Stockdale & Proctor who will present it to him on Thursday, but should it be granted our Son of a b of a Judge I think will dissolve it.

You are a non resident and can get out an injunction in Federal Court. In that way we can stop them & get the case into Court sure & if you authorize me to sign your name to petition & stand in with me, I will have injunction papers gotten up and presented at once, but that will be very expensive you know & then this fall Election we will beat the entire business & that will wind up the case. But you must be the judge about going into it. I have left not a stone unturned to stop them so far & have not had but little success.

Peareson and Peareson were employed to assist Stockdale and Proctor. Judge Peareson wrote that he was "regretful that Masterson was so particular," and Proctor said he felt "satisfied that I can accomplish nothing," but, when the petition was presented, Judge Pleasants surprised all of them by granting a temporary injunction, transferring the case back to Wharton County, where it again came under the jurisdiction of Judge Burkhart. Augustus Kountze got interested and wired Pierce: "Go ahead. I concur in everything you do by advice of counsel, sharing expense equally with you." When the case was again heard by Burkhart, Peareson came to grief. "I did my best before Judge B," wrote Peareson, "but he smashed us worse than I expected & I had expected him to do us up pretty thoroughly." There was nothing left to be done

"I recognize no obligation"

now except to take the case to the federal court and try to defeat the "Court House gang" at the fall elections. Again, Pierce was away from the ranch when the votes were counted, but McCroskey wired the news: "The Wharton Click carried the Day on the Cort House."

The courthouse and Richmond troubles had consumed much more of Pierce's time than he had intended giving these matters; consequently, as was usual when the season turned warm, the Colonel had taken Hattie and his daughter for a trip to the East. Miss Mamie's cousin Grace accompanied them as far as North Trenton, Rhode Island, where Mamie and Grace left the party and went unaccompanied to Bridgetown, New Jersey. The Colonel stayed on at North Trenton, "sulking in his tent" over a spirited discussion he had had with his daughter upon the arrival of the marriage agreement. Mr. Proctor had written:

> I send you inclosed the paper, and also accompany same with an agreement which your daughter should make with you. This latter must be executed in advance of the others, as you will note that the marriage contract recites that it has been heretofore executed.
>
> I need not tell you why I have not attended to the matter sooner —the fact is, I have never written a paper about which I have thought more, studied harder, and worried more intensely.
>
> I know what you wish to accomplish by it—how much is involved in it—and what results may follow from it—and I further know what anxiety it has occasioned me. It is not a perfect instrument, but it is the very best I have been able to do. I have consciously done my very best, and send it to you, trusting it may serve your purpose, but I am not an insurance officer, and know that the arrangement is accomplished with wiles; but life is made up of such; and as I have worried over this, I have sometimes thought it were best to be in my *cronick* condition "without this world's goods."
>
> I hope you are having a splendid time. Hamilton, doubtless, wrote you about the Richmond troubles. I think there is a silver lining in the cloud and that all will come straight.
>
> Give my very kindest regards to Mrs. Pierce & Miss Mamie. Should write more but it is too dark to see.
>
>   faithfully yr frnd,
>   D. C. Proctor.

Shanghai Pierce

Pierce continued to sulk over in Rhode Island, until he received the second letter from Miss Mamie. She wrote:

> My dear Papa
>   Not withstanding the fact that you have not written me a word since I saw you, and are no doubt carrying out your threat not to write, I am going to send you a few lines this morning to let you know that you are not forgotten by me. . . .
>   Trusting this will find you and Mama both well, and enjoying yourselves, I am with much love to both,
>   yours devotedly,
>   Mamie.

Miss Mamie's letter thawed out the Colonel, and they were soon on their way to Kansas City, where the bridegroom met them for the trip back to the wedding at the ranch. When the rites were completed, Mrs. Withers took "dear Papa" aside and, handing him a package, stated: "Papa! I want you to do me a favor. Keep this for me, please." And when the package was opened, the Colonel found the marriage agreement to which was attached Pierce's own note in favor of his daughter, in settlement of her mother's estate, for the sum of $150,000.

Letters of congratulation from Shanghai's friends found their way into his mail. The ever faithful Tom Nye "was glad," so he wrote, "that the man Miss Mamie is to marry is a good man, and I Hope that he will always be Kind to her. The Price Dull got for his Cows is More than I Expected. Waugh's Ranch is my Headquarters now. It is a good job for me and a healthy country. I have been in fine health ever since I have been here. I Expect it is the hard living —goat & bread—Flour and Corn & Coffee—beans—but a Mexican cook & that spoils the whole—it is Hard to teach a Mexican to cook our way. Cut up a few chunks of goat & put it in a pot of water & boil about ½ hour & then it just suits a Mexican. This is a sample of their cooking. I would not give a good Negro cook for all the Mexicans in Mexico. This is the meanest Stingiest ranch I Ever saw It is nothing to have Meal issued to us full of worms & no Sifter to get the rascals out Either. I wrote Mr. Dull about the Meal."

Ike Pryor took notice of the wedding by writing "Friend Pierce":

"I recognize no obligation"

Today I am Wrangling with old man Snyder while you are giving away your girl. I intended to have sent down a present but have just returned from the Panhandle & had no chance of securing anything appropriate for her. Hope she will take the will for the deed. I have been too busy to eat.

George Washington Miller, founder of the 101 Ranch, added his mite to the event. "My Dear Sir and Friend, A. H. Pierce," said his note, "I received your Leter Sum days Sence. I hope you have gotten well and got a great big sun-in-law & will be pleased with him & he will make Miss May a Good husband & the first baby may be a Boy & named for his grandpa AHP and make a good rustler as he is."

Almost a year after Pierce wired Kountze that a storm had broken over the K and KO ranches, freezing their cattle to death in large numbers, the Colonel told him again that Texas was experiencing a "norther of great severity." Kountze acknowledged that he "was not without considerable anxiety whenever any cold waves strike Texas"; and "the mischief is," said he, "these blizzards are now coming in too quick succession to bode you or us any good. I am constantly feeling quite uneasy."

The new snowstorm continued for three days, after which the weather moderated, and Pierce found that Kountze had lost four hundred "Little Eastern Swamp Angels," while his sea lions had survived the bad weather much better. Jay Forsythe took advantage of the appearance of the cattle to visit the K and KO ranches and make an offer. The Colonel rejected the offer and advised Kountze that Jay Forsythe "does not have money enough to buy a Nigger's supper." He told Kountze, however, that Forsythe's offer should be accepted, provided Forsythe could get his partners, Smith and Jot Gunter, to endorse his notes. Jay Forsythe returned to Houston, and from the Capitol Hotel he wrote Pierce: "After studying the matter over thoroughly we have concluded that the proposition made you is the best we can do, that is, $17.50 per head for the K brand of cattle delivered at Red Rock, Indian Territory, $50,000 cash, when the shipment is commenced, the balance on or before 15th of October, 1888, with 10% interest until paid, the cattle to be yours until paid for."

Shanghai Pierce

Kountze refused to let Pierce close the deal with the buyers, on the basis of their proposal, but called a meeting of all concerned at Kansas City, where Henry Withers drew a contract selling to R. M. Smith, Jay Forsythe, and Jot Gunter "all the K brand of steers, supposed to be about ten thousand head, for which the second party is to pay $17.75 for each animal so delivered, at Red Rock, Indian Territory; Ten Thousand dollars is to be paid at the signing of this contract; Forty Thousand when the shipment commences, and the remainder at any time on or before October 15, 1888."

On the third of April, Jay Forsythe instructed Pierce:

> the Wether has turned of[f] Warmer and the grass is Coming fast think we can commence receiving the K Cattle about the tenth of this month Want you to Bill them al to Mendota Station that is the first station South of Read Rock they have Mutch Better Yards ther for unloading I wil arange My out frit there to receve them You can run them just as fast as you Want to I wil be prepared to handle them.

Pierce forthwith applied to the Santa Fe Railway to provide a chute so that his cattle might be unloaded without delay. The general manager replied that the railroad "was pushing to get through" with its construction, and said, "We will not ship any Stock for Jesus Christ or God Almighty until 10th April." The Colonel sent back his blistering reply: "Until the receipt of your letter I did not know that either Jesus Christ or God Almighty was in the cattle business, but Shanghai Pierce is, and he is going to stay in it. Build the chute, I tell you."

On the morning of the tenth of April, J. E. Pierce and A. P. Borden arrived in Fort Worth with two trains loaded with K steers. "Abel Lost three head," wrote Jonathan. "Beck, the Kansas City Bull Puncher, Lost 12. the cattle are very week, and it is hard to get one up when he is down. They pulled us throu a Whoo ping." Borden reported from Mendota that he had "turned 757 good steers over to Mr. F.—and 3 with the ribs mashed in, one has a leg broken, and another is minus ribs. Nep let one get away. Charlie Ellis lost his dude nigger. He had one of the worst kind of "big jaws" but I got him through without Mr. Forsythe seeing him. We are most

"I recognize no obligation"

through and I do not know what will become of me in the next six months. Can you tell?"

From New York, Kountze registered his complaint, first, because Forsythe did not make the forty-thousand-dollar deposit on the day the shipments commenced; then, when Forsythe deposited a check, he quarreled until the bank reported payment on the check. This was followed by a violent outburst when he discovered that the bank had charged him seventy dollars exchange on the check. His greatest disappointment, however, came when Pierce reported: "I have just returned from Fort Worth and find that things are very badly muddled so far as cattle shipments and railroad facilities are concerned. Up to date we have shipped all told 7,300 head of K brand cattle. We will be fearfully short. Unless I find 1,000 to 1,500 additional on the ranches we will come out the short end of the horn in this deal." And when Shanghai's draft on Kountze Brothers for $7,271, representing freight and feed charges, reached Augustus Kountze, the New York banker looked forward to the time when the "undisclosed one-sixth" contract could be brought to a close.

Pierce went on to New York. He presented Augustus Kountze with bills of lading showing that he had shipped 8,184 steers; that Forsythe received 8,040; and that he had rejected 56 steers. The freight bill had increased to $18,303.65. These Kountze deferred paying, "as I have forgotten whether the Railroad charges we have paid are net charges or whether we are, under our arrangement, entitled to a reduction from the amount charged by reason of the large shipments we have made." Kountze, however, paid the "bill of expenses incurred by Mr. Pierce in the matter of collecting and shipping the K brand steers, and one-third the expenses incurred by Mr. Pierce in the Wharton County injunction suit, the total being," he said, "$1,393.27." Before Kountze would go further with the consummation of the contract, Pierce must, so Kountze told him, file duplicate freight and feed bills, present an itemized statement covering all expenditures for gathering and shipping the K brand steers, get certain improper charges, made by the railroad company, corrected, advise whether this is the end of all the steers or not, whether any steers should be found, and whether or not Pierce would claim an interest in such. Then, giving Pierce a bit of admonition, he concluded: "The railroad companies, as you doubtless have experienced, are always slow to pay for reclamations, however just they may be. I notice there were too many cooks and hence the broth was spoiled."

The Colonel presented the claims to the railroad company, and, as Augustus Kountze had surmised, full "reclamation" was not forthcoming. Shanghai, however, pocketed a voucher for $876 and advised his New York partner, who immediately answered: "I am in receipt of yours advising me of the collection of $876 for K cattle which were killed by the Gulf, Colorado & Santa Fe Ry. Co. It is to be regretted that your modesty prevented the collection of the remaining 44 2/3 head of cattle which were lost in transit, and trust in future you may prove more courageous in matters of this kind, so as to avoid being victimized hereafter."

Upon reading Kountze's critical letter, the Colonel stroked his beard and then said, thoughtfully: "I don't think it is so bad. But Brother Kountze did not fare as well as Ike Pryor and I did the time we robbed the Santa Fe. We got paid for a lot of dead cattle. You know what that is in the cattle business. They died, considerable, and that helped us out. They were cattle without horns. A nigger took a rawhide string and tied their heads up to make them stand. The railroad paid us for them. they did not kick; thought it was a very reasonable claim."

A draft went forward, drawn by A. H. Pierce upon the account of Kountze Brothers, for Pierce's full interest in the "undisclosed one-sixth interest" in the Kountze Brothers' undertaking. Augustus Kountze again deferred payment, demanding that Shanghai provide a full statement of the cattle and an explanation of the shortage: "Now, I am desirous of your explanation which probably has become of the remainder of these cattle, as from everything I could ever ascertain the total death rate in no event ever reached a thousand head. I think that this is a matter which you will feel pleased to give me your best judgment, *inasmuch as you were charged with the care of the K brand cattle,* and therfore I trust will be able to give the most accurate explanation any party could give in reference to the discrepancy or loss in cattle."

While Pierce was taking time out from his correspondence with Kountze and securing certified copies of Kountze's own renditions of the number of the cattle they owned from the tax collectors, Dillard Fant, while on a visit to New York, called upon

"*I recognize no obligation*"
the banker. Fant immediately scribbled Shanghai a note, which read: "Well, Shang I Saw old Man Kountze. He Says you don't need any Guardian for a Neighbor Ranch Man!"

In due time Pierce sent the statement Augustus had demanded, the numbers being supported by Kountze's sworn statements made to the tax collectors.

STATEMENT OF K CATTLE BOUGHT, DIED, KILLED, SOLD, ETC.

1885 yearlings bought by A. H. Pierce	7944	
June & July 2 yr olds " " " "	1171	
July & Aug Yearlings " B. D. Crary	1056	
" " 2 Yr olds " " " "	771	
Killed & paid for by R. R. & a/c for by AHP		9
Hides Sold & a/c by AHP		187
Steers delivered to S & F—sound—		8040
" " " " " crippled		41
" died in transit to Territory		85
" with Big Jaws shipped & Rejected		2
" cripped badly & left in S & F pasture		10
" " " " " " ZV " (died)		6
" skinned by B Kuykendall, fee ½		3
" leg broken at Fort Worth paid fee		1
Bulls and Stags cut & Died before shipping		2
" " " " " sold Hewins		22
Big Jaws now in KO Pasture		8
Steers branded KO, 1888		89
Estimate loss in receiving & branding 1 & 2 year olds 1%		109
Estimate to be on range which we will find yet		200
KO Steers in Herd reported by Borden	19	
" " " " " " Gifford	4	
" " " " " " A. H. Pierce	4	
No. of Steers out in 3 years		2155
	10969	10969
To Loss Net a/c for about 20% in three years	2155.	

Attached to the statement was not only a draft for $4,561.89, but also a request that Kountze Brothers pay him twenty-five cents a

189

head for every animal accepted by Forsythe, the same being a "sales commission."

Of course the draft was not paid. It was, however, returned accompanied by a copy of the "undisclosed one-sixth" contract, and the provisions, thought by Kountze to be determinative, were underscored. They read: "A. H. Pierce shall be entitled to one-sixth of the cattle, or if sold, one-sixth of the proceeds of the cattle. Pierce shall make no charge for any individual services in purchasing and looking after said cattle."

After Augustus Kountze had placed this in the mail, he took his family and boarded a steamer for an extended tour of Europe. This absence gave the Colonel sufficient time to make his reply, which was waiting for the banker upon his return. It was positive and to the point:

> Your statement does not include any compensation to me in making the sale of these cattle. I think, and shall, and do now insist that I am entitled to a Compensation for effecting this sale, and that the contract, so far as denying me this, plainly provides for what particular service I shall make no charge, Viz.: "for my individual services in purchasing or looking after said stock." This I certainly did without charge to you, but in addition to this I did sell the cattle, and did so from personal effort, and attended with no inconsiderable expense.
>
> It is not my purpose to yeald compensation in this regard, for I recognize no obligation under this contract or under any law, human or divine, by which you should have the benefit of my labor, experience and acquaintance, without making me reasonable compensation therefor.

Pierce then informed Augustus Kountze that it was his intentions to be in New York in a short time, but, in the meantime, "you must honor my draft on you for the $4,561.89 with interest."

En route to New York, Shanghai received a telegram from A. P. Borden. It said: "Bob and John Stafford of Columbus was killed Monday night. Will send you the news containing the account when it comes."

Jonathan Pierce also relayed the news: "Staffords got their Just Desserts in the Long race." To these comments, Tom Nye added his approval: "The Staffords, R. E. and John, have won their

"*I recognize no obligation*"

race at last, and have got what they worked for so long and so hard. You have no doubt seen the account in the papers."

The account of the double killing was carried in great detail in the daily newspapers. There had been a long-standing animosity between the Stafford brothers and members of the law firm of Foard, Thompson and Townsend. Two of Townsend's kinsmen, on the fatal day, stood on the streets of Columbus, heavily armed. The Stafford brothers appeared. A barrage of "Nigger-loving" epithets ensued; and then there was a spray of lead, and the Staffords were no more.

Shanghai made a hasty concession to Augustus Kountze, deposited his money, and struck back to the ranch. There he found a letter from L. S. and M. H. Hope, who had been indicted for the double murder:

> Mr. Pierce
> Dear Sir   I have under stood from Some of my friends that you would let us have one thousand dolars to help us out of our trouble in the Stafford killing   we are very poor and both of us have families to take care of   If you will be So kind as to let us have the money you can Send it to T. L. Townsend and he will see that it is used in the proper way   he is our oldest unkle   if we live and git out we will repay.

Following closely upon the request for financial assistance came the Sheriff, who served Shanghai with a subpoena to appear as a witness on behalf of the Hope brothers. Pierce, too, thought it was time to go to Europe, so he ordered staterooms out of New York and prepared to take himself out of the jurisdiction of the courts of Texas.

15. "*That damn Dutchman Bosky*"

Early one hot August morning in 1884, Shanghai rode around by way of the new town of Mackay, en route to the BU Ranch. He had heard that someone was building a new house. From the ranch, the Colonel went on to Fall River where he was to spend his summer vacation. "That damn Dutchman Bosky" troubled him as he rode eastward, and, from Fall River, he told Hamilton what to do about it: "When I left the Ranch and Came up to BU Ranch I Saw old Bosky the Dutchman that owns the R R Land in BU Pasture building a house at Macky   he told me he was going to Moove Some Cattle in in Septr.   I told him he could put in 300 or 350 and no more before I left for the North   but he wanted to put in 700   I told him if he did I would turn them out & also that he must not

"*That damn Dutchman Bosky*"
put in a lott of Common Bulls   I told Dowdy if he turned in over 350 to turn them out & Say nothing about it   So if he does Put them in, they will all drift down to Lower End of Pasture & you post Willie, when he is going up there to Work, Should he go before I get home, to Say Nothing about when he is going up there to Work, but to Commence Soon as he gets in-Side the gate & make a big work & turn all out at Lower gate he can get & Say Nothing about it & tell him to tell his Men to keep their Mouths Shut."

The house-builder was none other than Joseph Boschi, a native of Italy, and close personal friend of Count Telferner. To Shanghai, he was "that damn Dutchman Bosky," the man who advised Italian cattle owners not to sell to A. H. Pierce and the owner of a large acreage within the Pierce Circle. "That Damn Dutchman" had come to Texas with Count Telferner and J. W. Mackay, as one of the builders of the "Macaroni" railroad. He had purchased land script on the New York stock market and succeeded in having 8,402 acres allocated to himself within the Pierce pre-emptions. After the railroad was completed, Boschi remained in Texas, not only to represent himself, but to serve as resident agent for both J. W. Mackay and Count Joseph Telferner, as individuals, and the American agent for the Swiss-American Company, a foreign corporation which had bought both land and cattle along the newly constructed railroad and sold its shares of stock widely in Italy and Switzerland. The principal stockholders of the Swiss-American Company were Joseph Boschi, Joseph Telferner, and J. W. Mackay. This corporation, under the guidance of Boschi, had bought and leased in such a way as to interfere with Pierce and Kountze Brothers in their efforts to push aside all small owners.

After Pierce wrote Hamilton to have Willie "make a big work & turn out" all Boschi's cattle, he waited impatiently at Fall River ten days for news. He employed his time, however, as usual, riding about the countryside, visiting the scenes of his youth and chatting with boyhood friends. One day, while on the west road out of Little Compton, he came upon a "private graveyard—the burial place of my father and mother." No care, he saw, had been given his mother's grave. As to his father's grave, he made no comment, but his observation caused him to change his route back into Providence, where he called upon Charles H. Brown at the Monumental Works, 268 Cranston Street. He gave an order then and there for a family monument. He instructed Mr. Brown to notify his sister, Miranda, "after the monument is erected, [and] I will send you a check for the same."

The first information any of the Pierce family had concerning the monument came through Mr. Brown, who was ready for his check. Miranda was not pleased with her brother's presumption and hasty action but supposed: "Now that it is done, it is all right, but I do not know." The incident was not closed, however, until she had written:

> If you had taken a written agreement, showing just how every part of it should be, and sent it to me I should have known if it was not what you agreed, and would not have received it. However, I suppose it is a good idea to have a family monument, for I have been good for nothing this spring, and Julia is at Maria's sick—has the doctor every day—and Horatio is really feeble this Spring, and cannot do much of anything, and if he does he is sick in bed; and after I have eaten my dinner I can't keep my eyes open. I have been asleep half a dozen times while writing this note. Here I am asleep again and must stop.

It was many years, however, before Miranda closed her eyes for her eternal sleep. Then the family monument was ready to receive the Pierce family history.

Despite his interest in monument-making, Shanghai could wait only ten days before repeating his instructions about "Bosky." On the fourteenth of September, 1884, he penned Hamilton another note from Kansas City:

> Your two favors rec'd on arrival here last night and was glad to here that all things was going nicely. hope you and Pleas made a good drive on Boskys Cows if you can go up there & take Some men with you that you can rely on before I get home, or be at BU Ranch when I come, & we will make a round & turn out all we can find. if Willie Should go up there to Brand he could make it so as to be at the Lower gate by noon & work all the Evening & turn out all he could find & Say nothing about it & it would be done before any one Knew it. Tell Willie to Work Slow & work the Cattle Clean.

"That damn Dutchman Bosky"

In the meantime, good news about "that damn Dutchman Bosky" came to him through brother Jonathan, and he hastened to write Hamilton about it:

> John Pierce Just arriaved Says Everything looks well. I wish you would have Rubin wash my old buggy off Clean & brush it out Inside Clean & put under the Shed & I want Rubin to Rub off My harness & Put it away nicely & First time any one goes up to BU Ranch in buggy, Send it up. John Tells me old Bosky has left BU Ranch—that Mackey owned the Land Instead of Count Telfner —if so it will Probably Save me Some Trouble.

Hamilton was soon able to mail along news that sounded better than that relayed by Jonathan. "Monserratt superceeded Allen McCoy yesterday on this R. R.," read Hamilton's message, "and everybody rejoicing." Pierce also rejoiced, for McCoy had been the Colonel's good friend while working for the railroad. Now that he was in need of a job and was well acquainted with the affairs of the Swiss-American Company, Pierce invited the former general manager to meet him down the river. There they had a conversation which was shrouded with greatest mystery. Both were in good humor when they parted.

Pierce's first move against Boschi was made by B. D. Crary, who pretended to act for Kountze Brothers. He offered to exchange land with Boschi, tendering him sections far removed from the Pierce and Kountze properties. Crary, however, was not successful, and he reported to Shanghai:

> I could do nothing with Bosky, but suggest his V/L notes be bought of[f] King, and they will surely bring the land or money back.

The conspirator next reported from San Antonio, where he had gone in search of King. Before going to San Antonio, however, he had called upon Attorney Townsend, at Columbus. From the Menger Hotel, Crary wrote of his progress and plans:

> Arrived here late last night, the train being behind time. Saw Townsend at Columbus, made known to him my business, but he wanted a little time to consider the matter and he promised to write by todays train to Austin, giving me his determination.

> I had a three hours sitting with King, and finally secured the 477 acres No. 62, provided I find matter at the Land Office tomorrow as he stated them to me, then it will be a trade.
>
> We get the Bosky notes, which are secured by Vendor's Lien and also a Deed of Trust. Bosky has paid $569, and if he lets his payments go by, you will get the land. If he does pay, you will get your money back and 10 per ct interest. King is to make up the necessary papers, so as to transfer to you the entire tract. I also got the GC&SF Section joining the lands we bought. The above was the very best I could do with him.
>
> I will work hard tomorrow to get through with the *Govenor*, Spence, and the Land Office.

W. W. King carried out his agreement with Crary by notifying Joseph Boschi, who was now living at Victoria:

> I have sold to A. H. Pierce, the notes due by you to me in the purchase of land—and will please pay same to him. I Shoed you the tax title held by me on Section No. 73. The owner of same can redeem it at any time within 2 years by paying to you double the taxes & costs. I do not know who the owner is.

Crary called at the BU Ranch after he returned from Austin, and had a confidential talk with bookkeeper Hamilton. He had discovered, while in the Land Office at Austin, that Pierce was preparing to file on a vacancy between the two surveys which lay wholly within the Kountze properties. For Pierce to put himself into ownership of property within Kountze's fences while Crary was helping him put Boschi out of the Pierce Circle was more than displeasing to Colonel Crary. Hamilton listened to the angry man, promised to say nothing to Pierce about the matter, then wrote:

> Col Crary said in regard to the vacant land that he Knew it was there long ago, and would have filed on it but that you beged him not to, as it would open up something that you wanted to Keep covered, and he said that he did not think you would file on it without letting him Know it. He says he has studiously avoided doing anything that will conflict with your interest, and says that if you have done this work intentionally that it is likely to result in a Serious Row among the Ks and you. I write you these particulars to let you know how he feels about it, and I will not let him

"That damn Dutchman Bosky"

Know that I have told you. I dont think that Colonel Crary has written a word to Kountze about this matter. I do not think that it would be good pollicy for you to invite their displeasure for a Small Matter.

Regardless of Hamilton's opinion as to his employer's "pollicy," Shanghai became enraged at the Land Office when he learned that McReynolds, acting for Crary and Kountze Brothers, had filed upon the vacancy. And he let his position become known to the Land Commissioner: "I am very much Supprised. The records show the survey was for A. H. Pierce, patent to which you turned over to von Rosenburg on an order from F. C. McReynolds, a Hireling of a Corporation & you admit you have no Evidence of any ownership from him or Texas Land & Cattle Company.[1] I was not aware that it was the duty of a State officer to Make Fish of one & Fowl of another or that this state were run Solely by & to the Interest of Corporations. Please send Pattent & Oblige."

Some time elapsed after Pierce and former general manager McCoy held their confab up the river, and McCoy, fearing he might be left out of developments, became restive and wanted to hear from Shanghai: "In case you have a little time I would like to know what you found out about the matter we spoke of up the river?" Much more had developed than Pierce had divulged to McCoy. Boschi, who had been feeling the pressure and was anxious to come to terms, wrote Pierce:

> Dear Sir! I had to wait a few days to answer your esteemed letter in order to consult with some of the Gentlemen you named. I am very anxious to come to an understanding with you about our business down at Mackay & So I did examine very carefully the propositions you submitted for the settlement of same.
>
> The company I represent ow[n]es & controls on the west side of Colorado River about 10,000 acres of land, some of these being leased. To ascertain the number of acres of land required to feed a cow, I beg of you the permission of taking Mr. Reeves average as that which would suit us, viz: As Mr. Reeves with 6,000 acres can support 1,000 head of cattle, I, with 10,000 acres, would put about 1,500 head & would agree & bound myself to this.

---

[1] Kountze Brothers incorporated their Texas holdings under the name of Texas Land and Cattle Company.

Shanghai Pierce

I would agree also, as your letter says, to have my cattle moved in your new pasture in the Six Summer months & per contra you shall put in my pasture 1,500 head of cattle for the six winter months.

You tell me you have built a new pasture north of the R.R., so you must have enclosed in same 1 2/3 Sections, or about 1,100 acres owned by me: per contra you possess acres 1,458 about in my pasture. I submit to you the proposition to exchange said land with due compensation for the difference.

Finally, I am also willing to pay you for the fence you have built around your land & this I will do in proportion of what is generally in use.

About giving you the management of my Co's cattle down at Mackay, I must state again (& I am sorry for it,) what I told Col. Crary Sometime ago, when he made me the same proposition in your name, viz: That at present I am unable to decide on the subject, but as soon as I have arranged & straightened my Co's business, I think I will be ready to come to an understanding about it.

Hoping you will find my counter-propositions good & liberal, while awaiting for an answer, I remain, Dear Sir
Respectlly Yours
Jos. Boschi.

Shanghai withheld the disclosure of his intentions regarding Boschi's counterproposals and sought a talk with the old Italian. Boschi was invited over to the BU for the talk. Accepting he answered:

Mr. A. H. Pierce, Esq.,
Wharton, Tex

Dear Sir
Replying to your favorite of 16th I will tell you that I will come to your Ranch tuseday 22th and we will speech about.
Respectfully yours
Jos. Boschi.

The "speech about" resulted in nothing; consequently old Boschi decided to turn over the management of his affairs to an agent, other than the anxious Shanghai, of course. Hamilton heard of Boschi's decision; therefore, he rode over to Mackay for a "friendly" visit with the Italian and to give him some neighborly advice.

"That damn Dutchman Bosky"

What he did there went forward in a letter to the Colonel: "Only three days ago I heard that Boschi had engaged old Abe Kinchelow to take his ranch & farm and I rode over before breakfast the next Morning to see him about it. I told him what an old rogue Abe was and he put a boy on a horse while I was there and sent him to tell Abe Not to Come. he was to move the next day. Boschi thanked me heartily for telling him about Abe. Mr. Boschi told me while I was at his house that you told McCoy that he [Boschi] did not have more than 600 head of Cattle on this range. Boschi has on his Memorandum about 1,100 head including calves. Clays count is 871. Boschi asked me if I knew and I told him I could find out from Clay. Shall I tell him anything? Boschi is very anxious to ship 2 cars of his Cattle, and the old man is so clever I have promised to help him get them: will only work the Cattle below first dam and Jones Creek."

Two weeks later, Hamilton reported to the Colonel: "I shipped 2 cars old Cows for Mr. Boschi to Chicago. I charged him $7.50 per head expences."

Some months after Boschi received his "expence" account from Pierce, Boschi and McCoy had a chance meeting on the train. From the town of Hungerford, Allen McCoy jubilantly reported the incident to Shanghai: "Mr. Boschi came over on the train this morning and I will send this to you by messenger from Mackay—I had an engagement here today, or I would have stopped over myself to have seen you. Mr. Boschi informs me that his company owes you about $200 for pasturage or Something of the Kind in connection with the care of the Co's Cattle."

Then McCoy gave Shanghai the news he had been wanting so long to hear: "Every arrangement & all matters pertaining to the Swiss Co. now requires *my* approval as Agent & Atty in fact in Texas for the Curator [receiver] in Switzerland—I Expect and hope that it will soon be determined over there to put the whole matter in the way of Entire Liquidation & close it out. Now what I would like is this—that you take in payment of this bill—Say—100 head of Steers deliverable in the Spring at whatever price rules at that time for such steers. They will, I think, be three years old then—and *advance* now on them—Say—$500. If this meets your views, please, send by bearer, Check and Contract which I will execute for the Delivery in the Spring.

"You have always wished to be released from this Neighboring interest & now you Can do much to assist me in closing its affairs out."

Then, as if by mere unimportant afterthought, McCoy remembered: "I need a little accommodation from the bank for 60 days. So, I would like if you would favor me with your good Endorsement to the enclosed note for $1,378.94, and place me under renewed obligations."

Despite Pierce's aversion to signing the "accommodation paper" he lent his "good endorsement."

Shortly after McCoy secured the signature of endorsement, Boschi got good news from Italy. He had "come into possession of his funds"; and, leaving the United States immediately, he was next heard from at Milano, Italy. In the meantime, Pierce's endorsement note came due, and for one and one-half years McCoy evaded payment. Finally the bank sued, including Pierce, of course, as endorser. This brought forth McCoy's assertion:

> Colonel:
> I most sincerely regret any annoyance the circumstance has caused you, But aside from this, I beg to assure you *most positively* you shall not have anything further to do with the matter. The Bank treated me most contemplably, as I think, and they did you, too; I would have paid them long before this but for their *threats* of suit, first, and suit afterwards when there was no necessity in any sense of such action. They claimed they were obliged to take such action to carry out *Banking principles*. I do not care to pay them since they sued until they get *judgment*. Of course, the annoyance to you I cannot in any way mollify at present but the *Whilijig* of time may possibly bring about an opportunity when I can show my appreciation.

Aften consulting with his Houston lawyer, who advised that there was no way to defeat his liability as endorser and "to look to McCoy looks rather slim," Shanghai paid in full and charged it up to losses.

McCoy's "whilijig," however, turned Pierce's way in a short time. From Milano, Italy, came a letter from Boschi, who would "have written sooner but I have been so exceedingly busy that I have hardly any time to spare." He informed the Colonel, however:

"That damn Dutchman Bosky"

    Now, I allow me in notifying you, that I have consented after mature judgment to the dissolution and liquidation of the Swiss-American Company.
    I beg to inform you, too, that whenever you might settle with my friend and representative, Mr. Jasper Fossati, the purchase bargain of the sale of land, formerly King, and now my property, I have authorized him to do it, and I bind myself to rectify what he will agree.

In due time, from Liguous, Switzerland, came notice of the appointment of Emelio Ruscovia as liquidator of the Swiss-American Company, and the confirmation of the appointment of E. D. Linn, Jasper Fossati, and Allen McCoy as liquidating agents of the company in Texas. McCoy could not decipher his power of attorney, for it "is written in *Italian*," but he "sent it off for official interpretation," after which he placed it on record. Fossati wrote to Pierce that he "had tried to persuade Boschi to sell, but I new beforehand that he would not at your price, after he went in possession of his funds, still I retain the power to Sell, and I claim to See more than Boschi does, the necessity for him to dispose of his lands—and selling to you. Add 25¢ to your offer and the land is yours."

    "I don't care about the cattle," wrote Pierce to his lawyers, "but have to buy the land in self defense." Then came the news: "Boschi has died lately; the original holders of stock are scattered through Italy, as are also the creditors. Most of the stock is owned by Count Telferner and Boschi."

    Attorneys Glass, Callender, and Proctor called Shanghai to Victoria for a conference. The purchase money was paid over to the resident agents, their deeds having been accepted. Proctor thought their signatures, under the circumstances, failed to pass good title, but, he counseled: "Take the land, Colonel, and sell it, and we'll keep it going to purify the title."

    Pierce went back to the BU Ranch and ordered McSparren to get the boys out and clean the Bosky range, to shove every animal not owned by him beyond the fences. Shanghai went along to see the fun. During the drive, the cattle passed a farmer's cow lot, and his milk cow was "permitted" to go along. When evening came, the farmer went with his pail to do his chores. Failing to find his cow, he made inquiry of his son, who told of the passing of Shanghai's herd. The farmer pulled down his gun and soon overtook them. He asked for Shanghai, who was pointed out to him. Unlimbering his Winchester, he gave positive evidence that he intended to kill the Colonel, then and there.

"Hold on, here, son. What's the trouble?" asked Shanghai.

"You stole my cow," angrily spoke the farmer.

"Well, well," said Shanghai, "that's all right. Take your cow. Cows have been here before you and I came; and they will be here after both of us are gone; but remember, son! There will never be another Shanghai Pierce."

16. "*We will rob them Yankees*"

"Mr. Pierce, it is very hard work. Stock very seldom sells above par, you know. We will issue the stock. I will take it up to New York and we will rob them Yankees!"

Daniel Sullivan was rubbing his hands very gently together as he spoke.

Shanghai and Little Dannie were standing at the corner of the Indianola Mercantile Store, looking out upon the waters of the Gulf of Mexico. Little Dannie, however, was not seeing the roll of waves upon the beach. He was seeing, in his mind, "a soft thing." In fact, he was feeling it as he rubbed his hands together. It was "velvet"—this thing he had proposed to Shanghai.

Ever since Pierce had settled up with Sullivan after the sale of cattle to Mathis in order to go to cheaper money markets, there had been a void in the banker's "1 per cent per month compounded monthly." What made this void ever so much more painful was the common knowledge that Pierce was more prosperous than when utilizing "credit unlimited" with Sullivan. To make things worse, Little Dannie had suffered some reverses while Shanghai had prospered. A great tidal wave, following in the wake of a hurricane, had almost swept Indianola off the beach. Sullivan's merchandise loss had been heavy. Many of his debtors had suffered irreparably. Some had died in the storm. Collections were at a minimum. Security for new loans was scarce. Besides these calamities, bankers from large cities were beginning to invade his territory.

There was a bright spot, however, in the outlook for Sullivan. Thomas O'Connor, the banker and Big Pasture Man of Victoria, had invited Sullivan to join him in a banking partnership with headquarters at San Antonio. Sullivan had accepted Mr. O'Connor's invitation, but he was loath to leave such a fertile area to the "ravages of the Cattle Kings." He would like to retain an association with his friend Shanghai, now giving promise of becoming the "king of Cattle Kings," who made money so readily. Therefore, Little Dannie proposed that Pierce, also, go along to San Antonio, as a partner.

"Little Dannie, it is too far off."

"Well, then," coaxed Sullivan, "why not form a million-dollar cattle company. A. H. and J. E. Pierce could subscribe for three-fourths of the stock. I will take a quarter, and I will take the stock up to New York and we will rob them damn Yankees!"

Pierce heard Sullivan's proposal to the end, then, mounting his horse, he called back to Little Dannie: "I go you, if 'my Counsellor' approves." Mr. Proctor counseled secrecy and, at the same time, admonished Shanghai that the land found necessary for the formation of the corporation should be speedily bought. He also suggested the impropriety of forming a corporation which would be predicated wholly upon selling stock to northerners. To this objection, Shanghai replied: "As a matter of course, he is to do the robbing. If I get my share, why should I cut up?"

Another meeting was held at Indianola. The Colonel and Sullivan agreed that Colonel John Dennis, an attorney at Wharton, should be employed to purchase some twenty thousand acres; that all land titles should be taken in names of persons other than

"We will rob them Yankees"

Dan Sullivan, to maintain secrecy, but that ownership would ultimately be conveyed to A. H. and J. E. Pierce, three-fourths, and to Daniel Sullivan, one-fourth.

Colonel Pierce had coveted the Duncan plantation for many years. This body of land, comprising 16,066 acres, lay east of the Colorado River and astride the Matagorda-Wharton County line. It was close to Shanghai's BU Ranch, both ranches skirting the river. "I can buy the Duncan Ranch," Pierce enthusiastically told Sullivan, "at a very low rate—$2.50 per acre. Mr. Duncan was offered $800,000 for it before the war. We can get it for $50,000. It is a bargain. It is worth four times the money we are paying for it—a bargain doubly so!"

Sullivan was cautious in his committal. Imbued with confidence in his own judgment and unwilling to risk any disruption of his fast forming scheme, Shanghai threw caution to the winds and made Little Dannie a promise: "We will buy it, and whenever you want to turn that back, *I will take it and pay you your money and 12 per cent interest.*"

Mr. Duncan met Pierce at Wharton, by appointment, to consider the sale of the plantation. Shanghai offered $40,000. With apprehensions that Shanghai might not let his offer stand for future acceptance, Duncan declined the offer and passed negotiations over to the following day, hoping that such an act on his part would bring a higher bid. That night Shanghai occupied a room jointly with a friend in the town's flimsy-walled hotel. Unknown to Pierce, in an adjacent room was a close friend of Mr. Duncan. The trade was on the Colonel's mind, and he could not sleep. During the small hours of the night, Shanghai whispered to his roommate (and when Shanghai whispered the windows fairly rattled): "By God, Sir. I am going to buy that plantation if I have to pay $45,000 for it!"

The man in the next room arose quietly from his bed and, in his bare feet, moved silently down the hall to tap on Mr. Duncan's door. Morning came, and Duncan let the Colonel seek him to renew his offer. Duncan firmly declined, not even intimating that he would consider a counteroffer. Then Shanghai raised his offer to $42,500. Duncan shook his head. Pierce came again with $45,000, and Mr. Duncan accepted. After Colonel Dennis had drawn the conveyances, Duncan told Shanghai of the midnight walk of his friend down the hall. Pierce sat in silence for a few moments before speaking: "Yes sir, Mr. Duncan. I have always known that I have a valuable voice, and here is an instance where one sentence from my mouth was worth five thousand dollars. By God, Sir. I ought to have it trained."

The Colonel rode over to Victoria and stopped in at the Brownson and Sibley Bank. He was feeling pretty good, now that he owned the Duncan plantation, but he was melancholy over the loss of the $5,000 to Mr. Duncan. He, therefore, decided he would take a fling at the stock market and recoup some of the $5,000 he had so glibly "whispered" away. At the close of the day, Pierce pulled out of the market with $9,500 profit.

Sullivan heard about Shanghai's gamble and directed:

> Send two thousand of my one-fourth to me at Indianola. Place the remaining $375 to my credit in the National Bank. You must let it go on the Duncan Ranch account.

Just as Shanghai was considering what to do about Sullivan's intrusion into his personal gamble, Reed Whittaker passed the bank, leading a sorrel horse. Pierce called out to him: "What will you take for him, Reed?"

"One hundred and twenty-five," answered Whittaker.

"Come and get it," shouted Shanghai, as he began counting out the money from Sullivan's "quarter interest." Then, depositing $250 in the National Bank to the account of Daniel Sullivan, he swung himself up on his newly bought horse and headed toward the Duncan Ranch, calling back over his shoulder before he got out of range: "O, Mr. Brownson! If Brother Sullivan kicks about the shortage, ask him if he knows what a carrying charge is."

As soon as Shanghai arrived at Wharton, he went down to the Duncan Ranch on an inspection tour. "Everybody is prowling," he grumbled. "It has been run by a man who has allowed everybody to run it. I cannot convince them I own the property. They all seem to think it is there, and they have the right to divide it." He found the fields grown up in Johnson grass. The many Negro cabins were falling down from neglect and decay. There were no fences. What had once been a fine, three-story brick residence was now a shambles. The upper stories were useless because of the leaky roof. The basement was damp and uncomfortable from

"We will rob them Yankees"

seepage out of the near-by Caney River. Willie LaBauve had already arrived from Dayton with 1,400 steer yearlings. McCroskey was bitterly disappointed in what he saw. Disconsolately, he observed: "They are steers from Eastern Texas. We never got a cow. There is not a female cow in the bunch." McCroskey felt better, however, when Logan arrived, driving 1,352 head of cattle, only fifty-seven of which were steers. When the two herds were mixed, they stampeded, two thousand "little Eastern devils" running in all directions. Finally, Logan and Labauve got them quiet, and Hamilton sent Shanghai a note: "Logan says the cattle left were in good shape. He stayed two days up there and they did not a single one come back. They stuck in bunches. The first lot took up are improving."

Shanghai then made a decision. He would make John McCroskey manager of the ranch. "John," he said, "I am going to nail you in it."

Just as soon as John was "nailed" into the Duncan Ranch, he made an inspection of his living quarters. Forthwith he complained to Pierce:

> That fine house on the Duncan Ranch, it naturally fell down. Nobody can live in it. When I got here it was an old plastered house, and it cracked. There is a big cellar on the bottom. It is right on the bank of Caney. The water gets six inches deep underneath the cellar. It is a large, old barn of a house. Duncan has kept his dogs in it for some years in some parts of the rooms. I cleaned it up. Doors are out of fix. I will live here a while. You will have to get me out of here. We will all die unless we drinked a barrel of whiskey every day. I dont want to do that, so you just build a little house out on the prairie. So far as the house is concerned, it is no account at all. We cant live in it. My wife is sick all the time. I am sick all the time unless I am plum full of whiskey. If I keep three thirds drunk on Caney, I am all right.
> The house is plastered. The plaster is cracked. The roaches have taken it. They crawl all over everything. They got bed bugs in there too. You can't kill them. I can't do anything with that house.

Before the new house was finished, McCroskey had to report more bad news to the Colonel. This time it had to do with his wife.

> Matt is very sick, but I hope that She will be better in a day or two. I had Mr. McCamley with [her] for two days, but she is a little

better this evening. I will have to give him an order on you for the money when he gets threw. I will also have to take her to galv as Soon as She is able.

McCroskey did not make the trip to Galveston, for he too was soon unable to travel. Stoically, McCroskey kept his own illness to himself, but Borden heard about it and relayed the information to Shanghai up in Kansas. Immediately Pierce wrote solicitously:

> am terrible Sorry to here of John McCroskeys Sickness but hope he will soon be better you Best Write him Word when he gets better to Come over & bring his Wife & Stay with you a few days & you Can order Some Ice & such things as he wants & recuperate him up a little.

McCroskey "recuperated up," but Matt did not. She was never able to make the trip to Galveston; they soon took her to the Deming's Bridge cemetery, where she was laid to rest within sight of Jonathan's El Rancho Grande. McCroskey went phlegmatically about his ranch duties. Even when the big snowstorm broke over the range and cattle died by the hundreds, the ranch boss stayed around the fireplace as much as he could. "It was terrible cold," he explained. "Skinning cattle was no nice job. I never hurried much. Never tried to skin them. I could have skinned a world of them if Pierce had issued the order, but he did not issue the order. It was not money in my pocket. Him and Sullivan were rich, and I did not hurry about it at all."

McCroskey found out that there were other things about the management of the Duncan plantation he did not like, now that he was "nailed in" down there. He was particularly displeased with the "free niggers" who were supposed to be cultivating about five hundred acres which had been set apart for farms. Consequently, John went over to the BU Ranch to have a talk with the Colonel.

"I told him," said McCroskey, "Mr. Pierce, we had better quit farming. It is running us behind. In his way of speaking he said: 'It is a hell of a note! We have the Duncan Ranch and have to buy corn to keep a horse alive. We had better plant more corn. It looks like a fine ranch! We should, at least, raise enough to feed a pair of mules and horses.'

"'I want to quit,' I told him.

"We will rob them Yankees"

"He shook his head and said: 'No! No! Go ahead and farm a little more, and I'll buy some corn up north and ship it down to you.'"

Then McCroskey brought up the matter of marketing the cotton the Negro tenants raised on shares, demanding that Pierce sell the cotton immediately after it was picked so he could settle up with the Negroes. Again, the Colonel disagreed with John and ordered him to ship the cotton as it was picked, after which it would be sold on the Galveston market when the price was right. McCroskey went back across the river to the Duncan Ranch. From there he complained again about the cotton: "I am in a little better humor this morning, since I have just got returns from the cotton I shipped. it brought a good price, but I will not be worred with the nigroes, like I am, for all the cotton, for [from the moment] it lease [leaves] Wharton they want to know how they stand and arrangements must be different as I will not ship no more cotton."

McCroskey, who rated himself as "general roust about, superintendent of the ranch, brander of calves, attendant to the farm and everything else," thought it would be a good idea to start a commissary on the Duncan Ranch, so "I can feed them free niggers living down in the bottoms." In order to have a storage room away from the residence, he built a cabin and sent off his order for "a little bacon and molasses." "We'll feed them bacon and molasses, dried apples and rice—the same as Mr. Pierce feeds me and the other Duncan Niggers, now that beef is too high and we don't each much of it," observed the Duncan Ranch boss.

Shanghai rode over to see how things were progressing. First, he saw about a thousand head of cattle that were not fat enough to suit him. "John," he said, "we will have to take some of those old sisters down to the bay. They will die here." Then, he turned his attention to the commissary venture and complained: "McCroskey, you rent that land to them Niggers too high. They can't make anything on it when they pay you four or five dollars per acre rent. No Nigger can take that land and make anything. First and foremost, of course, we aim to get the rent. If there is anything left it can go to the supply account. Now, as to that stuff. I see I have been buying it by the car load. The flour will get weevils in it; the bacon wormy; the loss will be mine. I do not want any supply account in mine. No man can supply Niggers and keep even. You reduce the rent and try to keep even with them. We have a landlord's lien, you know. Between the land and the lord, they get all the Niggers makes. The poor Nigger comes out naked. That's about the sum and substance of it—the poor Nigger is left. Besides that, I am not out doing a mercantile business for the Pierce-Sullivan Pasture & Cattle Company. I think you are a little ultra vires on that point. I had an old gander once that could not get any goslins, and the judge said he was ultra vires! I think you are a little ultra vires. The company was not chartered to do a mercantile business."

When Shanghai went back to the BU Ranch, he did not forget to buy McCroskey's corn. The following instruction went to Winfield, Kansas: "Please Ship me one Car good old Mixed Corn in good Sacks, as it has to be hauled some distance. Also Ship me in Same Car *Covered up in the Car,* 10bbls—if to be had in Bls—if not, in 50 lb Sacks—*Eclipse Flour,* & Aim to bill the Car about 3,000 Pounds less than there is. I want the best flour & Eclipse was Kind I shiped with Corn before."

Shanghai placed Jonathan in charge of a crew as soon as the ranch was bought and directed that the Duncan Ranch be resurveyed, then fenced. Jonathan employed the county surveyor, but rains came, and Jonathan sent his first report: "I had to Abandon Duncan Survey act Rain." Then, not to be defeated, the versatile brother put his own talents to work, and on June 23, 1883, he recorded his activities: "I returned from Caney on the 21st June we had a big Job. Done the Surveying Myself traced the old Lines."

While the boundry lines were being traced, Joyce was put in charge of a crew to cut a fence row through the timber, but, three days before the survey was finished, Jonathan wrote in disgust: "Joyce cut about 5½ miles fence row & flickered," but, he added hopefully, "Frank Rugely is getting along very well hauling posts. Wire is in town will put up prairie end first. the weather is dry & beautiful No worms no flies Nor Mosquitoes, but have had hard time digging the holes it was like Iron." Sixty days later, Jonathan turned in his final report: "The prairie end is all fenced. My hands I had from this side over there is all but two & Myself sick with Billious fever & Chills & fever although I myself have escaped this far. it was the bad water that made them sick & the terible heat."

The "cow sense" G. C. Gifford had shown while on the trail for Shanghai had pleased Uncle Abel immensely; therefore, when

"We will rob them Yankees"

Gifford announced his intentions to branch out into the cattle business on his own account, Pierce gave him encouragement and lent him a substantial sum of money with which to buy a herd of cattle, branded Half Moon. He told Shanghai that he could buy them for thirteen dollars each. The Colonel thought they were worth the money, and Hamilton wrote Gifford a check to cover the transaction. A few days later, when Willie Labauve and Clay McSparren were branding over on the Duncan Ranch, Gifford rode up with the Half Moon branding irons tied to his saddle. He tendered the irons to Willie, telling him he had sold the entire brand of cattle to Mr. Sullivan and that he had already turned the herd into the Duncan pasture. Clay liked the Half Moon brand and adopted it for the Duncan Ranch. Colonel Pierce heard about the delivery of the Gifford cattle by Sullivan, so he looked at the company books to see what had happened. Then he swore volubly: "O, my God. O, My God! Sullivan bought them at thirteen dollars and turned them into the company at thirty-five dollars. *I think he made some money out of that!*" After cooling down a little, he chuckled to Hamilton: "Well what of it? I'll make no objection. Cattle are booming."

Some days later, Pierce discovered that Little Dannie had thrown him another left-handed curve. This time the news came through John McCroskey. Years later Shanghai gave his own colorful version of the incident, stating:

> One time when I was going in my gallop across the country, I saw a lot of sow yearlings in a corner. There was a lot of sow yearlings and I said to McCroskey:
> "Jesus Christ, where did you get those sow yearlings?"
> He said: "Carson brought them here."
> "Carson, hell! What did he bring them here for?"
> He said: "Mr. Sullivan sent them here."

By George, if it had not been for their horns you could have put one in each pocket of your shooting jacket when you are out hunting with the Honorable E. H. R. Green with your hunting suit on. I tell you, you could have put one in each pocket! I think it was the hardest lot of stock I ever saw. I would not have given $4.00 for them. I would have given $1,400.00 each for them just as quick as I would have given $4.00. But they were branded. There was no use for me to cut up. I took my medicine and went on. But when

I looked at them little innocent, damned looking jackasses with
my naked eye, that had been sent down from Espirito Santo Bay
that he called yearlings, that had little horns like your finger with
wrinkles at the ends! Yearlings! It was the rag-tag and bob-tails
and the scum of creation. Sullivan knew it. He picked them up
for debts. But they were branded. There was no use cutting up,
and they had the Duncan brand on them. But of course, I give
McCroskey hell!

McCroskey's only comment about the incident was:

> Mr. Pierce said: "John, where in the hell did you get them damed sow yearlings?"
> "That is the cattle that Sullivan sent here," I said.
> "Dan played hell," said Mr. Pierce.

"That," concluded McCroskey, "was the starter of the Duncan Ranch cattle—the female part."

Pierce's land agents continued to buy until 54,915.25 acres belonged to the partnership. Pierce, therefore tried to consolidate his holdings. H. H. Kirkpatrick, while not serving as clerk to the United States District Court, was employing his talents in concocting schemes through which he and Colonel Pierce could turn an easy dollar. Although Shanghai now had all the land he wanted, still Kirkpatrick's lure was too strong for him. This was especially true since it was being rumored around that a new city was to be built across the bay from Galveston. It was to be called Texas City. The land involved in Kirkpatrick's scheme lay within that region. Here is the proposal received by Colonel Pierce from Kirkpatrick:

> I wrote a few days ago about giving me discretion to buy at any price under two dollars, and if you will, it will be well to advise the bank to pay my drafts for the purchase money recited in any deeds that I may present for land lying between Highland Bayou and Halls Bayou.
> I enclose a sketch of land in the pasture. The tracts marked "B," we have bought, and we have bought those marked "E," "F," and "G." The tract marked "I" is for sale. The tract marked D is the Collett land. The one marked C is for sale. The one marked "K" is *mine*.
> Now I direct your attention to a plan to adopt. By purchasing

"We will rob them Yankees"

the tracts marked I, A.M., C & L (or P and R instead of M) we could fence on our own land from one Bayou to the other and Tucker [Tacquard] would only have 2,500 acres in the pasture, and you can see that he would have but little between our fence and his, and much of that is fenced in small places or owned by men who have cattle on it, and not an acre of it for sale.

Now my idea is that we must have the tracts on the line to enable us to make him see how formidable we are. As you know, if we own the fence, we can expel all of his cattle except what his own land will sustain, while we will get the benefit of such land as neither of us can buy; but if he owns the fence, it will be reversed.

It may be very important to act promptly, as Tucker will be stirred up when he suspects what is up, and that is why I ask for discretion to buy at any price under $2.00.

Of course, we do not expect to build any fence, but it will be well to be able to make him think so. There are only about 50,000 acres in the pasture now, and there are said to be 10,000 cattle on it, 9000 of them belonging to Tucker, so you see he can't stand much crowding. I wired you this evening to wire the bank to cash my check for the Collett land. If we could get all the other land, so as to run the fence as indicated, we could make much better terms than we calculated upon.

Finally, as Pierce said, "after many a flicker and flaw," Secretary of State J. W. Raines issued a corporation charter, No. 2319, to Pierce-Sullivan Land and Cattle Company. On May 5, 1882, the following year, an amendment was approved changing the name to Pierce-Sullivan Pasture and Cattle Company. The incorporators named were A. H. Pierce, J. E. Pierce, and D. Sullivan. The joint-stock company was created, according to the authority, "for the purpose of buying, selling, and owning lands and pastures, and of raising, breeding, buying and selling neat cattle, horses, sheep, goats, and hogs." The business of the company was to be transacted in the city of San Antonio and at the pasture of the company in Matagorda and Wharton counties, Texas. The corporation was to exist for a period of twenty-five years. "The capital stock shall be one million dollars."

After the business of the corporation had gotten well under way, Shanghai began to worry about their bookkeeper; so he walked into Sullivan's bank one day with a troubled look on his face. "Dannie," he said. "I am no bookkeeper. You know that by now. Hamilton will occasionally take a little too much tea. You know what I mean. You have seen men who have got a little too much tea! He might make some mistake. You are a bookkeeper, look over his books."

"No, Mr. Pierce," cheered Sullivan. "It is useless to look over a good bookkeeper's books. If he wants to rob you, he will rob you anyway, unless you stand and look over his shoulder all the time."

"You ought to know," slowly acquiesced Shanghai. "If you don't know about the books, what is the use of me trying. I am no bookkeeper. I never get anything without paying for it. I have lived on the prairie all my life. Dannie, I have worked hard. It has taken a good deal of my time. It is no little job to run a ranch all the time. They have cut our fences. They have killed my cattle, raised hell. Everybody knows the pressure brought against a pasture man, and they have all been goin' for me. I was the only one in there that could stand it; no one else! I lived it out. I am there yet. But when I go home at night, I want to sleep. I've had a heap to do. Mr. Sullivan, you would not have done it for $10,000 a year; neither would I—*for money*. Dannie, I could not keep them books *right*, much less *wrong*."

"*We will rob them Yankees*"

After the conversation with Little Dannie, Shanghai left the city with the feeling that he had his partner's confidence, and he felt better as he rode the train toward the ranch. The train conductor came along and disturbed his thoughts by handing him a telegram from Sullivan. The Maverick Bank had closed its doors and there was a run on Sullivan's bank. Little Dannie was in real distress. He wanted to know if Pierce would lend him some money.

"You can have what you need, and more if you want it," wired the Colonel.

Within less than an hour the conductor came back with the second message. "You are a prince. D. Sullivan."

Holding the message in his hand, he left the train at Victoria and hurried to the Levi Bank, calling out as he entered: "Look, Levi! Look! He calls me a prince."

17. "My shotgun went off in the Pullman Palace Car..."

"No. Sir; Miller is known to be the biggest liar on the American continent, and not only the biggest liar, but the biggest thief, there is no dispute about that. He is not only the biggest liar, but the biggest thief and a son of a bitch. He is under indictment now—he is under sentence." (Page 1246, transcript of record, U. S. Circuit Court of Appeals, 5th Circuit: No. 1053. *Daniel Sullivan v. Abel H. Pierce.*)

The George Washington Miller who had the distinction of having his reputation thus sworn to in the United States District Court at Galveston, Texas, is best known as the founder of 101 Ranch and father of four sons who became equally well known through their 101 Wild West Rodeo and Show. Miller's birthplace was Crab Orchard, Kentucky. He was born January 22, 1841. By the simple expedient of subtraction, it is ascertainable that George lacked but a few months of having attained his majority when the

"My shotgun went off in the Pullman"

Civil War assumed the shooting stage. For reasons which he did not take time off from his feverish money-making efforts to explain, both presidents, Lincoln and Davis, were deprived of his services as a combatant. It is a matter of record, however, that he patterned after General Grant's father and made money in army trade. His specialty was buying and selling government mules. As he bore no title, he, like Shanghai, annexed the synthetic rank of colonel. This was in line with the vogue of the time, according to Miller's biographer, as "such was attached without official decree to the names of prominent men as a mark of respect."

Within less than a year after Lee's surrender, George had not only acquired a synthetic colonelcy, but also Molly, the daughter of Judge David B. Carson, and they were on their way out of Kentucky, "since the Negro slaves had been freed and severe conditions were imposed upon my state." He was described as being "fully six feet tall, of powerful frame, and most loquacious." Nothing was said about his handwriting, which readily baffled all experts.

In 1870, George and Molly, with their two-year-old son, Joseph C., were on their way toward California, driving a pair of mules "in search of a location where I can realize my ambition—a mammoth livestock ranch." Miller was the forerunner of that type of American found throughout the cattle country who could walk to Sunday school with a chunk of lead on the end of a double-breasted, brass watch chain, and ride home on a mare, followed by a yearling colt, displaying a new gold watch and chain. Thus, when the Miller wagon reached the frontier town of Newtonia, Missouri, he began to exercise his talents. He found the town over-rooted by fat hogs, and he began trading the proverbial watch chain and chunk of lead for hogs, much to the satisfaction of the local people. The hogs soon became "Kentucky hams," and he started down the trail toward Texas with ten wagonloads of hams and "sow bosom," which he converted into mossy-horn steers. These he fattened on free Indian lands.

On one of his rides southward with cow-hunters, he went as far as Brazos County, where he met and entered into a mercantile arrangement with H. B. English, who was an extensive cattle buyer and small-town merchant. The name of the firm was changed to Miller and English. They proposed to sell to drovers "coming and going"—English, as they went northward, Miller, as they returned. Miller and Pierce did not become acquainted while Miller was in Texas, although Shanghai was then buying large numbers of cattle through English. On the first of September, 1883, however, Shanghai instructed his bookkeeper:

> If we need any provisions for Cow-driving you can order them from Miller & English we will be driving about 6 weeks & Probably no Longer So you can see what is on hand & Know how to Calculate.

Colonel Miller was well aware of the value of the Indian free range in the Indian Territory, and, although the land could not be bought at the time (should he have had an inclination to make purchases), he pre-empted some 60,000 acres, according to the fashion of the time, and began to get ready to put Texas cattle into his two pastures. Miller's first move was made immediately after he met Shanghai, who was then in Kansas straightening out a partnership deal with Jay Forsythe.

The sale of cattle by Shanghai to Smith, Forsythe, and Gunter had resulted in profits to all of the parties. Jay Forsythe was encouraged as a result of the deal and made two trips to the BU Ranch in the attempt to get Pierce to stake him for $65,000. Jay took the cattle to Indian Territory and began grazing them on free Indian lands. Imagine Shanghai's wrath, then, when he received notice the cattle were being billed Forsythe and Pierce.

Shanghai went immediately to Forsythe and told him: "Forsythe, you have got to re-amend the charter. There is no flicker and flaw about that! I've staked you with $65,000, without a dollars worth of security. You've made $20,000. When I picked you up, you did not have money enough to buy a nigger's supper. Now you start to run my cattle off and ship them in another man's name. I'll hop you. I'll stop you quick. I've known all the Forsythe family, and you are the only one I ever saw of the name that was not a gentleman, but black sheep get in all flocks, and you happen to be the black sheep of this flock. You've billed the cattle: Forsythe & Pierce. You did not say Pierce & Forsythe. You did not put a dollar in the world in it. You are a little too premature. Got the cart before the horse. When I put up all the money, I do not want you to

George Washington Miller (Courtesy Western History Collections, University of Oklahoma Library)

Joseph G. McCoy
(Courtesy Denver Public Library Western Collection)

"My shotgun went off in the Pullman"

put your name before mine. You would not like to be the tail of the kite if you put up the money."

When Miller heard about Shanghai's liberal loan to Jay, he made it a point to see the colonel and buy a small herd of steers. From Winfield, Kansas, he scribbled Pierce a note:

> I am having a lot of fun poked at me about Pierce "Sea Lions" by parties having some good North West steers to sell that have not sold, or had an offer made, and very anxious to get one at Sea Lion price. I would like for you to let me know as much as ten days before you want me to come to pass on the cattle. We are having splendid wether ever since you was here. Pasture in big demand.

When Miller went to the BU Ranch to "pass on the cattle," he learned, so he said, that Shanghai really had three grades of cattle. The Half Moon cattle belonged to the Pierce-Sullivan Pasture and Cattle Company; the BU brand belonged to Pierce's daughter; but the D's were personally owned by Pierce. "When I first went to see Pierce's cattle," commented Miller, "I objected to the cattle. I told him they were inferior cattle, and not as good as I expected to see, but he says: 'They are not as good as the cattle you *haven't* seen. Wait until you have seen them, and then you will be better satisfied. They are worth $5 more than these, and that makes them come pretty cheap.' So, I waited until the cattle came over, and they were really better cattle than I expected to see. When I saw them, they were big nice cattle, and I took them all at the same price. The cows that would come from the Duncan Ranch would be great big, square-built, fat cows, and the cows he would put with them would be old 'Shelley' cows that he would get around his pasture. He said he had to ship them to save their lives! He would put them in with the good cows, and sell them, and strike an average. Sullivan was not a friend of mine, and I didn't care particular whether he got robbed or not. I bought the Half Moons. I wouldn't let a good thing go by. By reason of getting these cattle mixed, I was making about five dollars a head."

After cutting back as many "shells" as Pierce would permit, Miller went west. At Sargent's Hotel, in Uvalde, he met the "ex-widow" of one of Shanghai's army friends. This chance meeting brought forth a long letter from the "ex-widow":

Shanghai Pierce

Dear Mr. Pierce

Do you remember Rolden Borden who lived on Mustang Creek before the War? Well, I am his ex-widow, Mrs. M. Branden Carter of New York. I came down here about four weeks ago to sell out a small brand of Cattle. The people are determined that I shall neither gather my cattle, nor get any price for them. They won't bring them in; they have made every excuse about not getting them. I was almost in dispair, when fortunately Mr. Miller of Kansas came to this Hotel—he has just shipped 400 head of fat cattle for a ranche adjoining where my cattle are. He told me he had bought a large drove from Mr. Pierce. and found Mr. Pierce *the best man in Texas*, to trade with; then told me how tricky these people were here; how they had treated him in such bad faith; said he was not surprised they had treated a woman worse. I felt so glad when I found you were Roland's old friend and fellow cowdriver. I determined at once to write you to come to my assistance. This town is three hours ride on the Southern Pacific from San Antonio —Now good Mr. Pierce won't you come to a widow's assistance? You can have all my cattle at your own price, if you will get me out of these people's hands or clutches. Please, won't you come to my assistance for the sake of the friendship you once bore to my dead husband Roland. Save me from these Western Sharks. I suppose you know that Captain J. C. Borden took everything that Roland left and sold it for his own use. When I see you I will tell you how the family treated Roland's children.

The "ex-widow's" appeal fell on deaf ears, since, previously, Miller had given him another task. A group of a "few chosen" cattlemen had formed The Cherokee Strip Association, and they had leased from the Indians the entire Cherokee Strip. This effort to grab the Reservation raised a furor within the ranks of free-range advocates, as well as from nesters who were importuning Congress to open the entire area for white-man settlement. Shanghai and Miller, consequently, appealed to their congressmen. Texas Congressman Joseph D. Sayers held out less hope than did the Honorable William Henry Crain to his cattleman constituency. "It will be my duty," Sayers told Pierce, "as well as a great pleasure, to do all I can to protect the interests of our people, whenever endangered by *unjust action* upon the part of the Federal authorities. In this matter, I am very much afraid that my effort will be in

"My shotgun went off in the Pullman"

vain, and I would earnestly advise our cattlemen to be very careful lest they be severely injured by orders from the Interior Department. The pressure to open the Indian lands for entry and settlement is very great, and this may lead to a peremptory to vacate such lands with but a moment's warning."

From Washington, Congressman Crain sealed his personal relationship with Pierce a little tighter by soliciting a courtesy from him.

> Governor Coke has repeatedly asked me for a pair of nice, large, Symetrical, well shaped steer horns. I would esteem it a great favor if you would Send him by express a nice pair at your earliest convenience

The horns went forward to Governor Coke, and, at the same time, Pierce requested that his congressman do a couple of favors for him. Back came the reply:

> A letter from the P.O. Dep't indicates that the route will be established. I will comply with your request in regard to the Sec'y of the Interior and advise you of the results.

Then, Crain added:

> I have a special personal favor to ask of you, and if you grant it, please notify me by telegram, at my expense. Mr. Regan of Victoria volunteered to loan me some money, and I got $5,000 from him at 12%. When the interest became due, I wrote him for time on it. His reply was: "Bank demands interest, send it immediately." Now, Mr. Pierce, will you pay him the interest and take my note payable when my mileage will be due? Will you also oblige me by seeing whether you cannot borrow enough money for me, so that I can pay up, in all, about $8,000.

Two weeks passed before Shanghai heard again from his congressman. This time he said:

> Your telegram reached me. I do not know how to thank you for your Kind and prompt response to my appeal to you for assistance. Enclosed please find communication relative to the trail. As soon as the reply from the War Department is received I shall forward

it to you. As this will be of interest to stock raisers generally, perhaps you had better send it to The News which has no correspondent here now. If you can possibly do so, please help me pay Regan by securing a lender in his place. Again thanking you for your prompt Kindness in sending the money asked by me without note, without security and upon my mere request, I remain your friend.

Congressman Crain pursued the interests of his constituents industriously. Acting on behalf of "Miller of Gonzales" and Pierce and Miller, he formulated a report of conditions as he found them in Washington. This he relayed to "My dear Mr. Pierce":

After numberless interviews, arguments, discussions and communications, I can at length give you a statement in regard to the trail matter. I am not yet in receipt of replies to my last communications but Know their contents by having learned them from personal interviews with the writers. Under the red tape process which obtains here I may get them in the course of a month.

Mr. Miller had written me to secure permits to carry two droves through the Territory, and I was operating for him and you both.

It became necessary for me to make formal statements of what I desired to accomplish. These were filed by me with the Secretary of the Interior, by him transmitted to the Indian Cmr., after passing through the hands of the Land Cmr. By the Indian Cmr. an adverse report was made, which was transmitted by the Sec'y of the Interior to the Sec'y of War, by whom it was referred to Lieut. General Sheridan, who indorsed upon it, in substance, that a five mile wide strip and ten days were sufficient, which ended the matter.

The Department holds that the Trail is not intended for fattening purposes, but simply as a highway over which may be driven in a reasonable time, and both the War and Interior Departments maintain that ten days constitutes a 'reasonable time.'

Now for the trail matter about which you particularly wrote in your last letter. The Department absolutely refuses to establish it.

It is contended that the country through which the proposed trail would pass is under the divided jurisdiction of the Interior and War Departments, and that the former having called upon the latter to take charge there, no interference with the management of affairs of the War Department will be exercised by the Interior Department. The Interior people further say that the proposed trail would pass in close proximity to some Indian colonies which have been established by Capt. Lee, U.S.A. and that disturbances would inevitably follow.

However, I succeeded to this extent, viz: they agreed to consider the matter in conjunction with the War Department, for the next year, provided you furnish a formal application, setting forth exactly what you want, that is, showing the trail by red or blue lines on a *map* to accompany the application, marking the prominent points by which the trail will pass.

Your letter was read carefully by the representative of the Department in my presence and we compared it with the Map in the Office, but could not find the places referred to on the map.

He stated, however, that the office had no accurate map showing the trails and admitted that the one he was using had been cut out of some Kansas or Colorado Stock Journal.

From all this, my dear Mr. Pierce, you can understand the difficulties which I had to encounter. The prejudices against the drovers is very strong, owing to complaints from the Indians, from settlers, and from parties interested in Keeping Texas cattle from market, while the drovers have had nobody here to present their side of the case, excepting our delegation, all of which are practically ignorant of the country, the trails, the settlements, etc. The best we could do was to repell in general the accusations made against our people, but not having been through the Indian Territory with cattle, of course, we could give no definite or reliable information. The Interior Department officials are in equal ignorance, and Gen. Sheridan is doubtless influenced by his experience and observation of two years ago when he visited the Territory.

I would suggest that a few prominent stockraisers from Southern Texas meet and agree upon a trail, cause a nice map to be prepared in accordance with my views and then come on here and have a talk.

It is needless for me to say to you that my services in this behalf are at the command of the Stockmen.

In regard to the permit requested by Mr. Miller, the Department replied that the established trails would be kept open but that the police regulations were under the control of the War Department, and that he would have to apply for a permit to Col. Sumner, Comg. officer at Fort Reno. I do not see the necessity for the permit, but as Mr. Miller requested one, I tried to get it. I am sure you will not attach any blame on me for the failure.

It is useless to argue with military men who have been on the ground and imagine they know all about matters.

Has Mr. Regan sent you a draft for $600? He wrote me an apologetic letter for crowding me to the wall.

Mrs. Crain is not in good health. The "boy" is a girl.

Pierce and Miller ran into Indian troubles very shortly after their cattle got into the Territory. The Chickasans stopped them and demanded that a fifteen-cent-per-head levy as grass tax be paid before the cattle would be permitted to move. Shanghai again referred his troubles to Washington, and Crain answered that the Commissioner of Indian Affairs had ruled that the levy was a "tax on commerce" and therefore unconstitutional, provided the cattle were merely passing through to market, but if they were being held for fattening purposes, the levy would be a grass tax and legal. He therefore told Pierce that he might pass his "uninfected cattle, free and uninterrupted through the Chickasawans on public highways," but, he concluded: "Your cattle are not allowed to go outside of said highways, and you need not pay the tax, however, you must keep them on the trail."

There was a sixty-day silence while Pierce and Miller located the cattle on Miller's White Eagle range. Then came another urgent and personal appeal from Washington:

> Dear Col: Personal
> I need five hundred dollars *immediately and urgently* I write to you to ask you to wire me whether I can have it or not as soon as this reaches you.
> If you say "Yes," as I know you will, I shall draw on you. You responded so promptly when I last asked a loan from you that I have no hesitation in requesting another; but don't disappoint me as my need is urgent. I will fully explain the matter in my next letter. Enclosed you will find my note and you are hereby authorized to fill the blanks.
> Yr friend
> W. H. Crain.

Pierce waited until Miller got seven thousand steers located in the "Egal Country." As he held a lien for an unpaid portion of the purchase price, he then availed himself of a provision in the contract to have a "Pierce man" with the cattle as long as Miller owed anything on them and sent his most trusted nephew, Abel Pierce

"My shotgun went off in the Pullman"

Borden, as observer at the 101 Ranch. At the same time, he dispatched Abel's brother, Frank, to the Snyder Ranch, as supervisor. Frank registered displeasure over his assignment, agreeing that "the grass is fine and the cattle filling up," but he was constantly finding the carcasses of dead cattle. "I've found three," he said, "since I last wrote." Besides that, the ranch was not operated according to his ideas, it being run when Mr. Snyder was away "by a 16 and 12 year old boy—a regular Ben Ward lay-out, and Mr. Snyder himself is not hurt with cow-sense."

Abel Pierce Borden got along better over at the 101 Ranch, but he took occasion to warn bookkeeper Hamilton not to place too much reliance in Miller's statements, saying: "Mr. Miller told me he had sent A.H.P. $10,000, hope you have received it *as he said.*" At the same time, he expressed pleasure in being able to state that people living in the Territory were becoming more careful about getting their branding irons mixed up. Both G. W. Miller and his son Joe had been indicted for unwarranted carelessness in cattle branding. "However," reported Borden, "Joe had his trial the other day and came clear, the case being dismissed. Was glad for both of them."

Borden's stay on the 101 Ranch was short. He tried to walk the ketch-rope up a horse's neck one day so as to "pin his head down," but the animal had a different idea about it. Rearing back, he flung the heavy man up into the air, and he came down with a fractured leg. Borden was carried over to a small sod house, where a doctor made an effort to set the bones. Shanghai heard about the accident and came blowing in one stormy night with a snowy blizzard. He bundled up the injured nephew and struck across the prairie to Gueda Springs in a flatbed wagon. Between curses over slow going and curses over fast and rough driving, Borden made known his thanks to his uncle for removing him to the care of doctors and more comfortable quarters. From Gueda, Hamilton got Borden's letter: "The trip helped me a little but not much.   my leg is pretty sore yet. The lower part of my leg is partially paralyzed. I used a battery on it with a secondary current full force. I could not feel it in some places."

When Shanghai realized Borden's condition, he ordered him to go to New York for attention. From there he wrote: "The bones were not properly set, were not even, the ends sticking by each other. The doctor says he can patch me up a little but can never make a good job of it as it has been done too long to break it up. I am flat of my back without being able to turn over for three weeks."

During the time Borden was an invalid, G. S. Hamilton checked over his own condition and found himself "too long addicted to too much tea and the curse of cards." He also waked up to the fact that he was two years behind in posting the Pierce-Sullivan Pasture and Cattle Company books. He, therefore, concluded it was the opportune time to let Colonel Pierce know something of his future intentions and advised him that "I have decided to take a half interest in the Furniture Manufacturing business with my bro in Ga." Then he stated unequivocably: "You can not get a better man than A.P.B. to attend to your business, and you will do well to secure the *promise* of his services right away so he will be on hand when needed. I will show him all he does not know. After mature deliberation on your part, I would be pleased if you would let me know what you think of my suggestions. The contemplated change is not on account of any dissatisfaction with you or yours, but with the hope of securing, while I may, a better moral and Social position for my declining years. I fully appreciate all you have done for me, and while we live, I am at your command."

Colonel Pierce accepted Hamilton's presumptuous suggestions and tendered the management of the BU Ranch to his injured nephew. Obviously, Borden was not in the best of humors when he replied: "You make me an offer to go there and run the ranch the year around and want my answer yes or no which I will make reply that I would not return to Texas and work for any price and have to work as hard in the summer as I have always had to in the winter. I do not want you to think I am afraid of work, for *I am not* but think I can get along without working like a nigger in the summer. If you are not in a big hurry for an answer, I think that perhaps after seeing you and talking with you about it that we could come to an understanding by which it will be agreeable for me to return. If you have some one you want to *break in*, take him along, as I am in no way bound to return. If I should return to you [I] should expect to stay so long as I perform my duties satisfactory to you. I am still flat on my back and will have to remain so 10 days or two weeks longer; if nothing happens, will be up on crutches the last

"*My shotgun went off in the Pullman*"

of the month. It will be some time before I am able to do much."

Pierce followed his nephew to Tiverton, Rhode Island, where he went under the care of his mother. The two men had their talk and Borden joyfully wrote Hamilton: "If nothing happens I will start for Texas on Dec. 3rd. I will get there and do what I can. I am getting around today with just the use of a cane."

Borden's injury had left a vacancy with the Pierce cattle at the 101 Ranch. D. M. Stapp was sent to fill it. Hamilton rode over with Stapp on the train as far as Rosenburg; there he gave him a ticket to Arkansas City, Kansas, where he was due to meet Mr. Miller, and he told him to file an itemized account of his expenses. The trip obviously had unrecorded pleasant incidents not wholly connected with Duncan Ranch business, for the expense statement was returned to Stapp with a request for clarification. This he furnished:

> Kind Boss:
> Your short and most welcome note Came, and was glad to here from you but am sorry you are going to leave Old texas, and may you have all this world Can afford in pleasure and good luck. I will tell you this is dullest place I ever Saw. I just got back from down on Red Rock and was cought in Snow Storm but am all right once more.
>
> I did not leave Roseburg untill fore in the even after you left me, so I had to take dinner there, and taken Super in Temple, and bought me a 25 cts worth of lunch for my breakfast, and got Dinner in Purcell, and then arrived in Arkansas City fiv o Clock in the evening, which cost me $1.75 and the totle was $22.30, and the Balence went to some pretty little girls, and you may bet it has cost me Somthing too."

The Millers were displeased with Stapp almost immediately; so within less than a month G. W. Miller gave vent to his feeling in a "plane" talk to Colonel Pierce:

> I rote you the 22 inst. I did not Say any thing about your boss hand Stap But now I will talk plane to you When we traded you promist to put a Good hand at the ranch Wich you fald to do I am Sorry to Say Stap is the D——Shirk I ever had on my ranche. I cant depend on him. I do think he is an awfull Lyer or you ar a *bad man* That is what the boys Sa at the ranche What

he has told would make a pretty good book. I think if I would Cuss him Like you do, he would be all rite. He is worth Less than any Granger I ever had.

But the opinion of the Millers did not disturb Stapp in the least. He thought "something else is the matter with them and I will find out as soon as I see G. W. Miller." He renewed his fidelity to Shanghai, promising:

> You may bett I will See and look out for you in spite of him as they will bear watching somewhat. I saw a steer that was Killed and butchered and the brand was cut out and years cut of and threw a Way, and I asked Charley why he done it, which he denied doing, and I asked who done it, but he said nothing. It looks bad, you bet, and I have been told lots lately, which I will tell you when you come up.

Ernest E. Dawdy relieved the boss hand and Miller thought Dawdy "a very good hand I like him better than Stap I think he is well satisfied up here," but Stapp was indignant at being replaced. He defended himself stoutly: "I never Spoke a hard word to them Since I came up here and never got Rolicy Christmas either, but I have made severl mashes lately and had lots of fun."

Dawdy stayed with the Millers for even a shorter period than either of his predecessors. Casper Bell was next in line. Casper was Shanghai's "fightin' man," and he was quite willing and able to carry out Pierce's minutest wish. As a consequence Miller turned his attention to other matters.

Shanghai and Miller both got copies of the order of the President of the United States, which Congressman Crain called "the ouster order." Crain quoted the Secretary of the Interior as saying:

> The Proclamation directs the removal of all cattle, and other live stock, now on that portion of the Indian Territory, commonly known as The Cherokee Strip or Outlet, which has been for several years occupied by an association or associations of whitemen, under certain contracts, said to have been made with the Cherokee Nation, in the nature of a lease or leases for grazing purposes, and does not include the reservations of the Poncas and Nez Perces.

Miller thought "the Strip looks blue, but what is OK is that we

"*My shotgun went off in the Pullman*"

will get the time extended." Dillard Fant, on the other hand, had been misinformed regarding the scope of the President's proclamation and, thinking that he was going to be swept off the Strip, told Shanghai, "I sold 5,000 last week to a Colorado man so cheap I could taste it." Then, learning through Pierce that grasslands might yet be had from the Poncas and Nez Percés, he hastily wrote Shanghai: "I've got to do something to counteract my trade. I am not sleeping very well at night. Now my beloved Friend how cheap are you going to sell yours. It is time you was giting a move on. Such is life for a man that works with Dan. He only eats one meal a day and don't smoke or drink, so he has a big advantage over me and you. O! how I would like to see you cool."

Miller was no cooler than Pierce after the proclamation. A large number of white men, being misinformed as to the scope of the order, and thinking that the Strip was wide open for squatters, made a run into the region to stake out their claims. Miller was in the path of the invasion. He wrote Pierce:

> I no you have be Excited over the news of the boom on the Cherry Kee strip   I am happy to tell you I am all rite   The Boomers burnt Every ranche from Cold Well to Ar Kans City and burnt a few cattle. I am Like Lot in the City of Sod dam   I was Saved. They did not cut fence or burn grass   You know I have fed the Boomers for the last Eight Years   And the Good Lord is on my cide and my cattle or all OK but a Little thin. I want 2,000 Moore to fill up my Ponca pasture. Would ove paid you sum moore money if I had not ove bought more cattle.

Pierce expressed his intention to go to Kansas and the Territory to see for himself how Miller was caring for the cattle and to determine whether or not he wanted to let him have "2,000 Moore" cattle. Before leaving, Jonathan broke his spectacles and asked Shanghai to have them repaired and express them back to him. He did so, inclosing a statement:

Repairing Specks	.25
Expressage	2.00
	$2.25

Jonathan stormed over the charge, claiming that his brother was just like his brother-in-law Wiley: "he is a fool, Yes, and a Knave, and a Son of a Tinker besides."

When Shanghai reached Arkansas City, he found conditions ominous. Not knowing, and probably not caring, that Jonathan was momentarily angry at him, he wrote him to come to Kansas where "the Grangers around Cedar Vale & Elgin is threatening & raising a little Hell with Cattlemen   I want you to bring my Bowie Knife, and bring up my Pistol that I Loaned you, and when you Come I can put it together here." Jonathan remembered the "expressage" and told Borden: "You had better write you uncle Abel to buy him one—as he might need it before I get there. I have never shot his yet—had it fixed up & cost me two Dollars & fifty cents; however, when I go north, I will take it but will have to charge him something for amt paid out for repairs."

The Colonel took notice of his brother's attitude and commented: "I note J.E.P. remarks about the Pistol, which are liberal."

Miller waited at Winfield, Kansas to hear from Shanghai. From there he sent off three letters to the Colonel, in one of which he said: "I Sorter Like my Self Sum what Less. I guess you have Saw Father Ben's[1] orders not to put any more cattle in the I.T. That done me up in good Shape. I have a thousand cattle in Texas I will go down and Sell, but I cant Set Still, so Don't give your cattle to no one but me. This is about 3 Letters I have rote you   If you are dead say so   If you are not let me hear from you. Don't Let a Little things Like Father Ben's order bother you. Everything will work out rite and if you dont bother yourself you may live two or *three years yet.*"

When the two got together, Miller decided he wanted to take another cut at Pierce's Half Moon steers, so Pierce offered to let him "pick the pasture at $15 per head for 350 Head." Almost frantically the Colonel sent off his instructions to Borden:

> Ship out all the Little Eastern Texas devills. I want to get rid of them, as they wont get any bigger. Should you of gathered & shiped a car or two out of beef pasture before you get this, Say nothing about it, as Miller will not take them if he knew any of the tops had been taken out. When he comes take him all through

[1] President Benjamin Harrison.

"My shotgun went off in the Pullman"

the Pasture & Show them to him & do it in the evening, after 3 o clock, or very early in the morning, as they Look better at that time of the day.

Borden made an effort to get the "tops" away from the ranch before Miller arrived but failed to get all of them. He therefore had to report to his uncle, now resting in Rhode Island:

> Clay arrived here at 12 A.M. yesterday with 300 cattle, all in good fix. I shipped 3 cars, one load was the tops and the other 2 straight Swamp Angels. Miller got here in time to see them in the pens but I did not let him know but what the 3 loads was all I took from the wire pasture.

Miller knew what was going on, for, just six days later, he told Pierce:

> Well I just arrived from BU Ranch. I received the cattle out of the west pasture. Then I went to See Brother Wiley K— and got his tops. He gave me a Squar deal. I got from him the best cattle I ever got in Southern Texas. Able shipt a Lot of fine Steers out of the wire pasture the day I come up. I told him I thought It would be *Sorter hard on huffs next Spring* to Ship them sort out now. I will ship trane Seelynes today. Will ship another to morrow, one next day. They will all go in Cide of 20 days. I will be fixt to Settle with you when you come.

The cattle traders met at the Hutchins House, in Houston. Mr. Benn and his son, Russell, were present. The talk in the lobby drifted from cattle to things eternal. Finally, a lull came in the conversation in which Colonel Pierce had not been taking part. Russell, the youngest man of the group, spoke up timidly: "Mr. Pierce, do you really think there is a Heaven?"

"I doubt it, son. I really doubt it," he replied, looking steadily at Miller all the time. "You know, son; I don't see why the good Lord would voluntarily take upon himself the immense task of cutting back so many culls."

Miller disclosed to Shanghai his real intentions before they got to the ranch. "The soldiers are hooping up the cattle off the Strip. No foolishness this time. They have to go. They are not allowed to come on either Ponca or Osage. The soldiers say they have orders to shove them all to the Panhandle of Texas. I've got all I need now, something over a thousand head, and I'm going to feed them at *Tolberts."*

Eugene Talbot, who owned a substantial herd of cattle which he was fattening on cottonseed, lived below the Duncan Ranch, and he was well equipped to undertake the care of Miller's one thousand Half Moon and BU steers, as well as his own. Upon arrival at Pierce's Station, Miller instructed Borden to have John McCroskey make the delivery to Talbot. The weather was warm, and the cattle did not wish to be disturbed, consequently, they stampeded. McCroskey reported the incident to Borden: "I have turned the Steears ove to Tolbert as he was cossing the River with KuyKendall cattle the run in the lake and Some bog down and Some got a way—I will let you Know how many I am Short." Another man was passing the lake when the stampede took place, and he reported: "Talbot had a time with Kuykendall's cattle as soon as he got them on the other side of the river.   twenty-five can just be seen by their horns in the lake and forty cannot be accounted for, and the supposition is, they bogged out of sight."

Colonel Miller stayed around the BU Ranch during most of the fall and winter, registering a part of the time at a small hotel at Mackay and at other times accepting Shanghai's hospitality over at the BU Ranch. In general, he made a nuisance of himself by using Pierce's cattle pens and stirring up trouble around the ranch. One day Borden saw Miller passing the ranch house, tagging along behind a small herd. The cattle seemed familiar to him, so he looked more closely as they passed. He recognized them as a bunch that Pierce had in a near-by pasture. He, therefore, called to Mr. Miller:

"What are you going to do with them?"

"Ship 'em," nonchalantly said Miller.

"The hell you are," angrily said Borden, as he called the Colonel to the scene, at the same time, mounting his horse and cutting the cattle back where they came from.

"Miller," stormed Shanghai, "I can't stand you. You have got so bad you take my cows before my own eyes. You have got more gall than any man I ever saw. When a man gets this bold, I can't watch him. I'm a Yankee myself. Borden is a Yankee; and I have had to send north to get another Yankee, and I tell you, all three

"My shotgun went off in the Pullman"

of us can't keep up with you. Mr. Miller, I can't keep up with you. I will have to quit you. You bother me too much."

Miller rode away to pay a visit to G. C. Gifford, who had 4,000 steers on which Pierce had loaned him a substantial sum of money. Despite Miller's information concerning the lien, he contracted to buy the cattle and started moving them from the country. He had made little progress, however, before a rider overtook him, handing him a curt note:

> Mr. G. W. Miller,
> Dear Sir: I hereby give you notice that G. C. Gifford's cattle must not leave the county without my being present, if they do, they will be brought back.
> *This letter is nothing private.*
> Res. Yours,
> A. H. Pierce.

Fortunately, for Miller, just after he received the note from Shanghai, one of Gifford's steers came to his rescue. It saved his face, but it almost ruined his leg by a resounding kick on the shin! Incapacitated by the blow, old Miller—not the Gifford cattle—left the county. From Temple, the injured stockman tried to make light of the incident by writing: "Shang: I am on my way home. It [the leg] is as Lag [large] as two Legs. Joe will be ther to morrow night Whatever Settlement you make with him will be all rite. Tell Gifford Joe will settle with him."

And then, he added: "Please don't turn back in any moore of them cut backs then you Cant help." He must have been enjoying himself, despite the pain of the sore leg, when he concluded: "I met Mrs. ―――― at Ebell Hotel as I came hom Mrs. ―――― has a boy Just Like you. Now, I hope Hot Springs will get all the Rheumatism and Sin out of you that you Live a Long Life & I may be able to get back a part of that $8000.00 I lost on the Se Lynnes 3 years ago."

Pierce went on to Hot Springs, Arkansas, to try out the salubriousness of the waters of that health resort. He did not have a reservation at the hotel and was refused one by the manager, obviously because of his blustery mannerisms. Incensed at the affrontery of the manager, Shanghai bellowed out: "Then by God, Sir. Is this hotel for sale?"

Shanghai Pierce

"Yes," said the manager-owner. "I own a half-interest. I'll sell it to you for $15,000."

"Sold," shouted Shanghai, as he reached for his checkbook and drew a draft on Weekes-McCarthy and Company, at Galveston.

The Colonel stayed quietly in his hotel for a few days, but, learning that the weather had turned bad down in Texas, he informed Borden: "I shall leave here one week from this morning. You Send my annual Santa Fe pass here. Enclose my Southern Pacifick pass to Galveston. have Vic Scour out the privy good before we come home   tell her to Scour the Seat good with Sand & Scrubbing brush."

To Miller, he wrote almost peremptorily. The Campbell Commission Company had interceded for Miller (who was also badly in debt to the company), and it wanted Pierce to continue financing Miller.

> as regards the Cattle trade, we will consider it off. Campbell is a good man & means to do what is wright, but owing to the Sringency in Money matters he may not be able to come up to his Expectations & I am afraid of the Ponca County anyway (as it is Sorounded by Grangrs) as I have had trouble with Grangers before. I am Sorry times are no better but they are Just as hard with me as with you. I will do as I agreed: See you through on the Cattle at Tolbotts, but as to running you at home that is out of the question.

Imporuned by the Campbell Commission Company, Shanghai met their representative, Mr. Black, along with Mr. Stoddard of the Independent National Bank of St Louis, and Miller. They gathered in the law office of Henry Withers. There it was disclosed that the Campbell Commission Company owed the bank a large sum of money, and Mr. Stoddard was pressing Black to continue financing Miller, that the profits might go through the commission company to the bank. Shanghai interposed his views: "Mr. Black, you are just trying to work it out of Miller, and like everything of that kind, when a man get into you, and you go and furnish stuff to work him out, you had better give it to him first as last. I refuse to make another contract with Miller."

"If Campbell Commission Company," interrupted Withers, "will put up the freight, advance enough to insure that the market price will not drop below the lien Mr. Pierce takes, and if Campbell will let me get the lien money each day as the cattle are sold, before Campbell gets anything, Mr. Pierce will trade with you."

"That, Mr Withers," scowled Miller, "is all turkey for Campbell, and all buzzard for Miller"

But "buzzard" it went, and, according to the agreement, 7,000 head of cattle—freight prepaid and protected with a sufficient advance—were contracted to go forward in the name of the Campbell Commission Company If there was any turkey left, Miller was to have it, but he had not forgotten that Pierce had said: "No one can get any sugar out of them after I have got done with them."

In preparation for the delivery of the large number of cattle to the Campbell Commission Company, Pierce was again forced to enter the market in East Texas. First, he bought from W. H. P. McFaddin, who sought to extend the delivery date and give him "average age" cattle. To this, Shanghai objected: "The change of date of delivery I can stand, but the average age won't do. If not it is useless for me to buy them & Old fellow you ought to be a little more broad gaged in your vices. I got you a good buyer & you made a good Sale to him, So I think you can afford to deal a little liberal with me. All I want is what is wright & if you Cannot Stand that you Can return the check."

Shanghai was inclined to be more liberal regarding the age of the cattle he bought from L. B. Pipkin, who was an experienced lumberman, and not an expert cattleman like McFaddin. However, when lumberman Pipkin questioned Pierce's status as a cattleman, he drew forth a withering rebuke: "Your favor Just to hand & 11 points fully noted. I am about as old & Large a Cattle dealer as there is in the State & have dealt in Cattle nearly 40 years & up to the present have gotten along with Everybody Satisfactorily. I have given you plenty of Lee way to be of full age. Any Summer or fall Calf is no better than a Calf that Comes the following Feby or March & if not a yearling by July 1st, I can buy him & Keep him 12 months & he is nothing but a yearling then—the same rule will apply to your own business—*When you buy logs, you Neither Expect Poles or Wait for the trees to grow to Make Logs.*"

Miller learned of the death of Eugene Talbot, so he showed up at the Talbot feeding pens just before a severe norther swept into the region. After the weather moderated, neither Miller nor the cattle were to be found, except about fifty head which remained around the pens. The suggestion was offered to Mrs. Talbot that perhaps the others had wandered off and died. However, old Miller wrote Shanghai from Kansas, intimating that Pierce should make a settlement with Mrs. Talbot. This brought forth the blunt refusal: "I cannot pay Mrs. Talbot, or anyone else, except the normal expenses incurred on the cattle in the Territory." And to the Commission Company he also made himself perfectly clear:

> Now, Mr. Miller is Broke & his Indebtedness is to Lawyers, Drs., Bankers, Fidlers & Com. Men & while My lien is First & good here —where I have an even Brake with anybody—but when you get me up there all the Creditors have got the advantage of me—as I am off my base & besides to fight a Suit up there is very Costive & my money is due here & *here I must have it.* I have between 7 & 8 thousand Beeves, Coast Range, I Expect to Ship to your firm & if I was afraid of you I certainly would not do it.

On May 3, 1895, there were 159 stable cars, filled with Miller cattle, billed to Campbell Commission Company and carrying $1372.50 freight charges, leaving Pierce's Station for Kansas City. As the cattle passed through Perry, Oklahoma Territory, attachment, then garnishment, papers were served on Pierce. The Colonel went on to Kansas City, where Stoddard told him that the Campbell Commission Company had failed and that his St. Louis bank, which had underwritten the venture for Mr. Miller, was now involved in the litigation. Shanghai called on Mr. Black, who had been appointed receiver for the commission company, and refused to invest any more money in the cattle, while at the same time getting himself appointed receiver. He stated his position:

> Black you have let Miller and a crowd like him drive you to the wall and while I would like the best in the world to accomodate you and know the cattle are more than ample security, I don't consider I have any claim on them for a new debt. If I commence paying Miller's claims, I will never get through and be bankrupt myself.

As receiver for the cattle, Pierce discovered that the railroad had made an overcharge. He presented his claim for refund, which

"My shotgun went off in the Pullman"

was declined. In lieu of payment, the railroad tendered him with an overpayment charge which had accrued on some previous shipment. To this Shanghai replied:

> Your statement shows up very nicely for the R.R. Side but it is a Vacuum in my Equiliberum which it fails to fill. No doubt, if you will write Mr. Miller at Winfield Kans he will send you Check for Amt overpaid him. I shall never return one cent & if you wish to bring suit don't delay, as I hire my Attys by the year & they are about out of business.

Now that Pierce had a large herd of cattle on hand, he had need for some of his trustworthy employees. He therefore applied to the railroad companies for passes for Dick and Neptune. The railroads operating south of Gainesville, Texas, complied, but transportation north of that station was not forthcoming. Pierce, consequently, instructed Borden from Arkansas City what they should do: "Enclosed find passes for Neptune & Dick. When they get ready to come on the 17th, they will arrive at Gainesville about Midnight & may be they can Sleep the Conductor through, if not, they will have to pay fare from Gainesville, to Purcell."

Rumors came to the bank officials that Miller was preparing to dissipate their security. Consequently Pierce said: "Mr. Young came to me one night in a hurry with a telegram from Stoddard requesting him to see me & get an armed body of men & go down & Keep Miller from Stealing & running of the Cattle. I told Young I had a man that Would Hold them in Spite of Hell or High Watter, if he would pay for it, & would be cheaper than to Hire other fighting men (as they are expensive Services) & Young said all Wright & this agreement was made & I was to pay Bell & it was to come out of the money in my hands."

Casper Bell took charge under the direction of A. H. Pierce, Receiver. As a result, the bankers and commission merchants fell under Miller's wrath. They took no notice of his threats. The situation was different, however, when Miller turned his attention to Shanghai, and he got the warning:

> Mr. G. W. Miller:
> I am sorry you have got afraid of me. I play second tune to nobody's fiddle. I cannot pay anything except the expenses incurred on the cattle now in the Territory in charge of the New York and St.

Louis banker's fighting man, which I hired by their positive instructions.

Now Miller, I have tried to treat you Wright all the way through, and in your letter you say you think that you and me are enough armed men. Now the extent of my arms, you will know, are the corkscrew you gave me and a barlow knife. I know you have been threatening the life of Black and Neal for the las thirty days, and now I suppose you fire has been withdrawn from them and centered on me. If so, write me at once without fail. Now, understand me fully: I am no fighting man, but I do not propose to be bulldozed or murdered by anyone if I can help myself.

Respectfully yours,
A. H. Pierce

Miller exploded to his friends, who relayed the assertions to Shanghai, that the cattle "could not be taken without a shotgun." Armed with a shotgun, and Casper Bell sitting by his side, the Receiver started toward Indian Territory. Miller met the train, and, when Shanghai did not disembark immediately, he started up the train steps. There was a terrific explosion, and Miller left *post haste*. The conductor found old Shanghai sitting quietly in the Pullman, with the car full of smoke and the end of the car full of bullets. He asked what was the trouble: Pierce chuckled: "My shotgun went off in the Pullman Palace Car and made a little noise."

A few days later Miller was told that Shanghai was coming back. Again Miller was at the depot, carrying two Winchesters and two boxes of cartridges. "I am going to give him one," he shouted, "and I'll take the other. We'll see who gets the cattle." But the shouting that day was in vain. The Colonel was not on the train. Shanghai explained his view of the situation: "I went down there, and he stood me off the first time, and I fell back and re-inforced."

The "re-inforcements" accompanying Shanghai the next trip consisted of Casper Bell, with a cocked Winchester across his arm, and an order from the United States District Court, empowering Shanghai, as Receiver, to sell the cattle under the purchase lien.

"I had the orders from the Court," explained Shanghai, "to sell the cattle and get my money. *I was holding them by the tail with one hand, and getting the money with the other.* I had a man standing there all the time. I gobbled it up."

18. *"Every potentate in Europe except the Pope was gone from home when I called"*

On the night after Daniel Sullivan wired Pierce, "You are a Prince," $20,000 of Shanghai's money left Galveston by express, consigned to D. Sullivan and Company. That was followed by another $20,000, and Shanghai wrote, tendering $30,000 more if needed. To the offer of the loan, the Colonel pinned a notation of a more personal nature. It said: "I wish you would Engage State Rooms for us on an Outgoing Steamer that leaves on or after 25th June on Some good line   give attention at once as we want good quarters   I dont want my ticket & My Wifes bought from San Antonio. I will

239

run up Some day about June 1st & See you then we can arrange about tickets to New York."

Mrs. Pierce thought she would enjoy the companionship of Daniel Sullivan's daughters on their contemplated tour of Europe; therefore, when Shanghai made his visit to Little Dannie, he carried along an urgent invitation to the Misses Sullivan, asking that Mrs. Pierce be permitted to have the pleasure of their company on the journey. Miss Annie Sullivan was attending school in New York at the time, and she was advised that Mr. and Mrs. Pierce, accompanied by her sister, would meet her in New York, and the four would travel together.

Miss E. A. Sullivan met the Colonel and Mrs. Pierce in St. Louis, and the three left for New York, June 22, 1891. Miss Annie joined them, according to plan, and the four went aboard a Cunard liner. Belfast was their first point of debarkation. The Colonel was much interested in the sights, but the ladies were hard put to it to prevent him from wandering off to look at some cattle. He made inquiries concerning their weight, growth, what diseases they were afflicted with, and "did they take Texas fever?" From Ireland, the party journeyed on to London; then they crossed the Channel to France. Although the railroad station was fairly seething with attendants, he could find no one whose duty it seemed to be to care for the numerous bags which the ladies were taking with them and which now lay on the dock ready to be loaded on the train for Paris. He stormed up and down but finally solved his problem by grabbing up the luggage and depositing it on the train himself. Then he sat down on a "cramped up seat" in disgust.

The stay in Paris was short. From Paris, they moved on up into Holland; thence to Germany. Here Shang took time out from sight-seeing to answer his mail, which had overtaken him. From Berlin, the troup rode into Austria, and finally to Rome.

Throughout his travels, Shanghai inquired about the most important people in the countries and never missed a chance to look at a strange cow. At Rome, he decided in favor of a visit to the Pope, so, taking the ladies in tow, he set out for the Vatican. "We walked down the long hall," he said; "I was leading the way, the ladies following. A guard stopped us. I tried to tip him. I offered fifty cents . . . I offered six bits. I knew that if six bits would not bribe an Italian, it was useless to offer more. I started to push by.

"Every potentate in Europe"

Then I saw them men with fixed bayonets charging at me, and I just threw up my hands in good old Texas style and backed out backwards faster then I had come in forwards.

"It was peculiar," he concluded, "how every potentate in Europe, except the Pope, was away from home that summer when I sent in my visiting card!"

Then, travel-weary and worn, the ladies quarrelled. For another thirty days, they journeyed on, the Colonel doing the best he could to maintain the peace. He visited the gown shops, looked at the art galleries, bought a statue in Paris, and finally took passage for New York.

After the quarrel in Rome, old Shanghai wrote a long letter of explanation to Little Dannie. At New York he had an answer. The Colonel would leave the Sullivan daughters at a certain New York address. "I left them there; saw them inside the house where he told me to leave them in New York. I came home. Of course, I knew people fall out and get very bitter on family matters sometimes, so when I got home, I wrote Little Danny 'how we should meet.' I did not want to go up there to San Antonio and get killed. I did not know how it would be. I attached to my letter a statement of the expenses of the trip.[1] Mr. Sullivan wrote right back: 'Glad to hear from you and that you are back safe. I enclose draft for $879.78, amount due you. That was a very economical trip; better than I could have done. I am very thankful for your kindness to the children. I am very sorry that matters was not more agreeable amongst the ladies, but that is something a man can't control, but

[1] The statement of expenses read:

D. Sullivan
        In Account with A. H. Pierce:

To Cash pd for Sleeper meals and Carriage from St. Louis to N.Y. (Miss E.A. Sullivan)	10 08
" Expenses of the Misses Sullivan from June 22nd to Oct 6th Incl.	1031 90
" Amt Pd for Mrs. D. Sullivans Paris Dress	105
" Cash pd to Miss E. A. Sullivan	650 04
" " " " " A. M. Sullivan	777 76
By Amt drawn on Letter of Credit	16 95
" Balance	879 78
To Balance due A.H.P.	879.78

Expense of A. H. Pierce and party from June 22nd to Oct 6th, 106 days—2063.81, or an average of $4.86¼ per day. Total Expense of Party, including Steamship passage $2943.81 or an average of $6.94¼ per day.

that need not effect us. We have been friends too long for anything less than a revolution to sever our friendship. Got your photo. It is fine. You must have been benefitted by the voyage. No more!'"

Thus finding out "how we should meet," old Shanghai looked forward with pleasure to his visit to San Antonio. There he regaled his friends with his travels. "I have," he said, "visited London, and Paris, and Vienna, and Florence, and Milan, and the duece only know where else. In Rome, I stood near the spot, so they told me, where Rienzi addressed the multitude. I rested within the shadows of Saint Peter's. I saw the Vatican and the Quirinal, and I gazed out on the 'Seven Hills.'"

Just at that point, fat old Dillard Fant inquired: "Shang, did you see any of the Papal Bulls at the Vatican?"

"Nary a damn critter. Nary a critter," he answered, "but I did see some fine old cows out there, just out of town."

19. "*Pluck my locks for souvenirs and charms*"

When Shanghai got back to the BU Ranch from San Antonio, he found a notice from J. P. Rossa, collector at the Port of New York. As he was looking over the notice, a small, stooped man, speaking with a definite German accent, stopped at BU headquarters, and asked if he might stay over during the night. "Come in, come in," shouted Colonel Pierce. "Make yourself to home." Introducing himself as Frank Teich, of San Antonio, he told the Colonel that he was stopping at the suggestion of his brother, Jonathan, with whom he had been estimating the cost of erecting markers at the Pierce burial plot near Deming's Bridge. "By all means," invited the Colonel, "stay all night. There will be no train until tomorrow. I can make you more comfortable here than over at such a place as Wharton."

After dinner, Clay McSparren came in to talk about ranch af-

Shanghai Pierce

fairs and listen to Shanghai tell about his recent trip "to the continent." While talking, Shanghai picked up the collector's notice again and announced. "Bill for my statuary. It cost me 540 'franks' —in American money, about $67. While in Paris, I passed under the Arc de Triomphe. I saw Venus de Milo, but what impressed me most was the Wacht am Rhine."

"Yes," modestly stated Mr. Teich, "while a lad I assisted in making the Wacht am Rhine."

Suddenly, Pierce arose from his chair and began pacing up and down the floor. Finally, he stopped before his guest and asked: "Then you could make a real statute of me, so when people passed they would say, 'There stands Old Pierce.' " Mr. Teich was sure he could. "Then I want one, a big one, not one you can't hardly see on the mantel piece with the naked eye, but one I can be buried under, so people can say, 'There stands Old Pierce.' "

The negotiations continued. Teich asked a commission of $2,500. Pierce offered $2,250, and the sculptor accepted. And it was to be "higher than any statute of any Confederate general, a fair likeness of myself."

"But who shall say it is a fair likeness of me? I can't see myself!" questioned Pierce.

"That," countered the sculptor, "may be determined by a person of your own choosing. Otherwise, you shall not have to take it."

The bargain was made. The morning train bore the sculptor back to his Monumental Works, north across the street from the Alamo, in San Antonio. He took with him every available photograph of the Colonel, and he diligently went to work with his chisels. Following him, in the mail came Shanghai's final instructions:

Mr. Frank Teich,
   San Antonio,
      Texas

Dear Sir:

Your favor of the 7th inst at hand and would have answered before but for the quarantine which kept me from home.

Your suggestions are all satisfactory to me and you can do as you suggest, and put but my name on the monument. on the marker put

"Pluck my locks for souvenirs and charms"

A. H. Pierce
Born June 29 1834
Died

Mr. J. E. Pierce will send you the lettering for the other two markers. You need not send the curbing but put down the cement walk.

Yours truly,
A. H. Pierce.

In the meantime it was rumored that Shanghai was to erect a "statute" to himself. The Colonel took great pleasure in advertising his intentions. In fact, he told how he had stopped off in New York after his "tour of the continent, looking at statutes in Paris and Rome" and had a bigger and better one made by a great sculptor. It was to be "an exact likeness of myself, cast in bronze." "In fact," he said, "to get it 'exact' I stood in plaster-of-Paris, whiskers and all, so they could get it lifesize. Paid twenty thousand dollars for it."

Nearly three months later, the Southern Pacific set out a freight car at El Campo. With hoists and tackle, a heavy gray marble monument was removed to a wagon. Six oxen pulled it slowly toward the Deming's Bridge Cemetery, while Clay McSparren rode along to point the way. Workmen set the plinth and mounted thereon a ten-foot section of highly polished, gray granite, into which had been cut:

A. H. PIERCE
BORN
JUNE 29 1834
DIED

Resting upon this granite section stood a ten-foot Palladian pilaster, which was topped with the "likeness" of the Colonel, cut from the finest gray marble. Lifelike, with hat in right hand dropped naturally downward toward the knee, his left hand clutching the lapel of his coat, and with eyes fixed slightly upward, "There stood old Pierce," scanning the future.

The workmen were finishing their toils; the scaffold was being dismantled; and old Shang rode down to the cemetery with Mc-

Sparren. Dismounting, they seated themselves upon a carpenter's sawbuck. Neither spoke as they studied the handiwork of Frank Teich. Finally a small Negro boy, Green Duncan, wandered aimlessly over to the monument. Several times he peered long and silently, first at the statue, then, at Mr. Pierce. Then he walked completely around the structure and stopped before the two white men. In a piping voice he addressed himself to the Colonel: "Mr. Shanghai, dat shore do look like you up there."

"Ugh, by God, Clay," snorted old Shang, as he arose to his feet. "I'll take it." And immediately he scribbled his acceptance:

Dec. 28th —7

Mr. Frank Teich,
San Antonio, Texas

Dear Sir:
The monument and statue for which you contracted with me to erect at Deming's Bridge Texas has been completed to my entire Satisfaction and is a fine piece of workmanship and art, and far exceeds my expectations. I shall always take pleasure in recommending you to my friends who want anything in your line.

Yours very truly
A. H. Pierce

The story went the rounds that there was to be a big unveiling. When cowboys inquired when the event was to take place, Shang would solemnly say: "Sorry boys, sorry. You are too late. We've already had it. Too bad you were not there. Little Dannie was there, and you know, that little rascal, just as they pulled the sheet off my statute, he reached up just as high as he could and poked me under the coattail and said: 'Shang: You old son-of-a-bitch, that's as near to Heaven as you'll ever get.' And what's funny about it, for once in his life, Little Danny may be right."[1]

Turning from "statute-erecting" back to his cattle business, but with the monument fresh on his mind, Shanghai rode along with the men as they made "a work" in the O'Connell pasture, east of

[1] An unveiling of the monument did not take place. Also, Mr. Sullivan swore in the U. S. court at Galveston, that never in his entire life was he on the Pierce property in that region; besides that, Mr. Sullivan was not "a cusser," like Shanghai. Obviously it was just one of Shanghai's big tales.

"Pluck my locks for souvenirs and charms"

the Duncan Ranch. The boys "scooped em up" as they came along, using little care to see that other people's stock stayed at home. A new rancher in the region missed his cow and followed after the herd. Quietly and courteously he approached and asked for Mr. Pierce, stating that Shanghai's crew had inadvertently taken along one of his cows.

"Hell," said Shanghai, "I don't have time to bother with your cow. I'll cut her out tonight."

"But," said the stranger, "I want my cow *now*."

"Take 'em on, boys," called out Shanghai. "We don't have time to fool with one old cow."

As quietly as he came, the man moved away, only to reappear with a double-barreled shotgun held firmly over the saddle horn. He stopped at a point within easy speaking distance for his mild voice. He raised his gun and took a steady bead on the bridge of Shanghai's nose, speaking very softly as he did so: "Mr. Pierce, I came after my cow."

"O, boys," instantly called out Shanghai. "Stop the cattle. Stop the cattle, I tell you. Cut out this gentleman's cow. Sorry I troubled you, Sir. I might have known you'd need that old sister, *now*."

As the man with the cow disappeared, the cowmen gathered around to laugh.

"He bluffed you, Shang!" said one.

Without hesitation, Pierce solemnly replied: "Men, I recently built a statute to myself down in my pasture." Then, cupping his hands, as if to imitate one looking through binoculars, he said, "And when I looked down that double-barreled telescope through the big ends, I saw way down to Deming's Bridge and that statute had written on it:

A. H. PIERCE
BORN
JUNE 29, 1834
DIED
TODAY."

The quarantine which was referred to by Shanghai in his letter to Teich, resulted from what Shanghai referred to as "Yellow feaver Scare or Gitter [jitter] feaver.' The "Gitter feaver" caught him away from home, as it did Borden also. Not being allowed to return to the ranch, Pierce, too, became jittery, and, riding the G.C. and S.F. to Fort Worth, he took notice of the "epidemick," which was actually smallpox, and wrote Borden:

> 7 Cases Small Pox at Rosenburg & one more death
> 2 Cases on Boden Hamer place at Wharton
> that is Where Old Isaack lives & Where Robt Staid night before last, I Suppose, as I Saw the Woman on train yesterday that had the baby at Isacks
> Read the Riot act to them all
> Allow no one to Return that leaves the place
> & if that dont Suit them let them leave
> & tell Robt not to allow anyone to come to his House
> & if he does let them Come & not report it run him off
> Wire me by return train to Ft Worth Care Pickwick Hotel.

While excluded from the ranch headquarters, he rode around the country inspecting the condition of things. His holdings were so extensive that he found it difficult to keep the property under observation. "I don't know how much land I own," he said. "I could not guess within ten thousand acres. One hundred and fifty thousand is pretty near to it. Fifty-five thousand in the Duncan Ranch. I've seen that list made up. On the west side of the Colorado, I own a whole slough of it. I own a lot on the east side, also, below the Duncan Ranch. And I own a great deal of land in Galveston County." In fact, he owned so much land that it was becoming a source of annoyance to him. He could neither keep it under observation nor prevent depredation.

Two sections of Pierce's holdings were grown over with cedar trees. These were the only cedarbrakes in the entire coastal area; and since the advent of barbed wire, cedar posts were in the greatest demand. He therefore hired E. M. Sojourner to cut posts for the ranch. While in Wharton, he was informed that one of Vi's sons had run away from the BU Ranch and was staying with Sojourner's cedar-cutting crew. Shanghai, consequently, went down the river to the cedarbrake. Before he got to the cutters he met John McCroskey, who told him that "some other cedar hands were camped about 400 yards from the line and some one else was stealing cedar from your land." He then dispatched a message to the campers, saying: "Now, Gentlemen, I give you due notice never

"Pluck my locks for souvenirs and charms"

to cut or haul another stick of cedar from my premises, for I will use the law on you to the fullest extent & if there is no law in the Statutes to protect my property, I will have it protected myself. This wholesale robbery of my property shall stop sure."

Then he had the land surveyed and cut a road entirely around it. This he said he did "to keep the cedar thieves off but it Looks Like Impossibility, and I give a liberal reward for anyone that can be Caught & Put in Penitentiary."

His attention next went to his Brazoria County cedarbrake. "We caught," said Pierce, "Conrad France stealing the cedar—not stealing it—just taking it, which is strictly legitimate in Brazoria County. I wrote to a lawyer down there, a Mr. Shepherd. He had been a reverend brother. Told him that they were selling all my cedar and he said: 'I know of no law on the statute whereby I can stop him.' He was evidently a better preacher than a lawyer! A man that lives in Brazoria, and he don't steal cedar, he is not in it. He is bound to steal cedar if he has a fence."

Next in line came Joe Pertrika. Joe's offense was that of being the father of a son who had been caught in the act of stealing firewood. Pierce placed the blame squarely upon the father:

> Mr. McSparren Caught you Son yesterday morning in my Pasture Stealing wood. My Pasture is posted according to law as you well know & You have been pulling down my fence & trespassing on me for last two years. You best come down and arrange matters at once & Sin no more.

These "sins" Shanghai reported to his Galveston advisers, who suggested that all his timberlands be enclosed in theft-proof fences. Pierce demurred to this solution. "There is no law in Texas," he informed them, "against stealing timber, and nothing but a shotgun fence will stop them, and I don't want to build such fences in a foreign land."

With timber-stealing off his mind, he visited the Duncan plantation. John McCroskey's faithful Negro, Arthur Green, met him. He dated his connection with the Duncan Ranch from "Ever since Mr. Pierce owned that ranch I rolled in there and have been knocking around ever since." Shanghai approached Arthur with the idea of finding out how things were progressing on the Half Moon Ranch and, specifically, how many acres the Negroes were cultivating.

Shanghai Pierce

"Boss, God knows," stammered Arthur, "it's too hard for me to tell how many acres there are."

"Just tell me as near as you can, just *about* how many," coaxed the Colonel.

"God Almighty! You see it's funny, but I just want to tell you the truth, as near as I can. For me to tell you how many acres—I couldn't do it. It's too much for my brains. If I would go to say 'how many,' I would have to go to them 'bouts,' and 'bouts' won't do. I can't say exactly, how much land they has. The Guinea grass ran them out of the old field, and they just cleared up back of the woods, and got a little fields backwards and forwards in there. They has got other land opened up—right sharp of it."

"Well, then," questioned the Colonel, "how many calves did you brand before the storm?"

"We branded a right sharp bunch, but I'm the fellow to do the work, you see, and somebody else is the man to keep the count, but we branded a good heap. I might tell you how many, and I might be lying. I mustn't do that. I might give you enough and I might give you too many."

Turning his attention to McCroskey's commissary, Shanghai inquired about the bacon and the molasses.

"He sells the things there to the farmers, the tenants. He sells some of it. Just as well give it to them," volunteered Arthur. "It's safer to give it to them, 'cause if you look for them to make a crop on that ground, they don't do it. I reckon he gives it to them. The Guinea grass cuts them off, so he hasn't got any pay yet."

As Shanghai rode out of hearing distance from Arthur Green, the old Negro mumbled, "See the Old Man goin' there. He's all the time growling about the fellow's behind—fellows behind—fellows behind. He ain't as rich over here as he thinks he is. He's way behind in his bacon. He gives out more than he gets back. Them Niggers is just like me. Them scound'els is black. Pretty near all of them black as me. If he crowds them, they go away and leave him that way. I got over here when Mr. Pierce bought this ranch, and got stuck—drank some of that water—and ain't been away since. Sorry I stayed."

As the Colonel headed back to BU headquarters, he saw a big, elderly man riding a racking horse. When within hailing distance, he called out: "By the holy Latter Day Saints! If it isn't my

"Pluck my locks for souvenirs and charms"
illustrious old Irish friend, Michael O'Connell! Making your yearly pilgrimage to the shrine of Little Dannie, eh?"

Michael O'Connell had immigrated from the "auld country" with Dan Sullivan and had remained his true friend throughout the years, even refusing to deposit his money in any bank other than Sullivan's. O'Connell owned a large ranch adjoining the Duncan plantation on the south and east. Each year he sold his cattle and demanded payment in "specie"; this he placed in his saddle-bags, mounted his racking horse, and headed steadily westward on his two-hundred-mile trip to Little Dannie's bank. On the sixth day after his departure, he would show up on the horizon again, his horse fagged and barely able to trot, but Michael O'Connell would be sitting as erect and fresh as when he started.

"You are just the man I've been wanting to see for a week," spoke the Colonel. "Sojourner tells me that Vi's little nigger ran away from the cedar camp and went to work for you?"

Michael nodded.

"Then," scornfully continued Shanghai, "this has become a hell of a country, when a nigger will leave free grub at Shanghai Pierce's ranch and run off to *work* for Michael O'Connell!"

O'Connell spurred his horse and soon disappeared westward. But when Pierce reached the ranch, he inked up his pen and wrote:

Mr. M. O'Connell

Dr. Sir

Greatly to my Supprise I am reliably informed that you have started a D Brand and are running over my D brand a fresh & putting Crescent over my D; you, and boath your Sons, are fully aware that I have been giving the D brand for last 20 years & you give, or allow your sons to give the Crescent D brand alongside of me & *giving the Rogues mark*, both ears cut to the head, is no more or less than Highway robery & I hardly know what action to take in the premises but will consult my Atty on the Subject. It is still fresh in the memory of all fair-minded men, the 13 Steers your boys turned below Green C. Duncans, the time Dick Johnson roped the U that got its shoulder broken putting them through the lower gate.

I have always considered you my friend, but this does not Look much like friendship.

Mr. W. T. Taylor is my author. Let me hear from you
           & oblige,
                A. H. Pierce

Shanghai Pierce

Michael O'Connell obliged Shanghai by maintaining a silence. However, as Clay McSparren worked through Pierce's "wire pasture," he found a neighbor's steer with Pierce's D freshly burned on it. The Colonel gave order to Clay "to take the steer so that we will know where he is and save him from the hands of any unscrupulous person." Then the Colonel wrote J. F. Walker, the owner: "Some person has undoubtedly branded this steer to make trouble. I will deliver him to you, or make any other disposition of him that you may suggest." When Walker asked for his steer, search as hard as Pierce's men could, they did not find him. He, therefore, was forced to report: "My boys cannot find him again, and I herewith enclose my check to pay for him." Then, while the incident was fresh in Shanghai's mind, he rode up on another big fat D steer. To his utmost astonishment, burnt across the full length and height of the steer, was another brand:

A. H. P.
is a
S. O. B.

"Well," commented Pierce, "they know me. Let him run, boys. He's good advertisement."

Meanwhile, the 'Gitter feaver' scare caused N. M. Uri and Company, wholesale liquor dealers in Louisville, Kentucky, to receive several hurry-up orders. From Shanghai came the following letter: "Enclosed find my check invoice of whiskey to J. E. Pierce. Today, I ordered 10 gal of same whiskey to be sent to W. M. Kuykendall, at this place, and papers to be sent to me. I wish, you have not already shipped this, that you would fill the order with an article to cost $3.50 per gal but make the bill as you did mine, $4.00, or rather make two bills for me, one at $3.50 and one at $4.00, and it will answer my purpose just as well."

When the whiskey arrived, the Colonel sent it along to his brother-in-law, accompanied by the Uri bills and a note: "Sue told John you had leased Giffords pasture. I own land in there also, and own and keep the lower fence. I have some cattle in there but there is splenty of grass for mine & yours also. Now wiley Old Fellow, I don't want my cattle disturbed. So don't turn any of them out."

Back came the reply, signed by "wiley, Old Fellow," but obviously written by Shanghai's sister Susan:

"Pluck my locks for souvenirs and charms"

>   I am not going to run off or get broke or bankrupt. You have got a beef of mine up there. What are you going to doe with it. I did not intend to youse your pasture, as I have ground enough to hurd on. I was a mity good fellow last spring when you could youse me. What has turned up now you are so hostile. I am the same old Wylie. I will come up and stay all night and we will settel our business
>
>   Respt Yours from
Wylie M. Kuykendall.
>
>   P.S. Col Pierce
>   I do all my husbands writing, so wrote to you what he directed me to write, as I do not correspond with you
>
>   S. E. Kuykendall.

When the quarantine was lifted and Shang was readmitted to the BU Ranch headquarters, he found an inquiry from Sullivan, couched as a mild complaint at Pierce's failure to send to San Antonio the last yearly report on the cattle company's activities. Barking out to Borden that "forbearance has ceased to be a virtue and my entire stock of patience exhausted," he ordered the statement prepared "instanter." When it was finished, he took it and caught the train for San Antonio. This was the first time during the existence of the corporation that he had delivered the account in person. Sullivan's reception was cordial but not enthusiastic. He took the statement without comment, other than to invite Shanghai into a room in the back of the bank. There he alternately paced the floor and peered critically at different items on the account until Judge Charles Ogden arrived. He then asked if the cattle market wasn't up a little. "It has been down a long time," responded the Colonel, "but there is a little spring in the price right now."

"Then," bluntly said Sullivan, "let's sell ours!"

"Mr. Sullivan," said Pierce, "I am in the business. I am bound to keep mine."

"How many cattle are down there?" inquired the banker.

"Our stock are badly overestimated—eight or ten thousand; worth about $80,000," replied Pierce. "I'll give you $20,000."

"I'll take $25,000," rejoined Sullivan; but there was no trade and the meeting broke up.

Shanghai Pierce

Colonel Pierce discussed his affairs with his brother. Now that Mrs. Withers was living with her lawyer husband in Kansas City and Jonathan had a large family of his own down at El Rancho Grande, they decided to dissolve the partnership, A. H. and J. E. Pierce. Consequently, Shanghai traded lands with Jonathan and took his Pierce-Sullivan Pasture and Cattle Company stock as part consideration. Immediately, Shanghai requested Dan Sullivan to transfer the stock formerly owned by Jonathan Pierce to Mrs. Mamie Withers. At the same time, Pierce made inquiry of Dan Sullivan, whether or not he had any objection to Mrs. Mamie Withers' being elected as a director to succeed J. E. Pierce. To this inquiry Sullivan made no reply. Sullivan did, however, press Pierce, again, to purchase his one-fourth interest in the Half Moon cattle, though styling Shanghai's "offer a hard one." To this Shanghai replied: "It is more than you are getting out West & top price in this Section. You must not forget, my offer was to collect them, which is 50 cents per head; that is just what it would cost you if you Sell to any outside parties; as you well know, it would not do to let Everybody be running My Cattle around & that I will not permit."

The time for the annual meeting of the directors and stockholders of the Pierce-Sullivan Pasture & Cattle Company came on February 11, 1895. The session was held, perfunctorily, in the office of Judge Ogden, in the Kampmann Building, San Antonio. The accounts were approved, and Mrs. Withers was elected to supplant J. E. Pierce, while Little Dannie sulked. When the meeting adjourned, Dan Sullivan walked into the hallway, ahead of Pierce. Instead of turning to go down the stairs, Shanghai reached out and caught Sullivan by the arm, continuing down the hallway with the banker in tow, saying: "Dan, I want to see you a minute." They walked together—Dan very short—Shanghai very tall. Neither spoke until they came to the window. Then in stentorian voice, Shanghai called down to him: "I would like to know what you are bellyaching about!"

"You mistreated my daughters in Europe," said the small man as he threw back his head and glared upward into the eyes of old Shang.

There was a barrage and counter salvo of retorts which could not be understood by those near by. Then Pierce, standing on his tiptoes, with forefinger pointing at Sullivan's nose, shouted into

"Pluck my locks for souvenirs and charms"

his face: "By God, Sir! I shall never come into your bank again. Right here I quit. *I tell you I do not thank any man to be my daddy.*"

Little Dannie quietly returned to his bank, choosing to make no explanation regarding the incident. Pierce, however, amplified: "We walked right out of Judge Ogden's office . . . instead of turning into the elevator, I asked him to step down into the hall of the Kampmann Building. . . . As we walked into the Kampmann Building, there is a continuation down to the window. I saw he was bellyaching about something. I said: 'Dan, I want to see you a minute. . . . I would like to know what you are bellyaching about!' I used a little stronger language than that. . . . I will leave it to you to put in what I said. I try not to use profanity. As to what I said, you can put in anything you please! The conversation was not pleasant, anyway . . . and I told him! 'Right here I quit. I tell you, I do not thank any man to be my daddy. Never again shall I come back into your bank.'"

Old Shang was troubled in spirit as he rode back to the BU Ranch. There he dug around through his files until he found Sullivan's letter. He read it several times: "I am very thankful for your kindness to the children. . . . I am very sorry that matters was not more agreeable among the ladies . . . that is something a man can't control. . . . We have been friends too long for anything less than a revolution to sever our friendship. . . ." Then, taking up his ink-daubed, blunt pen, he copied the letter, word by word, and, placing it in an envelope, he rode down to the depot to mail it. Although Shanghai anticipated an answer, there was none.

In the meantime, Easter Sunday, 1895, came. On that day, R. B. Houston, a merchant of Wharton, received a telegram notifying him of the death of his brother-in-law, Colonel H. B. Andrews. Mr. Houston hurriedly left to attend the funeral at San Antonio, and, finding he needed funds while in the city, he presented himself at the office of Daniel Sullivan. The banker was especially cordial and inquisitive as to financial affairs in Wharton County. He casually inquired if Mr. Houston happened to be acquainted with Colonel A. H. Pierce, president of the Pierce-Sullivan Pasture and Cattle Company. Mr. Houston stated that he had known Mr. Pierce for ten or eleven years and that he was also acquainted with the corporation property. Whereupon Sullivan stated that there were "about 18,000 or 19,000 acres of land in there—my part—and

Shanghai Pierce

Pierce claims there is 12,000 cattle. I will," he stated, "sell you my part for $125,000."

The merchant thought "the deal a little big" for him. Then Sullivan confided: "Pierce says there are 12,000 cattle in there. I think he has more."

"Well, how am I to determine?" queried Houston.

"I suggest you hire a sharp Negro and send him down there and see about it, and count them," slyly offered Sullivan.

A short time after the conversation in San Antonio, Mr. Houston was sitting on the sidewalk in front of his store. His heels were hooked back over a rung of a laced cowhide-bottom chair. From down the street came the clear high-pitched voice of Shanghai Pierce. The merchant pointed his finger at Colonel Pierce and the retinue of cowmen who followed him.

"Always entertaining the crowd," murmured Mr. Houston. "Talking loud . . . a big crowd . . . a typical cowman . . . likes to talk *big* and loud. He seems to rather like the idea of attracting a crowd by loud talk and jocular sayings, and impresses one as announcing: '*Here I am.*' But I don't believe Mr. Pierce would say anything he doesn't mean, unless it were in a jocular manner. I'd rely on him, and would feel perfectly safe in doing so. Would you, men?"

By that time Pierce had come abreast of the loungers before the store, and Houston arose to address the Colonel: "Mr. Pierce, I would like to speak with you a moment, Sir." They went inside, Houston leaning against the counter, Shanghai towering over him.

"I was in Santone the other day," began Houston.

"Yes?" queried Pierce.

"I heard one of your partners talking about you," continued Mr. Houston.

"Who?" said Shanghai, rather sharply.

"Sullivan," answered Houston.

"What did he have to say?" asked Pierce, now obviously interested.

"He wanted to sell me his stock," informed Houston.

"Did you buy it?"

"No, Sir: I did not want it. Something I could not handle. He asked me how many cattle there were. Said *he* didn't know; had

"Pluck my locks for souvenirs and charms"

never been on the ranch; never been among the stock. I told him: 'Pierce knows.' He said: 'Pierce says there only 7,000 or 8,000 head. Can't you get some pretty sharp nigger to work in Pierce's crowd and get him to make an estimate of them?' "

"No gentleman," snorted the angry cattleman as he turned on his high-heeled boots, "no gentleman would have asked a man to send a nigger down in to my crowd to look over and estimate my stock—an old cowman." And he was gone.

In strict compliance with the legal technicalities, the president gave written notice to each of the directors and stockholders of the company that "the regular annual meeting of the stockholders will be held in the City of San Antonio, the third day of February, at 9:30 A.M., the place to be the law office of Chas. Ogden, in the event same shall be agreeble and convenient to Mr. Ogden, if not so convenient and agreeable, then the parlor of the Mahncke Hotel in said city," to which was affixed the signature "A. H. Pierce. Done and issued this the 13th day of January, 1895."

At the appointed time, two young lawyers, F. C. and V. B. Proctor, armed with powers of attorney from A. H. Pierce and Mrs. Henry Withers, walked into "the law office of Chas. Ogden." Between them was Daniel Sullivan. It was announced that Mr. Ogden, for the moment, was away from his office, but that it was agreeable that the meeting of the corporation should be held there instead of in the parlor of the Mahncke Hotel. Mr. V. B. Proctor displayed his authority from A. H. Pierce to vote 740 shares of the corporation, and the meeting was called to order. F. C. Proctor exhibited his credentials, suggested the absence of the president, Mr. A. H. Pierce, and moved the election of Daniel Sullivan 'temporary chairman.' Chairman Sullivan took his seat, and F. C. Proctor was made secretary; whereupon, V. B. Proctor introduced resolutions changing the place of meetings of the corporation from Judge Ogden's San Antonio office to "the pasture of said company in Matagorda County, Texas," and amending the by-laws so that thereafter they would read: "The officers of this corporation shall receive no salary, except the president and superintendent"!

These proposed amendments, with only the Proctors voting (Sullivan, the chairman, according to rule, being allowed to vote only in the instance of a tie—which was not to be), passed just as Judge Ogden appeared and began frantically to wave Mr. Sullivan from his chair as presiding dignitary.

Interspersed between Mr. Ogden's shouts of "Fraud, fraud! Pierce is perpetrating a fraud upon the company—moving it to some place in the pasture—in Matagorda County," the presiding officer quietly stated: "Gentlemen, I wouldn't be surprised. There are grounds for the accusation. If I said otherwise, I'd have to apologize for saying it. With all the confidence and friendship I've had for Mr. Pierce he did not have the cheek to come here himself, so he's sent these two young men. Until now I did not think Mr. Pierce was an ingrate. If these two lawyers—two Mr. Proctors—can't take care of him, I can't help him."

One week passed before Sullivan broke the silence which fell upon the adjournment of the stormy stockholders and directors' meeting. Sullivan filed a written request for a final statement of the accounts, and Pierce complied eleven days later, showing a cash balance in the hands of A. H. Pierce of $18,111.81. Sullivan drew a draft, immediately, upon Pierce's Galveston bank, Weekes, McCarthy and Company, for his one-quarter interest, $4,527.90. Shanghai promptly wired the bank: "Let Sullivan's draft go to protest," but he explained to Sullivan: "The reason I did not make distribution of this surplus was, that during the winter of 1894 and 1895 fully 40% of all the stock on the ranch died, and I shall purchase young steers with it this spring and help restock the ranch."

Four days later, Pierce complied with all the legal formalities in notifying Sullivan that "there will be a meeting of the board of directors of the Pierce-Sullivan Pasture & Cattle Company in the pasture of the company in Matagorda County, and you are requested to be present at that time." Then Sullivan observed: "I do believe he is trying to dissatisfy me!" At the same time, he directed Mr. Herman Brendel, his secretary, to make a thorough investigation of the corporation's affairs. Armed with a written directive from Sullivan to Pierce that the latter "furnish him every facility in your power to make full investigation into all the affairs," Brendel left by train for the BU Ranch. At Rosenburg he met a jovial talker who introduced himself as Asa Dawdy. He professed to know everything about old Shang and encouraged the large-nosed, big-black-moustached investigator to tell him the details of the brewing squabble. He also prevailed on Brendel to leave the train at Whar-

Fred C. Proctor,
My Counsellor

J. Clay McSparren,
"Mr. Clay,"
trail boss for Shanghai

"There stands old Pierce"

"Pluck my locks for souvenirs and charms"

ton and use the new telephone which Pierce had just installed at the BU Ranch. This, he said, had been done by Pierce over the protest of Mr. Monserrat, general manager of the Southern Pacific, as being "an expensive luxury!" Brendel was invited by telephone to come on to the ranch but was also informed that Mr. Pierce would not be at home until the beginning of the week, Sunday, and furthermore, that Pierce was due to be at the Duncan Ranch, Monday next, to preside at a Pierce-Sullivan Pasture and Cattle Company director's meeting.

On Sunday morning, Brendel went by train to Pierce's Station. At the ranch house, he was met by Colonel Pierce, in his best mood. Mr. Brendel was most welcome. "Mr. Borden will take you out; drive you around to see the nice cattle we have out there. You can stay as long as you want to. I have some good old Log Cabin whiskey. I'll give you the best there is in the house. We have plenty of room, lots of grub and plenty of niggers to cook it. . . . O, God; you may want to look at the books. There is the books; any papers you want, ask for them. Borden will give them to you, if they are here."

"About that time," later stated Pierce, as he described the incidents of that Sunday, "dinner was ready, and we went and got it and while we were eating, a messenger came with a note from Asa Dawdy who wrote that he had just been to San Antonio, where he had heard that Sullivan was intimating that I was hiding out some of the cattle, and that Brendel had stated while on the train that 'Pierce is robbing Sullivan.'"

The diners were quiet after the messenger left, and soon Pierce pushed back his chair, and, crooking a finger at Mr. Brendel, stated: "I want to ask you one question." Striding out of the dining room, he led the way upstairs, while Brendel followed, twisting the ends of his bushy black moustache downward with both hands.

"We'll go upstairs," said Pierce almost fiercely. "I'm not blowing my business around where others can hear it. I want to know whether Dawdy is blowing or not; that is all!" At the same time, he showed Brendel the note which had been handed to him by the rider.

Mr. Brendel gave the statements an unequivocal denial. Pierce looked at him for a moment, then said: "That is all right, Mr. Brendel," adding, as if an afterthought, "If people need killing, they can be accommodated. I once had a squatter on some land, and couldn't get him off. Offered to give it to a party if he'd get him off. He started to put up a post against the gallery of that man's house—on the property line—and the other party came out of the house. He shot at him; he killed him; and it cost me five hundred dollars to clear him."

"I have heard that kind of talk before," responded Brendel. "If I am not welcome, I will travel."

Colonel Pierce's talk then turned milder, and they descended the steps to meet Borden in the office, where Brendel wanted to know how much land the company owned. Pierce did not know. "I will have to look it up. I once knew, but for the last year, I have had such intense pains in my head I cannot recollect six months back." Borden and Brendel then checked very carefully over the company books, finding an error of one dollar against the interest of Mr. Pierce. They laughed over the singularity of that fact, and Brendel congratulated Borden for his accuracy in bookkeeping; then they retired for the night, agreeing that corporation matters would be pursued further next morning.

Old Shanghai was up early Monday morning, and, while breakfast was being served, he told Brendel that he had to go over to McCroskey's ranch house to hold a director's meeting and that, if there was anything else he wanted during the day, Mr. Borden would give him all the information he needed. Then he ushered Mr. Withers into the buggy and they drove away.

Turning to Mr. Borden, Brendel asked if the company had a bank account. "No," said Borden, "Mr. Pierce is the banker. He charges himself with all money that comes in that belongs to the company and credits the company with it, and when he pays out anything, he charges to company and credits himself."

Brendel then asked to see the account-sales, but Borden stated that he would not have time to go over the sales; he had to go to Wharton to court. Then he too rode off. Mrs. Pierce came into the office, and, finding Brendel sitting alone, invited him into the parlor, requiring him to stay for lunch with her; then, she sent him to the depot in a buggy.

Back in San Antonio, Brendel enlarged upon his experiences in Wharton County. "You know," he spoke earnestly to Sullivan, "Mr. Pierce is a dangerous man. He is the czar of that country down

"Pluck my locks for souvenirs and charms"

there. Why, he told me: 'As far as I can tell, this country belongs to me. I have two lawyers—Brooks and Brown—employed by the year, to attend to my legal business. That relieves me of trouble hiring lawyers every time I have a lawsuit. I own all the country, and everybody that wants to stay around has to do as I do!' Then, too, he has a pain in his head, and he cannot recollect anything that happened six months back."

From San Antonio, Brendel sought again to get the sales accounts into his possession, offering to guarantee their return if Pierce would send them for his inspection. Pierce replied: "The account sales would be about as much Greek to you in your office as your business would be in mine, and under no condition will I send them." Then he added: "However, if you desire to send a detective down here and inspect them, he shall be shown every courtesy, and shall have full access to all papers and accounts, and can remain as long as he pleases. If I have been robbing you as long as you have reported I have been, why have you never discovered it before. Heretofore my acts have been approved by every regular meeting without any dissenting voice from you. I have always looked after this business for the company the same as I would my own, and I stand pat that I am the best cowman in the state today. I see no way of arriving at the number sold, except to take my word for it, and if you can take that, I guess you can take my word for the price they sold for. All cattle that have not been stolen, died or sold are on the ranch today, and no more, and I, myself, never saw a man that made any money out of cattle on paper."

Sullivan knew that the end was near; therefore, he suggested: "In order to avoid all controversy, I propose to sell my interest in the Pierce-Sullivan Pasture & Cattle Company to you for cost and eight per cent per annum from date of my investment."

"As your price is so exhorbitant," countered Pierce, "I hardly deem an answer necessary, but I will sell on the same terms and throw in my fourteen years of good hard work to boot, half of which time I have had to carry my life in my hand. There is not another cattle company organized during the balmy days that has paid their original stockholders ten cents on the dollar. Ninety per cent of them went under. I will give you six months to go from the North Pole to the Gulf of Mexico to find another stock company that has paid the original stockholders back their original money put in. There is never one on earth that I ever heard of that got anything like their original money back. But if you will come within the bounds of reason, I will buy your stock. I will give you fifty thousand dollars for your interest to be paid in Galveston or New York exchange. My offer is my ultimatum and includes last year's revenue, most of which has already been spent."

But "to arrange our ranch affairs amicably as it looks we cannot reach conclusion by correspondence," replied Sullivan, "I suggest you come up, and we talk our affairs." But Pierce was about to leave for Hot Springs, and, besides that, he had sworn never to enter Sullivan's bank again, so he consented to meet Sullivan at the Tremont Hotel at Galveston, Saturday May 9.

On the seventh of May, Dan Sullivan put in much of his time reading the political developments in the presidential race. The presidential aspirant, William Jennings Bryan, captured the big headlines. Bryan, the Nebraska lawyer, who recently was a sharp critic of the Cleveland administration in the halls of Congress, was now making preconvention speeches, urging that the Democratic party adopt a platform of free coinage of silver at the rate of sixteen silver dollars to one gold dollar. Dispatches in newspapers disclosed that the Silver-Republican party, as well as the Populist party, were pressing the leaders of the Democratic party to nominate the big-voiced Nebraskan on a coalition ticket. Foremost in the ranks of the solid Republicans was William McKinley. He stood staunchly for a high tariff on imports, especially on cattle and hides. It seemed certain that McKinley would be the Republican nominee to oppose "that gar-mouthed Bryan," as Shanghai spoke of him, "who will ruin the cattle business unless somebody sews his mouth up." Sullivan figured the notes held by his bank, payable in gold only, and multiplied the sum by sixteen. "If Bryan wins," he told Brendel, "gold notes will be worth sixteen to one." He read the San Antonio *Express* financial section. There he saw: "Gold Shipments Not Likely to be Excessive." From off the Alamo Brokerage Company's private wire, he took a telegram: "The market closed steady at recoveries from the lowest reports that shipments of gold on Saturday would be trivial, or perhaps would be postponed entirely."

In the same paper he read: "Washington, D. C.—ALL SHOUT-

"Pluck my locks for souvenirs and charms"

ING FOR MCKINLEY. Republican atmosphere at Washington today was redolent for McKinley."

To this Southern Democrat, who had put in four years with the Confederate cavalry, the "redolence" of an anti-sixteen-to-one, high-tariff Republican was devoid of fragrance. Sullivan, then, turned back to the money report of May 2. It said: "New York— All shipments of gold were below expectations." And, on the face of the "Financial Report," May 4, Texas Section, he saw: "Hogg on Silver Issue. (Waxahachie)—Ex Gov. James S. Hogg spoke for two hours and a half at East Side Park, beginning at 1:30 this afternoon. A tent was erected with a seating capacity of 2,000 while the pavilion accomodated as many more. A long procession of white horses, on which sat staunch silver men waving their hats, accompanied the Governor to the grounds." On May 5, the New York report by private wire to Sullivan advised: "Gold Exports Cause Renewal of Caution by Traders." And on the sixth, the same source reported to Sullivan: "Dealings were strictly professional, the cause of the restrictions of business being alleged due to Gold Export."

"If McKinley is nominated," said Sullivan, "there will be a great demand for gold to pay indebtedness. If he is elected, the shortage of gold will be increasingly critical: its purchasing power will be great. There is real money to be made in controlling gold." Then he left the bank for his train, en route to meet Pierce at Galveston.

On the train his eyes fell upon an Austin news dispatch which read:

> May 6 — Brother Jones Prying Out the Devil. Populists like a Billy Goat! Evangelist Sam Jones says a Populist is like a billy goat. He doesn't want ideas. Take a goat by his whiskers and try to talk ideas into his head, and he'll pull away and go to eating grass. Try to talk to a Populist and he'll do the same thing; but just tell him about the way the rich are getting richer and the poor, poorer, and he'll stay with you all day and listen with both his long ears.

Sullivan smiled and said that there were enough long-eared Populists to listen all day to Bryan-the-peerless when he cries out, "Sixteen to one," and gold will be at a premium in a very short time.

Shanghai Pierce

Mr. Sullivan arrived at Galveston on the early morning of May 9. He went to the Tremont Hotel, registered, and sat quietly in the lobby. Mr. Pierce left the BU Ranch at noon on the eighth. He arrived at Galveston after dark, and went to the residence of his daughter, who, with her husband, was spending the summer at the seaside. Withers and Pierce then went to the Tremont but failed to find that Sullivan had arrived. Early the next morning, he again inquired at the Tremont and, not finding Sullivan, walked over to the Weekes-McCarthy Bank, impatiently inquiring of McCarthy and Withers: "Wonder where Sullivan is? I've been waiting all day." At noon, Shanghai, with great reluctance, left his waiting post to go to dinner with Withers. After dinner, his son-in-law suggested that they ride down to the city in the streetcar; Withers would get off at the Tremont to see if Mr. Sullivan had registered. The Colonel was to continue on the car around the block, and, if Sullivan was located, Withers was to flag Pierce off the streetcar. When Withers entered the lobby, he saw Sullivan quietly waiting, with his hands folded across his lap, so he signaled Shanghai, who told the son-in-law to go back to the bank and hold himself in readiness to draft any necessary papers, and into the hotel he went. Withers waited from one to four in the afternoon at the bank. McCarthy closed the bank at four, and Withers took up his watch in the Tremont lobby until five, when Sullivan and Pierce joined him.

When Pierce entered the lobby, Sullivan was the first to speak, courteously suggesting they go to his room for the conversation. Once within the room, Colonel Pierce proffered Mr. Sullivan a large and comfortable chair, taking a less comfortable and lighter one himself, which he tipped against the wall with only two legs resting on the floor. Then he sat down, hooking his boot heels over a chair rung folding his arms, he waited.

"I have come down," spoke Mr. Sullivan, "to see if I can make a satisfactory deal of the ranch with you."

"All I will give is what I offered," snapped Pierce. "That's my ultimatum."

"Let's divide the property—divide the cattle."

"No, I will not do it," came the Colonel's answer. "It is useless to talk," continued Shanghai. "You will have to take my offer or let it stand as it is. I am sick. Dr. Fly has been doctoring me all

"Pluck my locks for souvenirs and charms"

winter. I am going to Hot Springs. He thinks I have Bright's disease. I think I may die. I have all the land and cattle I want. I have worry and trouble enough ahead. I don't need any more. Don't need it in my business. Mr. Sullivan, it is useless to argue any more. I will either give you $50,000 for your quarter interest or take $60,000 each for my one-quarter interests."

The men sat quietly, Pierce with his arms folded, and Sullivan making elaborate figures on a piece of paper. Then, in an intemperate outburst, the banker said: "Mr. Pierce, you are robbing me, sir. You are robbing me."

"Rob!" shouted Shanghai. "Rob, Good God Almighty Damn! Talk about robbing *you!* You have robbed every man in western Texas you ever touched but *me.* I admit I rob you, but you will get even by Saturday night. Turn out and do a little robbing yourself."

Mr. Sullivan arose quietly from his chair, placed his pencil back into his pocket, then announced: "I accept your offer made to me at San Antonio." Pierce unwound himself and started down the steps to the lobby, Sullivan following dejectedly. There they were joined by Henry Withers, and the three went over to the Weekes-McCarthy Bank, where Ed McCarthy had remained in expectation of their arrival.

Withers dictated a memorandum of agreement which McCarthy typed. Then two notes were prepared, each dated May 9, 1896, one being payable on or before July 1, 1896, for the sum of $10,000 and drawing no interest until after maturity, the other payable on or before January 1, 1897, for the sum of $40,000 and drawing 6 per cent interest from July 1, 1896. When Withers tendered them to Sullivan for his inspection, he shook his head and stated emphatically: "They must be made payable in gold." The Colonel acceded, and Withers interlined into the notes the words "in Gold."

Now, with just fifty-two days in which to get his hands on ten thousand dollars in gold, and with "gar-mouthed" Bryan making speeches causing bankers to grasp their gold hoards a little tighter, Shanghai found he had a task suitable to his talents. Abandoning his trip to Hot Springs, despite the warning of Dr. Fly, he pressed into service old Neptune. It savored of the days of his first cattle buying. They went out again together; Shanghai rode his big bay; Neptune followed in his wake. It was not a journey from cow camp to cow camp this time, but from town to town. Pierce was in earnest. Entering each town at a canter, he would rein in his horse, while Neptune drew up quietly to stand behind his master. "I am Shanghai Pierce," he would call out so his voice would carry the full length of the street. "Anybody got any gold for sale?" In this manner he bought gold, paying the premium, and passed on to the next town to buy again. At the end of the sixteenth day of his search, Shanghai was ready to make Little Dannie another proposition. He would, so he wrote, pay Sullivan *now*, if he would discount the ten-thousand-dollar note at the rate of 2 per cent and the forty-thousand-dollar note at 8 per cent.

But no! Sullivan had been reading his election horoscope again, so back went his refusal:

> Yours of 5–25th to hand. In reply beg to state that if McKinley is nominated in June on a silver platform, *gold* will command twenty-five percent premium at once, and if, in November, a silver president is elected, *gold* will be way up, probably 2 to 1.
>
> With these prospects in view, I could not entertain your proposition to discount your notes, as the chances are I will make more by waiting.

On June 26, banker Sullivan called upon Brendel to get the two Pierce notes from the vault. Sullivan took the forty-thousand-dollar note and pinned to it a slip of paper on which he wrote: "Collect only in Gold." Passing the note to Brendel, he instructed: "Fix the other the same way." Then he wrote instructions to Ball, Hutchins and Company, bankers, at Galveston: "Collect in Gold only and place to our credit, *under separate account in gold*. Protest. Do not hold for convenience of parties. Deliver only on payment of drafts." Then he smilingly dropped the letter into the mail.

On the early morning of July 1, a few minutes before banks were scheduled to open for business, old Shanghai came out of the Weekes-McCarthy Bank. Following him were four men, three Negroes and Mr. W. G. Jones, a trusted employee of Weekes-McCarthy. The five men carried a sack of gold in each hand. The procession moved straight to Ball, Hutchins and Company, Pierce, of course, leading the way. Arriving, Pierce swung a sack of gold over to the grasp of his left hand, while he yanked on the door. It

"Pluck my locks for souvenirs and charms"

was locked. Quietly lowering the two bags to the sidewalk between his feet, he raised both fists and struck violently and repeatedly until someone called from the inside. "What is it? Who is it?"

"I am Shanghai Pierce, by God sir. I want my notes."

Waiving the few moments until opening time, Mr. H. A. Robertson, Jr., swung open the doors of Ball, Hutchins and Company, and Shanghai Pierce, gold bags in hand, led the procession to the note-teller's window. He hoisted the bags to the sill, commanding: "Count it, by God sir, and give me my notes." Mr. Jones nodded his countinghouse fraternal guarantee, and Robertson walked leisurely to the note case, and, extracting the notes, stamped them: "PAID, per H. A. Robertson, Jr." Having done this, he passed them through the wicker. Pierce's hand was there to receive them. He took a quick glance at each of them, then pinched off his signatures. This he put into his mouth and chewed violently for a moment; then he spat the paper residue upon the floor: "There, by God, sirs!" The mutilated notes were returned to Jones with the request: "Put the notes in the bank, please sir."

Old Shanghai was in rare good humor that night as he passed through Houston to go back to the ranch. He was talking boisterously as he approached the gate guard at the Southern Pacific station.

"Tickets, please," sharply called the gateman. "No admittance to trains without tickets."

"The hell you say!" retorted Shanghai. "I have a ticket here that will pass me anywhere in the world." Then he waved a ten-dollar bill under the nose of the gateman and passed on into the train with "Big Belly" Asa Dawdy. Dawdy took a seat so he could face Shanghai, who had seated himself with "a Drummer." Diagonally across the aisle was a stranger and a woman who chose to leave the car shortly after the conversation got under way.

"Dawdy," said Shanghai, "I squeezed Sullivan this time. I got him in the 'nine-hole' where I could squeeze him. By God, he had to settle my way. Little Dannie was inclined to get mad, but I said to him: 'By God, I don't see why you should get mad. You have been robbing me, and now I've got you where I can down you. All you have got to do is rob a few more widows and orphans, now, and get it back.'"

Shanghai then directed his remarks to his traveling-salesman seatmate, shouting: "I consider a man a God damned good one that can down Little Dannie in any transaction. I think it is the best commercial record a man can make if he can prove in court that he had robbed little Dannie Sullivan. I'll be very popular for this. The people will descend upon me and pluck my locks for souvenirs and charms."

Nearly three weeks later Mr. W. E. Watson, a customer of D. Sullivan and Company, withdrew his deposit from the Sullivan bank. After gaining possession of his money, he explained his action to Sullivan. He had been on the "Macaroni," so he said, and had heard a conversation between Mr. Pierce and Asa Dawdy. "I will give you a full account of it," stated Watson. "I am timid, Mr. Sullivan, and a little afraid of you. From what I heard, perhaps he has injured you and you have lost heavily."

Sullivan was profuse in his thanks for the information; however, he remained silent until the returns showed that McKinley had been elected. Business went on an upward surge. Cattle prices trebled; people began buying land and ranches, and rumors came that Shanghai was selling off portions of his vast holdings for enormous profits. But Daniel Sullivan's gold was worth no more than it had ever been. Then, without notice, suit was filed in the United States Circuit Court, Eastern District of Texas, styled *Daniel Sullivan v. Abel H. Pierce*. It was alleged that Daniel Sullivan was a subject of Great Britain and that Abel H. Pierce had designedly and fraudulently "robbed" the plaintiff in the sale of the Pierce-Sullivan Pasture and Cattle Company stock while Plaintiff Sullivan was imposing implicity confidence in him, "not believing that Pierce would wrong me the first time he got a chance or rob me after I built him up." For relief through the court, Sullivan asked that his stock be returned.

When news of the lawsuit reached Johnnie McCroskey, he smiled and observed: "The lawyers will get good picking out of them two big roosters," and, true to the McCroskey prophecy, the "lawyer picking" began. Fred Proctor, in Shanghai's language, "contributed to my future welfare" by demanding a fee of ten thousand dollars. Shanghai protested in writing:

> I think you have placed your values Pretty high Considering the Many years I have Patronized Stockdal & Proctor and your present

"Pluck my locks for souvenirs and charms"

> firm but I want to Continue my business with you & want you to make your fees reasonable as possible. Remember I am not S.P. or Sap R.R. Corporation & My business nothing in Comparison with either of them, but I will be just as *prompt in Paying as they are* & Probably more so. Scale it as much as Possible & Remember I never ask Something for nothing & was not aware that I was such a hard customer, but if the *Kicking Cow* does Kick, the bucket is Empty.

Despite the inclination of the "cow," she did not kick the bucket empty this time; and immediately an array of witnesses began giving testimony before the court and by deposition. One hundred and four witnesses, in all, were called.

The first session of the court was scheduled for December 27, 1898. Shanghai registered at the Tremont Hotel on the afternoon of the twenty-sixth. As he walked down the hallway, he was thoroughly surprised at having G. W. Miller accost him. This was the first time he had seen Miller since his shotgun went off in the sleeping car and made a little noise. Miller was making motions as if to remove something from his hip pocket. Old Shanghai surmised Miller's intentions and called out that he was not feeling well: "Let's go down stairs, Miller"; and before anything could be done about it, Pierce accepted his own invitation and was down in the lobby, surrounded by his friends. Miller was greatly displeased over Pierce's hasty departure and declared: "He got down where somebody stood between him and me and talked might big."

After unbosoming himself of "the mighty big talk," Pierce left for the rear of the hotel under the guidance of a friend. It was buzzed around the hotel that Miller was going to shoot Pierce, and hangers-on lingered to hear the fireworks. Finally the Colonel reappeared. This time he was guarded from a respectful distance by a small Negro boy, who was "all dressed up for the parade." He wore a much-too-large livery of green, which had been furnished by the head bellboy of the hotel. The green suit was embellished with braid of gold. "He was," so said Shanghai, "the hotel field-marshal." Over the shoulder, the little Negro carried a worn-out broom. He strode manfully to synchronize his steps with those of his six-foot-four charge as they marched off to the courthouse, while onlookers laughed and knew that old Shanghai was lampooning effectively, though silently, Miller's display of bravery.

Shanghai Pierce

Sullivan was the first to take the witness stand. He tried to impress the court with his belief that Pierce had robbed him, that his trust in his business associate had been implicit, but that "Everybody is afraid of Pierce. The czar is a dangerous man to tackle. He is a dangerous thing." But that he [Sullivan] only made a living: "that is about all."

G. W. Miller next appeared as a witness on behalf of Sullivan, but, before he could unburden himself of his version of Pierce's frauds on the Pierce-Sullivan Pasture and Cattle Company, he was confronted by Mr. Proctor with a certified copy of a criminal conviction in the United States Court. The conviction certified that "George W. Miller, in the Territory of Oklahoma, Noble County, did, on the 12th day of July, 1897, then and there knowingly, wilfully take, steal, and carry away by stealth, with intent to steal and purloin the same, one cow, against the peace and dignity of the United States of America," for which offense, "having been tried by a jury and found guilty, he was sentenced to pay a fine of three hundred dollars and costs and to be imprisoned in the Federal Jail, at Guthrie, and confind there for the term of six months."

Miller protested his innocence, that the conviction was a "frame up," and that, besides, the sentence had been reversed.

When Pierce was called to the witness stand, he snarled at Miller's testimony and shouted: "Miller is known to be the biggest liar on the American continent, and, not only the biggest liar, but the biggest thief; there is no dispute about that. He is not only the biggest liar, but the biggest thief and a son of a bitch. He is under indictment now—he is under sentence."

Shanghai then turned his attention to Jay Forsythe, also from the Indian Territory. As to him, Shang swore: "Mr. Forsythe got up at Tulsa, swore to a big lot of stuff, because he was mad at me. I staked Forsythe when he did not have money to buy a nigger's supper. I have known all the Forsythe family and he was the only one I ever saw of the name that was not a gentleman, but black sheep get in all flocks, and he happened to be the black sheep of that flock.

"Now, Mr. Proctor, you make a great deal of fun of associates of mine in the Territory. A man that goes to the Territory in 25 years and only struck two sons-of-bitches, he is a wonder."

The fervency of Colonel Pierce's assertions resulted in the

court's declaring a recess. During the adjournment, Pierce's attorneys admonished him to desist from the use of profanity, which he assured them he would do. When he again resumed his testimony, he addressed himself to the court: "Judge: Mr. Proctor and Mr. Terry say I did considerable cursing this morning. I call it 'cussin.' Mr. Proctor calls it 'profane language.' I was not aware I was cussin. I had cause I admit, still using cuss words don't do any good. I wish to withdraw my 'profanity.' I will try to keep from doing it again. I tell you what I'll do. I'll make a trade with you: If you will hold up your hand, I'll stop."

Finally, Judge Ogden questioned Pierce regarding the difference that developed between the ladies on their tour of Europe. Shanghai angrily retorted: "I would just as well have by-gones be by-gones, to let that pass, and Judge, you might as well die without hearing it." When, however, the court required Pierce to answer the question, he made this statement:

> About five years ago, I went to Europe. My wife took Mr. Sullivan's two daughters. We went over to Europe, travelled all around. We got to Rome. The young ladies fell out with my wife and would not speak to her. There I was, ten thousand miles away from home with three women, and had to eat at the same table, ride in the same carriages, and stop in the same hotels, and they would not speak! Now then, you can just imagine the situation I was in. I sat down, wrote Mr. Sullivan a letter; told him the women had fussed; had fallen out; but he might rest assured his daughter would find every attention in the world. I went on, and we traveled six weeks or a month, afterwards, until we returned home to New York. We all got back together. Mr. Sullivan wrote me a letter where to leave the young ladies, and I left them, and saw them inside the house where he told me to leave them in New York. I had no animosity to the girls. When I wrote to Sullivan to know how we should meet—I did not want to go up there to San Antonio and get killed—I did not know how it would be, but he wrote me a letter in which he said that women's quarrels men should not pay any attention to; that nothing short of an earthquake could break our friendship. I went up there and met Mr. Sullivan. He said I had done very well; got through very reasonable. We had enough to eat—not the finest—I did not like that kind of eating—but we lived respectable, and we got back, and he thanked me for taking care of the young ladies, but of course Mrs. Sullivan never

Shanghai Pierce

asked me out to her house.... But the third time I went up there he treated me cooly. I saw he was bellaching about something. As we walked down the hall in the Kampmann Building, I said "Dan, I want to see you a minute. I would like to know what you are bellyaching about." *Judge! I used a little stronger language than that. I have agreed not to use any profanity. I will leave it to you, Judge, to put in what I said.* He said: "You mistreated my daughters in Europe." After that, the conversation was not pleasant! and I said: "I shall never come into your bank again." And right there I quit. I tell you, Judge, I do not thank any man to be my daddy. It was an unpleasant trip, but I certainly treated the ladies the best I knew how. Of course, I am not a ladies' man. I took extra pains after my wife fell out with them, and if I showed them too much attention, my wife jumped on me; and when I showed my wife too much attention, the girls jumped on me. There I was between two fires, But I did the best I could; and *that is the bottom of this lawsuit. There is nothing else in it.*

On June 15, 1900, The Galveston News printed the news item:

The big Pierce-Sullivan suit has been on trial this week before U. S. District Judge Bryant, in Galveston. The trial will close this week, but the decision will not be reached for some time yet.

When court adjourned, Colonel Pierce rode the train back again to Pierce's Station. On the train was Mr. W. L. Hall, county attorney of Wharton County. Colonel Pierce was apprised of the fact that Mr. Hall had given Brendel advice during his investigation of the Pierce-Sullivan suit. "In fact," said Pierce, "I knew Hall was around picking up all the skalley wags he could find in the country, raking the barrooms, and everywhere else he could to get them for witnesses against me." But despite this knowledge, Pierce liked Hall; and, too, Hall had a couple of bottles of good whiskey which he was just at that time sampling, and Shanghai, after such a long trial, took a tongue-moistener. Almost immediately the Colonel's guard was down, and he launched off into a dissertation on Sullivan. "Sullivan, poor Sullivan," he said, "I pity the youth to have his feelings so larcerated as he did at Galveston. Yes, sir, Hall! I ought to have a cromo for robbing Sullivan. But I am almost sorry to have to beat Little Dannie. I have had a large monument erected

"Pluck my locks for souvenirs and charms"

down at Deming's Bridge. It is in one of my pastures, and people will come from the far end of the world to look at it, to see the statute of the man that beat Little Dannie. They will tramp down my grass. . . . They will starve my cattle to death . . . to see the statute of the only man who ever beat Little Dannie."

20. "Trust in Providence if the breaching breaks"

Just before the political termites finished gnawing out the supporting piers of the Island City Savings Bank, causing that institution to collapse, Ed McCarthy, pledging A. H. Pierce to secrecy, told him of the impending disaster. As a consequence Pierce withdrew his thirty-thousand-dollar deposit and placed it again in the American National Bank, which was organized by a number of wealthy Galveston citizens with a capital stock of one-half million dollars. Captain Nick Weekes became its president; Ed McCarthy, its cashier; and W. C. Skinner, its teller. Pierce bought stock, but he was not elected to the directorate.

Nick Weekes, a Confederate who had served with Shanghai

"Trust in Providence"

in the war, was Shanghai's trusted friend. Both Weekes and McCarthy were quite popular in the Island City and they sought to increase their popularity by delving into Galveston politics. Captain Weekes was elected state and county tax collector, and McCarthy got a friendly board of aldermen to appoint him city treasurer. Thus, as custodians of public money, they were able to enlarge the deposits of the bank and, at the same time, direct many political manipulations. But, when there was an adverse reaction in the city to the political schemes of these officers, they were served with notice by the directors that they must withdraw from politics or the affairs of the bank would be closed.

Captain Weekes took his troubles to Colonel Pierce, who bought the bank, paid off the stockholders in full, and created, out of the residue of the old institution, Weekes-McCarthy and Company. For about four years, it was Shanghai's banking institution. With the exception of "that cow out there," Shanghai had no greater love than Weekes-McCarthy and Company. Captain Weekes became "My Partner," while Ed McCarthy was "My Son." Shanghai's letters were replete with solicitations for his bank. "Old Partner," he wrote John Elliott, "we would like to do your banking business in Galveston you Shall be treated Wright"; "Enclosed find my check on Galveston," he told another, "We do no banking business with Wharton." "Take care of Kuykendall if he needs money," he wrote Weekes-McCarthy and Company, "I hope *I* will not break the bank drawing on it, but it appears Everybody I am carrying is broke." And again, to Weekes-McCarthy, he wrote: "I came from St. Louis with G. C. Duncan. He told me he had opened an account with us. He is first class & C. D. Kemp, whom I stake; send him a check book, he is a good man." And to his old whiskey wholesalers, he announced: "The Banking house of Weekes-McCarthy & Co of Galveston belongs to me and if you have any business in this section, would be pleased to have you do it through my bank." And "If R. G. Kuykendall should be overdrawn, you need have no uneasiness, for he is perfectly good."

On the other hand, T. W. Bundick did not occupy the high status in the Colonel's affections that his banking institution did. This is evidenced in the instance when Bundick found it convenient to ride through Pierce's pasture on his way to Elliott's Post Office. Bundick was in no hurry, consequently he tarried in the pasture during the night, staking out the horse he rode and one he led on Shanghai's grass. This intrusion came to the ears of old Shang while he was at ranch headquarters resting up after completing the organization of his bank. Old Shang stormed at Borden and instructed him to send Bundick a bill. Back came Bundick's reply:

> Yours of 24th ultimo. was duly received and contents noted on regard about the horse pasturage, the amt. which you will Please find Enclosed is $1.00 for two days pasturage for 2 horses, and give me credit for the amt. that is paided.

Pierce next concerned himself with "Old Robert's" troubles. This old Negro had commended himself to Pierce when he took a rawhide string and tied up the heads of the Pierce and Pryor cattle to enable them to stand; when those cattle later died they were paid for by the Santa Fe as cattle "killed in transit." Old Robert was also Mr. Borden's favorite around the ranch. It was of him he wrote: "Robt has been with nearly all the cattle this year, and some of them were loaded heavy, and he looses none, and sure is a good man. Can't you afford to bring him a suit of cloths. He will thank so much of them."

This time, however, Robert was not "thanking about his cloths." Down in Matagorda County, near where Robert had been caring for some of Shanghai's cattle, a foul murder had been perpetrated. A white woman "of low grace," according to the newspaper, was found dead. The coroner had pronounced that she had come to her death by murder at the hands of some unknown party. It was known that Robert had been working in the vicinity; besides that, he was a Wharton County Negro; and worse still, he was a Shanghai Pierce Negro, either of which was sufficient cause for him to be arrested and placed in jail. Shanghai read the news and went to Robert's rescue as fast as Forest and Robbin would draw him. He railed, first at the sheriff, then at the district judge, for trying to bring "my Nigger to trial in a Whiteman's Union County." Such a furore did he kick up that Robert was transferred to Jackson County and put in jail at Edna. Shanghai followed on to Edna, and when the Negro's bail was set, he took the bail bond down to Mr. Benn.

"Trust in Providence"

"Sign it, Mr. Benn," demanded Pierce. "He ain't guilty. I'm going to see him through. If he jumps his bond, I'll pay it, Mr. Benn!"

Mr. Ward accommodated with his signature, and Old Robert went over to live at the Crescent V Ranch. With the Negro out of the county, the case against him for the murder of the woman of low grace was forgotten, and Robert worked faithfully on for Ward until he died at a ripe old age.

Much to Pierce's astonishment, he found Borden in rebellion at the ranch. He was ready to turn in his resignation as manager. "I have tried my best," Borden told his uncle, "to keep things straight for you, but when you speak of sending Bell here to work, I sever my connection with the ranch. You can hire whom you please, but when Casper Bell comes here, I quit. I have tried for two winters and favored him every way I could, and he kept me in hot water all the time, and kept the hands discontented, and worked against me all the time to his utmost ability, and I will never try to get along with him again. I am ready to pack up and leave."

Shanghai placated his nephew, however. "About Casper coming to run the ranch: That is all bosh. I don't need any more men for that purpose, but I have got to have pens built & well bored down on Mad Island & want a couple bourd at Duncan Ranch & of course, you cant leave the ranch to do it & I am certainly to old to Lay out all Winter & My Idear was to put Casper down there, but he will not be there to interfere with your business. So don't fret about that."

Borden quit fretting and turned his attention to a menace which had developed almost overnight and which gave promise of making much trouble. The Land Office at Austin declared a vacancy between two surveys on the Duncan Ranch, and the rumor spread that the Big Pasture Men had been pre-empting land to which they did not have title. Land-hungry men took the ruling as a signal that there were other such vacancies. Consequently, County Surveyor Carrington, under the prodding of Matagordians, took up his transit and went into the Pierce and Kountze pastures on an exploratory expedition. Shanghai warned Jonathan immediately: "Your County Surveyor, Carrington, is up here surveying off claims and locating settlers in Kountze's pasture, and I hear he is coming on into mine. If you are on his bond, better get off at once, for someone is going after Carrington and will make someone responsible."

The inroads were worse than even Pierce had foreseen. Like hungry grasshoppers they came. They opened gates, cut fences, drove out the cattle, and staked off claims. "The grangers have taken our country," moaned old Shanghai. Then he called upon his "counsellor," writing:

> A lot of boomers have discovered that all my land is vacant land and have squatted all over it. They had the Matagorda County surveyor at work locating for them in Braman's pasture, and then came on up into the Kountze pasture, and then on up into mine, and as soon as he came on the inside I had an injunction out against him, and the three that filed first in it, and the sheriff went down and served papers on the sureveyor, but failed to find the three that had filed, but found from twenty to thirty others that had taken claims in my pasture. I want you to come over and give me your ideas how to eject them all. They are a desperate set of men and will not listen to any reason, and we cannot find out their names or anything else concerning them except they are in my pasture and refuse to moove. The surveyor has opened a strip a mile wide right through my pasture, and has torn every survey apart and does not regard their calls at all and I know that I have had them surveyed correct, and that there is not a bit of vacant land in there. Come over and see if you can't devise some way whereby I can get rid of this set of boomers.

Proctor came to Shanghai's relief, and the "surveys were put back together" again, but the onslaught had put him in a general bad humor. Some of this he vented upon his friend of old, H. B. English, who was having difficulty in paying Pierce $21,225.15, an indebtedness which had grown larger and larger during the period when English was acting as his cattle purchasing agent. "In the past," commented Pierce, "English has been like the Nigger—he reduces it every year—he pays me the *entrust*." But the amount had become too large, and Shanghai demanded: "You best pay or secure the account, for when I pay the fiddler the guests must dance to the Musick or quit Dancing."

J. S. Todd, a cattleman at Checotah, Indian Territory, picked this inopportune time to lay claim to a steer which had gone to market with the U U brand on it. An inspector had cut the animal

"Trust in Providence"

back to determine ownership before it was sold, both men being notified. Pierce fairly frothed at Todd's presumption of ownership, writing:

> You are a very smart Latter Day Saint when you tell me I never owned a steer in U U brand. I have raise, young man, more cattle than you ever saw in Every brand that was ever on the face of the Earth. this Section of Texas was Settle[d] in 1821 & the brand business started here & I owned UU cattle before you were born, which the record will show. Go on with your suits. I am not afraid of them. Lawsuits are good Collateral. Pop your whip. In your County you all claim the Earth wheather it belongs to you or not.

On top of that, Barse Commission Company of Kansas City sold some steers on the market for him for two cents a pound, while six thousand other steers sold on the same market for $3.35. Pierce "worked them from the shoulder," as he said, when he acknowledged receipt of the Barse sales account:

> I rec'd the two sales accounts. Now gentlemen, forbeareance has ceased to be a Virtue & if that is not Wholesale Robery I am no Judge. All I want is What my Steers brought Less Frt & Commissions & Yardage & if I don't get it, I will know the reason why. I have heard of gall but there is more Gall in these sales accounts than I ever Immagined any Kansas City pimp had in Stock.

In the effort to improve and conserve the large acreage held by Pierce, Borden suggested that the rich black bottom lands be cultivated. Shanghai demurred with: "You know I am a pasture man," but during the summer of 1897, he met Major L. A. Whatley, Texas penitentiary agent, on the train, and they discussed the feasibility of using convicts to clear the lands and plant crops. Whatley persuaded him, inasmuch as there was to be a "letting" by the Prison Board in a short time, to apply for the hire of a sufficient number of convicts. On July 4, Shanghai wrote Whatley that he was going to be wanting fifty convicts, and "I see there is to be a letting soon & I would like to get that No. & Knowing the Position you hold & the Confidence in your good Judgment I would like for you to Speak a favorable word for me when my bid comes up." As an inducement, he reminded the penitentiary agent that his "place was split wide open with the railroad and that he would be caused no expense and delay when he came to inspect them and that he would always get his money at the moment and without any trouble." Besides that, he avowed: "I will always try and see that you shall be royally entertained when here." The "letting" resulted favorably for Pierce, whereupon a petition was circulated by Wharton citizens recommending certain Wharton men for employment as "Sargent of Guards on the Plantation." The Colonel hurriedly filed his protest with the penitentiary board:

> In regard to the force that will be employed on my place, I beg to say that I have no pets, or anyone whom I wish to furnish with a soft berth, and oweing to the general feeling of prejudice [against me] that exists in this County, I would much perfer that you send a man here for Sargent that is an entire stranger, and a man that means business, and if such is the case our relations will be of a pleasant nature. Wharton has no guards, or at least I think so. There is not a laboring man around Wharton but what is against Pierce & it is strictly against my religion to Pay money to my enemies. I want good gards and foreigners to this section. Now try & get you a doz of First class gards that will take good care of the Mules & have Pierces Int at Heart. Come out & see me when you have time.

Then, as an afterthought, he concluded that he would, however, like to put in a good word for Dr. B. R. Valls of Wharton for state convict physician. "He has been my family physician, and attended all cases on my place for several years, and has always been very successful, and reasonable in his charges. One of the best evidences of his skill is that he has cured me, when others have failed, and is cussed by everybody for it."

Now that he had convicts to cut the timber from the land and cultivate the farms, he needed mules. He therefore wired an order to Chicago for one hundred mules. He wanted them: "Half and half, horse and mare mules at sixty-five dollars—fourteen-three to fifteen and a half hands high, all gentle to work, good black mules, and don't get any that are split too high up between their hind legs." When the mules arrived at Rosenburg, he and R. A. Rich, who had decided to go into the wood business with the Colonel, went over to inspect them. There he saw them come to grief. The

"Trust in Providence"

G. C. and S. F. switching crew made a "flying switch" of the animals over to the Southern Pacific, and the shunted cars struck a "Heavy Standing train & Piled up." As a result of the "pile up," Pierce presented his bill of damages in these terms:

N.Y.T.&M. Ry
To A. H. Pierce, Dr.
To Damage Done 4 cars mules at Rosenburg by G.C.&S.F. Ry by making a flying switch, crippling several and skinning one from stem to stern . . . $75.00.

When he inspected his bills of lading, he found a charge for horse collars and other similar items needed on the convict farm for "Expressage, $10.05." This, he told the penitentiary board, "Could of been shiped by Freight for about $2.50 or $3.00 & Arrived here in due time. It appears to me it is about as much out of Keeping to Send Such Stuff by Express as it would be to of Shipt my horse in Pullman pallace Cars. I am no kicker but have made a living looking after Minor Matters."

As soon as Mr. Rich began cording up firewood at Shanghai Station, Pierce reported that the Southern Cotton Oil Company at Houston was ready to receive it. Next, he appealed to the Southern Pacific to make him a special rate on shipping the wood to Houston, saying: "If I can get the rate I would give you 400 cars freight during the summer when but little is doing, but if nothing but the $10 rate is to be had Could you give me Big Cars & allow me to ship $12\frac{1}{2}$ cords per car & Not Measure them & Who of the Railroad Commission would be the Wiser & I will sell the Wood & you get the business." Wood shipments went out of Shanghai Station rather rapidly, until five thousand cords had been delivered; then something went wrong, for he wrote one of his consignees: "On yesterday we shiped you a car of wood, trust you can use it. I will not be able to ship any more as we are very busy planting. The last two cars we have pact in 13 cords, so you can get the benefit of one cord. For a while the Conductors got the Devil in them & Wanted to be as mean as possible, but have made no kicks lately."

Burning off the canebrakes, cutting down the timber, and plowing up the land had resulted in diminishing the wildlife of Wharton County, but deer and bear could yet be found. It, therefore, became the fashion of the time to belong to a hunting club, and such men as Judge Barbee, Girard Harrison, and others were very fond of the sport. Club members would go into the timber country, camp, run bears, and celebrate, generally, for days at a time. On one such occasion, when Governor James Stephen Hogg was much in the political limelight, Judge Barbee, who, unlike Pierce, was the Governor's admirer, invited him to go with them and "follow 'Old Slim' whose certain nose will turn up the trail of a bear." The Governor's enormous avoirdupois must have been the underlying cause of his sending regrets that "I will be abroad on business, but nothing would be quite so enjoyable."

The Barbee bear hunt took place on schedule, despite the absence of the Governor. This time "Old Slim" failed to smell out a trail, and the hunt was about to be called off when news came from the Pierce Convict Farm that a prisoner had escaped. Colonel Pierce, so the messenger said, would like very much to have the assistance of "Old Slim's" never-failing nose, and off went the entire party on the trail of the fleeing Negro. His trail was soon picked up, and the baying pack headed up the Colorado River toward Columbus, the convict crossing and recrossing the water to throw the dogs off his scent. Finally, the Negro hastily borrowed a farmer's horse, but Slim was so close upon him that he had to abandon his mount and take to a tree, from which he was retrieved and returned to his woodcutting. Sometime later, Governor Hogg and Colonel Pierce met in the Menger Hotel. Hogg took the opportunity to repeat his regrets at not being able to attend the bear hunt, but Pierce consoled him with the assurance that the hunt had been wholly unsuccessful, "However," he added, "we did tree a two-legged coon."

After Colonel Pierce saw that A. P. Borden was a successful agriculturist, he put no obstacles in his nephew's way when he set forth to turn grazing land into rice farms, although Shanghai still contended that he was a Big Pasture Man. The Bay City *Tribune* thought more of the project than did the Colonel. In its December 9, 1899, issue the paper set up in big headlines:

"*Trust in Providence*"

> THE RICE INDUSTRY HERE
> NOW BEING FORMULATED BY MR. BORDEN
> IS DESTINED TO EXPAND INTO A GREAT FACTOR
> IN OUR FUTURE PROSPERITY
>
> A. P. Borden, of Pierce's Station, sent down a force of hands and teams Friday, and began breaking land on the A. H. Pierce property just below Elliott's Ferry, on the west side. We learn that Mr. Borden will put in a pumping plant and open up a rice farm. He will begin with three or four hundred acres this year and extend the plantation as circumstances may justify.
>
> LATER: Just before going to press The Tribune learns from a reliable gentleman, who has talked with Mr. Borden, that the latter will put in at least 600 acres of rice and possibly several thousand. This friend gives it as his opinion that he will not stop short of 2500 acres. *The fact that the enterprise has started on A. H. Pierce's land* [part of the Wire Pasture] *means much.*

On the twentieth of January, the *Tribune* indicated the extent of Borden's ambitions by printing:

> It is said that a gentleman representing a syndicate of experienced rice growers recently waited upon A. H. Pierce and proposed to take 25,000 acres of his land and prepare it for rice culture.

The rice land was in the general neighborhood of John Pierce's El Rancho Grande; and Borden was thus engaging more of the popular attention at the time than was his uncle. As a consequence, Jonathan turned reporter for the *Tribune*, drawing attention to himself. He wrote: "This region had a hail storm last week, which broke all records—and nearly everything else in the community."

The "syndicate of experienced rice growers," mentioned by the *Tribune*, turned out to be Jonathan Lane, attorney for the Gulf, Colorado and Santa Fe R.R. Co. Pierce told Lane: "I have 23,000 acres of Land in Wharton County. It includes all I own north of McCroskey's Ranch   it is a fine Bodie of Land & I will take $5 nett to me, and if you want 15,000 more, I can sell you that East of Caney. Please make no mention of Price named as I will not price it to anyone else at that figure as unless I am badly mistaken you prefer to do what is wright & have some grattitude in your soul, a virtue which is a stranger in most of Humanity."

Shanghai Pierce

The deal was made, and, when the news got talked around, it became the signal for land-buyers to descend upon Pierce in such great numbers that Borden was hard put to it to show the land and close land trades.

Land sales, which looked so "rosey" to Borden, were, to Pierce, colored according to the purchaser. "Borden," said the Colonel, "I am to get a good deal in the future out of them deals. A great deal of it I'll have to take back. A man will come along and pay you a dollar per acre, and a world of them people will just stay one year. If he is a Bohemian, charge him a pretty good price; I have him safe! If he is a Dutchman, I have him pretty sure! If he is an American, I know he is gone! I'll have to hunt him the world over to get service on him and get my land back. The American, he flies off; he is gone; he goes in the night; and you don't get your money. I expect to get it, and maybe sometime I will, but the lawyer's fees, and court fees and getting service will cost us a lot of money to get our land back."

Jonathan Lane's interest in the Pierce property had been encouraged by Nick Weekes, who, ever since the American National Bank days, had spent time, periodically, in New York trying to interest financiers to build a railroad from Galveston through Pierce's pasture. Augustus Kountz, in 1888, had tried to see Jay Gould and get him to send his man, B. S. Wathen, of St. Louis, "who is in charge of all railroad construction in Texas with which the Gould parties are connected," to see Pierce; but Kountze's efforts were fruitless. Things were different, now. Weekes and McCarthy, bankers, interested the Santa Fe in building its line from Eagle Lake to Bay City; and then they induced Jonathan Lane to buy rice land, through which the new railroad would be built.

With a great deal of railroad-building talk in the air, Shanghai went to San Antonio to be in attendance at another stockman's convention. Colonel Pierce's name headed the list of arrivals at the Mahncke Hotel on convention day. With him were J. E. Pierce, Wiley Kuykendall, Jot Gunter, and that tall, suave merchant and stockman, E. A. Arnim, of Flatonia, who, when tendered a bottle of beer by one of his friends, courteously declined but answered: "I thank you, my dear sir, but I never drink beer, but I will take a leetle drink of straight whiskey to hold in my mouth and sweeten my terbacky." When the "terbacky" formalities were over, the San

"*Trust in Providence*"

Antonio *Light* sent around a reporter, who wrote: "A. H. Pierce, J. E. Pierce and W. M. Kuykendall of Pierce, Texas, are here to talk sheep and cows. Everything has been arranged by the Citizen's Committee on entertainment to give the Live Stock Association lots of music. Carl Beck's *full* band has been engaged for three days. Headquarters at the Southern Hotel. The band will serenade in front of the *Manche* Hotel." (No mention was made whether it would be "full" or otherwise during the serenade.)

Then "The Big Convention Opened in the Grand Opera House." There was "Eloquent Prayer and Eloquent Speech," so said the *Light*. "Rabbi Samuel Marks invoked the Divine blessing in a very eloquent manner—'Be with them O! Eternal! Satisfy them with Thy bounty! Give them full and ample success in all their undertakings, and on the fields of their lands send the rains and the dews for them, and let the precious beams from Heaven fall, too, in the right season, that they may be blessed.'" After which, stated the *Light*, the presiding officer announced that "Officers Kneeland and Khouri have been placed on duty at the Convention Hall during the meeting."

Probably there was nothing amiss about the presence of the police officers, for the San Antonio *Express* took notice of the profusion of diamond studs shimmering upon the white-shirted bosoms of the delegates. The *Express* headline read: "Race Between Sheepmen and Cattlemen for Biggest Diamonds." Most noticeable of all was the sparkler which glinted from beneath Colonel Pierce's beard, which was described by his niece, doubling up her dainty fist: "Just that big."

During the convention tenure, Shanghai returned to the Manchke Hotel one night by streetcar. In his effort to alight he collided with several men who seemed to try to board the car before he could get off. At the same time another man pressed the Colonel, rather rudely, toward the entrance, thus blocking the aisle. "By God, Sirs," shouted the Colonel, "Either get out or come in!" Thus admonished, the men apologized and broke away. Upon entering the hotel one of his friends noticed the conspicuous absence of his shirt stud. It had been clipped from its fastening. His cattlemen friends and a few sheepmen gathered around and laughed heartily at his misfortune. Pierce remained grave until they had had their fun. Then he laughed big and loud. One of his friends wanted to know why he would laugh. "By God, sirs," he shouted. "Because I'm the only one entitled to laugh . . . the only one in the crowd who can afford to buy another one like it."

Banquet-time came. San Antonio's mayor bowed himself out as toastmaster in favor of diminutive Edwin Chamberlain, brother-in-law of Richard King, owner of a half-million South Texas acres. The toastmaster, however, was not without position in such an assembly, for he represented eastern life insurance companies who had money to lend on land and cattle securities. The printed menu showed "Oysters, tender loin of trut,[1] baked quail, veal cutlets with Champoignons, tenderloin roast, shrimp, chicken, salad olives, celery, cakes, Compott,[1] and wines—Rhine, Fench[1] Claret, Champagne—and coffee."

None, however, took notice of the absence of A. H. Pierce, and few saw or understood the news item from Galveston which stated that the newly elected directors of Gulf and Interstate Railway Company were Nicholas Weekes, Edward McCarthy, and H. S. Spangler, the latter "formerly in the auditing department of the Southern Pacific, then with the Texas Railroad Commission as expert accountant." Neither had many attached any importance to the item in the *Light*, saying that the railroad-builder "Mr. Yoakum is in town."

Both cattlemen and sheepmen were well on their way home the next day before Shanghai opened the door of railroad promoter Uriah Lott's Menger Hotel quarters, where a San Antonio *Express* reporter interviewed them. Colonel Lott acted as spokesman. Next day, the *Express* had the headline:

COLONEL LOTT'S ROAD IS STARTED
Active Operations began at Alligator head Tuesday.
Colonel Uriah Lott's projected railroad System, having Victoria as its center, has received a very substantial start off. The first dirt on the new road was thrown on Alligator Head, Tuesday morning, and the work will be pushed through from that harbor to Victoria without delay. There was an important meeting held in The Menger yesterday in regard to the railroad. The meeting was between Colonel Lott and a number of wealthy stockmen. The extension of the road from Victoria to Alvin, a distance of 113 miles, was under

[1] As spelled in the San Antonio *Daily Express.*

"Trust in Providence"

consideration. The meeting resulted in raising $2,000 per mile for the building of the road. There were present at the meeting, Colonel A. H. Pierce, A. Pierce, jr., Wylie Kuykendall, L. Ward, B. Ward, Colonel Keeran and Jim McFaddin.

Many times, Pierce had observed: "I would like to have the County seat of Wharton County at Pierce. That Wharton Combine is dangerous. Those Wharton Shysters try to beat me. We do no business with Wharton," but he knew that to get the county seat located at Pierce must be done by enlarging the facilities there. It could not be done merely by his contribution of "$20,000 to the first railroad that toots a whistle west of the Colorado on my property." He had therefore told Colonel Lott: "I want a R.R. & know full well if we can get the thing in tangable shape you can build it, but for myself, I am sick & in no condition at the present to build a railroad and do not intend to back any wildcat scheme."

Ed McCarthy, however, buoyed his hopes when he informed Pierce that, after investing $550,000 of the Weekes-McCarthy and Company funds in Gulf and Interstate Railroad Company stock, Mr. Weekes had been elected its president and that he was a member of the board. Uriah Lott had been giving evidence of falling under the influence of Kountze Brothers and changing the route of the road to the Kountze property, instead of across the BU and Half Moon Ranches. To be able to link up the Gulf and Interstate with Lott's contemplated road, the Colonel thought, would surely make Pierce the county seat. He, consequently, poured his heart out to the railroad promoter:

> Your favor to hand & found me sick, but I am up again but not in very good shape to talk Rail Road. I note your remark about changing your route & that it would suit the Kountzes better for you to cross below El Campo. That is all wright, You are not building R.R. for your health & if the Kountzes pay the fiddler, you must dance to their musick, but any route you select west of the River is bound to hit Huntington. Of course, I would like to have the Co. Seat at Pierce and from Gal[veston] to San Antonio Via Yoakum, I am on a direct line, but you Miss Matagorda Co. Entirely the Rich[est] Co in the State & not a R.R. in it & you would run through a long Stre[t]ch of County from Brassos [Brazos] to Colorado without a cent of Bonus & I doubt if you would not have

to pay mos[t] of the way for the right of way & further you would be parelling [paralleling] the S.P. & Hugging it all the way from Beaumont; to[o], Huntington is a bad man to Hugg, as he is Soule less & Would Squeeze the breath out of his Grand mother for the Almighty dollar. You want to get as far from him as possible. I am very Sorry Breckenridge decided not to go in with you as he would of given the thing more Height all through this Section than any man in Texas.

I note what you have to say about the Interstate. *We hold all the bonds* & the terminal facilities at Bolivar would pay us our money four fold.

I think if you can Build a road from San Antonio to Galveston, you will have your hands full, as talk is cheap but it won't build R.R. Remember one thing more; not more than half that agree to give donations ever pay up. As for myself, I am willing if the Road runs, as we talked it, to do what I told.

I leave today to take a 60 day Rest & let the world wag. I am now out & must have some rest.

During Colonel Pierce's absence from the state, the world did wag. In fact, Jonathan Lane, on behalf of the Santa Fe, projected his Eagle Lake-to-Bay City extension and called on the people of Wharton to pay a bonus of fifty thousand dollars for locating the line east of the Colorado and through the town of Wharton. When Shanghai arrived at the ranch, he found an invitation from bonus solicitors to attend a dinner in Wharton, at the residence of one of the Wharton railroad boosters. Shanghai decided to attend, and he was placed to the right of the hostess. During the dinner, when it became evident that the railroad would be built through Wharton, instead of passing on the west side of the Colorado, Shanghai grabbed up his knife and sliced off an ample portion of the butter on the butter plate, observing as he did so: "Well, Wharton should pay the fifty-thousand-dollar bonus, if the road is to pass through *your village*."

The hostess quietly spoke to the maid, saying: "Please remove the butter. The gentleman has had his knife in it."

"Ugh," said Pierce in rejoinder to the rebuke, as he picked up the biscuit platter, "Take this with you, too. The lady has had her fingers in them."

Rumor came to Pierce that things were not going well with

"Trust in Providence"

Weekes-McCarthy and Company. Shanghai went to Galveston and employed Adoue and Lobit to make an investigation. Among other things, not only had the Gulf and Interstate cost Pierce the original $550,000, but Weekes-McCarthy and Company had let the property absorb another $160,000. That, however, was not the worst part of the picture. The Gulf and Interstate bonds had been bought with an outstanding option to sell in the hands of Winnie, Featherstone, and Minor. These option-holders were not only unable to sell the property at Pierce's price, but they held on tenaciously to the option, thus preventing anyone else from buying from Pierce. Then, too—and this shattered Pierce's faith in "my son Eddie" completely—instances were found where the money from the bank had been lent and the collateral taken in the names of Weekes and McCarthy, rather than that of the corporation.

Shanghai decided immediately upon liquidating the bank. Mr. Adoue was appointed liquidator, and the Chemical National Bank of New York agreed to furnish the necessary funds. All depositors were promptly paid in full: then began the scramble to collect the sums due the old Weekes-McCarthy firm. Messrs. Mann and McLemore were among its hundreds of debtors. Pierce offered to settle with them for fifty cents on the dollar. They did not reply, and Shanghai complained to his liquidator: "Close it up—I offered to settle with them for 50%. If they have a spark of Honesty or Honor in their soules they will Pay it. It is useless to tody to Judge Mann any further. Get him down to your bank & give him a big rounding up."

Mr. Calloway held a claim against the liquidating institution, and he was particularly obstreperous. As to him, Pierce wrote Adoue: "I see no way to get rid of the Old Cuss but Pay Him & trust the Lord may remove him from my sight forever; I want to be rid of the old deciple & trust the Good Lord will bless him & strike him with lightening for his extreme liberality." Then he wrote solicitously to Mr. Alex Easton: "I have written to Mr. Adoue in regard to the matter & he will let the matter rest & we will try to fix it up, but Easton, you are honest & a man takes but one chance on that class of men, that is, his dying. Men of your class are scarce but S. B.s & D. R. are Plentiful."

Mr. Adoue reported that, in lieu of a settlement with Sweney, he accepted a life insurance policy as security. This pleased the

Colonel, who said: "Liquidator—I note your remarks about the amt. Paid on Sweneys Life Policy—you done wright, as the Lord takes care of those that take care of themselves & He may remove Sweney from Earth to Heaven which would be very beneficial to us." And to another who did not wish to meet his obligation in full, he snarled: "I would not give 10 cents on the dollar for the paper of 60% of your Galveston Citizens. They are fine Collectors but D—— Poor paymasters." On and on it went until the time came when he must settle with his "Liquidator." To him he wrote: "Liquidator— I can truthfully say—well done good faithful servant—Enter Thou into the Kingdom of Heaven. You know you work for 3 things— Glory, Charity & Money. So all I say say about liquidation is: Mix up [as] Much Glory & Charity as Possible."

The Bay City *Tribune* took final notice of the liquidation by notifying Matagorda County depositors that the canceled checks issued by depositors in the late bank of Weekes-McCarthy and Company of Galveston had been sent to Judge Hamilton to be turned over to those who called for them. It then observed: "This is another instance of the value of dealing with a reliable home man instead of foreigners, for not a man has lost a cent."

When the affairs of the liquidated bank were in such shape that he could give his attention to the Gulf and Interstate Railroad, Pierce sought to cut Lovejoy, Winnie, and Featherstone loose from their crippling sales contracts. To Lovejoy he said:

> Now, Colonel, you are a good lawyer. I am a good Cow Man & Winnie, no doubt, a good Lumber Man & Featherstone, *you can name for yourself*, but one thing is self-evident, he cant Sell a Rail Road. The talk of Extravagant Expenditures by Spangler is all Flobb. he has had nothing to be Extravagant with, except to run the Road on Wind & what little Money I put up & When the thing winds up, Winnie will go to sawing Lumber, Instead of selling it if he can get it to saw & Pierce wont go to *Banking* & the Lawyers will have but D—— Little. Winnie is foolish not to take all he can get out of me in cash, go back home & Dream of the Eruptions of Mt. abissurious & Atnae, forget he ever heard of the Gulf & Interstate—that is what I would like to do.

Winnie took the Colonel's advice, partially, at least. Whether he

"Trust in Providence"

dreamed of any volcanic eruptions is not known, but he took what he could get out of Pierce and journeyed on up to Kentucky.

As soon as the property was free to be sold, Shanghai sent "My Counsellor" off to New York to try his hand at a sale with George Jay Gould. Day after day the young lawyer called at the Gould offices, only to be told: "He is not in today; he is expected tomorrow"; or "He is in conference and cannot be disturbed." These reports Proctor relayed to the anxious Colonel, who wrote Fred to return, remarking to those at home: "You know he stayed there quietly smoking my twenty-five-cent cigars, at so-and-so per day, and it didn't bother Fred a bit."

During the time Fred Proctor was smoking Shanghai's twenty-five-cent cigars, the Colonel made a trip up to San Antonio, thinking that it would not be amiss to chat with George Breckenridge a little about Lott's railroad. George was absent when the call was made and, knowing that Shanghai was playing in tough financial luck, surmised that he wanted to borrow some money. Breckenridge, therefore, wrote Pierce offering to take care of his needs. Back came Pierce's reply: "I had nothing special in mind. I just called in to see all the boys, and thought I might view the body of the Old Cock Roach, and feel his pulse on finances. Your kind offer is not accepted now, but I may have to call on you later. Incidentlly, I am sending my old Friend Monseratt today a Jugg of my old XX Rhode Island Vinegar. So I thought I would send you a Jugg as it is very fine & Splendid in Sallads & will sharpen up your *appetite, but not your wits,* as they are *not in need of any stimulants.*" In passing these letters along to Fred Proctor, he wrote on the bottom of the banker's letter "It was good of the Old Cock Roach, but he did not forget his good and valuable friend, Old 8%."

September came, and Pierce observed that the Cane Belt railroad was being built, "but the elements seem to be against these people." On the sixteenth of September, the Colonel came out of the house after the so-called Galveston storm had struck down everything on the Texas coast and had devastated the country for hundreds of miles inland. He looked about and quietly said: "Well, I have turned Rice Boomer. I see that Borden's crop has stood the storm without damage when everything else is blown to atoms." Then he went back in the house and penned a personal note to D. T. Beals, president of Union Nation Bank at Kansas City, asking

Shanghai Pierce

that $80,000 be sent to his nephew G. C. Gifford, to be used for the relief of Wharton County people through his bank. "The Terrible Calamity," he wrote, "which has just befalled our county, in which we were in the middle, has caused the need of this money. The People are Wrecked, and instead of having money to deposit, they are bound to draw out Every Dollar they have. Wire me as soon as you receive this." Then he drew his check in favor of C. D. Kemp for $1,103, to tide him over his misfortune, and said: "Friend Kemp: We got pretty badly torn up here, but My Galveston Loss is Perfectly Enormous & Kemp, you and two other men are the only men that could get a dollar from me now."

Next, Colonel Pierce turned his thoughts to G. G. Williams, president of the Chemical National Bank, New York, who had so readily come to the rescue when Weekes-McCarthy and Company was in trouble. Chuckling, he said, "I have Old Man Williams of the Chemical in good humor and think to try to keep him so." Then he wrote:

Septr 23rd 1900

Mr. G. G. Williams
   Chemical Nat. Bank,
   New York City, N.Y.

As you have seen the full accounts of the fearfully o[r]deal we have Just passed through & are no doubt somewhat worried in regard to it—if you will have a little Patience & Listen to my tale of woe I think I can satisfy you so you will loose no sleep as to my Indebtedness to your bank, but remember in our Present Condition, it takes Patience & oddles of it. Firstly we have been nearly swept from the face of the Earth and at Least 8,000 People have gone from this World to God only Knows what Port they Landed at. here at my ranches I was badly torn up Many houses Barns Feed Houses & C flat to the ground & I had built a very nice little Church for my people, all at my own Expence & the Good Lord saw fit to give it a H—— of a lick & nearly wreck it, so my first thing is to replace my buildings next my Wind mills of Which I have dozzens to Water my stock all of which are more or less wrecked many entirely gone we had had Excessive rains & overflows ever since March until the storm more rain than had fallen in any one year in Last 48 years which had damaged my Crop very much & then to Cap the Climax the storm swept the entire crop clean from the face of the Earth the crop on my Convict Plan-

"*Trust in Providence*"

tation 1800 acres in cultivation alone would of have been worth $30,000 & then the worst Of all I have about 100 negroes on my Plantation, East of Colorado River which I am bo[u]nd to take care of until August & at Least 100 German & Bohemian Farmers to whom I have sold Land that cannot pay their int nor notes maturing, but I will get every dollar of my money & Int by being Lenient   the Gulf & Interstate R R I Put into the Hands of a Receiver a few days ago   it is a wreck   about 25 miles of the track gone   over 100 cars blown from the track & 5 Engines turned bottom up. My Galveston City Property in bad shape   My assetts of Weeks McCarty & Co are of not much Value out of which I probably by an abundance of Patience [can] get $100,000 in next 3 years the *Hightoned Honorable Gentlemen,* as they term themselves, that could Pay dollar for dollar take compromise at 20 to 25 Cents on the dollar & with our damnable Bankrupt Law all I can do is take it. Galveston was as rotten as Sodom & I think that is one cause of the Lord's visiting it with His wrath. I will Enclose you a rough schedule of my assetts in which there is no Wind or Water if Let alone. The storm covered an area of about 100 miles Wide. My Nephew & Private Secretary has been very sick & is at Hot Springs & on his return, if you desire, I will give you an exact statement. Now, Mr. Williams rest easy & I will pay you every cent I owe you & Int. & I ask no Sympathy as Sympathy is collatteral for nothing, but I do ask this of you: when you have your board of directors together, state them my case fully & ask them when I have Paid you every dollar of Principle & Int due you that they give me a rebate of 2%, making my Int 4% Instead of 6% & if the Lord, in making them, finished his Job & put a soule in them they will do it without a word. If you will give them a solid talk, one thing you bear in mind, there is no Liens of any kind against any of my property & My Credit anywhere in Texas, good as it Ever was.

Forgive me for this Long Letter & would be pleased to hear from you

I am Yours Truly,
A. H. Pierce.

P.S. It takes a barrel of money to run my business. Don't fail to give your board that talk about reduction of Int 2%, which no doubt the Lord will give them 2% Credit in Heaven. The Good Lord Knows they are going to need it.

For several days thereafter Colonel Pierce engaged himself in attempting to collect unpaid accounts. To Honorable John Lovejoy

Shanghai Pierce

he wrote once more: "Now, Colonel, I am in Hard Line for Cash & I know you can raise the amt due me. If you have not friends enough in a city like Galveston to Lend you that much money I would shake the dust from my feet and leave the city forever. I deserve better treatment from Citizens of Galveston than I am getting & I think the corruption of your city had much to do with the Lord's visitation of His wrath upon you of late." His next request was that Spangler, as Receiver for the Gulf and Interstate Railroad, stay clear of "the Galveston Ring," and especially of Minor. "I don't want him," he said. "He is as cold blooded as a rattle snake. When the Lord made him, He did not complete the job. He omitted to put a soule in him." After that tirade, he interceded for R. V. Davidson, saying: "Davidson owes me a large amount & if you can get him appointed [to a job with the Gulf and Interstate] his fur will come to me!"

Colonel Pierce made a trip over to Beaumont and there he was interviewed by W. C. Averill, general passenger agent of the Gulf, Beaumont and Kansas City Railroad. The Houston *Post* reported the interview:

> Mr. Averill had a rather interesting interview with A. H. Pierce, owner of the Gulf & Interstate. Mr. Pierce said: "I have the road placed in the hands of a receiver, and I have given the receiver $5,000 with which to get the engines and other machinery under shed, and there I expect to let the matter drop."
> "But you have to do something with it, Mr. Pierce, or the State will take away your charter," said Mr. Averill.
> "If the State wants the charter more than I do," countered Pierce, "they can have it; I'm done with that road. You see [laughed Pierce], I'm only working on this earth for my board and clothes, and other things do not matter."

When Shanghai opened his mail at the BU Ranch, he found a letter from an old-time friend who wanted to pay his indebtedness by delivering some personal property, all that was left to him after the devastating storm. Pierce declined to accept it, writing encouragement instead: "You will make a good Crop next year & need them, so don't get discouraged." In the same vein, he addressed a letter to one of his old army captains, J. K. White, who

"Trust in Providence"

offered to sell everything he had and pay the receipts over to Pierce as a credit upon his overdue account:

> Captain, No:
> Just go ahead and fix up your Houses. I will carry you over another year. We will make a Crop someday & will come out all OK. The storm nearly wiped me off the face of the Earth, but we must trust in Providence if the Breaching Breaks.
> Very res Your old Friend
A. H. Pierce.

Next, he turned his attention to some notes held by Attorney George P. Robertson of Meridian, Texas, for collection. He asked Robertson to advise him what he had done about them and then admonished the lawyer: "Please wind them up on some terms & also sell the little balance of Land I own there *as I am administering on my Estate* & Wish to get all these little matters settled up so as not to give my administrators any trouble looking after these little minor matters."

To the president of the Third National Bank of St. Louis, he wrote with a great deal of feeling. The bank was still holding a residue of money which came to it as a result of the Miller receivership, and Shanghai wanted his money immediately: "Your favor rec'd & note from the Tennor, of which I am very much supprised, that Mr. Stoddard is going to Pay me when the litigation is ended. The Litigation will End in all probability in about 5 years, but I have very serious doubts that the bank will ever get a dollar but I wish to administer on my Estate & have never had any such agreement with Stoddard that I was to wait until the reseriction of Christ for my money, so I have ordered suit Brought and the Court can decide the Matter."

Mrs. Pierce's nephew Allen Butler was at the ranch, spending the summer vacation months before returning to Virginia to school. As it was about time for the boy to go back to school, the Colonel took down his file of papers and looked over his admonition to the president of the school, a letter which he had sent along with the youth when he entered the eastern school the previous year. This he read aloud to Allen: "Enclosed find my check on Chemical Nat Bank of New York to Pay Tuition of Allen Butler for ½ Semester. Now, Mr. Abbott, Everything must be in its place as tomorrow may never come, So he must not Put Off Nothing for tomorrow that can be done today & he Must Neither Chew Tobacco nor Smoke Cigarets, but I want him to learn Arithmatick thourough; the Extras, such as grand rush at Foot Ball, Broken Ribs & Eyes knocked out, can be dispensed with."

Despite Pierce's disapproval of his lack of progress, Allen expressed a desire to return to school, and as a consequence Pierce again addressed himself to Mr. Abbott:

> Yesterday Allen Handed me one of your Catalouges & I note you take no pupil unless for full term; now I wish you to inform me if the Rule is Carried out strictly.
>
> I want to return Allen for one half the session & if he Improves no more in future than past then I wish to take him out of school for good, as according to his last year's reports he has done nothing & it is a useless waste of money for him to continue any longer.

When he had finished writing to Abbott, he called in the necessary subscribing witnesses and wrote a codicil to his will, which he placed in the vault with the original and a list of his assets. The codicil struck out the name of Edward McCarthy as executor and substituted that of Mrs. Mamie Withers; it provided liberally for "the children born of the body of my brother, Jonathan E. Pierce, except his son, Abel B. Pierce, who shall in no event receive any part of said property"; and it also reduced Allen Butler's legacy. "It is now my will," he wrote, "and I wish to change it, and I do expressly declare it to be my will to give to Allen G. Butler one thousand dollars," instead of ten thousand dollars.

On December 10, Pierce sent an order to H. Runge, Cuero, Texas, stating:

> I wish you would buy & ship to Sargent Barr, Wharton, by freight, as it comes through same day it leaves there, one Dozzen & a half of this year Turkeys, at least ½ goblers or more if can be gotten, without extra cost. I am in no hurry for them, as I want them for my Convicts Xmas Dinner & Please advise me what you can get me ½ Doz Goblers of Crop of 1899 at, as I want to eat them Myself.

One week later he saddled his horse for a ride to the Duncan Ranch.

"Trust in Providence"

Roads were almost impassably muddy as a result of the storm, and Forest and Robin, his prized buggy team, got a rest. He was determined to find out whether or not the Southern Pacific Railroad had killed one of his mules. He expressed it as his opinion that "all Railroad Men, from [Superintendent Richard] Jones down swear in Line, as they always do, as their Bread and Butter depends on it." He also thought that "a man of great Prominence & a bitter Enemy of mine, Just because I wont join their clan—White Men's Union—has offered to Loan [the railroad] a waggon & team to haul off any animal they kill of mine." He therefore warned the railroad company of his determination: "I go to Duncan Ranch Monday & if facts are as have been stated to me, you will hear from me *but not by letter or Phone* you killed my mule beyond a doubt."

While riding down in the lower ranch country, he called upon his friend Mrs. May Cleveland, chatting with her while he rested. When he was ready to leave, he found some difficulty getting into his saddle. Mrs. Cleveland set out a chair. He stepped upon it, then into his saddle. When seated, he looked down at her and remarked: "Imagine Shanghai Pierce using a chair to get on a horse when the time was I could stand flatfooted and jump into any saddle!"

As he rode away, Mrs. Cleveland observed: "Yes, he is as uncouth as the cattle he drove, but with all his blustering ways, there is no harm in him. He is at heart one of the best men in this or any other land."

Christmas Day came, and the Colonel had his turkey. For the evening meal, he ate rather heartily of raw oysters. Then he sat in Borden's office for a time reading a book by Archibald Clavering Gunter entitled *Mr. Potter of Texas*, a book in which the main character was modeled after Shanghai. After reading for some little time, he closed the book and chucked it away, complaining, as he went off to bed: "I've got a headache."

During the early part of the night, old Vi heard a groan coming from Mr. Pierce's room, and when she reached him she found him unconscious. Immediately she summoned Dr. Valls, who sent distress calls to Dr. Joe Ruess, at Cuero, and Dr. Allen Smith, at Galveston, but all efforts to save him were futile. At three in the morning a message went out:

Shanghai Pierce

Pierce, Texas,
December 26, 1900

Mr. A. J. Compton, Galveston.
    Mr. Pierce died this morning.
        Hattie Pierce.

A. H. Pierce's will was read two days after the funeral. After providing substantially for some of those of the Pierce Circle—notably, John McCroskey, the man whom he always was willing to trust behind the mountain, Abel Pierce Borden, his sisters Mira and Mary, his invalid brother Horatio, Mamie Withers, and others—the will stipulated that Hattie might withdraw her entire community interest, either in cash or in property, or become a one-third-interest legatee in a trust which included all the Pierce property except five hundred shares of Pierce-Sullivan Pasture and Cattle Company stock, which went to his daughter. The remainder of the trust went to the son and daughters of Mrs. Withers. In the will, Pierce expressed the hope "that my wife will appreciate the motives that prompt me, and that she will acquiesce in my better business judgment and accept as a beneficiary under the trust." This she did, until the affairs of the estate were stabilized.

Federal Judge Bryant rendered his decision in the suit of *Daniel Sullivan v. Abel H. Pierce,* denying Sullivan the right to recover his stock. This decision, of course, vested the majority of the corporation stock in Mamie Withers.

A. P. Borden became coadministrator with Mamie Withers of the Pierce estate. Under such competent management, "Old Man Williams of the Chemical" was soon receipting the estate and giving his board of directors that "solid talk," that they could claim "their 2 per cent in Heaven."

Thus ended the dramatic career of Shanghai Pierce. He was the symbol of his era, and he passed away with that era. He was big; he was rich; he was selfish; but he could also be kind. His humor was as brilliant as that of any character Mark Twain or Bret Harte ever fashioned; and his cunning, masked by apparent naïveté, was seldom matched. Business, whether involving a quarter-million-dollar loan or a twenty-five-cent pair of sox, was his lifeblood. His country, his state, his family—nothing was as important as "that

"Trust in Providence"

cow out there." His "statute," which he himself erected, is still a perfect memorial to, and a reminder of, the westward-moving American—the man who pulled up his own roots and fled to the West, where there was room and opportunity.

Appendix: Bos Indicus

The influence of a man of Shanghai Pierce's stature does not die with the man, any more than a blast furnace cools overnight. The power of his estate, under the guidance of A. P. Borden, the man who "trained" under Shanghai, will be evident for a long time to come. Among the few really beneficial and far-reaching contributions to the cattle business in recent years was the introduction of a small herd of Braman cattle into America by A. P. Borden, acting as director of the Pierce Ranch.

Having already made one fortune in the cattle business, Shanghai, in his later years, looked to new industries. Among the new enterprises in which he became interested shortly before his death was tea. He had already grown rice on his "Wire Pasture" and had shipped carloads of cordwood from his forests. At the suggestion of his manager and namesake, Borden, he had thought of tea-growing. One of the many products that the United States still had to import entirely was tea, and it promised to be extremely profitable if it could be produced at home. Unfortunately, Shanghai never lived to develop his ideas about tea-growing. That was left to his nephew Able Pierce Borden.

The Congress of the United States also became interested in the fact that this country did not grow tea, although the American importation of tea was heavy. As a result, the Department of Agriculture secured an appropriation. George F. Mitchell of New York became "tea examiner" for the United States government, and experimental tea farms were started at Summerville and Tea, South Carolina. Mr. Borden heard of the experiment and tendered his cooperation as well as six hundred acres for tea culture. By 1905, there were 105 acres of tea growing under Borden's supervision at Mackay. The plants for five hundred more acres were in the Pierce Estate barns ready for planting when the Colorado River overflowed and killed them.

By a strange coincidence, just at this time horticulturist Fairchild, author of *The World Was My Garden*, traveling in far-off Australia, made some observations regarding the breeding of Brahman cattle. He knew of the Secretary of Agriculture's interest in cattle and sent a write-up to Washington with photographs which he had taken. The Department of Agriculture was so impressed with Fairchild's observations that they were published in a bulletin. "So far as I know," later wrote Fairchild, "only one cattleman paid any attention to this publication. He was Mr. A. P. Borden of Pierce, Texas, a very resourceful ranchman, who had a Brahmin bull which he had bred with native stock. He claimed that the Brahmin cattle are not only the best range cattle, but great walkers, but are far less subject to ticks than are our native cattle. Mr. Borden came to Washington and plead his case with Dr. Melvin, Chief of the Bureau of Animal Industry. As a result, Mr. Borden was given permission to bring in a shipload of Brahmin cattle."[1]

Borden's study of the culture of tea had apprised him of the fact that the best tea is grown in high altitudes and that the best quality of tea then on the market was grown at Darjeeling, India. He therefore concluded that, should he make a trip to India, he could study both the culture of tea and the breeding of Brahman cattle. The venture, he knew, would be an expensive one, so the matter was discussed with the Pierce Estate's attorneys, Proctor and Vandenburg. These lawyers also had Mr. Thomas M. O'Connor, a wealthy Victoria cattleman, as their client, and he was induced to share the financial venture with the Pierce Ranch.

The *Bos indicus* species of cattle is distinguishable, in one manner, from the *Bos taurus* by a general profusion of sweat glands over the body which the *Bos taurus,* or indigenous American cattle, lack. The cattle belonging to the *Bos indicus* species in the United States are generally known as "Brahmans," "Brahmin," or "Brahmas," and sometimes as merely "Brahma." In fact, the term Brahman has been officially designated by the Department of Agriculture for all breeds of so-called "Indian cattle," or sacred cattle.

[1] *The World Was My Garden* (New York, 1938).

Bos Indicus

Shanghai Pierce was aware of the fact that "Bremmers" (as he wrote it) did not carry ticks as native cattle do. "Bremmers" had been among his herds from the early days of his cattle-raising. Just where he got the strain is not clear. However, Brahman cattle were by no means strangers in the United States. As early as 1849 there was one small Brahman importation; those went to South Carolina. Later importations are claimed to have been made into Georgia, Louisiana, and Texas. The Twenty-sixth Annual Report of the Bureau of Animal Industry (1909), Department of Agriculture, states in its first sentence: "About thirty years ago a number of the so-called Brahman cattle of India were introduced into southern Texas by A. H. Pierce, a stockman of Pierce, Texas. These animals were crossed with our domestic cattle, and the resulting influence on the herds was markedly apparent." Since there is no evidence that Pierce imported into the United States any sacred cattle during his lifetime, the presumption must be made that the word "introduced," used in the government report, meant that he brought Brahman cattle into Texas from other states.

One of the subjects to which Colonel Pierce gave much thought during his life time was the elimination of Texas fever. It is, therefore, of more than common interest to note that The Bureau of Animal Industry Report (1909) stated also, regarding the first Brahman cattle owned by Pierce:

> One of the most interesting observations was that their progeny remained relatively free from ticks while other stock in the same pasture would be literally covered with these pests. The Brahman grade cattle appear likewise to be less affected by other parasites and pestiferous insects. . . . Since this first importation by Mr. Pierce the Indian strain of blood has gradually deteriorated, and after his death, one of the executors of his estate, Mr. A. P. Borden, requested a permit from this Department to make a further importation of Indian cattle for the Pierce ranch with a view of restoring this strain of blood.

Shanghai Pierce's efforts to solve the problem of Texas fever first took the form of greasing his little imported bulls with lard, which he and Johnny McCroskey applied with a paintbrush. Later, of course, he saw the possibilities of eradicating the disease by crossing the native cattle, or *Bos taurus*, which sweat chiefly around the mouth and nostrils, with the *Bos indicus*, or Brahman species, "which secrete a sebum," according to the Bureau of Animal Industry, "by the sebaceous glands of the skin, which has a peculiar odor and seems to be repugnant to insect life." Colonel Pierce's information was confined to the fact that he saw that the "Bremmers" sweated and the ticks fell off, and the cattle got fat thereafter. He expressed the opinion that the salt in the perspiration when exposed to the sun "scalded" the ticks. He had no way of knowing that the oily sebum was nature's way of "dipping," a process which did not come into vogue until after the Colonel died. The information possessed by Pierce, however, was passed along to his forward-looking nephew, who enlisted the co-operation of Thomas M. O'Connor in a daring venture.

Mr. Borden's trip to Washington resulted in his getting the consent of the Secretary of Agriculture to import other sacred Indian cattle, an importation which had been stopped in 1884 by an Act of Congress outlawing foreign cattle except upon order from the Department of Agriculture. The Secretary impressed upon Mr. Borden not only the danger of financial loss incident to the failure of the importation experiment, but also the danger of bringing contagious diseases into the United States. Therefore, he made it a condition requisite to the authority to import that an inspector from the Bureau of Animal Industry should go to India, at the expense of the importers, inquire into the history of the cattle bought there, inspect the cattle before purchase, and accompany the animals purchased to the United States, making periodic tests for contagious diseases. Mr. Borden agreed to the conditions imposed, and Dr. William Thompson, inspector for the Bureau, once in the veterinary service of the Philippine Islands, was chosen to perform the duties.

A landing site was selected on Simonsons Island, adjoining Staten Island. There, special quarantine quarters were provided. The Island lies across a salt marsh, about one mile distant from New Jersey, and it would not have been possible for the cattle to reach the mainland during the proposed quarantine period.

On March 31, 1906, Mr. Borden and Dr. Thompson met at Bombay, India. From Bombay they went to Miraji, where twenty-two bulls were purchased. These cattle were then shipped in clean and disinfected cars to a farm at Poona. Nine Brahmans were

Bos Indicus bought at Ahmadabad, and six others were secured from Madras. Then the two men took a two-wheel cart, drawn by Zebus (a species of the Sacred Indian cattle), and they drove several hundred miles until they had acquired fifty-one cattle—forty-six bulls, two cows, one heifer, and two calves. At Poona, microscopic examinations for diseases were made. This had been impossible before they were placed on the farm, because of the prejudice of the Hindus against bleeding the sacred cattle.

From Poona, the animals went in disinfected cars to Bombay. By means of a loading chute they went immediately into the waiting steamer. At no time before loading was there any indication of disease among the herd. However, Mr. Borden recognized the risks he was taking, and he reported his accomplishments in a letter, which stated:

TAJ MAHAL HOTEL
BOMBAY

TELEGRAPHING ADDRESS PALACE BOMBAY

Apr 26th 1906

Mr. V. B. Proctor
   Victoria
      Texas

Dear Mr. Proctor:
At last I have my cattle on board and if nothing prevents will sail from here tomorrow night at 10 P.M. We go to Kirriche and remain there a week, but with the delay we will make Hamburg in about 35 days which is good time for a tramp and I am on a good new ship. I certainly will be glad to get away that far. I am free from any disease and if it was not for this port would not feel uneasy but one can't tell what might happen here, and I could not get hay that I could guarantee was not infected. I am shipping without insurance as the rate is 15%, and in case any disease should break out I am up against it, and the insurance would do no good, so I decided I would take the risk my self, as it is all one big gamble whether I land them in Texas or not. I am having a time getting men to go with them. I hired a German who has been on a U.S. transport six years and four coolies and yesterday the German struck one and they all quit but I guess I will get some more. The

ones that quit had been with the cattle and were regular herders and understood the cattle and I hated to loose them but the trouble occurred before I could prevent it. Now I will have to depend on seafaring men as I had brought the hearders from the interior and I can't get more now from there. I am sending you a news clipping so you can have some idea what I have been up against. I also enclose you photos of a part of the cattle taken last Sunday the day before they were loaded on trucks for Bombay. I wish you and Mr. O'Connor could have seen them then. I have 46 bulls 3 heifers and two calves. Am sorry I could not meet Mr. O'Connor's wishes in regard to cows but I have had a time to get what I have. I am sending you photos which will serve to give you and Mr. O'Connor some idea of what I have. I have about eight different breeds. As I do not care for the opinion of the public in this affair I had just as leave they did not see the photos. With kindest regards, I am

    Yours very truly,
    A. P. Borden

P.S. Some of these Bulls have considerable sheath but all the large bulls have it.

The cattle ship left Bombay on April 27 and reached Hamburg on June 2, where they were transshipped, arriving in New York on June 16, 1906. At New York, without putting them on the land, they were transferred, by the use of a cage, to a barge and removed to Simonsons Island. No cattle had been lost in transit, and they all went into quarantine. Mr. Borden left them and returned to the Pierce Ranch.

As soon as the Brahmans were sufficiently recovered from their ocean voyage, additional tests were made to determine whether they carried any harmful diseases. These tests were made on June 29 and June 30 with no reactions. Finally on the fifth and sixth of July, a number of rabbits were taken to Simonsons Island. Individual rabbits were innoculated with the blood of individual Brahmans. Blood was drawn from the ear of a Brahman and injected into the thigh of a similarly numbered rabbit, under extreme sanitary conditions.

A few days later the temperatures of the rabbits were taken. Rabbits numbered 16, 39, and 42 showed a marked rise. The blood of each rabbit was then examined microscopically, and the *Try-*

Shanghai Pierce, hunting for society

Abel Pierce Borden, Shanghai's nephew and namesake

A "Brahmin" bought by A. P. Borden in India

Bos Indicus

panosoma evansi, the causative agent of the dreaded disease surra, was found. The gravity of introducing surra into the United States was, of course, known to John R. Mohler, chief of the Pathological Division of the Bureau of Animal Industry, and to William Thompson, veterinary inspector, who had remained with the cattle from the time of their purchase; consequently, it was decided that the infected animals should be killed and repeated tests made on the other animals.

Mr. A. P. Borden was in Texas, and the infected animals were killed on July 20, he being notified by wire of the action taken. He was also informed that all other cattle which demonstrated surra would likewise be killed.

The message directed to Borden was relayed by his secretary to the Pierce Estate's attorneys, Proctor and Vandenburg, of Victoria, since Mr. Borden was en route to New York to receive his cattle and bring them to Texas and since Mr. O'Connor was not available that day. The telegram from the Secretary of Agriculture caused a veritable furore in the offices of the Victoria lawyers. Telegrams were, consequently, directed to every person who it was thought might assist in delaying the execution of the Brahmans, including cattlemen's associations and ranking politicians. Senator Joseph Weldon Bailey reported that he had stormed the office of the Secretary of Agriculture without avail; that the veterinary in charge had condemned the cattle and their "liquidation will proceed."

The prospects of saving the cattle looked gloomy to the Victoria lawyers. Finally, Mr. Vandenburg said: "We have wired everybody but the President."

"That," said V. B. Proctor, "is an idea!"

"He ain't God," observed Vandenburg. "Let's go."

Then, the story was retold to President Theodore Roosevelt, the two-hundred-word telegram winding up with the assertion that "it would be a calamity to the cattlemen of the United States to slaughter those cattle just because one little rabbit caught the sniffles from one of them."

Among those who had received the calls for assistance was Mr. Mayer L. Halff, a New York lawyer and former Texan. He described his action as follows:

Shanghai Pierce

On a Tuesday morning of a summer during the administration of the late Theodore Roosevelt I received a long telegram from Mr. F. C. Proctor, an attorney at Victoria, Texas. In this telegram Mr. Proctor stated that Mr. Pierce had imported forty-nine brahma heifers and one brahma bull from India into the United States at a very great expense; that these animals had been landed at the Government Animals Quarantine Station at Carteret, New Jersey; that upon landing at Carteret these animals had been tested; that a number of them had been found to be infected by the tsetse fly; and that the Department of Agriculture had ordered all of the animals be destroyed on the following Friday. Mr. Proctor requested me to go to Washington and spare no expense or effort in an attempt to have as many of these animals as possible admitted into the United States. He said that the Honorable Cecil Lyons of Texas had arranged for me to have an audience with President Roosevelt on the following morning.

I went to Washington on that Tuesday evening, and on the following morning, called on President Roosevelt. He received me very cordially, and upon hearing of my mission introduced me to the Secretary of Agriculture over the telephone and suggested that I take the matter up with Secretary Wilson.

When I called on Secretary Wilson, he received me rather brusquely, asking me at the outset why I had gone to the President, and why I had not come direct to him. After the amenities had been straightened out between us, the Secretary asked me the purpose of my visit and I told him that I wanted to prevent the destruction of these animals pursuant to his order. He asked me what I wanted him to do; whether I wanted him to allow these animals to go to Texas and infect all the cattle there. I told him that I certainly did not intend to make any such unreasonable request. He then asked me what suggestion I had to make, and I made the following suggestion: that he permit me to construct on the Island of Carteret at the expense of Mr. Pierce a cattle barn which would provide separate stalls for all of the animals that had not proved to be infected on the original testing, each stall to be separate from the other by close wire mesh running to the top of the building and insuring against the contact of each animal with anything outside its stall; that the animals which had already been found to be infected be destroyed; that the other animals be periodically tested; and that all of the animals which had developed negative tests up to the time of the first frost be permitted to be sent to

Bos Indicus

Texas. I told the Secretary that I would gladly pay the expense of two Government physicians whom I asked him to assign to this particular importation and that I would also pay for all rabbits used in making the tests.

The Secretary told me that he thought this was a fair and reasonable suggestion, and that he was willing to go along with me in carrying it out.

I promptly caused the cattle barn to be erected on Carteret Island at an expense of approximately $7,000. The cattle which had been found infected . . . were destroyed on the Friday set for the destruction of all the animals.

Mr. Pierce had brought over three or four Hindu cowmen to insure proper care of the animals. These Hindus emitted unforgettable wails when these animals were destroyed, prostrated themselves on the ground, and went through their religious ceremonies in connection with what to them was an unpardonable destruction of sacred animals.

The other animals were promptly transferred to their stalls and were kept absolutely separate from each other. Two Government physicians took up their residence on the Island. I paid for countless rabbits which were used for a period of months in testing out the animals which had been placed in the stalls. As I recollect it, in the early stages of the tests of these animals about six or seven were found to be infected and were destroyed. The balance . . . were released after the November frost of that year and were taken down to Texas.

As I recollect it, the expense of Mr. Pierce, in this matter, exclusive of my fee, amounted to approximately $10,000. Mr. Borden, who was at that time general manager of Mr. Pierce's cattle interests, and who came to New York during the detention of these animals, told me that these animals cost Mr. Pierce approximately $100,000 landed on the Island of Carteret.

The Brahman-rabbit chart kept by the attending physicians showed:

POSITIVE REACTIONS OF RABBITS TO SURRA, FOLLOWING INOCULATIONS WITH BLOOD OF ZEBUS

Date of inoculation	No. of Animal	Date of Diagnosis	Period of Incubation
First test, July 5 and 6	39	July 15	Ninth day
	42	July 16	Tenth day
	16	do	do

POSITIVE REACTIONS OF RABBITS TO SURRA, FOLLOWING INOCULATIONS
WITH BLOOD OF ZEBUS

Date of inoculation	No. of Animal	Date of Diagnosis	Period of Incubation
Second test, July 31	43	Aug. 6	Sixth day
	1	Aug. 7	Seventh day
	2	do	do
	50	do	do
	34	Aug. 9	Ninth day
	41	do	do
	44	do	do
Third test, Aug.	26	Aug. 11	Fifth day
	40	Aug. 12	Sixth day
	6	do	do
	47	Aug. 15	Ninth day
Fourth test, August 11	45	do	Fourth day
	5	Aug. 16	Fifth day
	37	Aug. 18	Seventh day
	7	Aug. 20	Ninth day

The Brahmans found to be infected were killed and their bodies destroyed with unslaked lime and pure sulphuric acid. On November 14, 1906, the Secretary of Agriculture issued a permit releasing the thirty-three surviving cattle from quarantine, and they went direct to the Pierce Ranch, in Texas, accompanied by Clay McSparren, who had been called to the quarantine headquarters by Mr. Borden, and these thirty-three became the foundation stock for the Brahman cattle in the United States.

Both nature and man have dealt kindly with Shanghai Pierce's little empire. Nature provided an underlying pool of oil, which, when discovered, increased the wealth of the Pierce Estate almost beyond calculation. The managers of the estate—A. P. Borden, Jack Hutchins, and Sam Cutbirth—conserved and increased the immense properties to the end that Shanghai Pierce's name remains a monument in the financial development of Texas. Many factors, of course, have gone into stabilizing the accomplishments of A. H. Pierce, but perhaps it may be crystallized in a remark of Manager Jack Hutchins. He stood one day looking out from BU headquarters

Bos Indicus

at oil wells and Brahman cattle, dotting the prairie for miles, all on the lands of "Pierce Ranch, Limited."

"Jack," said the friend, pointing to the oil wells, "those have been the real producers, have they not?"

With a typical Shanghai quip of humor, Hutchins replied, pointing to the Brahman herd: "Have you recently tried to buy a good Brahman steak?"

Bibliography

ABEL HEAD PIERCE was one of the most prodigious of letter-writers even though he had no formal education. A large proportion of his letters were written by him with pen and ink, letterpress copies of which he preserved. This practice continued until his death. As a consequence, many of his letters were kept and are now with the University of Texas Library, Austin, Texas. These original papers have been the groundwork for this biography. Pierce was also a perennial litigant; and the federal courts at New Orleans and Galveston, as well as the state courts, particularly at Wharton and Bay City, Texas, have furnished valuable historical material. Being a colorful character, who enjoyed public mention, his actions were chronicled currently in the newspapers of the Southwest. His friends as well as his enemies stored away many a tale, some of which, for obvious reasons, did not get the printer's preservative. Therefore, a host of people, some with a secondhand tale to tell, some with authentic information, have contributed to the preservation of his record, and it would be obviously unfair were I not to mention those who have wished to be helpful:

Paul W. Adams, San Antonio, Texas; Arda Allen, San Antonio, Mrs. F. K. Adoue, Galveston, Texas; Dr. John H. Burleson, San Antonio, Texas; Hy Bates, Bay City, Texas; C. Stanley Banks, San Antonio, Texas; Walter Billingsley, San Antonio, Mrs. A. P. Borden, Houston, Texas; Flora Bodington, Little Compton, Rhode Island; K. C. Cates, Velasco, Texas; Frank H. Crain, Victoria, Texas; Mrs. Ellan Dunn, San Antonio; Margaret Mame Emmett, Houston; Dorothy Foraker, San Antonio; Sterling Freeborn, San Antonio; Charles and Carrie Gilbert, Houston; Bradford R. Grimes, Kiowa, Kansas; Henry Hensley, Bay City, Texas; Octave Herman, Wharton; George Hammon, Houston; Elvira (old Vi) Miller,

Wharton; "Took" Haynes, Wharton; J. A. (Gus) Jamison, Victoria; Mrs. C. D. Kemp, Wharton; Mrs. J. F. Kilgore, San Antonio; William F. Koch, San Antonio; Ed Kilman, Houston; John P. Lowery, Albuquerque, New Mexico; C. S. Mitchell, La Ward, Texas; William H. Morrow, Mobile, Alabama; Mrs. Elizabeth McCarthy, Galveston; D. W. McHugh C.R.I. and P. Ry. Co., Fort Worth, Texas; Dr. Pat I. Nixon, San Antonio, Texas; John Norman, Bay City; Robert Norman, Bay City; Neptune Holmes, Pierce, Texas; Ida Malone, Wharton; Mrs. Houghton Phillips, San Antonio; V. B. Proctor, Victoria; Bill Parsons, Uvalde, Texas; L. W. Pollard, Kerrville, Texas; Mrs. George Sargent, Bay City; Dr. and Mrs. Fred B. Shields, Victoria; Edith Skeen, Kerrville; Gabriel Sims, Bay City; Jasper Singleton, Wharton; W. C. Skinner, Galveston; William Cloyde Tracy, Victoria; William J. O'Connor, Victoria; R. K. Traylor, San Antonio; Alicea V. Tate, Galveston; Dr. William Thompson, San Antonio; Clyde Wantland, San Antonio; John K. White, San Antonio; Benjamin F. Wilborne, Little Compton, Rhode Island.

Manuscripts and Papers

Athey, T. N., Papers. Oklahoma Historical Society, Oklahoma City.
Ballinger, Judge W. P. Diary, 1881. MS in the University of Texas, Austin.
Clark County (Kansas) Historical Notes. MS by Dorothy Berryman Shrewder. Copy in the hands of Chris Emmett.
County Records of Matagorda County. Records now at the University of Texas, Austin.
Douglas, G. L. "Famous Texas Brands." Copy of MS in the University of Texas Archives.
Ford. "Texas Cattle Brands." Copy of MS in the University of Texas Archives.
Indian-Pioneer Papers. 116 vols., MS collection, University of Oklahoma Library, Norman. 1937.
Inspection of Trail Herds. MS in the University of Texas, Austin. 1886.
Matagorda County Cattle Records; Criminal Records; and Civil Courts Records.
Moore, Lamar. "Cattle Brands of Texas with Historical Sketches." University of Texas Archives.
Payne Papers. Oklahoma Historical Society, Oklahoma City. 1879–84.
Pierce, A. H., Papers. University of Texas Archives, Austin.
Report on the Frontier of Texas. Committee of Investigation, New York. 1875.

Bibliography

Government and Miscellaneous Documents

House Executive Document 145, 47 Cong., 1 sess.
Senate Report 1278, 49 Cong., 1 sess.
.Farmer's Bulletin 1779, Beef Cattle Breeds, USDA.
Mohler and Thompson. "The Study of Surra," *Farmer's Bulletin 148*. USDA.
Francis, M. "Cattle Diseases," *Bulletin No. 53*. Agricultural and Mechanical College of Texas, Veterinary Section.
Roster of Jackson County (Texas) volunteers. Texas Library and Historical Commission, Austin, Texas.

Magazines and Periodicals

Baker, Armel Keeran. "3 X Brahman Ranch," *Brahman Breeder-Feeder*, Vol. 12, No. 9 (September, 1946), 44.
Boyle, Shirley. "A Cattleman Puts His Spurs to his Banker," *The Junior Historian*, Texas State Historical Association, Vol. 5, No. 2 (November, 1944), 7.
Bray, C. I. "Brahman Cattle in Southern Louisiana Pastures," *Breeder-Feeder*, Vol. 8, No. 1 (January, 1942), 5.
Connaway, Dr. J. W. "About Texas Fever," *The Texas Stockman and Farmer*, Vol. XVI, No. 29 (April 28, 1897), 3.
Crimmins, Colonel Martin L. "Lee Hall Gets His Men," *Frontier Times*, Vol. 18, No. 12 (September, 1941), 543.
Demark, Harry Van. " 'Old Shang' Pierce," *The Cattleman*, Vol. XXXIII, No. 10 (March, 1947), 60, 64, 65.
Douglas, C. L. "Cattle Kings of Texas—Abel Pierce," *The Cattleman*, Vol. XXII, No. 8 (January, 1936), 19.
Emmett, Chris. "Thomas F. Corry Had Land Deal With Shanghai Pierce," *Frontier Times*, Vol. 19, No. 4 (January, 1942), 167.
Gillett, Captain J. B. "Ben Thompson and Billy Sims," *Frontier Times*, (October, 1934), 1.
Gipson, Fred. "Son-of-a-Gun in a Sack," *Frontier Times*, Vol. 22, No. 2 (November, 1944), 57.
Graham, J. O. "The Book of Wharton County," *Southwestern Historical Quarterly* (April, 1942).
Grimes, William Bradford. "President's First Annual Address to The Commercial Club of Kansas City, Kansas," *Kansas Citian* (September, 1937), 7–8.
Halff, Mayer L. "First Importation of Brahmans to the United States," *The Cattleman*, Vol. XXXVII, No. 6 (November, 1950), 136.

Hatch, James. "More about the Career of John Wesley Hardin," *Frontier Times* (June, 1924), 6.
Nolen, O. W. "Shanghai Pierce," *The Cattleman*, Vol. XXXI, No. 7 (December, 1944), 31.
O'Neill, John. "Sacred Cattle in Texas," *The Texas Stockman and Farmer* (October 7, 1884).
Pierce, Margaret. "Shanghai Pierce, Cowman," *Frontier Times*, Vol. 18, No. 10 (July, 1941), 453.
Ramp, Peggy. "The Old Chisum Trail," *The Junior Historian*, Texas State Historical Association, Vol. 7, No. 4 (January, 1947), 5.
Records, Ralph H. "A Cowhand's Recollections of Southwestern Cowmen of the 1870s and 1880s," *The Cattleman*, Vol. XXX, No. 1 (June, 1943), 26-28.
Sartwelle, J. W. "Brahman Cattle Industry," *Houston*, Official Publication of the Houston Chamber of Commerce, Vol. II, No. 9 (October, 1931), 3.
Saunders, George W. "Outline of 1924 Old Trail Driver's Reunion," *The Pioneer*, Vol. V, No. 5 (October, 1924), 1.
Siringo, Chas. A. "A Texas Cowboy or Fifteen Years on the Hurricane Deck of a Spanish Pony," *Argosy*, Vol. 332, No. 2 (1951), 22.
Stone, E. C. "Brahman Cattle," *The American Brahman Breeder's Association* (September, 1941), 3.
Stone, E. C. "Brahman Adaptability," *Breeder-Feeder*, Vol. 7, No. 1 (October, 1941), 3.
Sweet and Knox. "On a Mustang Through Texas," *Frontier Times*, (October, 1933), 15.
Vandenberge, Joseph V. Sr., "The Pierce Brahman Importation," *Brahman Breeder-Feeder*, Vol. 10, No. 3 (April-May, 1944), 20-21.
Wooding, James Bennett. "Colonel Ike T. Pryor, Pre-eminent Pioneer Rancher and Empire Builder," *The Pioneer*, Vol. III, No. 9.
Wright, R. M. "A. H. (Shanghai) Pierce," *Globe Live Stock Journal* (April 3, 1887).

Newspapers

Austin American, Austin, Texas, March 28, 1920; April 30, 1944.
Bay City Breeze, Bay City, Texas.
Bay City News, Bay City, Texas, February 1, 1900.
Colorado Tribune, Columbus, Texas, October 29, 1849.
Corpus Christi Caller, Corpus Christi, Texas, October 25, 1946.
Dallas News, Dallas, Texas, April 2, 1924.
El Campo Eagle, El Campo, Texas, November, 1899.
Fort Worth Star-Telegram, Fort Worth, Texas, March 8, 1942.

Bibliography

Galveston News, Galveston, Texas, December 3, 1899; January 22, 1900; February 1, 3, 1900; December 27, 1900; January 23, 1916; January 3, 4, 1939; January 12, 17, 1951.
Galveston Semi-Weekly News, Galveston, Texas, June 14, 1900.
Galveston Tribune, Galveston, Texas, January 19, 1933; June 10, 1933.
Houston Chronicle, Houston, Texas, August 30, 1931; January 10, 1932; January 21, 1940; February 12, 1951; August 30, 1951; April 27, 1952.
Houston Post, Houston, Texas, 1900, 1943, 1944, 1948, 1950.
Houston Post-Dispatch, Houston, Texas, November 22, 1925.
Houston Press, Houston, Texas, 1935.
Independence County Globe, Dodge City, Kansas, June 20, 1882.
Jackson County Progress, Edna, Texas, December 2, 9, 16, 1899.
Matagorda County Tribune, Bay City, Texas, May 6, 1899; November 11, 18, 25, 1899; January 26, 27, 1900; February 3, 10, 17, 24, 1900; March 3, 10, 17, 24, 31, 1900; April 14, 1900.
Providence Sunday Journal, Providence, Rhode Island, April 19, 1942.
San Antonio Daily Express, San Antonio, Texas, January 11, 18, 20, 1898; September 8, 1888; August 17, 18, 19, 1889; July 8, 9, 10, 1890.
San Antonio Evening News, San Antonio, Texas, January 14, 1944.
San Antonio Light, San Antonio, Texas, November 13, 14, 19, 25, 1885; August 4, 1890; January 11, 17, 18, 19, 20, 1898; December 27, 1900.
Spectator, Wharton, Texas, September 21, 1900.
Victoria Advocate, Victoria, Texas, December 26, 27, 1900.
Williamson County Sun, Georgetown, Texas, January 10, 1883; January 14, 1938.

Books

Adams, Andy. *The Log of a Cowboy*. Boston, 1903.
Allen, Jules Verne. *Cowboy Lore*. San Antonio, 1933.
Barnard, Evan G. *A Rider of the Cherokee Strip*. Boston, 1936.
Bolton, Herbert Eugene. *Texas in the Middle Eighteenth Century*. Berkeley, Calif., 1915.
Braman, D. E. E. *Braman's Information About Texas*. Philadelphia, 1857.
Brown, John Henry. *History of Texas from 1685-1892*. St. Louis, 1892-93.
Bushick, Frank H. *Glamorous Days*. San Antonio, 1934.
Collings, Ellsworth. *The 101 Ranch*. Norman, 1937.
Cook, John R. *The Border and the Buffalo*. Topeka, Kan., 1907.
Cornelius, F., Sr. *Biography and Personal Reminiscences of F. Cornelius, Sr.* Privately printed, 1917.
Cox, James. *Historical and Biographical Record of the Cattle Industry*

Shanghai Pierce

and the Cattlemen of Texas and Adjacent Territories. St. Louis, 1895.
Cross, Joe. *Cattle Clatter*. Kansas City, Mo., 1938.
Dale, E. E. *Cow Country*. Norman, 1945.
Dobie, J. Frank. *The Vaquero of the Brush Country*. Dallas, 1929.
Douglas, Claude Leroy. *Cattle Kings of Texas*. Dallas, 1939.
―――. *Famous Texas Feuds*. Dallas, 1936.
Fairchild, David Grandison. *The World Was My Garden*. New York, 1938.
Freeman, George D. *Midnight and Noonday: The Incidental History of Southwestern Kansas and the Indian Territory*. Caldwell, Kan., 1892.
Graham, J. C., and Phillip Rich. *The Book of Matagorda County*. Bay City, Texas, 1946.
Gunter, Archibald Clavering. *Mr. Potter of Texas*. New York, 1888.
Halsell, H. H. *Cowboys and Cattleland*. Nashville, 1937.
Hawthorne, Hildegarde. *The Poet of Craigie House*. New York, 1936.
Helm, Mary Wightman. *Scraps of Early Texas History*. Austin, 1884.
Higginson, Thomas Wentworth. *Henry Wadsworth Longfellow*. American Men of Letters Series. Boston, 1902.
History of the Cattlemen of Texas. Dallas, 1914.
Hogan, William Ransom. *The Texas Republic*. Norman, 1946.
Hough, Emerson. *The Story of the Cowboy*. New York, 1897.
Hudson, Estelle, and Henry R. Maresh. *Czech Pioneers of the Southwest*. Dallas, 1934.
Hughs, Fannie May Barbee. *Legend of Texas Rivers and Saga of the Lone Star State*. Dallas, 1937.
James, Marquis. *The Cherokee Strip*. New York, 1945.
Lake, Stuart N. *Wyatt Earp: Frontier Marshall*. Boston, 1931.
Lawrence, A. B. *History of Texas: the Emigrant's Guide*. New York, 1884.
Lewis, Oscar. *Silver Kings*. New York, 1947.
McCoy, Joseph Geiting. *Historic Sketches of the Cattle Trade of the West and Southwest*. Kansas City, Mo., 1874.
Matthews, Sally Reynolds. *Interwoven*. Houston, 1936.
Osgood, Ernest Staples. *The Day of the Cattleman*. Minneapolis, 1929.
Pelzer, Louis. *The Cattleman's Frontier*. Glendale, Calif., 1936.
Phelan, Marcum. *A History of the Expansion of Methodism in Texas, 1867-1902*. Dallas, 1937.
Potter, Jack Myers. *Cattle Trails of the Old West*. Clayton, N. M., 1935.
Rainey, George. *The Cherokee Strip*. Guthrie, Okla., 1933.
Raymond, Dora Neill. *Captain Lee Hall of Texas*. Norman, 1940.
Ridings, Sam P. *The Chisholm Trail*. Guthrie, Okla., 1936.

Bibliography

Rister, Carl Coke. *Land Hunger: David L. Payne and the Oklahoma Boomers.* Norman, 1942.
Saunders, G. W., and J. Marvin Hunter. *The Trail Drivers of Texas.* Bandera, Texas, n.d.
Seymour, Flora Warren. *Indian Agents of the Old Frontier.* New York, 1941.
Siringo, Charles. *A Texas Cowboy.* New York, 1886.
Sonnichsen, C. L. *Cowboys and Cattle Kings.* Norman, 1950.
Sowell, A. J. *History of Fort Bend County.* Houston, 1904.
Streeter, Floyd B. *Prairie Trails and Cow Towns.* Boston, 1936.
Taylor, Ira Thomas. *The Cavalcade of Jackson County.* San Antonio, 1938.
Taylor, Thomas Ulvan. *The Chisholm Trail and Other Routes.* San Antonio, 1936.
Texas: A Guide to the Lone Star State.
Treadwell, E. F. *The Cattle King.* New York, 1931.
Underwood, Laura, and Mrs. J. Paul Rogers. *History of Brazoria County.* Brazoria County Federation of Women's Clubs. 1940.
Walton, Judge Buck. *Life and Adventures of Ben Thompson.* Austin, 1884.
Warshow, Robert Irving. *Bet-A-Million Gates.* New York, 1932.
Webb, Walter Prescott. *The Great Plains.* Boston, 1931.
———. *The Texas Rangers.* New York, 1935.
Wellman, Paul Iselin. *The Trampling Herd.* New York, 1939.
Western Texas: the Place to Live. (By a six-year residenter.) Cincinatti, 1860.
Wharton, Charles Ray. *Wharton's History of Fort Bend County.* San Antonio, 1939.
White, Owen P. *Them Was the Days.* New York, 1925.
Wooten, Mattie Lloyd. *Women Tell the Story of the Southwest.* San Antonio, 1940.
Wright, Robert M. *Dodge City, the Cowboy Capital.* Wichita, Kan., 1913.
Young, Samuel Oliver. *A Thumb-Nail History of the City of Houston, Texas.* Houston, 1912.
Ziegler, Jesse A. *Wave of the Gulf.* San Antonio, 1938.

Index

Abilene, Kan.: 64, 66 ff; described, 62, 70
A. C. Leverette, freighter, docks at Powder Horn, Tex.: 30
Ace of Clubs: see brands
Accommodation paper, signed by Pierce: 200
Adams, Andy: 126, 133
Adoes & Lobit: Pierce owes, 7; conduct investigation, 289
Alabama, freighter: 48–49
Alamo Bar, Abilene, Kan.: 62
Alamo Plaza, San Antonio, Tex.: 135
Alden, John, kinsman of Pierce: 12
Allen, Arda Talbot, Matagordian: ix
Allen, John, a Pierce cowhand: 133
Allen, Winnie, archivist: ix
Allen & Pierce Co.: 49, 51
Allen & Poole Co.: 56, 85; ship Pierce's cattle, 48–49; buy out Pierce, 59
Allred, Gov. James V., made records available: ix
American Hotel, Abilene, Kan.: 62
American National Bank: 274–75
Andrews, Col. H. B., dies: 255
AP: see brands
Arkansas City, Kan.: 227, 230
Army of the Republic: 81
Assets, list of Pierce's: 7–8
Aunt Eliza: 45
Austin, Tex.: 73, 106, 144
Avance Hotel, Hot Springs, Ark.: 7; purchased by Shanghai, 233–34
Averill, W. C.: 294

Babcock, T. W., gives opinion of Isaac Flagg: 122
Bailey, Senator Joseph Weldon, storms office of Secretary of Agriculture: 307
Ball-Hutchins & Co., bankers: 266
Banks, General: 41

Barbecue, held for parsonage: 171
Barbed-wire fencing: 135–36, 158
Barse Commission Co.: 279
Batch-shack: 25
Bates, Frank, of the Spade Ranch: 149
Bates, Henry: 57
Baucker, G. W.: 43
Bay City *Tribune*: 282 f, 290
Beans, Jack: 123
Beer Garden, The, in Abilene, Kan.: 70
Bell, Casper, a Pierce "hand": 122, 127, 133, 228; helps Pierce get cattle from Miller, 237–38
Big Pasture Men: activities aired by Texas legislature, 106–107; fight fence-cutters, 142ff, 163–64
Bishop, Carter, marries Mary Head: 18
Black, Mr., from Kansas, loses a herd: 54–55
Black Hills (cattleman's financial graveyard): 38, 40, 90, 93
Black Republicanism: 67
Blacksmith: 13, 25, 35, 37
Blagge, J. H., assists Shanghai in sale of Galveston property: 168–70
Blessing, Tex.: viii, 8
Blizzards: BU Ranch and Kountze Brothers suffer from, 169; three-day storm, 185
Blocker, John, cattle rancher: 126
Bombay, India, Brahman cattle shipped from: 305
Bonanza Queen: see Mackay, Mrs. J. W.
Boomers, annoy Shanghai: 227–78
Borden, Abel Pierce, nephew of Shanghai: viii, 6, 27, 52, 141, 173, 186, 260; coadministrator of Pierce estate, 5, 298; arrives at BU Ranch, 122; takes herd to Kansas, 123ff; quarrels with Gifford, 148; observer at 101 Ranch,

321

225; promoted to BU Ranch manager, 226; threatens to resign, 277; starts rice farm, 282ff; expands Pierce estate, 301; imports Brahman cattle, 304–11
Borden, Frank, nephew of Shanghai: arrives at BU Ranch, 122; supervisor of Snyder Ranch, 225
Borden, Captain J. C.: 37, 43, 220
Borden & Earle: 43
Borden Mercantile Co.: viii
Borden, Tex.: 113
Boschi, Joseph: *see* Bosky
Bos indicus: 301ff
Bosky, That Damn Dutchman: 147ff; negotiates with Pierce for sale of land, 192ff
Bos taurus: 302, 303
Boston and Chicago Batteries: 41
Brackenridge, R. J.: 84
Brahman cattle: 164, 301–11; rabbit chart, 309–10
Braman, Daniel Erasmus E.: 89, 90; helps Pierce clear land titles, 100
Branding: 18, 25, 26, 39–40, 51; illicit, 66
Brands: Ace of Clubs (J. E. Pierce), 36; AP (Abel Head Pierce), 25, 28, 49, 50, 53, 57; BU (Mamie Pierce), 43, 52, 53, 73, 99, 119, 125, 141, 219; Crescent V (B. Q. Ward), 28, 95, 99; D (Abel Head Pierce), 92, 132, 133, 219, 252; Half Moon (Pierce Sullivan Pasture & Cattle Co.), 211, 219; HL (George Stidham Hamilton), 119; HO (Frances Charlotte Grimes), 25; K (Kountze Brothers), 108, 110, 185, 189; KO (Kountze Brothers), 108, 110; RG (Captain Richard Grimes), 25; Star (brand of boots), 61; WBG (William Bradford Grimes), 25, 90; UU (Abel Head Pierce), 278–79
Bratton Hotel: 62
Brazos River: 18, 147
Breckenridge, George: 291
Brendel, Herman, Sullivan's investigator: 258–61
Bridgeport, Mass.: 41
Bronc-busting, on Grimes Ranch: 22–23
Bronc-peeler: 28
Brother Andy: *see* Wilson, Andy
Brown, Charles, erects Pierce family monument: 193–94
Brown, Hunky Dory: 54, 56, 81, 85
Brownson & Sibley, bankers: 206
Brownstone Bunk House, Abilene, Kan.: 62

Brush-poppers: 55
Brush-splitters: 51
Bryan, William Jennings: 262–63
Bryant, Dr.: 112
Bryant, Eva: 112
Bryant, Judge, hears Sullivan-Pierce suit: 272, 298
BU: *see* brands
BU Ranch: 99, 114, 119, 137, 147, 169, 205
Buchel, August: 37; is killed, 41
Buffalo: 74, 129
Buffer: 95, 99
Bull's Head Saloon: 62, 71
Bunch, R., acting chief of Cherokee: 150
Bundick, T. W.: 275
Bundick cattle: 52
Burchfield, Mr., hears Widow Ward obituary: 131
Burkhart, Judge: 90, 178, 182
Burton, Walter Moses, Texas senator: 178
Bushyhead, D. W., chief of the Cherokees: 150
Butler, Allen, tuition paid by Shanghai: 295–96
Byler, E. P., attempts to run quarantine: 82–83

Cabeza de Vaca, Álvar Núñez: 18
Caldwell, Kan.: 131
California: 111; gold, 85
Camp, Joseph W., to marry Fannie Lacy: 37
Campbell Commission Co.: 234ff
Canada: Pierce cattle go to, 94; toured by Shanghai and Hattie, 156
Cane brakes: 15, 52
Caney River: 42, 51
Capitol Hotel: Austin, Tex., 144; Houston, Tex., 185
Carancahua Bay: 85
Carancahua River (Karankawa): 26, 56–58, 81
Carolina: 67
Carpenter: 35, 45
Carpetbaggers: 177
Carrington, Matagorda County surveyor, starts boomers: 277
Carson, Judge David B.: 217
Carson, G. W., a Pierce "hand": 123
Catholic Academy, Indianola, Tex.: 32
Cattle rustler: 37, 80, 143, 216
Cattlemen's Association: 143; Shanghai joins, 144
Cattlemen's convention: at Austin, Tex.,

Index

144ff; at Denver, Colo., 171, 174; at San Antonio, Tex., 284ff
Cavalry: 40, 41
Cedar thieves: 248ff
Cemetery: 8, 20
Champaign, Illinois, protests against Texas fever: 166
Chariot: 47
Charley Morgan, Allen & Pierce's leased ship: 51
Charlton, Mr., "inside owner": 105
Chemical National Bank, New York City: 3, 5, 7, 75, 289, 292ff; certificates, 76
Cherokee Indians, unite against cattlemen: 150
Cherokee Strip: 220; "ouster order," 228-29
Cherokee Strip Association: 220
Chicago Stockyards: 156
Chickasans: 224
Chili Queens of San Antonio, Tex.: 135
Chin, William, a Pierce 'boy': 123, 127, 133
Chisholm, Jesse: 52
Chisholm Trail: vii, 52
Churches: Pierce's, 8, 173; Deming's Bridge, 42; Tres Palacios, 35, 54
Ciprico, George W., employer of Colonel Hungerford: 111
Civil War: 34ff, 44, 61
Clement brothers: 67, 82
Clements, Nelson, New York land agent: 91, 93
Cleveland, Mrs. May: 297
Clothing, cattlemen's described: 61-63
Coasters: 29, 95, 99
Coates, H. C., a Pierce trailman: 127, 128
Cobb pie: 102, 153
Code of the West: 64
Coe, Phil: Ben Thompson's partner, 62, 71; is killed, 72
Collector of Internal revenue: 131
Collins brothers: 21, 49
Colorado: 94, 133
Colorado River: 18, 25, 35, 89, 105
Colorado *Tribune*: 28
Columbus, Tex.: 43, 87, 88
Commissary, McCroskey's: 209
Commissioner of Indian Affairs: 150
Confederacy: 34, 37-38, 41
Confederate currency: 36, 38
"Congress shoes": 86
Connally, Senator Tom: ix
Connecticut: 28, 36, 37

Conventions: *see* cattlemen's conventions
Convict farm: established, 279ff; escaped prisoner, 282; Christmas dinner, 296
"Cookshack meals": 24
Coonie: 82
Corn: 92, 157, 208-209
Cornbread, Mrs. McSparren's: 172
Cotton: 19
Counterbrand: 26; Shanghai indicted for, 139
Courthouse: fight over building, 180ff
Craig, W. J., Southern Pacific official: 115
Crain, Congressman William Henry: 146-47, 228; negotiates with Interior Dept., 220-24
Crary, B. D., Kountze manager: 91, 108, 142, 195
Crescent V: *see* brands
Crescent V Ranch: 99, 137
Croom, J. L.: 100, 101
Croom, W. J.: 181
Cuba, Pierce ships to: 49
Curry, Mr., brings suit: 101-102
Cutbirth, Sam: 310
Cypress knee: 29

D: *see* brands
D Company, First Texas Cavalry: 34, 35, 37
Dago George: *see* Ciprico, George W.
Daniels, L. S., letter to Pierce: 115
Davidson, R. V., prominent Galveston: 294
Davis, Governor, of Texas: 67, 68
Davis Cattle Co., defaults in delivery of cattle: 149
Dawdy, Asa H.: 44, 52, 53, 123, 140, 267; peddles tales to Brendel, 258
Dawdy, Ernest E.: 228
Dawdy, Pleas, ordered to chase off Bosky cattle: 194
Dawdy estate: 140
Dayton, Tex.: 109
Dead-tree gallows: 58, 68
Death squad, Ranger McNelly's: 68
Decrow, Thomas, seafaring man turned cattleman: 18, 28
Deming, E. A., Pierce's friend: 21, 25, 43
Deming's Bridge, Tex.: 40, 42, 53, 208, 245, 247
Dennis, I. N., land agent: 100
Dennis, John, Wharton lawyer: 204
Dennis, Liege: 28, 57

323

Denver, Colo.: 69, 98, 133, 147, 164, 165, 173
Department of Agriculture: 301ff
Depot, built by Southern Pacific: 117
Devil's Addition, houses prostitutes: 70
DeWitt County, Tex.: 50, 67, 68, 90
Diamond stud, stolen from Pierce: 285
Doan's Crossing, Tex.: 127-28, 132
Docks, built at Palacios: 51
Dodge City, Kan.: 64, 126
Dogies: 26
Donnell, Lawson & Simpson Co.: brokers, 97-98; go broke, 99
Driskill, Tobe, rich Texas cattleman: 66, 68
Drover's Cottage, Abilene, Kan., erected by McCoy: 62
Duncan, Green, a small Negro boy identifies "the fair likeness": 246
Duncan, John: 18; cattle, 28; plantation bought by Pierce, 205-208
Duncan Ranch: 205ff, 219, 248ff, 277
Durham, Ranger George: 68

Earp, Wyatt, describes Kansas City: 64
East Texas, Kountze buys land in: 99
Eddleman, Mr., buys John Lowery cattle: 132-33
Edna, Tex.: 104
Edwards, L. E., lawyer, ejected from banquet hall: 146
Elliott's Ferry: 25
Ellis, Charles, Negro cattledriver: 123
Ellsworth, Kan.: 64, 72, 76; Hell in session at, 73
El Rancho Grande: 49, 58, 71, 78, 79, 86, 103, 106, 127; organized, 42; expanded, 46-47; outriders inspect, 50; wet ponies brought to, 54, banding at, 56; J. E. Pierce's management pleases Shanghai, 84; partnership dissolved, 254
Elwood, I. L., owner of barbed-wire co.: 135
Emancipation of Negro: 66
"Emporium for Dispensation of Liquid Tarantula Juice": 62
English, H. B.: 217-18, 278
English Co., is faked by Shanghai and Clements: 91
Estevanico: 18
"Etheopian Eden of America": 18
Ettar the bear, captured by J. E. Pierce: 153
Europe, toured by Shanghai and Hattie: 240ff, 271

Evans, Ira, land agent: 99
Evans, Sam: 133; challenges Pierce, 137

Fairchild, mentions Brahman cattle: 302
Fall River, R. I: 14, 102, 192
Fant, Dillard: 229, 242; borrows from Little Dannie, 96; buys cattle from Fleming, 142; in New York to visit Kountze, 188
Featherstone, Mr., railroad promoter: 290
Federal Court: injunction removed to, 91; Sullivan-Pierce suit, 272
Fence building: 89, 95, 136
Fence cutters: 143, 149, 157, 158, 161, 162-64
Feud: *see* Taylor-Sutton feud
First National Bank of Austin, Tex.: 84
First National Bank of New York City: 7
First Texas Cavalry: 37
Fish Brand Oil Skin: 61
Fitzgerald, Tod: 180
Flagg, Isaac: 122, 129
Fleming, Thomas N., plays joke on Fant: 142
Fleurry, I. N.: 43
Flora, Shanghai's cousin: 102
Fly, Dr., Shanghai's physician: 265
Foard, Thompson & Townsend, law firm: 191
Forbes, T. D., a Southern Pacific official: 117
Forsythe, Jay, buys Pierce cattle: 185-86
Fort Bend County, Tex.: 45, 106; political situation, 178-80
Fort Sill (Cil), Okla.: 150
Fort Sumpter, South Carolina: 34
Fort Worth, Tex.: vii, 127
Fossati, Jasper: 201
Foster, Jim M.: 21, 28, 29, 40, 42, 48, 49
France: 19
Fredericksburg, Tex.: 20
Free range: 218
Freighters: *see Alabama, Charley Morgan, Harlan*
Frost, Henry: 179

Gallows: *see* dead-tree gallows
Galt House, Louisville, Kentucky: 160
Galveston, Tex.: 7, 18, 42, 48, 75, 86, 91, 94f, 122, 147, 168, 264, 286, 291
Galveston, Harrisburg & San Antonio Railroad Co.: 113, 114
Galveston *News*: 178
Gambling: houses at Abilene, Kan., 70; organized, 75

Index

Gates, John Warne, barbed-wire company salesman: 135–36
Gayle, A., cattleman: 43
George, Moses B., operator of Drover's Cottage: 62
Georgia: 68
Gerkin, Mr., of the Southern Pacific: 117
German immigrants: 20
Gibbs, C. C., Southern Pacific official: 116f, 181
Gibson, Ned, of the Jaybird-Woodpecker feud: 180
Gibson, Volney, killed by Kyle: 180
Gifford, George C., a Pierce nephew: viii, 122, 292; takes herd to Kansas, 123ff; quarrels with Borden, 148; trail driving difficulties, 151ff; turns cattle onto K and KO lands, 170; buys and sells Half Moon cattle, 210–11; sells cattle to Miller, 233
Gitter feaver: *see* Yellow Fever
Glass, Callender & Proctor, attorneys: 201
Gold: Robbins, 17, 36, 42, 44, 47; Pierce sells cattle for $110,000, 59; Shanghai's, 69, 75; the Sullivan notes, 262, 265
Golden, Mrs., "inside owner": 105
Goliad, Tex.: 73
Gonzales, Tex.: 62, 82, 123
Gonzales County: 104
Gould, George Jay: 284; Fred Proctor calls on, 291
Grab game: 26, 143
Grand Jury, indicts Lunn: 59
Grangers: 125, 230
Grant, Sam, tries to kill Siringo: 57
Green, Arthur: 249–50
Green, E. H. R., wealthy Texan: 211
"Green horn army men," try to make a running count of cattle: 74
Green Lake, Tex.: 34
Greer, Mrs. Edith Borden, niece of Pierce: viii
Grimes, Bradford R.: takes over father's responsibilities, 91; turns merchant, 92
Grimes, Frances Charlotte (Fannie): 24, 28; Pierce brands HO for "my gal Fannie," 25; in Connecticut, 36
Grimes, Captain Richard: sailor and rancher, 16ff; refuses to employ Pierce, 20
Grimes, William Bradford ("Bing"): viii, 22ff, 33ff, 51, 56, 67, 85, 136, 142, 149; hires Shanghai, 20–21; characteristics of household, 23; in competition with other cattlemen, 28ff; pays Shanghai in Confederate money, 38; takes over stray cattle, 43–44; struggles against Shanghai Circle, 88–93
Grimes Ranch: 30, 38
Grimes Tallow Factory: 33, 42, 81; slaughter of cattle, 43; compared with El Rancho Grande, 56
G. T. T. (Gone to Texas): 159, 159n.
Guadalupe River: 18, 19, 48, 51, 88
Gulf, Colorado, and Santa Fe Railway: 114, 127, 147, 186, 188, 283f
Gulf Hotel, Abilene, Kan.: 62
Gulf and Interstate Railway Co.: 7; founded, 286; put under receiver, 293
Gulf of Mexico: 18, 48, 95
Gulf, Western Texas, and Pacific Railway: 115
Gunter, Archibald Clavering, novelist: 297
Gunter, Jot, wealthy cattleman: 173, 284
Guyle, A.: 43

Hackberry, Indian Territory: 123
Haley, J. Evetts, archivist-author: ix
Half Moon: *see* brands
Halff, Mayer L, helps Borden get Brahman cattle in country: 307
Hall, Ranger Captain Lee, at cattlemen's convention: 146
Hamilton, George Stidham: 119, 122, 131, 137, 157, 192ff, 214; hired as bookkeeper for Shanghai, 81; takes over Hunky Dory Store, 84; appraised by Shanghai's sister-in-law, 85; reports cattle purchases to Kountze, 109; moves to BU Ranch, 110; resigns, 226
Hamilton, Tex.: vii
Hamilton, Thomas Jefferson: described, 73; helps outwit the army greenhorns, 74; helps Pierce recover on bank certificates, 76
Hamilton's Point: 81
Hardin, John Wesley: trees Wild Bill Hickok, 65; in Abilene, 66ff; trouble with Wild Bill Hickok, 70–71; on the rampage, 72; back in Texas, 81f
Harlan, a freighter: 51
Harrisburg & San Antonio Railway: 113
Harrison, President Benjamin, clears Strip of cattle: 230
Hartford, Connecticut: 17, 23
Hazel, Jesse: 63

325

Head, Abel, Shanghai's uncle: 13, 18; employs Shanghai, 15ff; employs Chester Robbins, 16f; feeds Pierce sanctimony, 19
Head, Hanna: see Pierce, Hanna
Head, Mary (Mrs. Carter Bishop): 18, 19
Heard, Jim, cattle buyer: 140, 147
Helms, Jack: vigilante, 50–51, 57, 67; kills a Negro, 66; is killed, 81
Henry, O (William Sidney Porter): 62
Herd law, McCamley employed to lobby against: 106
Herrin, Mr., "inside owner": 107
Heyer the blacksmith: 27, 39, 40
Hickok, Wild Bill: 66, 67; treed by Hardin, 65; city marshal, 70–71; kills Coe, 72
Hides: 30, 33, 104
HL: see brands
HO: see brands
Hogg, Gov. James Stephen: speaks on Silver issue, 263; invited to bear hunt, 282
Holcomb, John, cattleman: 43
Holmes, Neptune: viii, 51, 101, 127, 130, 133, 172; wails at Shanghai's decease, 4; with Shanghai in Kansas City, 10; slips quietly into Pierce's activities, 47; makes trip to Saint Mary's, 48; the indispensable, 123; helps Pierce buy gold, 265–66
Holt, Mr., a cattleman: 18
Hope, L. S., kills Staffords: 191
Hope, M. H., kills Staffords: 191
Horse Creek, Colorado: 133
Hot cakes, establish friendship of Widow Ward and Shanghai: 21
Hot Springs, Ark.: 7, 233, 265, 293
"Hotel field marshal": 269
Hotels: at Abilene, 70; trouble at Victoria, 88; see also name of hotel
Houston, Dun: 126
Houston, R. B., Sullivan tries to sell Pierce-Sullivan Co. stock to: 255ff
Houston, Texas: 111, 185, 231
Hungerford, Colonel Daniel E., vice-president of Macaroni Railroad: 111–13
Hungerford, Edna: 111; marries Count Telferner, 112
Hungerford, Louise: see Mackay, Mrs. J. W.
Hurricane: encountered by A. C. Leverette, 30; at Galveston, 291ff
Hutcheson, Judge J. C.: viii

Hutchins, Jack: viii, ix; manager of Pierce Estate, 310

Immigrants: see German immigrants
Independent National Bank of St. Louis: 234, 236
Indian Free Range: 218
Indian Territory: 91; attempt to confine Indians, 129; cattlemen try to get control, 220–24; see also Cherokee Strip
Indian Territory Cattle Company: 176
Indianapolis, Ind.: 69
Indianola, Tex.: 19, 28, 29, 34, 37, 39, 40, 43, 50, 80, 82, 96, 159, 203; cattle business at, 30; shipping port, 31
Indians: 18, 25; agency buys Pierce cattle, 74; take cattle from drovers, 129–31; kill a Pierce "boy," 131; leases give trouble to cattlemen, 174–75; see also Cherokee and Chickasans
Injunction, Wharton County suit: 187
"Inside owner": 104
Interior Department, Crain advises caution: 221
International & Great Northern Railroad Co.: 97, 99
Intruders driven from Strip: 150
Ireland, Governor, calls fence-cutting session of legislature: 163
Island City Savings Bank: 274; patronized by Shanghai, 147, 149; bankrupt, 161
Island of Galveston: 18
Italy: Mackay-Hungerford party lands in, 112; Swiss-American and Macaroni Railroad incorporators from, 193

Jack-the-barber: see Hungerford, D. E.
Jackson County, Tex.: 41
Jacksonville, Tex.: 50
James, Hattie: see Pierce, Hattie
James, John G., buys land from Nye and J. E. Pierce: 161–62
James County, Kan.: 84
Jamison, Ella, cattle taken by Grimes: 43
Jaybirds and Woodpeckers: 179ff
Jerkin-and-slicker democracy: 62
Jesse, Wild Bill's girl friend: 72
Jim Crow outfit: 74
Johnson, Snake Head: 63
Jones, Sam, evangelist: 263
Jordan, J. W., United States Marshal: 150–51
Juanita River: 25
Judea schoolhouse: 12

Index

K: *see* brands
K Ranch: Crary becomes superintendent, 108; fenced, 137; fence-cutting damage, 162f; losses in blizzard, 169ff
Kansas: 53, 55, 66, 67, 88, 89; Pierce buys bankstock in, 75, 97; Byler works for Shanghai in, 82; litigation, 84; mysterious visitor from, 103
Kansas City, Mo.: 6, 69, 70, 90, 95, 122, 131, 153; Shanghai and Neptune arrive in, 10; St. James Hotel, 60; Shanghai hunts for society, 63ff; the metropolitan playground, 72
Kansas City Stockyards: 10
Karankawa River: *see* Caranchua River
Keller, Nolan: 57
Keeran, Mr., cattleman: 18
Kentucky: 73
Ketch-rope: 23, 225
King, W. W., sells Boschi notes to Pierce: 195-96
King-of-the-cattle-kings: 4
Kings of the Ranch: 100
Kiowa, Kan.: 91, 95, 132
Kirkpatrick, H. H., clerk of the U. S. District Court: 174; land agent, 100; participates in the Tacquard Squeeze, 212-13
Klopper Pasture: 7
Knight of Bovina: 135ff
KO Ranch: McReynolds to superintend, 108; established, 110; fenced, 137; fence-cutting damage, 162ff; losses, 169ff
Kountze, Augustus: 102, 108, 136, 157, 163, 169ff; "New York brother," 97; visited by Pierce, 98; in Wharton County courthouse fight, 181ff; informed of cattle loss, 185; refuses to close Forsythe cattle deal, 186; cattle lost in shipping, 187; quarrels over sales-commission, 189-90
Kountze, C. B., advises against anti-quarantine legislation: 174
Kountze, Herman: 103; confers with Pierce, 69; visited by Shanghai, 75; inspects purchasable grasslands in Texas, 97-99; visited by Mamie, 155
Kountze Brothers: 157, 287; bankers, 69; buy Texas lands with Pierce, 97-109; unsettled account with Pierce, 154-57; lose cattle in blizzard, 169ff; cattle sold to Smith and Forsythe, 185-90; preempt land with K and KO ranches, 196

Kountze Ranch: 108, 110
Kuykendall, James, competes with Grimes: 28
Kuykendall, Susan: *see* Pierce, Susan E.
Kuykendall, Wiley M.: 81, 87, 110, 252-53, 284; marries Susan Pierce, 45; the superb range-boss, 47; enlists Siringo, 55; recognizes John Wesley Hardin, 82; sues Shanghai, 139; gives Miller square deal, 231
Kuykendall, Wiley M., et ux v. Abel Head Pierce: 139
Kyle, William Henry: 100; forms partnership with Pierce, 51, 85; occupies range with Stafford, 88; dissolves Pierce partnership, 95; a buffer against Stafford, 99
Kyle-Pierce Range: 99

Labauve, Gilbert: 26
Labauve, Valcour J.: 26
Labauve, Willie: 27, 134, 211; joins Shanghai, 123; quits Pierce, 165; ordered to run off Bosky cattle, 193; brings cattle to Duncan Ranch, 207
La Belle France: 19
Lacy, Fannie: 29, 40, 41; marries Shanghai, 43; dies, 53
Lacy, Nannie: 41, 53, 57; marries J. E. Pierce, 45
Lacy, Widow: 43
Lake Charles, Louisiana: 117
Lambert and Bishop, wire dealers: 136
Land titles: 100
Lane, Jonathan, buys Pierce land: 283ff
Lariat: 53
Lark, Negro, gives Wiley a ride: 45
La Salle, René Robert de: 19
Leland Hotel, Caldwell, Kan.: 131
Levi, G. A., treasurer Macaroni Railway: 113
Levi trousers: 11, 61
Linn, E. D.: 201
Liquor: 34, 41, 45, 47, 63, 123, 175, 252
Litigation: Kansas, 83ff; against fence builders, 89ff; to clear land titles, 101-102; *Kuykendall v. Pierce,* 139; Grand jury indictments, 139; with Dan Sullivan, 268ff
Little Compton, R. I.: 13, 27, 153, 193
Little Danny: *see* Sullivan, Daniel
Littlefield, George W., of Texas Livestock Association: 143, 170
Liverpool & London & Globe Insurance Co., agents to oust Grimes: 93

327

Livestock Association meetings: *see* cattlemen's conventions
Lobbyist, McCameley at Austin, Tex.: 106ff
Lola, a girl friend of cattlemen: 63
Lombardi, Mr., buys land from Jonathan Pierce: 161ff
Longfellow, Henry Wadsworth, related to Pierce: 12
Longhorns: 25, 29, 33, 43ff, 51, 74, 82, 128–29, 166
Long-loop gang: 56
Lott, Uriah, railroad builder: 286ff
Louise, Texas, named for Hungerford's daughter: 112
Louisiana swamps: 29
Lovejoy, John, owed Pierce: 293–94
Lowery, John P., sells cattle to Eddleman: 132–33
Lowrey, Fred V., critic: ix
Lowrey, Janette, author-critic: ix
Lunn, Ed.: 26, 58
Lunn, Wilborn W.: 43, 65; escapes hangmen, 58; indicted for stealing cattle hides, 59; *State of Texas* v., 79ff
Lunn Brothers: 26, 66; join Pierce forces, 49; association with Taylor crowd, 50; watched by regulators, 57; hanging, 58
Lynching: 58, 66

Mabry, Major Seth: 12, 73; buys Pierce cattle, 127, 133, 134, 147–48; pays Shanghai, 155
Macaroni Railway: *see* New York, Texas and Mexican Railway
McCameley, Fred: 140, 143
McCameley, John W.: 34; pays forfeited bond, 79; lobbyist, 106
McCarthy, Ed: 274ff, 286ff
McCoy, Allen: general manager of Macaroni Railroad, 113, 114; superseded, 115, 195; connives with Shanghai, 195ff; receives accommodation note, 200
McCoy, Joseph, mayor of Abilene, Kan.: 62, 70, 73, 167
McCroskey, John: 122, 211, 298; takes herds north, 123ff, 149ff; Half Moon superintendent, 207ff
McCroskey, Matt, wife of John McCroskey: 207–208
McFadden, W. H. P.: 235
Mackay, J. W.: 193; mines a fortune, 112; builds Macaroni Railway, 113

Mackay, Mrs. J. W.: daughter of Jack-the-barber, 111; "Bonanza Queen," 112
McKinley, William, candidate for presidency: 262–63, 266
McNelly, Captain L. H., Texas Ranger: 68–69
McReynolds, F. C.: 142, 197; KO superintendent, 108
McSparren, J. Clay: viii, 4, 8, 117, 165, 310; learns of cattle rustling, 57; listens to conversation with Mr. Curry, 101–102; joins up with Pierce, 123; vouches for Half Moon brand origin, 211; hears trade made for statue, 243ff
McSparren, Mrs. J. Clay: 171–72
Mad Island Pasture: 7
Malone, Ida ("old Idar"): ix, 123
Manchke Hotel, San Antonio, Tex.: 135
Marbury, Ann, related to Shanghai: 12
Market Square at Kansas City: 63, 64, 72
Marshall, Billie, meets Pierce: 32
Martin, Thomas C., the mysterious stranger: 103
Massachusetts: 28
Masterson, Mr., attorney, gives Pierce trouble over land purchases: 100–102
Matagorda County, Tex.: 17, 34, 59, 91, 100; cattle in, 28; Negroes in, 66; courts, 78, 138, 257
Matagorda, Tex.: 17, 25, 34, 35, 37, 43, 45, 50, 65, 75, 79
Matamoros, Mexico: 40
Matanzas, Cuba, Pierce ships cattle to: 49
Mathis, T. M.: 164
Matthews, Mr., buys Pierce cattle: 96
Mavericking: 32
Mavericks: 49, 50, 51, 55, 56, 66
Mayflower, Pierce ancestors on: 12
Medicine man's show: 136
Melvin, Dr., chief of the Bureau of Animal Industry: 302
Mendota Station, Indian Territory: 166
Menger Hotel, San Antonio, Texas: 135; Governor Hogg at, 282
Merchants National Bank, St. Paul, Minn.: 134
Metropolitan Hotel, New York: 158
Mexican ponies: 54
Mexicans: 44, 67, 72
Mexico City: 111
Milheim Station: 127, 147
Miller, Bernard: 124

Index

Miller, Elvira ("Old Vi"), Negress: 86, 123, 297
Miller, George Washington: 185; characteristics of, 216–17; buys cattle from Shanghai, 219, 224, 230–31; writes letter to Shanghai, 227; trouble with Shanghai, 232–38; at court for *Sullivan v. Pierce*, 269–70
Miller, Joe: 217; acquitted of theft, 225
Miller, Molly: 217
Mine: 112
Minnich, Maggie E., "inside owner": 105
Minor, Mr., holds option on railroad sale: 289
Missionaries: 75
Missouri: 52, 83
Mitchell, George F., tea-examiner: 301
Mohler, John R. of Bureau of Animal Industry: 307
Mokehunne Hill: 112
Monseratt, M. D.: succeeds McCoy, 115, 195; gets jug of XX Rhode Island Vinegar, 291
Monte dealing: 75
Montgomery, Peyton, buys cattle: 147–48
Montgomery Baths: 111
Monument: the Pierce family, 194; Shanghai's, 243ff, 272
Morgan liners: 29
Morris, Alexander, within the Pierce Circle: 104
Mossy horns: 29, 34, 51, 52, 54, 55, 136
Mosquitoes: 18
Mullen, Priscilla, related to Pierce: 12
Muskets, Missouri: 83
Musselman's saloon, Victoria, Tex.: 39
Mustang grapevine: 29
"My Counsellor": *see* Proctor, Frederick C.
Mystic Knights of Bovina: 145

Navidad River: 54, 95
Nebraska: 53; legislature receives proposal from Pierce, 75
Negroes: viii, 4, 8, 10, 18, 22, 23, 44, 51, 66, 67; hold political offices in Wharton and Fort Bend counties, 178
Nep: *see* Holmes, Neptune
Nesters: 106, 220; hired by Pierce, 125; opposed by cattlemen, 145
New Braunfels, Tex.: 20
New England: 13, 17, 21
New Orleans, La.: 28, 29, 30, 40, 48, 49, 53
New York: 3, 19, 27, 32, 91, 98, 306

"New York brother": *see* Kountze, Augustus
New York Stock Exchange: 97–98
New York & Texas Land Company: 97
New York, Texas & Mexican Railway: 113ff, 148, 193, 281
Newell's Grove, Texas: 56; the hanging at, 58
Newtonia, Missouri: 217
"Nigger's supper": 185, 218
Non-enclosure law: 107
Norman, John, a Pierce supporter: 123
Norman, Robert, a Pierce supporter: 123
North Texas: 44
Nye, Thomas: 35, 37, 52, 54, 56, 156, 184; a vigilante, 50; appointed receiver, 90; buys land from Pierce, 101; delivers cattle, 127–29; witness in law suit, 139; buys land with forged title, 160ff; leaves Matagorda, 181

Oaks: 36, 41
Oath of allegiance to Confederacy: 37
O'Connell, Michael: 250–51
O'Connor, Thomas: 18, 21, 82; makes One Arm Jim pay, 84; in the Pierce camp, 85; invites Little Dannie to become partner, 204; shares Brahman importation expense, 302
Ogallala, Neb.: 124, 216f, 133f
Ogden, Charles, San Antonio lawyer: 254, 257; hears case of *Sullivan v. Pierce*, 271
Old Caney: 42
Old Clinton, Tex.: 81, 82
Old Dominion: 13
"Old Idar": *see* Malone, Ida
Old Prince, Pierce's horse: 43, 51, 59
"Old Slim," trees a two-legged coon: 282
"Old Vi": *see* Miller, Elvira
"Omaha brother": *see* Kountze, Herman
Omaha, Nebraska: 64, 69, 98
101 Ranch: 185, 216, 225
Outriders: 50
Oxen: 8, 38, 50

Palace Hotel, San Francisco, Cal.: 164
Palacios Point: 17
Palacios, Tex.: 51
Pancakes, Widow Ward's: 22, 28
Panhandle National Bank, interested in forged land title: 161f
Papal Bulls: 242
Partain, Ed., a Pierce "boy": 123, 151
Peareson, Colonel, Shanghai's lawyer: 102

329

Peareson, Dr. E. A.: 34, 35
Peareson, Phillip E., organized Young Men's Democratic Club: 178-79
Peareson and Peareson, attorneys: 182
Peeler: 133
Peirce, Thomas Wentworth, railroad man: 12, 113
Perry, Deputy Sheriff: 79
Perry, Mrs.: 79
Petersburg, Va.: 13, 18
Peticola, Mr., discharged by Pierce: 48
Philippi, Grace, librarian: ix
Phillips, J. Y.: 105
Pierce, Abel (Shanghai's son), died in infancy: 53
Pierce, Abel B. (Shanghai's nephew), left out of will: 296
Pierce, Abel Head ("Shanghai"): Emmett's boyhood impressions of, vii-viii; described, 4, 10, 11, 60, 64; will, 6, 7, 296, 298; list of assets and indebtedness, 7; funeral, 8-9; statue of, 8, 243ff; "Webster on Cattle," 11, 12; ancestors, 12; characteristics of, 12, 19, 20, 27, 29, 53, 63, 298; born, 13; philosophy, 14, 24; clerks in Uncle Abel's store, 15-19; works for Bradford Grimes, 21-38; schemes to ruin Grimes, 24, 26, 38f, 42, 85f, 87-93; the nickname "shanghai," 26-28; in Confederate army, 37-38; forms partnership with Jonathan Pierce, 42; marries Fannie Lacy, 43; partnership with Allen & Poole, 48ff; involved in Taylor-Sutton feud, 50-51, 57ff, 65-69, 78-82; difficulties with Andy Wilson, 75-77, 83-84; marries Hattie James, 86; land purchases and business deals with Kountze brothers, 97-109, 169-71, 185-90; relations with railroads, 110-18, 186; expands BU Ranch activities, 119-34; fights against fence-cutters and cattle thieves, 140ff, 158, 162-64; troubles with Bosky, 192-201; association with Sullivan, 203-15, 253-66, 268-73; dealings with George W. Miller, 216-38; as a banker, 274ff, 289ff; as railroad owner, 286-88, 290-91, 294; dies, 298
Pierce, A. H. and J. E. Cattle Co.: 44, 95, 108, 122; partnership formed, 42; company becomes a reality, 47; partnerships with Ward and Kyle, 51; assess 35,000 cattle, 56; Helms as foreman, 66; Hamilton to keep books, 81; accused of illegally possessing beeves, 104; partnership dissolved, 254
Pierce, Fannie: see Lacy, Fannie
Pierce, President Franklin, related to Shanghai: 12
Pierce, Frederick Horatio (brother of Shanghai): 13
Pierce, Hannah Head (Shanghai's mother): 13
Pierce, Hattie (Shanghai's second wife): 8, 119, 155, 168, 183; to discuss will, 6; managing father's estate, 75; marries Pierce, 86; tours Canada, 156; tours Europe with Shanghai and Sullivan daughters, 240-41, 271; legatee, 298
Pierce, Jonathan Edward (father of Shanghai): 13, 36
Pierce, Jonathan Edward (Shanghai's brother): viii, 8, 53, 57, 75, 79, 87, 110, 137, 153, 157, 169, 186, 283, 284; described, 30; at Grimes Ranch, 30-35; characteristics of, 36, 41; in Confederate army, 37, 41; partnership with Shanghai, 42, 46; marries Nannie Lacy, 45; rounds up cattle for shipment, 127, 147-48; Wichita County lands, 161ff; surveys, and fences Duncan Ranch, 210
Pierce, Mary (Shanghai's sister): 14, 298
Pierce, (Mamie) Mary (Mrs. Henry Withers): 79, 119, 154, 183; birth of, 52; takes trip with Shanghai, 164; requests statement of estate, 168; marries Withers, 184; elected director of Pierce-Sullivan Co., 254; executor of Shanghai's will, 296; legatee, 298
Pierce, Miranda (Mira): 13, 14, 18, 30, 42, 79, 102, 194, 298
Pierce, Nannie: see Lacy, Nannie
Pierce, Susan E. (Mrs. Wiley M. Kuykendall): 35, 41, 45, 87, 110, 252-53; files suit against Shanghai, 139
Pierce, Texas: 113
Pierce Circle: 88, 89, 104, 193
Pierce family motto: 42
Pierce-Kyle & Pierce: 85, 88
Pierce papers: ix
Pierce Ranch, Limited: viii, 311
Pierce-Reed, partners: 73-74, 75, 83
Pierce-Sullivan Pasture & Cattle Co.: arrangements for creation of, 203ff; expanded, 212; incorporated, 214; disagreement between Pierce and Sullivan, 253ff; Mamie becomes director, 254; by-laws amended, 257;

Index

affairs investigated, 258ff; Sullivan sells out to Pierce, 265
Pierce-Ward Range: 95
Pierce's Station, Tex.: viii, 148; named by Shanghai, 118
Pilkington Pasture: 7
Pinchback, Alley: 43
Pinchback, Mary: 43
Pipkin, L. B.: 235
Plank fence: mutual protectionists build, 89; Grimes' scheme, 95
Planter's House, Abilene, Kan.: 62
Platte River grass: 99
Pleasant Hill, Buchel killed at: 37
Pleasants, Judge, grants injunction: 90–91, 182
Podo, Kaffir of BU Ranch: 123
Poker: 63, 81
Police: 67, 70, 81, 164–65
Political conditions: in Galveston, Tex., 168; in Wharton and Fort Bend counties, 177–83
Pond Creek, Indian Territory: 148
Poona, India: 304–305
Pope: 239
Port Lavaca, Tex.: 19, 31, 34, 165
Porter, William Sydney: *see* Henry, O.
Potter of Texas, Mr., novel patterned after Shanghai's life: 297
Powder Horn, Tex.: 30
Prince Carl of Solms-Braunfels: 60
Proctor, D. C.: 39, 90, 168; prepares pre-nuptial contract, 183
Proctor, Frederick Cocke: 3, 6, 8, 22, 204, 278; nickname of "My Counselor" given to, 4; at Shanghai's funeral, 9; holds power-of-attorney, 257; attorney in *Sullivan v. Pierce*, 268ff; attempts to sell railroad, 291
Proctor and Stockdale: *see* Stockdale & Proctor
Proctor, Venable B.: holds power-of-attorney, 257; receives Brahman cattle letter from Borden, 305
Proctor and Vandenburg, represent Pierce's estate: 302, 307
Proctors, The: 6; attorneys for the Macaroni Railroad, 113
Pryor, Colonel Ike T.: 12, 126, 138; remarks on Pierce's cattle, 174; collects damages from Santa Fe, 188
Public roads: 29
Pullman Palace Car, Shanghai's shotgun goes off in: 216
Purcell, Indian Territory: 152
Puritanism: 18

Pybus, John: 43
Pybus, Joseph, indicts Shanghai: 139

Quantrill gang: 50
Quarantine: Byler to run the, 82; cattle winter below the line, 83; Brahman cattle at Carteret Island, 304
Quarantine board, controls Colorado cattle imports: 174
Quarantine laws, discussed at Denver meetings: 164ff, 174
Quebec, Canada: 156
Quirt: 23

Range brander: 24
Rattlesnakes: 49
Receiver: 236
Reclamations, railroads slow to pay: 188
Recorder of brands: 25
Red River: 55, 64, 128, 150, 165
Red River Campaign, Pierce in: 37
Red Rock, Indian Territory: 186
Reed, J. D. (One Arm Jim): 73, 75, 82
Reeves, John: 141
Regimental Butcher: 37–38
Regulators: 51
Renegades: 17
Republic of Texas: 99
Rhode Island: 4, 11ff, 15, 18, 28, 30, 35, 36, 98, 102, 153
Rice: farms started by Borden, 282ff; Shanghai turns boomer for, 291
Rich, R. A., forms Pierce partnership: 280ff
Richmond, Texas: 37, 111; Jaybirds and Woodpeckers, 178ff
Rio Tres Palacios: 17, 21, 28, 41, 43, 52, 93, 110
Riviera: 112
Robb, the Widow: 104
Robbins, Chester Hamlin: 16ff, 20, 25
Robbins, Mary Louise: 23
Robbins, Philamon: 17, 23
Robbins, Samuel: 16, 17
Robert, Old, charged with murder: 276ff
Roberts, Ed, cowboy: 123, 141
Robertson, H. A., Jr.: 267
Rocky Hill, Conn.: 16, 36
Roosevelt, President Theodore, intervenes for Brahmans: 307
Rosebush hedge: 46
Rosenburg, Tex.: 113–14
Royal Arch Degree: 26, 93
Ruess, Dr. Joe, called to attend Pierce: 297
Rugeley, Captain John: 18, 34

331

Running iron: 51
Ryan, Thomas: 175

Sacred cattle: 303
Saddlebags: 47, 48
Saddlepocket dogies: 109
Sailboat: 16, 17
Saint James Hotel, Kansas City, Mo.: 10, 11, 12, 60, 62
Saint Mary's, Texas: 40, 48
Salad, Jot Gunter's Honest Texas: 173
Salt Lake, Utah: 165
San Antonio, Tex.: 135ff, 204, 243, 261, 284, 291
San Antonio *Daily Express:* 135, 285f; report on cattle barons, 144-45
San Antonio *Light:* 110, 285
San Francisco, Cal.: 111, 112, 164
San Jacinto veterans, land holdings in Texas: 100
Sartwell, W. S., castigates Pierce: 107
Saunders, George, eminent cattleman: 52, 138
Sayers, Joseph D., Congressman: 220
Schooner: 19
Schultz, August: 43
Scott, General Winfield: 34, 111
Sea lions: vii, 95, 126, 219
Secession: 34
Shamblin, J. M.: 179
Shanghai Circle: *see* Pierce Circle
Shanghai hat: 32, 53
Shanghai rooster: 27
Shanghai, Tex.: 113
Sheep: 47
Sheepmen, race with cattlemen: 285
Shelly bellies: 26, 29
Shotgun settlement: 48, 238
Simon's Cafe, Austin, Tex.: 146
Simpson, John, hotel owner: 62
Sims, Gabriel, poker-playing cowman: 123, 127; disturbed by Indian, 129-30
Singleton, Jasper, Pierce cowboy: 123
Siringo, Charlie: 44, 53-54, 55, 57, 82
Sixth Texas Regiment: 34
Skeleton of Negro: 66
Slaughter, Lum, cattle rancher: 126
Slavens, L. C., Pierce's Kansas City lawyer: 69, 70, 83, 84
Slicker: 8, 61
Slicks: 51
Smith, Dr. Allen, Shanghai's physician: 297
Smith, John M. (All Jaw): 50, 57, 65; hanged by vigilantes, 58

Smith and Forsythe, cattle firm: 169, 173, 185-86
Snake Head Johnson's Special Blend: 63
Snodgrass pens: 54
Snowstorm: 208, 225
Snyder Ranch: 225
Southern Pacific Railway: 7, 12, 111, 115-17, 181, 281
Sowle, Captain, related to Shanghai: 102
Spade Ranch: 91, 92, 149
Spangler, H. S.: accountant for Gulf and Interstate Railway, 286; receiver, 294
Spanish pony: 22, 31
Sparks, Fred, "inside owner": 104
Speer, Tom, marshal of Kansas City: 65, 68, 72
Spoor, John, cattle taken by Grimes: 43
Sporting men: 70
Spurs: 23, 27, 61
Squatters: 62, 277-78
Squeeze: *see* Tacquard Squeeze Out
Stafford, R. L. (Bob): 87, 88, 95, 99, 108, 126, 137, 143; killed, 190
Stafford brothers: 67, 87, 190-91
Stage coach: 131-32
Stags: 35
Stake-and-rider fence, made by Pierce: 22
Stampedes: 55, 123, 129, 232
Stapp, D. M., sent to 101 Ranch: 227-28
Star: *see* brands
State News: 73
State of Texas v. *W. W. Lunn: see* Lunn, W. W.
Statue of Pierce: 8, 243-46, 272
Stephens, Henry, cattle rancher: 126
Stidham, George Hamilton: *see* Hamilton, George Stidham
Stock claims: 114
Stock pens: 116
Stockdale, Governor Fletcher S.: 39
Stockdale and Proctor, lawyers: 39, 40, 168, 182
Stockraiser's Association of Western Texas: 143
Stoddard, Mr.: 234ff, 295
Stolen cattle: 141
Strays: 44
Streetcar, Shanghai loses diamond in: 285
Stuart, Mrs. (General) J. E. B.: 154
Subpoena, Pierce under: 191
Sullivan, Annie, takes European tour with Pierces: 240f
Sullivan, Miss E. A., takes European tour with Pierces: 240f

Index

Sullivan, Daniel: 31, 32, 40, 42, 48; dies, 80
Sullivan, Daniel (Little Dannie): 32, 37, 40, 48, 52, 80, 82, 85, 95f; partnership with Pierce, 203–15; run on Sullivan's bank, 215; borrows money from Pierce, 239; daughters, 240; tries to sell Half Moon Ranch stock, 253ff; sells to Pierce, 264; sues Pierce, 268ff
Sullivan, Daniel v. *Abel Head Pierce:* 216, 268ff; decision, 298
Sullivan, Pierce, Pasture & Cattle Co.: *see* Pierce-Sullivan Pasture & Cattle Co.
Sullivan General Mercantile Store: 3
Summerville, S. C.: 30
Sumners, Major, watches Pierce herds: 153
Sutton, Bill, killed: 67
Suttons, the: 50, 81
Swamp angels: 29, 99, 109, 147, 148, 185
Swaybacks: 26
Swiss-American Co.: 193ff; liquidated, 201
Swiss Company: 199

Tacquard Squeeze Out: 213ff
Talbot, Eugene: 232; death of, 235
Talbot, Mrs. Ellas: 24
Tallow: 33; factory, 43, 57
Tax on cattle: 84
Taylor, Mr., cashed Pierce's notes: 49
Taylor, Ed: 122, 127, 143
Taylor, Jim, killed Sutton: 67
Taylor, Tom: 178
Taylors, the: 50, 67
Taylor-Sutton feud: 50, 67f, 81
Tea farm: 4, 301–302
Tea, South Carolina: 301
Teich, Frank, sculptor, makes statue of Shanghai: 243ff
Telferner, Edna: *see* Hungerford, Edna
Telferner, Joseph, Italian Count: 193; marries Edna Hungerford, 112; president of New York, Texas and Mexican Railway, 113
Terry, Kyle: 179; killed, 180
Texana, Tex.: 37
Texas: 11, 12, 16, 18f, 27f, 34, 41, 46, 61, 65, 76, 90, 99
Texas City, Tex.: 212
Texas Fever: 165–67, 303
Texas full dress: 62
Texas Land and Cattle Company: 197 n.
Texas penitentiary: 279

Texas tuxedo: 63
Texian: 61
"Thank God," suggested for name of depot: 8
"That old cow out there": 29, 52, 101, 269
Third National Bank of St. Louis: 295
Thirteenth Army Corps: 41
Thompson, Mr., agent for the *Alabama:* 48
Thompson, Ben: 62, 66, 68; described, 71; accident to, 72; in Austin during cattlemen's convention, 144–46
Thompson, Mrs. Ben, in accident: 72
Thompson, Isaac, introduces wild rose into Texas: 46
Thompson, Wells, lawyer: 178
Thompson, Dr. William: 304ff
Tobacco: 131, 296
Toddy: 39, 63, 69
Tomahawk, kills a Pierce "boy": 131
Town-naming: 110
Trail, Chisholm: *see* Chisholm Trail
Trail drives: 29, 48–49, 52–55, 61, 82–83, 123–34, 148–55
Train wreck: 115
"Treaty of peace," signed by Taylor-Sutton factions: 81
Tremont Hotel, Galveston, Tex.: 86, 87, 122, 168, 264
Tres Palacios Church: 35
Tres Palacios River: *see* Rio Tres Palacios
Tres Palacios, Tex.: 28
Truehart, H. M., and Co.: 100
Tumlinson, Captain Joe: 51, 56f, 81
Typewriter, bought by Shanghai: 103

Unbranded cattle: 42
Union: 35
Union Nation Bank, Kansas City, Mo.: 291
University of Texas Archives, Austin, Texas: ix
Up Duke of Matagorda: 100
Uri, N. M., and Company: 175, 252
Uvalde, Tex.: 219
UU: *see* brands

Vacant land pre-empted by Pierce: 196
Valls, Dr. B. R.: recommended for convict physician, 280; summoned to Shanghai's deathbed, 297
Vandenburg, Joseph Verlin: 302, 307
Vegetables, raised by J. E. Pierce: 34

Victoria, Tex.: 20, 35, 39, 48, 51, 82, 88, 91, 100, 111, 113, 305
Vigilantes: 65, 66, 69
Virginia: 13ff, 17f, 35f, 154
Virginia Female Institute, Mamie attends: 153-54

Wages: 18, 23, 28
Walking stick: Pierce's 63ff, 95; Podo's, 123
Walrous country: 99
Ward, Benjamin Quinn: 28, 50f, 56, 67, 107; Pierce's partner, 85; builds barbed-wire fence, 136; dissolution of partnership, 137
Ward, Mrs. B. Q.: ix
Ward, Dean, counts the cattle: 138
Ward, Mrs. Eleanor Shannon: see Ward, Widow
Ward, Lafayette: 22, 85
Ward, Russell E.: ix, 85
Ward, Widow: 21ff, 28, 85, 103, 131
Warren's Plantation: 7
Washington County, Tex.: 71
Wathen, B. S., railroad advisor to George Jay Gould: 284
Watson, W. E., hears Shanghai boast: 268
Waugh's Ranch: 184
WBG: see brands
"Webster on Cattle": 11, 12
Weekes-McCarthy and Co.: 7, 264ff; formed, 275; liquidated, 289-90
Weekes, Nick: 168, 170, 274ff, 284, 286
Well's Point, Tex.: 58
West, George: 143
West Columbia, Tex.: 51
West Port Harbor, R. I.: 102
Western Stock Journal: 143
Wet ponies: 54
Wharton Click: 183
Wharton County, Tex.: 99, 182, 287, 292; political troubles, 177-83
Wharton, Tex.: 87, 100f, 288
Whatley, Major L. A.: 279
Wheeler, Willie, cowboy: 44
White, J. K.: 294-95
White Eagle Range: 224
Whitemen's Union: 297
Whittaker, Reed, sold horse to Pierce: 206
Wichita, Kan.: 64, 82, 83
Wichita Falls, Tex.: 91f, 127, 148
Wild cattle: 18, 48
Wild game, in Texas: 18
Williams Creek, Texas: 89
Williams, G. G.: 3ff, 292ff
Williams, Robert H.: 34
Wilson, Andy (Brother Andy): 75f; brings suit against Pierce, 83-84
Winchester: 53, 125, 143
Windsor Hotel, Denver, Colo.: 165
Winnie, gives Pierce trouble: 289ff
Wire Pasture: 7, 252; planted to rice, 283
Withers, Henry, Pierce's son-in-law: 154, 167, 186, 234, 264
Withers, Mamie: see Pierce, Mary
Wood business: 281
Wood, John: 40
Woodpeckers: see Jaybirds and Woodpeckers
Woods' Range: 48
Wo haw: 129
Wren, Mr., "inside owner": 107-108
Wright Hotel, Dodge City, Kan.: 126
Wrinkle horns: 29
Wyoming: 95, 133

Yellow Fever (Yellow Jack): 19, 247, 252
Yellowstone Park, Wyo.: 164
Young Mens Democratic Club: 179

Zebus: 305

www.ingramcontent.com/pod-product-compliance
Lightning Source LLC
Chambersburg PA
CBHW020732160426
43192CB00006B/198